GERMAN FLAMETHROWER PIONEERS OF WORLD WAR I

GERMAN FLAMETHROWER PIONEERS

of World War I

Thomas Wictor

Schiffer Military History
Atglen, PA

Acknowledgments

Profound thanks are in order to the following people, without whose help this book would not have been possible.

Thierry Ehret, for his unparalleled research skills and the use of his photos. Maurice Sublet, for the generous use of his photos. A. Langley, for his cartoons and magazine covers. Robert Lembke, for sharing stories of his father's experiences in the Guard Reserve Pioneer Regiment.

For the use of photos, thanks go to Ronny Pobucky, Hans Schmidt, Antonio Rosetto, Cyrille Gaston, Daniel Griffin, Chris Boonzaier, and Gregg DuBois.

Thanks also to Jörn Fickert, Dr. Brian Wimborne, Tony Schnuur, Rainer Strasheim, Bruce Gudmundsson, and the translators of the Axis History Forum.

All photos from the author's collection unless otherwise credited.

Dedication

This book is dedicated to all the American military personnel who have seen their service distorted, misreported, denigrated, and perverted by those with agendas.

Book design by Robert Biondi.

Library of Congress Catalog Number: 2007931037.

Printed in China.
ISBN: 978-0-7643-2772-8

Published by Schiffer Publishing Ltd.
4880 Lower Valley Road
Atglen, PA 19310
Phone: (610) 593-1777
FAX: (610) 593-2002
E-mail: Info@schifferbooks.com.
Visit our web site at: www.schifferbooks.com
Please write for a free catalog.
This book may be purchased from the publisher.
Please include $3.95 postage.
Try your bookstore first.

In Europe, Schiffer books are distributed by:
Bushwood Books
6 Marksbury Ave.
Kew Gardens, Surrey TW9 4JF
England
Phone: 44 (0)20 8392-8585
FAX: 44 (0)20 8392-9876
E-mail: info@bushwoodbooks.co.uk
www.bushwoodbooks.co.uk
Free postage in the UK. Europe: air mail at cost.
Try your bookstore first.

CONTENTS

Chapter Six

Chapter Seven

Chapter Eight

Chapter Nine

Chapter Ten

INTRODUCTION

The climax of the film *The Lost Battalion* (2001) perfectly illustrates the popular conception of how flamethrower attacks were conducted during the First World War. German flamethrower pioneers walk upright and exposed throough the woods, heedless of cover, advancing in a slow-moving Napoleonic skirmish line. As they approach the American positions, they pointlessly spray their oil into the air. Most of these clumsy automatons are shot down, bayoneted, or even wrestled to the ground. As they fall, some spin and douse their comrades; others explode, engulfing more hapless Germans in flames and proving that the weapon is as dangerous to its users as it is to the enemy.

To many if not most modern-day military historians, this debacle rings true. German flamethrower operators are thought to have been too encumbered to move quickly, and their devices were little more than a pyrotechnic display born out of the doctrine of *Schrecklichkeit* or frightfulness, which at least one writer attributed to the 1902 war manual *Kriegsbrauch im Landkriege:*

> All measures which conduce to the attainment of the object of war are permissible and these may be summarized in the two ideas of violence and cunning. What is permissible includes every means of war without which the object of the war cannot be attained. All means which modern invention affords, including the fullest, most dangerous, and most massive means of destruction, may be utilized.[1]

The German flamethrower of the First World War is thus often interpreted as a failed instrument of terror, deployed with no real thought other than to burn men to death.

Deconstructing the conventional wisdom is not difficult. A moderate amount of research will reveal that the Germans developed comprehensive tactics designed to both minimize casualties among flamethrower operators and convince the enemy to surrender without a fight, and there were strict written orders for when *not* to use the weapon. In addition, German flamethrower pioneers were highly trained, extremely mobile assault troops who used speed and concealment to improve their chances of success and survival. Finally, flamethrower operators never faced the enemy by themselves. Instead, they were deployed with hand-grenade throwers, light machine gunners, and grenade-launcher squads who provided cover during the advance.

Many modern scholars would be surprised to learn of mass flamethrower assaults that included as many as 240 devices coordinated from the air. These experts cannot define a "combined stationary and pouncing attack." They are also ignorant of Indian-style Forward Stalking, covering jets, flame shock troops, and the Knife Tactic. In short, much of what the Germans accomplished in flame warfare from 1914 to 1918 has been forgotten, even though the information survives in libraries and archives.

This book is an attempt to shed light on a misunderstood weapon and the almost-universally mischaracterized men who used it. Far from being the suicidal fanatics so often presented in film and literature, German flamethrower troops of the First World War can arguably be called the first modern special-operations force, cautious and highly trained men with the same mental and physical qualifications displayed by their present-day counterparts.

The reader should understand that this book is not a general history of the First World War. Only German flamethrower attacks and their immediate tactical repercussions are covered.

Note on German Terminology

To make for easier reading, most German terms in the text are translated into English. When a name, title, or concept first appears, the original German is provided in parentheses after the translation. Exceptions include *Grof, Kleif,* and *Wex,* the abbreviations for the types of flamethrower; military terminology more familiar in German, such as *Jäger, Landwehr, Landsturm, Leib, Freikorps,* and, in some cases, *Ersatz;* and the names of individual *Freikorps* units, the English renditions of which are cumbersome.

Some German units and organizations had parentheses in their names. In the text, brackets are used as parentheses within parentheses. For example, *Jäger- (Sturm-) Bataillon Nr. 3* in parentheses is rendered *(Jäger- [Sturm-] Bataillon Nr. 3).*

Ranks of German noncommissioned officers do not correspond exactly to those of the American or British military. Since scholars disagree on how best to translate them, all ranks are given in German for the sake of consistency. The reader is presumed to have a certain familiarity with these terms.

CHAPTER ONE

Early Flamethrowers

The term "Greek Fire" has come to describe an ancient incendiary material that adhered to its target and could not be extinguished. Early hand grenades, firebombs, and artillery shells are said to have been filled with it. In reality, Greek Fire was a specific weapon first used in AD 673 to burn Muslim ships besieging Constantinople. More properly called a weapon system, it consisted of a distilled and pressurized naptha-based compound sprayed by a hand-pumped siphon through metal tubes.[1] Greek Fire was therefore a flamethrower, in the modern, technical sense of the word.

Flamethrower technology was lost and rediscovered several times in the millennium that followed the introduction of Greek Fire. Arab armies of the thirteenth century deployed "portable tubes that could burn a man to ash at thirty feet."[2] With names such as the "Dart of Cathay" and the "Chinese Flower," these weapons seem to have originated in the Far East. The Chinese of the same period had their own flamethrowers: the "*pao* that belched flaming powder, and the *fie-ho-tsing,* the 'spear of fire that flies.'"[3]

Early twentieth-century German workmen spraying whitewash with equipment that strongly resembles the wartime backpack flamethrower and lance. Berlin mechanical engineer and inventor Richard Fiedler conceived the flamethrower when developing nozzles for spraying pressurized liquids, including petroleum and paint.

The Prussian artillery experimented with a flamethrower in 1702. Called the Serpentine Fire Sprayer *(Schlangenbrandspritze),* it used bellows to blow an incendiary substance through a wheeled tube. The project was eventually abandoned because the compound was so viscous that it set the flamethrower itself on fire.[4]

In 1849 Representative Abraham Lincoln and Senator H. Hamlin presented to both houses of the United States Congress "a discovery of 'liquid fire' as a means of attack and defence*[sic],*" the invention of Professor B.F. Greenough of Boston.[5] This device was clearly a flamethrower, consisting of a metal pipe three-sixteenths of an inch in diameter connected to a small pump by twenty-five feet of rubber hose. A nozzle at the end of the pipe was fitted with wire gauze through which flammable liquid was sprayed. Newspaper articles reported that the ignition of the fluid took place several feet beyond the nozzle, but the process was not described. Congress apparently showed little interest.

The American Civil War, however, spurred the development of new weapons. Greenough resumed research on his flamethrower under the direction of a military board that included Captain G.V. Fox, the Assistant Secretary of the Navy. During an 1862 demonstration at the Washington Navy Yard, the apparatus produced a flame thirty to fifty yards long and two feet in diameter, the jet accompanied by a dense, suffocating cloud of smoke. Greenough's liquid fire was said to be inextinguishable, burning readily on the water and consuming the wooden targets. It is not known why such an impressive weapon never saw service.

At the start of the twentieth century, two Germans – an engineer and a fire chief – were inspired by Greek Fire to reinvent the flamethrower. Working independently of each other at first, as members of an industrialized and intensely nationalistic culture, they created a machine-age, mass-produced version of the ancient weapon that would never again be lost to history.

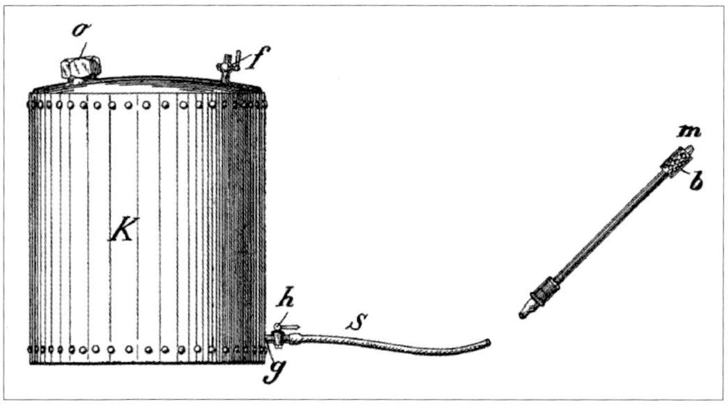

Richard Fiedler's first flamethrower patent, filed on April 25, 1901. Even in this design, Fiedler envisioned a "firing device" (b) or igniter for the lance. (German Patent No. 134348.)

Richard Fiedler

In 1900 a Berlin mechanical engineer and inventor named Richard Fiedler was studying nozzle designs for spraying liquids when he realized that gasoline fired from a pressurized tank could be ignited and used as a weapon. This prompted him to give up his initial research and focus on his new concept.[6] On April 25, 1901, he patented his first flamethrower, a kettlelike "Method for Producing Large Masses of Flame" *(Verfahren zur Erzeugung grosser Flammenmassen.)* That year he also approached the Supreme Army Command (*Oberste Heeresleitung* or *OHL*) and was awarded funds to continue developing his prototype.

Fiedler presented his flamethrower to the Prussian Engineer Committee *(Preusisches Ingenieur-Komitee)* in 1905, on the training grounds of the Guard Pioneer Battalion *(Garde-Pionier-Bataillon)* in Berlin. Although the demonstration was deemed satisfactory, the weapon itself was not yet ready for combat. The Engineer Committee suggested several improvements, which Fiedler duly incorporated. In 1908 the Fiedler flamethrower was assigned to the Pioneer Experimental Company *(Pionier-Versuchs-Kompagnie)*, the de facto 5th Company of the Guard Pioneer Battalion. The Pioneer Experimental Company carried out tests with a small, backpack model of flamethrower and a "large, mobile apparatus."[7] The small model would eventually be called the *kleine Flammenwerfer* or *Kleif,* while the large became the *grosse Flammenwerfer* or *Grof.*

Both devices consisted of a lance connected to an oil tank by a rubber hose. A fuse attached to the end of the lance was set alight with a flare igniter, activated when the operator pulled a cord. Fiedler submitted designs for his M.1908, M.1909, and M.1910 flamethrowers to the French patent office as well as the German. After the First World War the French general staff

Pionier Hermann Schmidt of the Pionier-Versuchs-Kompagnie, which developed flamethrowers from 1908 to 1912. Schmidt is shown here with his wife Johanna. During the war he fought at Antwerp, Ypres, Lille, Reims, and Verdun before being gassed and declared unfit for combat duty. He wears the M.1910 service jacket (Waffenrock) with Swedish cuffs, Guard lace (Garde Litzen), and a red embroidered V on the shoulder straps. Courtesy Hans Schmidt.

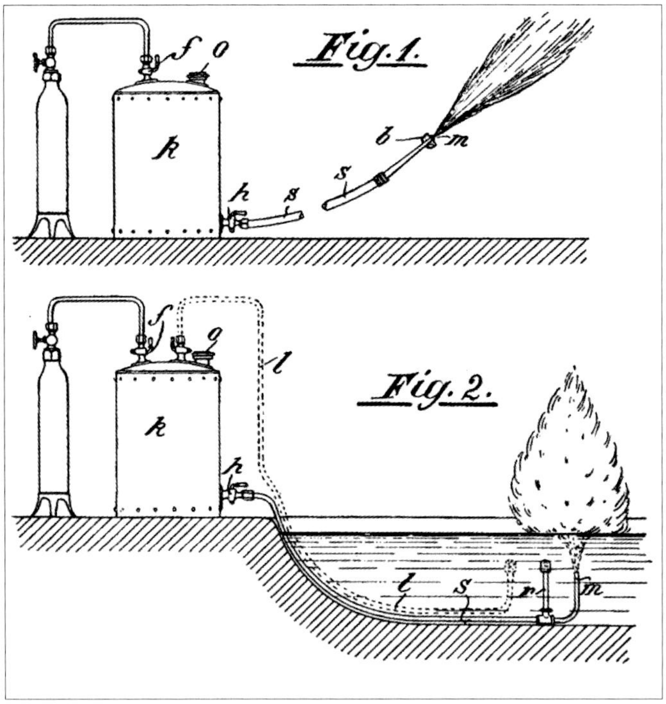

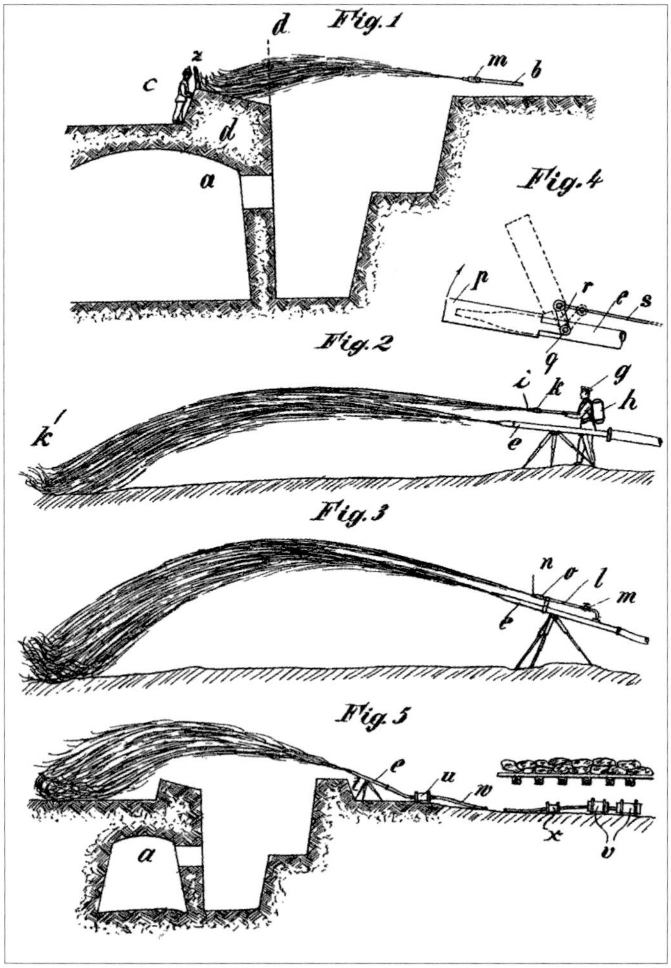

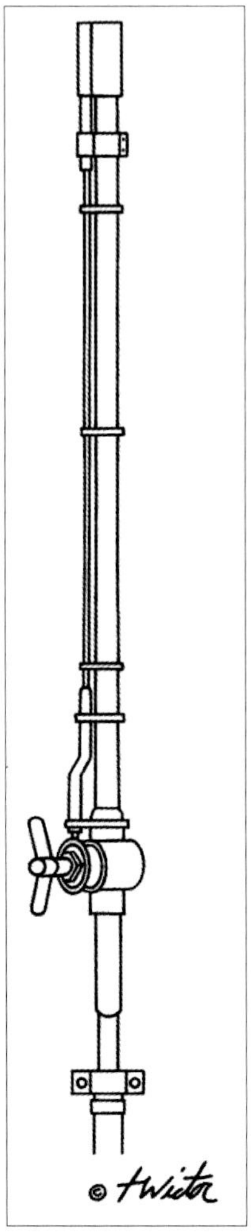

Above: Patent for Fiedler flamethrower, filed in Switzerland on January 3, 1908. It could be fired underwater (Fig. 2) as a maritime signaling device and could also be used as a military gas sprayer by mixing various chemicals with the flame oil. During the war the Germans used flamethrowers to spray poison gas on at least one occasion. (Swiss Patent No. 42243.)

Top right: Patent for Fiedler flamethrowers, filed July 18, 1909. Figure 1 shows a soldier deflecting a flame jet with a metal shield. Figure 2 is a large flamethrower ignited with a portable model. Figure 3 depicts a double-barreled flamethrower, the small model igniting the stream of the large. In Figure 5 the large flamethrower is shown with its oil supply protected by a fortified shelter. (German patent No. 256286.)

Right: Patent for the Fiedler portable flamethrower, filed in Britain on December 29, 1910. This "Apparatus for Producing Long Jets of Flame" was adopted almost unchanged by the Austrian army. Fiedler described it as "particularly adapted for military purposes." (British Patent No. 30161.)

Left: Fiedler flamethrower lance. To fire the weapon, the operator loaded an igniter into the cylindrical holder on the lance nozzle. He then turned the large handle at the base, which pulled a cable that cocked the spring-loaded firing pin in the base of the igniter holder. When the valve reached the full "open" position, the firing pin was released, detonating the percussion cap in the igniter and touching off the spray of pressurized oil.

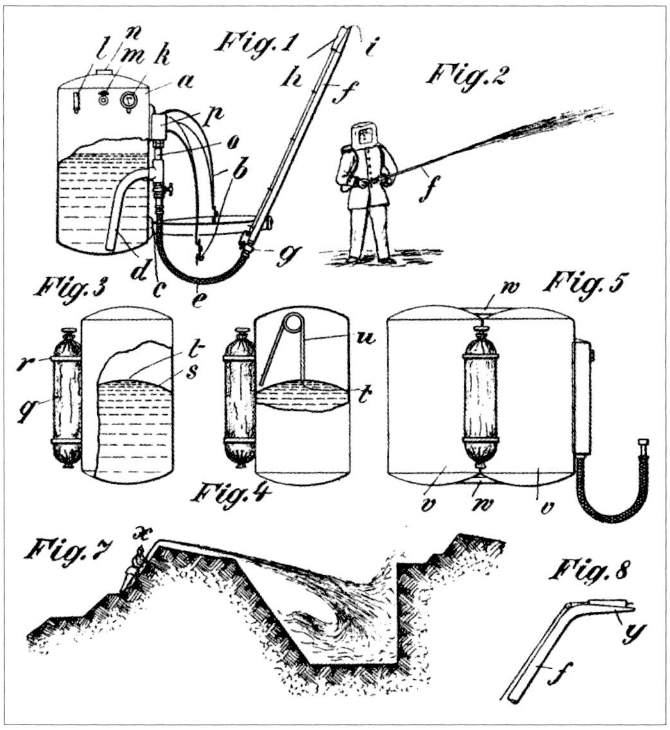

was criticized for not anticipating that the Germans would use flamethrowers in any upcoming conflict, given that Fiedler's patents included drawings of soldiers firing the weapons and explanations of the weapons' military value.

In his 1909 patent Fiedler predicted that the enemy might deflect flame jets with metal shields. The flamethrowers themselves were designed in such a way that the oil jet was ignited far beyond the nozzle of the lance. This protected the operator from excessive heat blowing back and reduced consumption of the fuel in flight, thus increasing the range. One large flamethrower employed a *Kleif* to light the jet, while another was a double-barreled model consisting of a small lance mounted on top of a large. Each had its own pivot so that it could be turned independently. Only the upper lance was fitted with an igniter, which produced a small, burning jet that was aimed at the large, unlit jet. When the large jet was ignited, the small lance was shut off. The large jet carried the flame to the target and continued to dump fuel on it, preventing the ignition from racing back toward the operator. Both large models of flamethrower were fed from heavily fortified reservoirs.

The 1910 patent included a sketch of a soldier wearing a protective facemask and operating a knapsack flamethrower, while another figure projected "fiery death into a trench by means of a bent pipe."[8] In his 1908 patent Fiedler also pointed out that chemical substances could be mixed with flammable liquids to transform flamethrowers into gas sprayers. According to the Swiss version of this patent (No.42243), the ability to spray "unbreathable gases" (*irrespirable Gase*) made the weapon very suitable in the event of war. For the British patent (No.216) of the same device, however, Fiedler chose the term "noxious gases" and gave as an example sulphur dioxide, which would merely irritate the enemy's lungs and eyes. Since the weapon would not spray poisonous gas, its use in warfare was therefore not a violation of international law.[9]

During the First World War the Germans would spray poison gas with flamethrowers on at least one occasion, reportedly to great effect.[10] Although the German military continually pressed for improvements, the Austro-Hungarian army adopted Fiedler's M.1910 flamethrower and lance designs almost unchanged.[11]

Requirements set forth by the Engineer Committee were difficult for Fiedler to meet. It was anticipated that the *Kleif* would be used in assaults, carried by men moving quickly into trenches by sliding down poles or climbing ladders. This meant that the apparatus had to be relatively light. The *Grof* would be used to attack and defend fortresses; because of its size, it was to be emplaced in a covered installation, while its lance operator and hose carriers moved forward.

Carbonic acid and water provided the carbon dioxide used as the propellant in these experiments. A design flaw in Fiedler's *Kleif* was that when the operator ran or jumped, the carbonic acid and flame oil mixed. The oil absorbed the gas and became a seltzer-like foam inside the apparatus boiler, which caused a decreased range of the flame jet. To overcome this problem, Fiedler welded a steel partition with an overflow pipe into the boiler, separating the flame oil from the carbonic acid.

Flamethrowers Versus Fire Tubes

In June of 1909 Fiedler was asked to demonstrate his flamethrowers to representatives of the War Ministry (*Kriegsministerium*), the General Staff (*Generalstab*), and the Engineer Committee. The object of the exercise was to test the inventions under combat conditions.

The demonstrations took place in September, at Fort Säpzig in the town of Küstrin. First, *Kleif* were used to attack two firing loopholes in a trench; for comparative purposes, two other loopholes were attacked with fire tubes (*Brandröhren*), sheet-metal cylinders that contained a combustible mixture set alight with a friction igniter. Producing a seven-foot flame and heavy smoke, they were held to the loopholes of bunkers and forts to drive out the garrisons. The burning time varied from forty to fifty seconds.[12]

Fire tubes were effective, but they were temperamental, complicated, and dangerous. They had to be left in their transporting box until they were ready to be used, and the box was to be set in the shade if possible to keep the tubes out of direct sunlight. In order for the flames and smoke to reach loopholes high off the ground, a long guide pole was used. It resembled a hangman's gibbet, with a cantilevered wooden beam attached to one end at a ninety-degree angle, to which the fire tube was tied. Before the weapon was fastened to the beam, a paper covering on the end was punched through and a friction igniter was screwed into a celluloid locking plate. The pole was raised to the loophole, and the igniter was detonated with a long lanyard attached to a pull ring.

Each loophole was attacked by a fire-tube squad (*Brandröhrentrupp*) of five or six men: an *Unteroffizier* as required; Number 1 and Number 2 carrying the guide pole; and Numbers 3, 4, and 5 each armed with a fused fire tube.

The *Unteroffizier* and Numbers 1 and 2 took the guide pole and hurried ahead at double time; Numbers 3, 4, and 5 followed behind. When the squad had gathered beside the

One requirement for the small flamethrower was that it be portable enough for the operator to climb ladders and slide down poles while wearing it. These pioneers demonstrate additional scaling techniques that would be difficult for a flamethrower-laden soldier to accomplish.

loophole, Number 3 tied the first fire tube to the pole, which Numbers 1 and 2 then raised. Once the fire tube was positioned in the loophole, it was detonated by a short jerk on the lanyard attached to the wire pull ring. The men holding the pole had to be sure that the jet of flame and smoke emitting from the fire tube were not blocked by the edge of the loophole. After the first fire tube burned out, the second and third were used if necessary.

One of the goals of the September 1909 demonstrations at Fort Säpzig was to determine if the *Kleif* operated by one man could replace the cumbersome fire tube with its guide pole and five- or six-man squad. To round out the exercises, the *Grof* was used offensively, hurling flames over a high barrier to strike the firing line behind; to test defensive capabilities, both *Grof* and *Kleif* engaged an assault column simulated with straw-filled dummies mounted on ladders.

The War Ministry and Engineer Committee pronounced the demonstrations extraordinarily successful. Flamethrowers were seen as such an improvement in incendiary weaponry that they were officially designated as replacements for fire tubes, and their further technical and tactical developments were to be pursued.

Matthias Erzberger (1875-1921), elected to the *Reichstag* in 1903, apparently recommended that the German army adopt the flamethrower.[13] The influential Erzberger was initially a pan-German and a supporter of an expansionist war, but he later led calls for a negotiated peace with the Allies and headed the German delegation that signed the Armistice on November 11, 1918. While serving as Minister of Finance for the Weimar Government, he was murdered by ultranationalists in 1921.

The Kaiser Rejects Flamethrowers?

Several American newspapers reported in similarly worded articles that Kaiser Wilhelm II was at first opposed to the flamethrower. The journalist Herbert Corey wrote that while he was stationed in Berlin in February of 1915, he heard from German sources that the general staff had kept their preliminary flamethrower experiments from the Kaiser. After the weapon was approved in 1909, Wilhelm was still not officially informed. When he inadvertently found out, he summoned the chief of staff:

> "I will not permit the use of such devices in my army," said the Kaiser. "They are devilish, monstrous – inhuman."
>
> "But Sire – " began the chief of staff.
>
> "Enough," said the Kaiser.
>
> At that time members of the staff were quoted as expressing regret that the weapon was forbidden them. One is compelled to wonder now if the Kaiser were in the end defied by the staff, or whether he assented to its use, and what particular epithets he now applies to a weapon of war that chars men's flesh from their bones.[14]

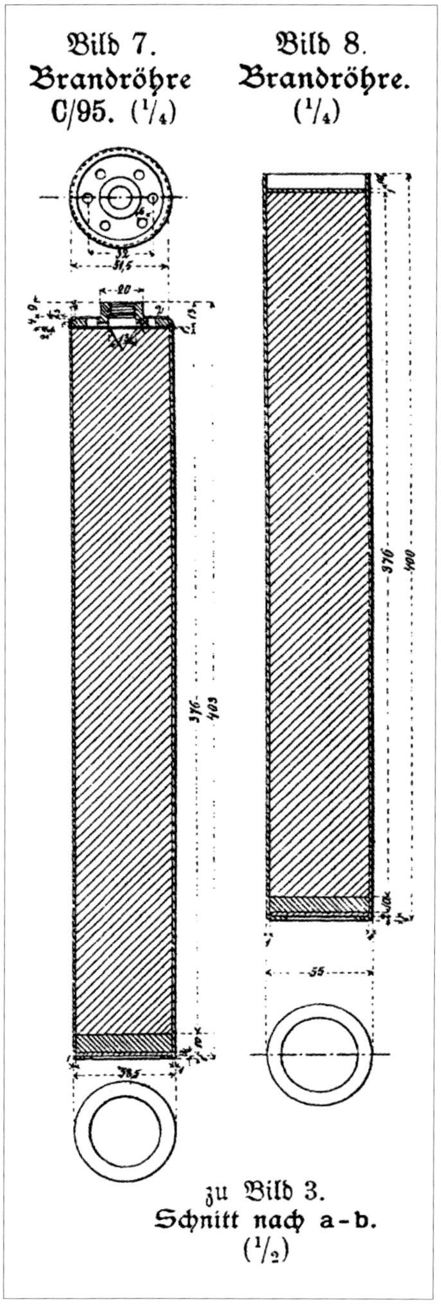

Fire tube (Brandröhre), an incendiary weapon used by pioneers to drive out the garrisons of bunkers and other strong points. The flamethrower was initially adopted as a replacement for the fire tube. Courtesy Thierry Ehret.

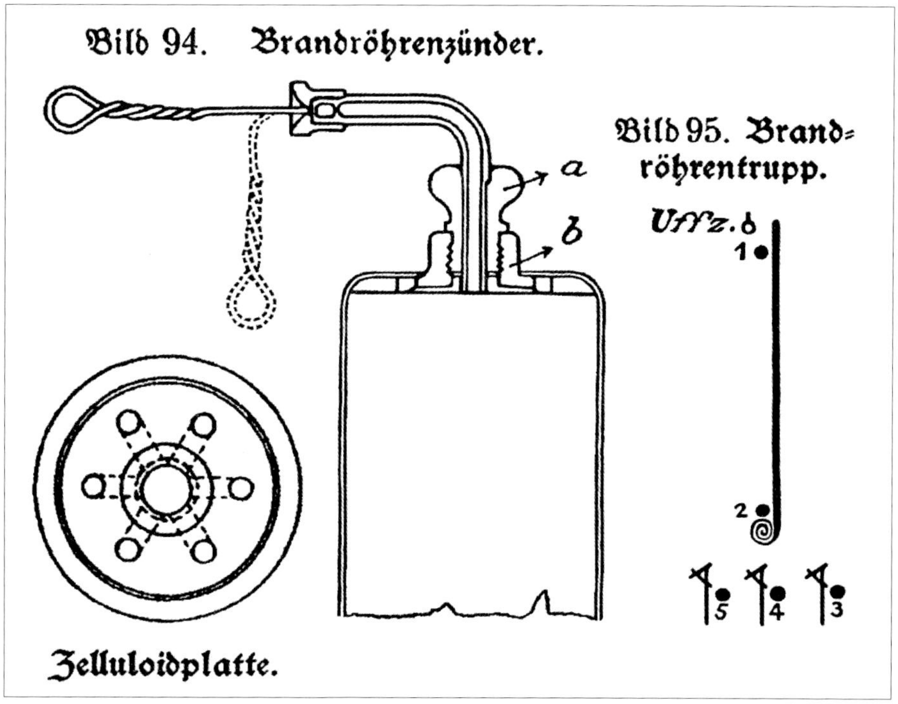

Figure 94 is the igniter for fire tubes, a friction fuse activated when the wire ring was pulled. Figure 95 shows a fire-tube squad consisting of an Unteroffizier (when needed); Nos. 1 and 2 carrying a guide pole; and Nos. 3, 4, and 5 carrying fused fire tubes. Courtesy Thierry Ehret.

Right: Italian sailor displaying the Austrian kleine 22l M. 15 Flammenwerfer, the production version of the Fiedler M.1910. Note the external propellant tank, the dual levers on the lance for spraying oil and detonating the igniter respectively, the padded backpack harness, and the coarsely woven shoulder straps.

During the war Wilhelm did indeed seem to change his mind about the weapon, jovially asking his flamethrower troops how many Frenchmen they had burned up.[15]

Ultimately Corey's colorful story cannot be authenticated. He himself was unsure of its accuracy, and he cast further doubt on his own reporting by stating that according to his German sources the flamethrower was invented by a "half-baked professor" at a German university.[16]

Bernhard Reddemann (1870-1938), future commander of the flamethrower pioneers, as Fire Chief (Branddirektor) of Posen. This portrait of the "Prince of Hades" was printed in a 1911 firefighting journal, on the occasion of Reddemann being appointed Fire Chief of Leipzig. (Feuer und Wasser.)

Bernhard Reddemann

The second seminal figure in the development of the modern flamethrower is Bernhard Reddemann, a man so unknown to present-day military historians that his first name is often mistakenly given as Hermann.

Born in Berlin in 1870,[17] Reddemann was commissioned in 1893 as a *Sekonde-Leutnant* in command of the 3rd Company of Lorrainese (Fortress) Pioneer Battalion No. 20 (*Lotheringisches [Festungs-] Pionier-Bataillon Nr. 20*).[18] He stayed with Pioneer Battalion No. 20 until 1903, transferring into the reserves in 1896-97. In 1903 he entered the *Landwehr* as an *Oberleutnant* of pioneers, First Military District Breslau (*Landwehrbezirk* I Breslau).[19] He became Fire Inspector (*Brandinspekteur*) of the city of Posen in 1906 and joined Military District Posen in the same year. In 1908 he was promoted to Fire Chief (*Brandirektor*) of Posen; three years later he became Fire Chief of Leipzig,[20] while serving as a *Hauptmann* of *Landwehr* Pioneers.[21] His final posting before war broke out in 1914 was with Military District Halle am Saale.[22] He earned advanced degrees in both law[23] and engineering[24] and attended Artillery and Engineering School in 1896.

Documentation on Bernhard Reddemann the person is scarce. One profile of this complex man was written in a firefighting journal on the occasion of Reddemann becoming the Leipzig fire chief in 1911:

> The *Posener Neuesten Nachrichten* express themselves as follows:
>
> "Fire Chief Dr. Reddemann was unanimously selected by the Leipzig City Council to be fire chief of Leipzig. Since Fire Chief Dr. Reddemann has accepted this very honorable offer, we must therefore expect his imminent departure from Posen. Thus our municipal fire brigade loses its impressive leader, who has such completely outstanding quick-wittedness and concern. Posen today can nevertheless say with pride that it possesses one of the best German fire brigades; that larger fires are extraordinarily rare here because the fire brigade smoothly and in no time at all hurries to the scene and puts out each fire as it germinates ...
>
> "Untiringly active in his official capacity, Dr. Reddemann also won for himself the pleasant agreeability of everyone with whom he interacted personally ...
>
> "Posen reluctantly accepts the departure of its fire chief; however, we wish this joyfully hardworking and eager-to-please official heartfelt good luck in his new, expanded office of enriched responsibilities."[25]

Reddemann Builds his First Flamethrowers

An engineer, soldier, and professional firefighter, Reddemann apparently became interested in flame weapons after reading a report describing the siege of Port Arthur, during the Russo-Japanese War of 1904-1905. His attention was caught by the fact that Japanese combat engineers used hand pumps to spray kerosene into the Russian trenches and then threw bundles of

Above: Members of a German municipal fire brigade in the early 1900s, displaying a large brass nozzle, hose, and breathing apparatus. Both Richard Fiedler and Bernhard Reddemann developed flamethrower technology based on firefighting equipment.

Below: Steam-pumper platoon (Dampfspritzenzug) of the Wilkau Municipal Fire Brigade in 1908. Bernhard Reddemann converted such a pumper into his first flamethrower, used to defend Fort Glowno in Posen.

burning rags to ignite the liquid.[26] It does not appear to have been an effective mode of attack, but it clearly stayed with Reddemann. In 1907, when the German army held a large-scale exercise in fortress warfare, he was given the command of a pioneer company and told to defend Fort Glowno of Fortress Posen:

> "So, Reddemann," said the governor of the fortress, *Generalleutnant* von Issendorf. "In a few days the attackers will assault the fort. You are to defend it in such a way that the attackers are routed! Now you will probably have to think of something new to make the attack fail. However you do it is your business!" [Reddemann] said to himself in astonishment: My God! So I have to instantly think of something new? But that is not so simple! Suddenly, however, it occurred to him. In ancient times, they had "Greek Fire" to spray at the enemy. Could it not be attempted here as well?[27]

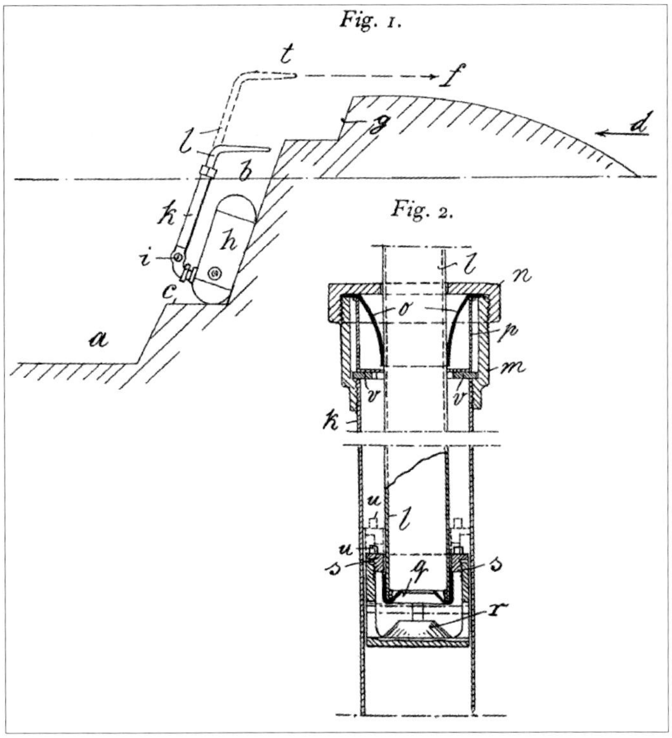

Fiedler patent for telescoping flame lance, filed August 19, 1911. It automatically extended to its full length when the oil stopcock was opened. Figure 2 shows a cross section of the nut that kept the lance at its full extension until it was retracted by hand. (German Patent No. 256832.)

Reddemann received von Issendorf's permission to deploy a steam-pumper platoon (*Dampfspritzenzug*) of the Posen Fire Brigade for the defense of the fortress. A small, unlimbered steam pumper was brought into a high bombproof vault and equipped with a number of barrels from which the hoses would draw liquid.

At the headquarters of the Posen Fire Brigade, Reddemann experimented with small hand pumps, filling the reservoirs with gasoline and petroleum mixed in different ratios. After much trial and error, he eventually produced long jets of liquid fire that burned continuously in the air. Stronger jets were achieved using the steam pumper in the fortress, the hoses of which led to positions on the tops of the walls and in small dugouts on the near slope of the moat. In preparation pioneers dug trenches, buried the hoses, and carefully covered them over with bricks. Reddemann did not describe his ignition source; presumably it was a burning brand, torch, or flare.

Firefighters were assigned the duty of hose operator (*Rohrführer*), a firefighting term later applied to flamethrowers. They were put in the dugouts to spray attackers climbing down ladders from the opposite bank into the fortress moat. Reddemann's plan was to substitute water for the burning oil-gasoline mixture. Trials using water went well, but on the day of the exercise higher command ordered that actual spraying not take place, fearing that the soldiers would be knocked off the ladders and break their legs.

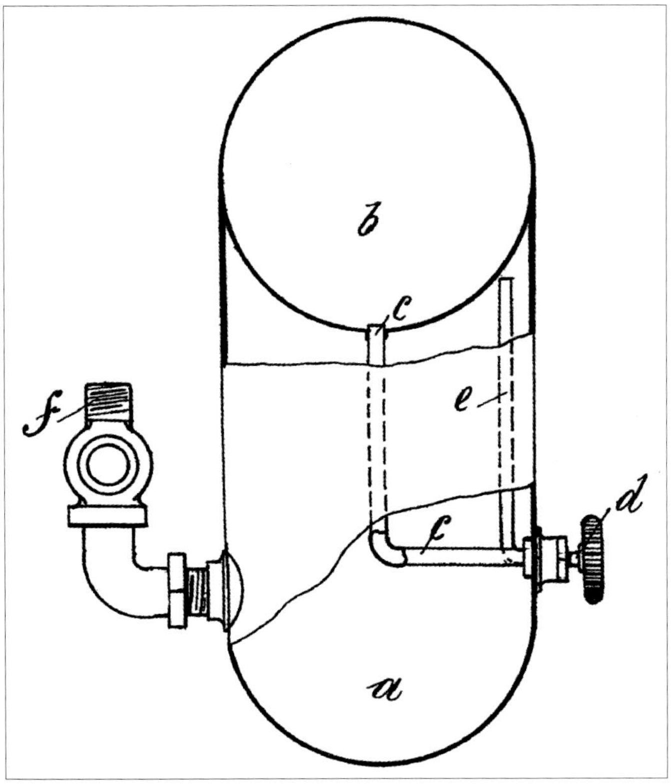

Fiedler patent for a flamethrower with an internal pressure chamber, filed August 20, 1911. This was the basic design for most German portable flamethrowers of the First World War. (German Patent No. 265400.)

Following the success of the fortress-defense exercise, Reddemann continued experimenting with oil mixtures, trying to find the perfect balance between flammability and a specific gravity high enough that the oil would spray as far as water. His designs were all based on hand and steam pumpers used by fire brigades.

In 1908 Reddemann met with Richard Fielder for the first time,[28] although details are lacking. The two kept in contact and began cooperating on flamethrower construction a few months after the start of the war. They do not appear to have worked together during peacetime; it can be deduced from their prewar activities that both were confident, strong-willed, and highly individualistic men, which could mean that they refused to compromise their visions. During the war, in fact, Fiedler and Reddemann often did behave more like rivals than colleagues.

1909-1912

Richard Fiedler continued developing flamethrowers after his successful demonstrations of 1909. In response to demands from the German military, he added separate internal chambers for the propellant gas, and lances capable of firing multiple shots. Engineer and pioneer officers in the War Ministry were impressed; one general said about this period, "There was someone called Fiedler who had a patent for a type of Greek Fire, and we were to wrack our brains to discover how this devilish thing could be used for military purposes."[29]

An important part of the testing process took place in 1911, when *Kleif* were assigned to West Prussian (Fortress) Pioneer Battalion No. 23 (*Westpreussisches [Festungs-] Pionier-Bataillon Nr. 23*), Westphalian (Fortress) Pioneer Battalion No. 24 (*Westfälisches [Festungs-] Pionier-Bataillon Nr. 24*), and Nassauian (Fortress) Pioneer Battalion No. 25 (*Nassauisches [Festungs-] Pionier-Bataillon Nr. 25*). These pioneer formations examined the flamethrowers for their "war usefulness" and collected their experiences in a report.[30] Although Reddemann was not involved in this phase of research, his defense of Fort Glowno may have influenced the War Ministry in its decision to assign flamethrowers to fortress battalions.

One-Year Volunteers (Einjahr Freiwilligen) of Westfälisches (Festungs-) Pionier-Bataillon Nr. 24. In 1911 Pioneer Battalion No. 23, No. 24, and No. 25 were ordered to evaluate the combat effectiveness of the portable flamethrower. The pioneer with the broom on the left wears an apron with the chalked slogan "Mama's little darling."

In 1912 Fiedler's *Kleif* was issued to Pioneer Siege Trains (*Pionier-Belagerungstrains*),[31] specialized units within pioneer regiments used to reduce fortresses. A pioneer siege train consisted of thirty-eight horse-drawn wagons loaded with mining equipment, surveying equipment, bridging equipment, scaling equipment, shovels, axes, trench mortars, battering rams, sandbags, barbed wire, grenades, and forges.

The flamethrower supplied to pioneer siege trains was fitted with a rigid telescoping lance attached to the right side by means of a swiveling elbow joint. Opening the oil-release valve automatically extended the lance, a design apparently thought to be more practical than the separate lance and rubber hose used on earlier models. It was not a successful adaptation and was withdrawn in the first months of the war.[32]

During this period Reddemann and Fiedler's research overlapped in that both men adapted existing firefighting equipment. As an example, the *Grof M.1912* produced by Fiedler was based on the "gas sprayer" (*Gasspritze*) of the fire brigades.[33] This device used compressed gas to pressurize the water that it sprayed. Curiously, Reddemann consistently claimed that the *Grof M.1912* had an oil capacity of twenty-six gallons, but documents found in the German national archives indicate that it held forty-five gallons.[34] Comparing images of

Russian soldier modeling a captured kleine Flammenwerfer (Kleif) M.1912, the first production model of portable German flamethrower. Note the angled nozzle with empty igniter holder. The oil-release block valve is visible at the base of the telescoping lance.

Opposite
Top: Kleif M.1912 being fired by its two-man squad. The operator carries the flamethrower and takes aim, while the assistant opens the oil-pressurization valve on the tank and the block valve of the lance. Unlike in the previous photo, the lance is fitted with the straight nozzle and an igniter. Courtesy Ronny Pobucky.

Bottom: Undated photo of the grosse Flammenwerfer (Grof) M.1912, developed from the "gas sprayer" (Gasspritze) of the fire brigades. Most of the personnel are from the Marinekorps, except for the officer in the dark glasses on the left. The weapon's twin propellant tanks have been removed and lie on the ground behind the sailor in the right foreground. It is not known if the Marinekorps trained extensively with flamethrowers. Imperial War Museum Q.51443.

Men of the Park Company of Pionier-Belagerungstrain 11. Pioneer siege trains were the specialized units within pioneer regiments whose duty it was to reduce fortresses. In 1912 these formations were assigned the Kleif.

the *Grof M.1912* to the twenty-six gallon *Leichtgrof M.1916* would seem to bear this out.

Automatic Igniters

Fiedler faced considerable obstacles in his quest to create a flamethrower igniter. The first was that the heavy, fast-moving oil stream was difficult to touch off; Fiedler solved the problem by targeting the petroleum vapor surrounding the jet instead. A functional igniter also had to be windproof and firmly seated on the lance nozzle so that it would not be knocked off in battle. Despite assertions by many present-day historians that early in the war German flamethrowers were lit with burning twigs, all devices after 1911 featured automatic igniters. This fact was once common knowledge, as shown by a magazine article from 1916:

> In the earliest models [of flamethrower], the combustible liquid was propelled by a gas-condenser out of a portable or fixt *[sic]* reservoir, and was lighted by some automatic device as it escaped from the nozzle of the projecting instrument.[35]

The burning twig or stick shown in period photos as a means of lighting flamethrowers was the makeshift stick fuse (*behelfsmässigen Stockzünder*). It was used only when the igniter supply had been exhausted.

Fiedler filed patents for automatic igniters in 1911 and 1912. Both devices incorporated percussion caps that were struck by firing pins, although the triggering mechanisms differed. The later igniter, a double-walled cylinder that fit over the lance nozzle, was used during the war. It contained a combustible compound that burned for approximately two minutes, allowing for multiple shots.

Several sources have described the wartime igniter as a "friction lighter" that used a flint, similar in design to a cigarette lighter:

> A short length of flexible hose ended in a nozzle in which was fitted the ignition device. As the oil emerged under pressure, it forced up the plunger of a friction lighter and ignited a core of fuze mixture surrounding the nozzle that remained alight long enough to enable a number of shots to be fired.[36]

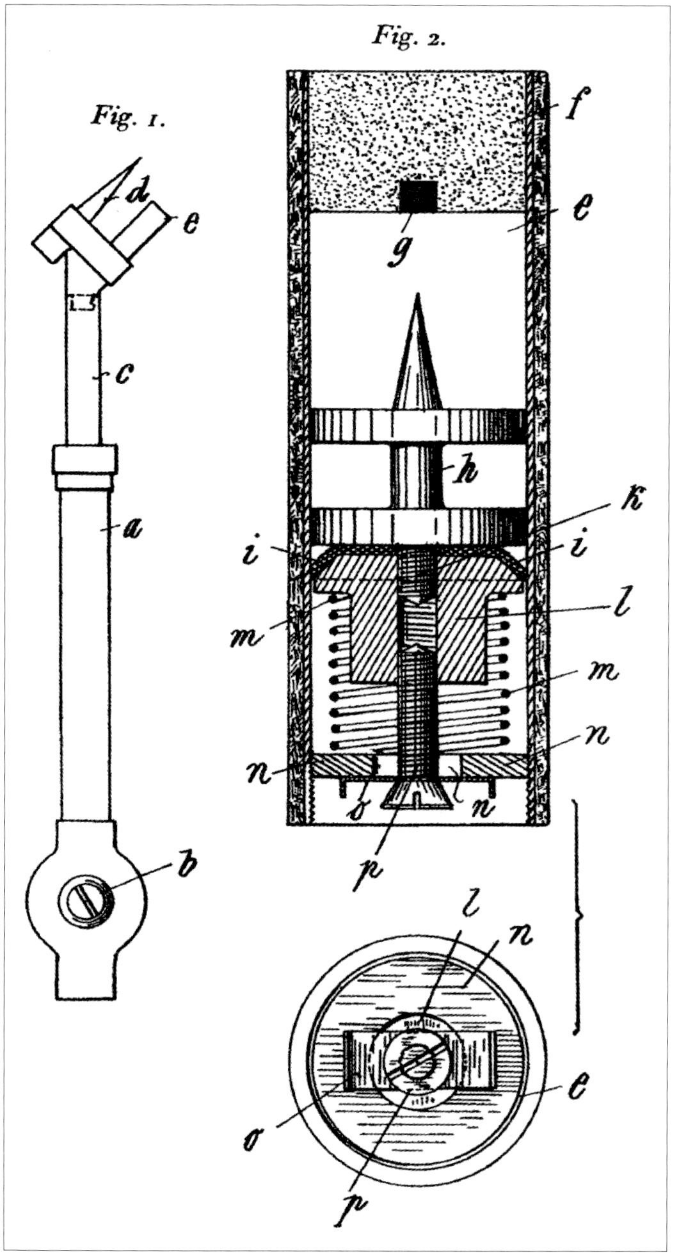

Fiedler igniter-holder patent, filed on August 20, 1911. It was attached to the nozzle of the lance and featured a spring-loaded firing pin (h) that when released, struck a percussion cap in the igniter (g) and set off a fusible compound (f). (German Patent No. 256285.)

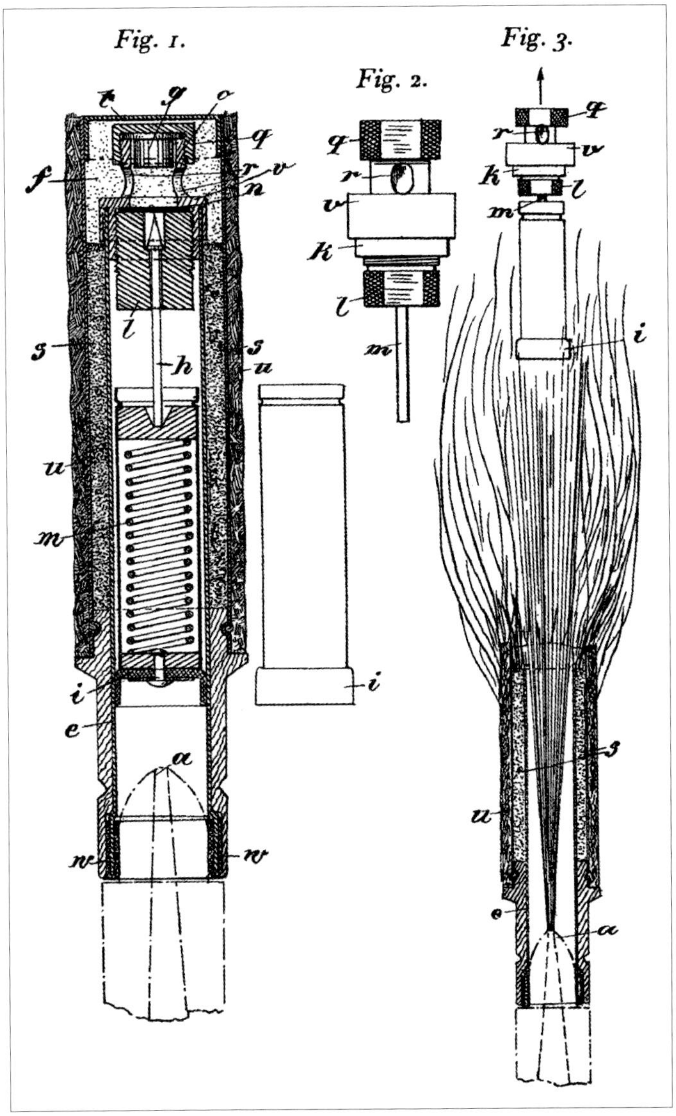

Fiedler igniter patent, filed on January 30, 1912. This model contained enough fusing compound to allow for multiple shots. When the operator opened the lance stopcock, the rush of pressurized oil propelled the firing pin into the percussion cap, which ignited the fusing compound. The firing pin and its base were blown out of the igniter holder at the first shot, leaving a clear passage for the jet of oil. (German Patent No. 270390.)

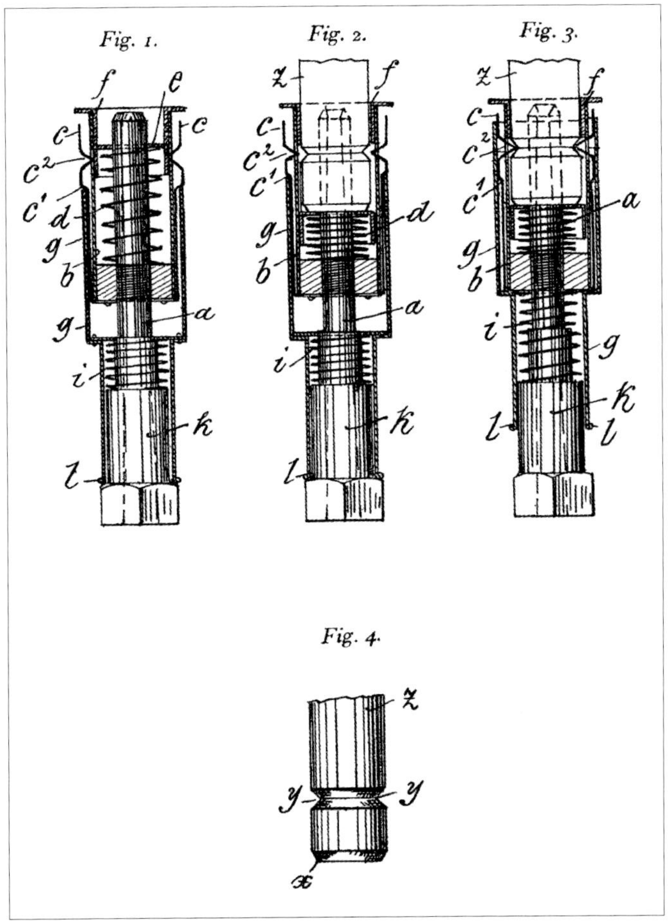

Fiedler patent for igniter holder, filed on January 31, 1912. It was a brass socket attached over the nozzle of the lance, with internal spring-loaded clips that locked the igniter in place. When the igniter was spent, the operator pulled the holder back along the nozzle, releasing the internal springs and ejecting the igniter. (German Patent No. 259566.)

Such a friction lighter has not been located in the German patent office, and it is not likely that a flint could ignite a high-pressure stream of oil. Friction fuses were used on fire tubes and incendiary hand grenades; they functioned as large matches and were activated by the pull of wire rings. Fiedler igniters operated more as firearm cartridges. In the case of the device patented in 1912, the oil jet propelled a firing pin into a percussion cap, which ignited the fusible compound packed inside the double walls. The initial jet also blew the firing pin and percussion cap out of the igniter, leaving a clear passage for the burning oil.

An important aspect of the carrying harness for the *Kleif M.1912* and most subsequent models of portable flamethrower is that it lacked a waist belt. There were shoulder straps and a steel waist support at the operator's back, but no strap across his middle. This was a safety feature that enabled the operator to instantly pull his arms out of the shoulder straps and drop the weapon if a leak or puncture caused spilled fuel to ignite.

Kleif M.1912. Note the disc-shaped oil-pressurization valve on the right side of the tank and the leather shoulder strap on the lance, which reduced recoil. The steel waist support lacked a belt so that the operator could instantly drop the flamethrower if it were punctured and began to leak oil.

CHAPTER TWO

The War Begins

When the Germans mobilized on August 1, 1914, flamethrowers were still weapons of the pioneer siege trains and were considered a means of conducting fortress warfare. It is not known if any pioneer siege trains actually used flamethrowers in combat. At the beginning of position warfare, flamethrowers were issued to "individual pioneer formations" as offensive weapons.[1] They were kept in the pioneer parks, vast storage and production depots that held and distributed weapons, equipment, and raw materials required by front-line troops.[2] The precise number of pioneer companies, battalions, and regiments given flamethrowers is not clear.

Men of Königlich Bayerisches Pionier-Park-Kompagnie 12. The sign reads "P.P.K. 12; 'Town' without fear; Sulzbach 1/Upper Alsace 1915/16." In August of 1914 flamethrowers were delivered to pioneer parks, to be kept in readiness for pioneer formations.

The German army of 1914 was well equipped with incendiary weapons of many different types. In addition to flamethrowers and fire tubes, it had incendiary grenades (*Brandgranate* or *Brandhandgranate*), sometimes called flame balls (*Flammenkugeln*), which were externally identical to the spherical smoke or tear-gas grenade (*Nebelgranate* or *Nebelhandgranate*). There were also the ground flare (*Flammenfeuer*) and, more insidiously, nitrocellulose tablets for burning houses. These small rings were strewn on the floor and ignited with a lighted match.[3] The incendiary hand grenades and ground flares were used as ignition sources during the first large-scale flamethrower attacks in 1915.

Multiple sources had the German army using flamethrowers to raze Belgian and French villages in 1914. The American ambassador to Belgium reported that the Germans who sacked the city of Louvain on August 25 were equipped with "apparatus for the purpose of firing dwellings, incendiary pastils, machines for spraying petroleum, etc."[4] In addition, an illustrated French postcard showed German soldiers setting fire to the town of Creil on September 6,

Pioneer park. Prior to 1915 pioneers trained with flamethrowers in the large open areas of such enclosures.

Right: Nitrocellulose tablets used by the Germans to set fire to dwellings.

Below: Wartime postcard captioned "Creil (Oise) – Burning of Rue de Gambetta (6 September, 1914)." In the background, German soldiers use two Kleif M.1912 to set fire to houses. It is not clear if this image is propaganda or a depiction of actual events.

spraying houses with *Kleif M.1912* as the panicked populace fled. Given the indisputably brutal German reprisals against civilians, it is difficult to discount all of these reports as anti-German propaganda.

Flamethrowers in Combat

At the time of mobilization Bernhard Reddemann was a *Hauptmann der Landwehr Pioniere* in military district Halle am Salle. With the onset of hostilities, he was appointed commander (*Kompagnie-Führer*) of the 3rd Company of Posener Pioneer Replacement Battalion No. 29 (*Posensisches Pionier-Ersatz-Bataillon Nr. 29*).[5] On September 24, 1914, he took command of the 2nd Company of Pioneer Battalion No. 29, which was sent to the Argonne region. After making stops at Sassey, Montfaucon, and Varennes, the 2nd Company was ordered to the *Barrikade-Rücken*, 1.2 miles east of where the flamethrower saw its first verified combat usage at Bagatelle-Pavillon.

On October 4, 1914, the German XVI Corps under *General der Pioniere* Bruno von Mudra launched an offensive in the Argonne that was intended to smash through the heavily wooded terrain and take the French positions:

> It was notable for being the first engagement of the war in which the Germans used everything in their arsenal: in addition to the 210 millimeter howitzers already used in the September attacks, which were normally part of the corps artillery, von Mudra added a new and extremely effective weapon, the Minenwerfer, known to subsequent generations simply as mortars. The infantry and the engineers used hand grenades and flamethrowers.[6]

For the attack on Bagatelle von Mudra sent Grenadier Regiment No. 123 (*Grenadier-Regiment König Karl [5. Württembergisches] Nr. 123*), the 2nd Company of Pioneer Battalion No. 13 (*Württembergisches Pionier-Bataillon Nr. 13*), and four light howitzers of Field Artillery Regiment No. 49 (*3. Württembergisches Feldartillerie-Regiment Nr. 49*), all of which were elements of the 27th Infantry Division. The 2nd Battalion of Pioneer Battalion No. 29, consisting of the 4th Company and 1st and 2nd Reserve Companies, was also attached to the Division for the mission. Army Command 5 (*Armee-Oberkommando* or *AOK 5*) viewed Bagatelle as a fortress and thus assigned the operation to *Generalleutnant* Kaempffer, its resident *General der Pioniere*. He quickly deployed siege weapons, including heavy, medium, and light

Major d. L. Reddemann,
Komp.-Führ. der 2./Pi. 29

Major der Landwehr Bernhard Reddemann. In 1914 he was a Hauptmann in command of the 2nd Company of Posensisches Pionier-Bataillon Nr. 29.

trench mortars and flamethrowers.[7] The 4th Company of Pioneer Battalion No. 29 used flamethrowers at Bagatelle-Pavillon on either October 4, according to a German source,[8] or October 5, as a French writer claimed.[9] From both accounts it is clear that the historic assault was not successful, though the former provided no details.

In the French version, German pioneers tried to drive the French back by setting fire to the undergrowth. First they threw packages of ignited nitrocellulose tablets, the kind used to burn houses. Since the thickets were still wet from recent rainfall, they did not catch fire. As a second attempt, the pioneers brought *Kleif M.1912* from Metz:

> These apparatuses launched a jet of burning liquid a distance of a score of meters. Their effects in a close-quarter fight were terrifying.
>
> However, all these means did not prevent the French from keeping their cool and their positions, and from

> obstructing the approaches of the Germans by musket fire and artillery, prohibiting any work on that day.[10]

This action took place not far from where Reddemann and the 2nd Company of Pioneer Battalion No. 29 were campaigning. On October 10, 1914, *Leutnant* Kienast became interim commander of the 2nd Company and Reddemann returned to Berlin.[11] Reddemann remained company commander until November 3, after which date he took on the project of creating a flamethrower detachment. It is not difficult to imagine that his October 10 trip to Berlin was made to lobby the War Ministry for a separate flamethrower formation that he would lead himself.

After the war Reddemann put in writing what he may have reported to the War Ministry, that flamethrowers had not lived up to expectations:

> Even then they exhibited a set of technical disadvantages. Above all, however, there were no officers and crews set up as specialists who would make as their principal occupation the versatile application of this close-combat weapon. They would thus also be able to collect organizational and tactical principles for the correct utilization of the new weapon and for fitting the infantry experiences into the mode of attack.
>
> The experiences made with the application of these first flamethrowers were therefore not encouraging.[12]

Around the time that Reddemann was conferring with the War Ministry about the future of the flamethrower, army commanders were defining the role of the weapon. Note 32, dated October 16, 1914, was sent from Saint-Quentin by the headquarters of the Second Army and titled "Arms Available to the Pioneers for Close Combat: Projectors for Flame and Smoke-producing Liquid":

> The commander-in-chief will place these arms at the disposal of the army corps according to their needs. At the same time, the corps will receive the absolutely essential personnel educated in the usage of these devices, who will have to be reinforced by pioneers of the field companies after they receive the necessary instruction for this purpose.

This pioneer of Pionier-Bataillon Nr. 29 displays a captured Schilt Number 3, the earliest portable flamethrower fielded by the French. On October 4-5, 1914, the 4th Company of Pionier-Bataillon Nr. 29 became the first unit to use flamethrowers in combat.

Right: Pioneer Unteroffizier armed with a Kleif M.1912 in 1914. Note the facemask, an item not described in any known German sources. The lance features the straight nozzle, here fitted with an igniter; the hose of a propellant bottle is visible on the wooden box in the background.

> The flame projectors are used by pioneers especially trained for this purpose; they are apparatuses similar to portable fire extinguishers, which project a liquid that immediately ignites spontaneously. The waves of flame have a working length and width of twenty meters. They have an immediate deadly effect and they force the enemy a long way back because of the heat that they produce. As they burn from one and a half to two minutes and can be stopped at will, short individual bursts are advisable in order to engage several objectives with only one filling of the tank. The flame projectors will be used mainly in house and street fighting and will be held ready at the position from where the assault will be launched.[13]

From this note, it appears that there were flamethrower pioneers who were attached to various army corps to serve as both assault troops and instructors. Field pioneers were trained as flamethrower operators when necessary.

No officially designated flamethrower-pioneer formation existed at this time, but a War Ministry order titled "Requirement of Pioneer Spare Equipment for Dispatch in the Field," dated November 11, 1914, stated that special weapons of the pioneers such as trench mortars and ammunition, flamethrowers, hand grenades, rifle grenades, and smoke charges were exclusively at the disposal of the Supreme Army Command. With the exception of flamethrowers, the weapons were to be held for use in the west by Pioneer Replacement Battalion No. 24 in Cologne, and for use in the east by Pioneer Replacement Battalion No. 29 in Posen. Flamethrowers and accessories were to be held by the Acting Engineer Committee (*stellvertretendes Ingenieur-Komitee*) in Berlin.[14] Thus the Supreme Army Command seems to have been the centralized authority that determined which pioneer units received flamethrowers and were sent into combat and/or to train other pioneers.

Note 32 was captured by the Allies in April of 1915 and the subtitle translated as "Flame or Asphyxiating Gas Projectors."[15] The Germans did not use flamethrowers to spray poison gas in combat prior to the document's capture, but British military intelligence may have read Fiedler's 1908 patents and seen how the devices had been designed to do so. In a British magazine article from 1916, Note 32 received extensive if somewhat exaggerated coverage. The writer called flamethrowers "fire-squirts" and insisted that they were "one of the Krupp secrets for blasting a road to Calais through the best armies of the Allied Powers." He also claimed that the sprayed oil "flamed spontaneously as it met the air," implying a chemical reaction instead of ignition from an external source. Finally, the range of the jet was said to be 100 feet instead of the sixty-six feet stated in the note.[16]

French soldier modeling a Kleif M.1912, captured in Alsace from a German line-pioneer unit. The top of the flamethrower has been painted a lighter color to camouflage it when the operator crouched in a shell hole or trench, and the retracted telescoping lance is missing the nozzle and igniter holder.

One of the pioneer formations that provided flamethrower instruction to other units was the 2nd Battalion of Pioneer Battalion No. 13, as shown in a memorandum addressed to an unidentified pioneer battalion, dated November 9, 1914:

> Until further notice, flamethrower training takes place from 8:00 A.M. to 2:30 P.M. at the pioneer exercise ground in Martin-Puich (southern end), conducted by the 1st Reserve Company, Pioneer Battalion No. 13.
>
> For that, one noncommissioned officer and six men from each company; if possible, two men from each platoon.

Vise Paris N° 122
CAMPAGNE DE 1914-1915
ND.
Matériel allemand. Crapouillots, mitrailleuse, réservoir pour liquide inflammable.

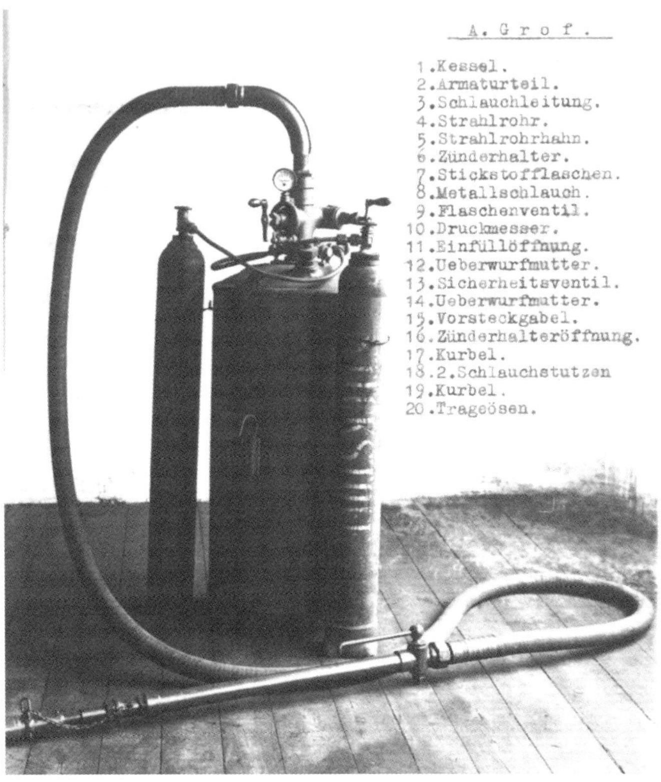
A. G r o f .
1.Kessel.
2.Armaturteil.
3.Schlauchleitung.
4.Strahlrohr.
5.Strahlrohrhahn.
6.Zünderhalter.
7.Stickstofflaschen.
8.Metallschlauch.
9.Flaschenventil.
10.Druckmesser.
11.Einfüllöffnung.
12.Ueberwurfmutter.
13.Sicherheitsventil.
14.Ueberwurfmutter.
15.Vorsteckgabel.
16.Zünderhalteröffnung.
17.Kurbel.
18.2.Schlauchstutzen
19.Kurbel.
20.Trageösen.

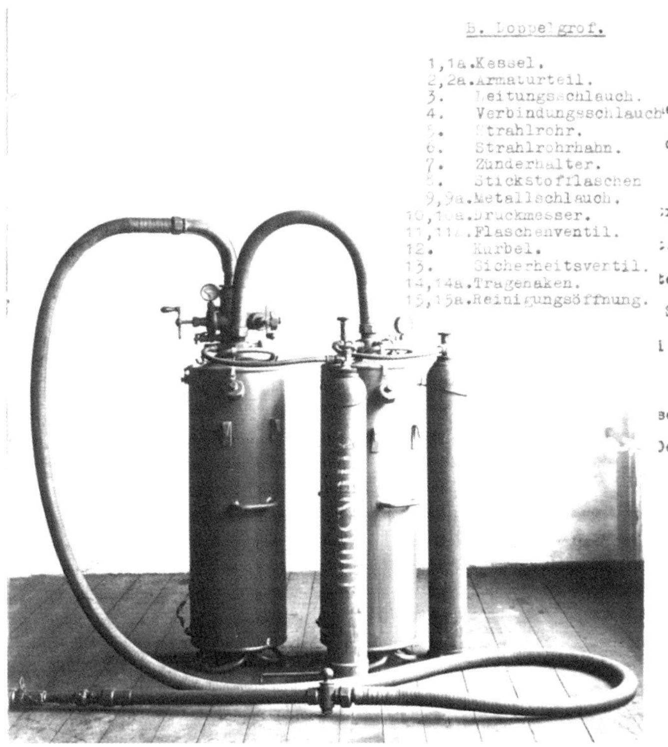
B. Doppelgrof.
1,1a.Kessel.
2,2a.Armaturteil.
3. Leitungsschlauch.
4. Verbindungsschlauch
5. Strahlrohr.
6. Strahlrohrhahn.
7. Zünderhalter.
8. Stickstofflaschen
9,9a.Metallschlauch.
10,10a.Druckmesser.
11,11a.Flaschenventil.
12. Kurbel.
13. Sicherheitsventil.
14,14a.Tragehaken.
15,15a.Reinigungsöffnung.

Opposite
Top: French postcard showing captured German weaponry, including a Kleif M.1912. As in the previous photo, the telescoping lance of the Kleif is retracted and missing the nozzle and igniter holder. The screw-on cover that protects the pressure gauge on top is also absent. Courtesy Cyrille Gaston.

Bottom left: Grof M.1912 and M.1914 telescoping large lance. The mechanisms on top of the flamethrower include a curved fuel outflow pipe to which the hose is attached; a pressure gauge; and the oil-pressurization and oil-release valves. This model flamethrower held forty-five gallons of oil. Bundesarchiv Militärarchiv PH5-II/496.

Bottom right: Double Grof (Doppelgrof) produced by the Selke company. Each oil tank held twenty-six gallons. On the floor is the M.1914 telescoping large lance. Bundesarchiv Militärarchiv PH5-II/496.

Right: Pioneer of Württemburgisches Pionier-Bataillon Nr. 13. In late 1914 the 1st Reserve Company of this battalion conducted flamethrower training for other pioneer formations and provided flamethrower squads for infantry units deployed to the western front.

> The officers must use the opportunity of this training to familiarize themselves with the apparatuses.
>
> Training will begin today at 2:30 P.M.
>
> 1st Reserve Company, Pioneer Battalion No. 13 must report when the training is completed.[17]

The *Kleif M.1912* was operated by a two-man squad; it therefore appears that in late 1914 pioneer formations included one two-man flamethrower squad per platoon.

During this period eighteen NCOs and 161 men of the 1st Reserve Company of Pioneer Battalion No. 13 were attached to the 55th Reserve Brigade, 28th Reserve Division, XIV Reserve Corps, near Mametz. These pioneers were divided into subunits assigned specific weapons or tasks:

> one rifle-grenade troop - one NCO and eight men
> one trench mortar battery - one NCO and twelve men
> four mining troops - four NCOs and thirty-two men
> three sapper troops - three NCOS and twenty-four men
> three construction troops for shelters - three NCOs and twenty-four men
> four hand-grenade troops - four NCOs and thirty-two men
> one troop for constructing brigade shelters - one NCO and six men
> two depot troops for supply depots - eight men
> one searchlight platoon - one NCO and thirteen men
> one flamethrower squad - two men[18]

The attached pioneer troops were under the overall command of a pioneer officer and two *Vizefeldwebeln*, who were responsible for the construction and technical work done in the sector. Orders for the trench-mortar battery, hand-grenade troops, searchlight platoon, and flamethrower squad were formulated by pioneer officers in the front-line position, in agreement with the regimental and battalion infantry commanders. Alone among the armed pioneers the two-man flamethrower squad lacked direct supervision by a pioneer NCO. This and the input of untrained infantry officers illustrate how flamethrowers were improperly or ineffectively used when first introduced. It is not known if the flamethrower squad attached to the 55th Reserve Brigade saw combat.

Flamethrowers Recalled

At the end of 1914, flamethrowers were mostly withdrawn from service, although some pioneer formations retained them well into 1915. The Supreme Army Command wrote in a report to the War Ministry that the apparatuses were unusable and the troops rejected them.[19] According to Reddemann and flamethrower-pioneer officer and author Charles Theune, there were two reasons why flamethrowers were a failure. First, the devices were a completely new type of weapon that required extensive training and understanding of its capabilities, neither of which the pioneers had at the time.[20] Second, the *Kleif M.1912* was technically defective. It was too fragile, too large and unwieldy, and could not maintain a consistent pressure.[21]

A comprehensive report on the shortcomings of the *Kleif M.1912* was filed by *Leutnant der Landwehr* Schenck of the 3rd Company, Bavarian 4th (Fortress) Pioneer Replacement Battalion (*Königlich Bayerisches 4. [Festungs-] Pionier-Ersatz-Bataillon*), on December 6, 1914. This secret document, sent from Ingolstadt, was titled "Remarks on the Training of Flamethrower Operators":

The armatures are poorly designed, presumably out of the intention that the apparatus be carried as easily as possible. It is therefore feared that the apparatuses will soon become useless in the field and/or require many spare parts.

Filling the gas tanks with air instead of Number 16 *Fl.W.*, which consists of nitrogen or carbonic acid, appears dangerous because the flame oil absorbs air and the apparatus leaks, creating an explosive mixture of air and flame oil. Since the propellant bottles are transported containing neither nitrogen nor carbonic acid, constant caution is required on site.

A disadvantage in handling the apparatuses is the fact that the lance is connected to the flame-oil tank by a swiveling elbow joint. It can be foreseen that handling the apparatus in its current form will not be particularly comfortable, and there is a danger that through an inadvertent movement of the carrier the elbow joint or lance will be bent, thereby rendering the entire apparatus nearly useless.

Teenage assault troopers of Königlich Bayerisches 4. (Festungs-) Pionier-Ersatz-Bataillon, which received flamethrower training in 1914. Note the shovels with shortened handles and the M.1915 Pickelhauben with spikes removed. The stick grenades are inert, as indicated by drilled heads painted red.

It may have to be considered whether or not it would be better to replace the swiveling elbow joint with a flexible hose. The weapon rarely achieves an effect of eighteen meters; the longest ranges are observed only in the first individual spray.

Apart from the direct influence on living targets, no particularly outstanding effects were observed. Only easily inflammable materials (straw, dry sticks, and such) immediately caught fire. In drills, individual flame bursts did not burn new wood at all, except in connection with the previously mentioned materials. To burn new wood, a continuous stream of flame must be thrown.

Of the enemy nothing much can be seen at short distances (about fifty paces in front of the flamethrower) because the burning flame oil produces a very intensive smoke cloud which goes into action very disturbingly and covers everything.

The applicability of the portable light flamethrower will therefore be quite limited.[22]

Flammenwerfer-Abteilung Reddemann

To deal with the problems of both the flamethrower and its poorly trained personnel, Bernhard Reddemann proposed to the War Ministry and the Acting Engineer Committee that he form a special unit devoted to the device. It would be armed exclusively with the flamethrower and would develop the weapon technically and organizationally. Just as importantly, it would create entirely new flamethrower tactics.[23]

Reddemann pitched his flamethrower unit as a means of driving the enemy out of nearby trenches, the weapon to be used strictly for close combat. Doubtless he reminded his superiors that he successfully defended Fort Glowno with flamethrowers in 1907. At the end of 1914 Reddemann was given permission to organize a small unit that later took the field under the designation Flamethrower Detachment Reddemann (*Flammenwerfer-Abteilung Reddemann*).[24] A Posen Fire Brigade *Feldwebel* named Ambrosius was recruited as *Offizier-Stellvertreter*; the remaining forty-eight men were fire-brigade personnel from Posen and young war volunteers.[25]

War volunteers of the 2nd Recruit Depot, Garde-Pionier-Ersatz-Bataillon in October of 1914. Flammenwerfer-Abteilung Reddemann was comprised of firefighters and war volunteers, possibly Guard Pioneers. In fact the young man standing in the center of the second row appears in another image as a member of the flamethrower replacement battalion. Most of the soldiers in this photo wear the M.1895 service jacket in dark blue (Dunkelblau).

Municipal firefighters from the town of Kattowitz. The age range of these men corresponds to that of Reddemann's flamethrower operators. Older, more experienced firefighters had lost the natural human fear of flame, while younger men were recruited for their energy and greater physical strength.

Reddemann knew from the beginning that having the right weapons and tactics would not be enough:

> Combat equipment alone does not bring success in war; on the contrary, above all it is the men that you must employ and the spirit that you must inspire. To make this new close-combat equipment into an effective instrument of assault, specially suitable tactics had to be devised, on behalf of which a specially created unit had to be organized in a suitable manner for the modern conduct of war ... but above all create in yourself the necessary heroic spirit of attack and keep it permanently[.][26]

This "heroic spirit of attack" could be found, incongruously enough, in firefighters. Many were older army reservists who were familiar with spraying equipment, were calm and cautious when dealing with fire, and understood the principles of the new weapon. It is likely that some or even most of the firefighters recruited into the new Flamethrower Detachment had worked with Reddemann on his hand-pumped weapons in 1907. As strange as it sounds that men devoted to putting out fires would enthusiastically volunteer to start them, a German pioneer general explained it in a postwar speech to the veterans of the flamethrower regiment:

> Even then we said to ourselves: The firemen must get their hands on something like [a flamethrower]. And that is what happened with some success, as you can see. We thought so and were proved right during the war. The pioneer, who in peacetime boringly gets used to "cleaning up," never feels as good as when he is in battle, for example blasting, and can blow something nicely in two without having to clean up afterwards. These firemen, used to putting fires out in peacetime, happily start them in wartime. You still seem to be proud of this tradition, and rightly so.[27]

Flamethrower Detachment Reddemann was formed in Berlin and assigned to the Fifth Army.[28] It traveled to Aachen on February 1, 1915, obtaining six automobiles that each towed three two-wheeled trailers for transporting equipment, reserves of flame oil, and personnel. On February 15 the

Detachment accompanied the VI Reserve Corps to Romagne sous Montfaucon to prepare for its first action.[29]

The First Large-scale Flamethrower Attack

In a memorandum dated February 12, 1915, two weeks before the first large-scale flamethrower attack, the General Inspection of Engineer and Pioneer Corps (*General-Inspektion des Ingenieur- und Pionier-Korps*) in Berlin addressed the issue of flame oil:

> The *Fiedler-Flammenapparat Gesellschaft*, the *Firma Chemische Fabrik* in Aktien (the distinguished E. Schering) and Professor Dr. Peppenberg were asked if flame oil will decompose if stored for a long time, and if explosive chemical compounds will form. The three agreed that flame oil stored for a long time will neither decompose nor form explosive chemical compounds. When using the flamethrower, an explosive compound can form only if oxygen or hydrogen are used [as propellants] in place of nitrogen and/or carbonic acid in conjunction with the regulation [oil] Numbers 2 and 16 for the light portable flamethrower, and/or if atmospheric air is introduced into the flamethrower. When nitrogen or carbonic acid are correctly used as the propellant for the flamethrower, an explosion of the flame oil is absolutely impossible.[30]

Richard Fiedler was thus closely involved in Flamethrower Detachment Reddemann's first operation, scheduled to take place in the woods of Malancourt where the German advance had bogged down. "When and where will we finally go forward again?" asked a pioneer officer named von Schaewen. "The pioneers cannot endure the sitting in place."[31] At Malancourt aerial photographs showed a broad sector where both sides were almost on top of each other across a battlefront that had been cleared of trees by artillery. There was nothing to obstruct jets of flame.[32]

Before the attack, scheduled for 11:00 A.M. on February 26, Reddemann reconnoitered the German position with the commander of the pioneers of the VI Reserve Corps. Von Schaewen of Pioneer Regiment 29 referred to the "well-known" *Hauptmann der Landwehr* Reddemann,[33] perhaps indicating that the nascent flamethrower commander was already somewhat of a celebrity in his branch of service.

Reddemann doubted that the Fiedler *Grof M.1912* would be suitable for the assault, given its bulk and duration of only forty-five seconds with the 0.4-inch (11mm) nozzle.[34] He decided to use small, hand-pumped flamethrowers instead, because they were connected by hose to reservoirs that could be refilled indefinitely, providing the three- to four-minute duration that he thought would be necessary. The Acting Engineer Committee therefore ordered ten portable, hand-powered sprayers. They were small enough to be carried through narrow, winding trenches and had a range of 100 to 115 feet. The French positions were fifteen to forty yards from the German sap heads, ideal for a flame attack.

At some point Reddemann changed his mind and supplemented his ten hand pumps with two Fiedler *Grof M.1912*. On February 25, 1915, the twelve flamethrowers were set up in the German sap heads fifty-five to sixty-six yards apart, across a front of 770 yards. Each flamethrower would "comb" a fifty-five-yard stretch of enemy trench.

Careful reconnaissance of the French line was carried out the night before the operation. Early the next morning the

Malancourt, the heavily wooded site of the first full-scale flamethrower attack.

French postcard depicting a mass flame attack. Note the hand-pumped flamethrower in the foreground, similar to the ones used by Reddemann's men at Malancourt on February 26, 1915.

Small hand pump of the type Reddemann converted to flamethrowers for use at Malancourt. One hose was connected to a lance and the other to an oil reservoir. Ten such weapons were deployed, along with two Fiedler Grof M.1912.

oil containers were carried to the emplaced flamethrowers by specially trained infantrymen who were ordered to contain their excitement and make no noise. The assault companies were "full of the best confidence in the outcome of the new devil's work of the Black Collars,"[35] a description which may have meant that the men of the Detachment wore blue municipal fire-brigade uniforms with black collars.

Immediately prior to the attack the flamethrower hoses were filled with oil up to the stopcocks of the lances. The infantry sentries stood behind steel trench shields, firing occasionally; according to Reddemann, the men of his Detachment were calm and confident of victory. At 10:59 German howitzer batteries pounded the first and second French lines, raising a solid wall of black smoke.[36] One minute later the flamethrower operators and squad leaders stood and exposed themselves above the breastworks, unleashing twelve streams of fire that fell onto the enemy trench with a loud hissing sound. Reddemann wrote that screams of pain came from the unsuspecting Frenchmen:

> Where they were not caught by the flames, they jumped out toward the rear of the trenches. Head over heels, without cover, they ran cross country. There was no time to run to the rear through the communication trenches. Only away, away, ahead of the frightful flames! Everything was left where it lay, except for their rifles. Untroubled by machine-gun fire, our infantry ran across the open ground. That is by far not as bad as the horrible flame-killed with whom they came to grips.[37]

The French were taken completely by surprise, as can be imagined. They simply had no idea what was happening to them. An account allegedly given by a survivor is horrifying, but its veracity must be questioned because the soldier claimed that the attack took place at dusk instead of in the morning. True or not, it captures the panic of the victims:

> Suddenly one of my comrades shouted, 'Hallo! what is this coming down on us? Any one would think it was petroleum.' At that time we could not believe the truth,

Above: Firefighters of an unidentified German municipal fire brigade. Note the black collars of their uniforms; one eyewitness account of the flame attack at Malancourt referred to Reddemann's men as the "Black Collars," raising the possibility that they wore fire-brigade uniforms.

Top right: The flamethrower attack at Malancourt, as depicted by Dutch cartoonist Louis Raemaekers. The caption reads, "Burning liquids. The marvels of Kultur."

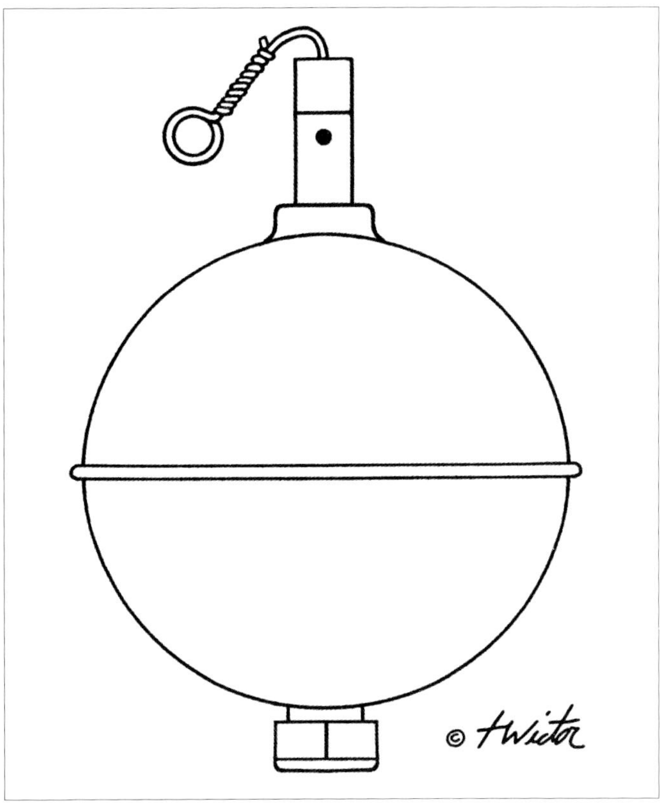

Right: Incendiary grenade (Brandgranate or Brand-Handgranate), also known as the flame ball (Flammenkugel), used by Flammenwerfer-Abteilung Reddemann at Malancourt. Externally identical to the smoke grenade (Nebelhandgranate), it had a five- or seven-second friction fuse that was activated when the wire ring was pulled.

but the liquid which began to spray on us was certainly some kind of petroleum. The Germans were pumping it from hoses. Our sub-lieutenant made us put out our pipes. But it was a useless precaution. A few seconds later incendiary bombs began to rain down on us and the whole trench burst into flame. It was like being in hell. Some of the men began to scream terribly, tearing off their clothes, trying to beat out the flames. Others were cursing and choking in the hot vapour which stifled us. 'Oh, my Christ!' cried a comrade of mine. 'They've blinded me!' In order to complete their work those German bandits took advantage of our disturbance by advancing on the trench and throwing burning torches into it. None of us escaped that torrent of fire. We had our eyebrows and eyelashes burned off, and clothes were burned in great patches and our flesh was sizzling like roasting meat.[38]

As is often the case in his writings, Reddemann declared total success. After three or four minutes of spraying, his men shut off their flamethrowers, picked up their rifles, and joined the attack as infantrymen, even though they had received no orders to do so. All four French lines were taken. Reddemann reported two or three flamethrower operators wounded but neglected to mention that one was killed and another died the next day.[39] Even with these losses, the men of the Detachment did not falter. "Courage in the face of death brought them forward."[40] They helped capture three machine guns and seven trench mortars, take many prisoners, and win terrain almost 700 yards deep. Not only was the flame-covered front cleared of the enemy, the French on the right and left flanks fled to an overall breadth of 2,400 yards. The laconic, black-humored observation of von Schaewen: "So once again the fresh pioneer spirit made things lively."[41]

According to American newspaper articles an apparatus resembling a fire engine was used in the attack,[42] and the Frenchmen felt a hot wind blowing in their faces seconds before the flames struck.[43] Unlike in Reddemann's account, the French were said to have stood their ground at the second line and counterattacked with a furious bayonet charge that forced the Germans to withdraw, leaving 150 dead and sixty

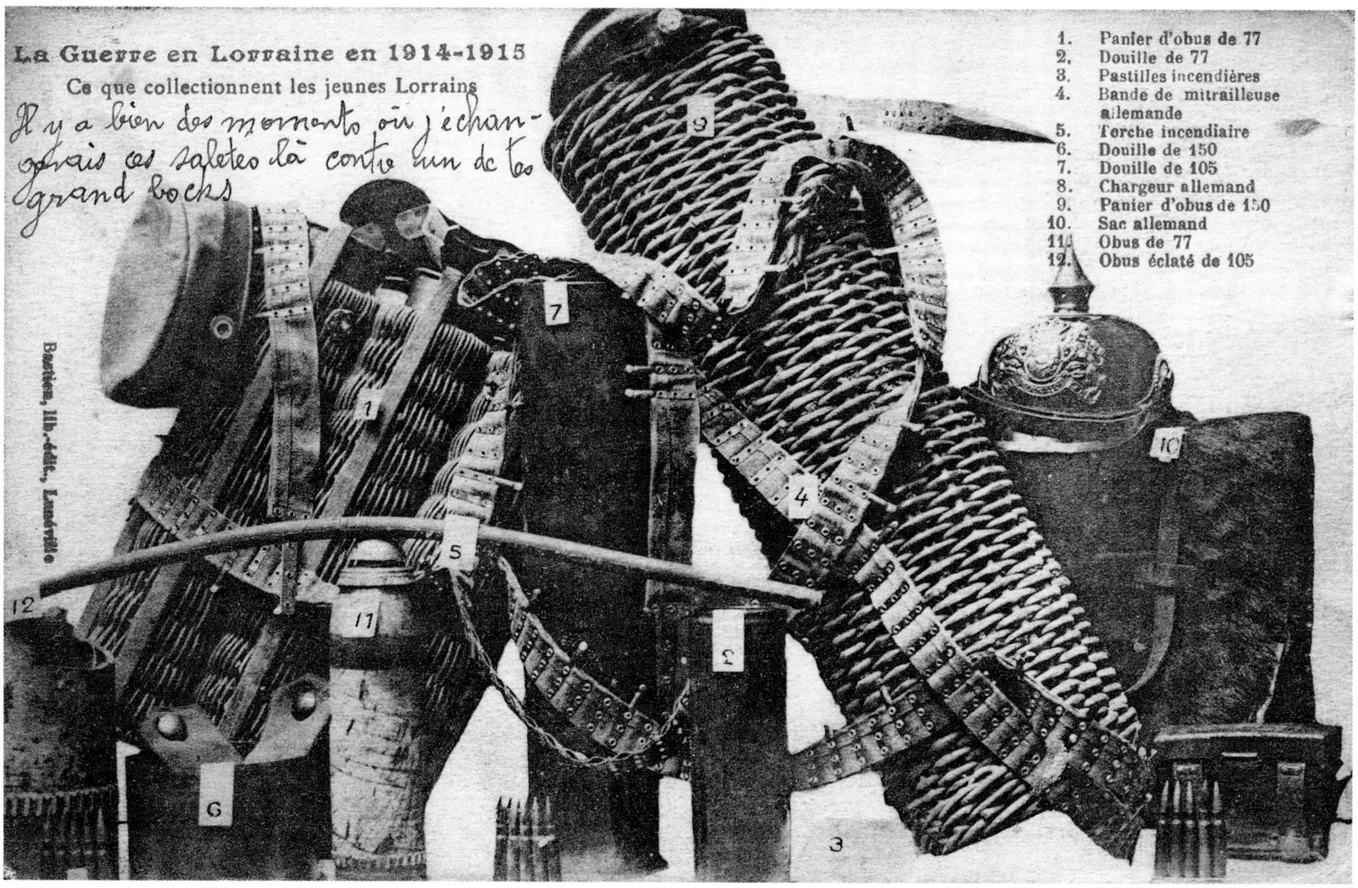

War material collected by Lorrainese children. Item No. 5 is a ground flare (Flammenfeuer), an incendiary device the Germans threw into the French trenches at Malancourt.

prisoners.[44] By the next day almost all the ground lost had been retaken.[45]

Aftermath

"Following this attack much recognition for the flamethrowers came from all sides," Reddemann wrote.[46] He himself learned several lessons from the experience. The most important was that all enemy resistance ceased within fifteen seconds of the first flame jet striking the trench, which made the three- to four-minute duration of the hand sprayers unnecessary. In addition, the assault troops should have been equipped with portable flamethrowers in order to carry the "terror of the flames" even further than the range of the large weapons, which would have broken the French resistance even more quickly and thoroughly. It was also apparent that superheated gases projected far ahead of the actual flames themselves and had a great effect on the enemy.[47]

Immediately after the attack *Oberleutnant der Reserve* Wolf of the Leipzig Fire Brigade was assigned to the detachment, along with two *Unteroffiziere* and twenty men of an unidentified unit;[48] they would likely have been firefighters, pioneers, or both. A second, smaller flame attack was carried out at Vauquois, near Verdun, following which Reddemann was recalled to Berlin by the Supreme Army Command and authorized to form an entire flamethrower battalion.

Some of Reddemann's first flamethrower operators may have worn the field-gray M.1910 service jacket of the Garde-Pionier-Bataillon, a young member of which is shown in this undated Berlin studio portrait. Note the plain field-gray shoulder straps piped in red, the service cap (Dienstmütze) with black band piped in red, and the long S98 bayonet.

CHAPTER THREE

The *III. Garde-Pionier-Bataillon*

On March 15, 1915, the Supreme Army Command ordered that a flamethrower battalion be established. It was raised in Berlin around a core of men from the Guard Pioneer Replacement Battalion (*Garde-Pionier-Ersatz-Bataillon*).[1]

Prewar pioneer battalions consisted of four companies, the 1st through the 4th. In the case of the Guard Pioneer Battalion, the Pioneer Experimental Company served as the de facto 5th Company. On mobilization the peacetime pioneer battalions were divided into two field battalions of three companies each, a move that created the *I. Garde-Pionier-Bataillon* (1st, 2nd, and 3rd Companies) and the *II. Garde-Pionier-Bataillon* (4th Company, 1st and 2nd Reserve Companies). In early 1915 each peacetime pioneer battalion received the 5th Company, which brought the total number of Guard Pioneer companies to eight.

The new flamethrower battalion was therefore designated the 3rd Guard Pioneer Battalion (*III. Garde-Pionier-Bataillon*), comprised of the 9th through 12th Companies and the Experimental Company (*Versuchs-Kompagnie*). On June 1, 1915, the Replacement Company (*Ersatz-Kompagnie*) was added.[2]

The 3rd Guard Pioneer Battalion had an initial strength of 800.[3] Its noncommissioned officers and men were drawn not only from the Guard Pioneer Replacement Battalion but also fire brigades, sixteen different pioneer battalions,[4] and most other branches of the service.[5] Volunteers from all over the empire,

Right: Line pioneers of different units recruited as flamethrower personnel. Sixteen pioneer battalions from all over the empire provided volunteers for the III. Garde-Pionier-Bataillon. Note the shabby uniforms and cloth reinforcing patches on the trouser knees. This undated photo may have been taken at flamethrower school.

Opposite
Top: 15. Corporalschaft, Garde-Pionier-Ersatz-Bataillon, posing grimly with beer, bread, and domestic accouterments; the small sign board reads "Cosy Hour of Finery." This unit supplied men who formed the core of the III. Garde-Pionier-Bataillon. Remaining positions were filled by firefighters and volunteers from all branches of service.

Bottom: Assault Detachment 27 (Sturmabteilung 27) of Infanterie-Regiment König Wilhelm I (6. Württemburgisches) Nr. 124. Assault troops such as these were given priority in the new flamethrower battalion. The cardboard sign is decorated with drawings of pistols and stick grenades, the trench raider's weapons of choice.

Gemütliche
Putzstunde
15. Corporalschaft
Nigrin

they were the "best and bravest"[6] and would fight *en masse* or in individual squads, on almost every conceivable terrain, and under any climatic, seasonal, or tactical condition.

Hauptmann der Landwehr Reddemann, soon to be known by his men as the "Prince of Hades,"[7] was the commander of the flamethrower battalion, while *Oberleutnant der Reserve* Fritsch was the adjutant. The company commanders were *Hauptmann der Reserve* Beck (9th Company), *Hauptmann der Reserve* Lewus (10th Company), *Oberleutnant der Reserve* Wolf (11th Company), *Leutnant der Reserve* Nitsch (12th Company), and *Oberleutnant der Reserve* Lindner (Research Company).[8]

The 3rd Guard Pioneer Battalion provided unique and exacting challenges for its members. Officers and men from diverse units and locales had to be welded into a unified force, create the technology and tactics of flame warfare, and develop the appropriate spirit for the use of the new weapon. The battalion was under the direct control of the Supreme Army Command, to which Reddemann addressed all of his proposals. He was also ordered to present written reports every two or three months, describing the organization and state of the unit, its engagements, the new practical experiences and extensions of this form of attack, and the new experiments and equipment. Finally, he delivered a monthly oral report to the Operations Detachment (*Operationsabteilung*) of the Supreme Army Command.

Individual flamethrower companies or the battalion as a whole were put at the disposal of the various armies and army groups for specific objectives. When at the front the battalion or its companies were subordinate to written order No. I 7791. op. of the Chief of the General Staff of the Field Army (*Chefs des Generalstabs des Feldheeres*). This decree stipulated in part that only the tactically responsible unit commander, in accordance with the particularity of the equipment and in agreement with the commander of the flamethrowers, gave the tactical order for the attack. The technical details of the flamethrowers' employment, along with the flame tactics, were left to Reddemann. The order also declared that the flamethrower was to be employed offensively; continuous introduction for a defensive purpose in the front line was prohibited.

Absolutely vital to the development of the 3rd Guard Pioneer Battalion was the support of Crown Prince Wilhelm, who lobbied for the new flamethrower unit and bankrolled it to an unknown extent, according to a former flamethrower pioneer.[9] Reddemann himself acknowledged the support of the Crown Prince and his father Kaiser Wilhelm II, referring to them as the unit's "highest friends and patrons."[10] The Crown Prince continued his close relationship with the flamethrower pioneers for the rest of the war and was instrumental in garnering the prestigious death's head (*Totenkopf*) sleeve badge that they were awarded on July 28, 1916.

Crown Prince Wilhelm[12] (1882-1951), friend and patron of the III. Garde-Pionier-Bataillon. Note the Prussian-style death's head badge on his service cap, the insignia of his former unit, 1 Leib-Husaren-Regiment Nr. 1.

Combat Equipment of the Flamethrower Battalion

Each 139-man field company of the 3rd Guard Pioneer Battalion was armed with twelve large Fiedler flamethrowers, the *Grof M.1912* that Reddemann called the "gas sprayer."[11] The range was deemed sufficient at 115 to 130 feet, but the size and weight of the weapon made it unwieldy in trenches, leading the experimental company to begin work on an improved model. In combat the large flamethrower was operated by a five-man *Grof* squad (*Groftrupp*) consisting of an *Unteroffizier* or *Gefreiter* in charge, a lance operator (*Strahlrohrführer*), an assistant (*Hilfsmann*) to help support the hose, and two *Grof* staff (*Grofleute*) to open the gas and oil valves.

In addition to the twelve *Grof*, each field company also received eighteen *Kleif* or small flamethrowers, a decision based on experience gleaned at Malancourt and Vauquois. Two models of *Kleif* were issued to the 3rd Guard Pioneer Battalion: The first was the Fiedler *Kleif M.1914*, converted from the defective Fiedler *Kleif M.1912* and operated by a four-man attack squad (*Angriffstrupp*) modeled on those of the fire brigades.[12] A *Kleif* squad (*Kleiftrupp*) consisted of an *Unteroffizier* or *Gefreiter*, a lance operator, a *Kleif* carrier (*Kleifträger*), and an assistant who also served as a replacement and a grenadier. To modify the *M.1912* into the *M.1914*, either Fielder or the battalion workshop replaced the telescoping lance with an M.1914 small lance (*kleine Strahlrohr M.1914*)

Soldiers of the III. Garde-Pionier-Bataillon displaying a Kleif M.1914 and the 4.6ft. (1.4m) version of the small lance (kleine Strahlrohr M.1914), armed with a live igniter. The swiveling oil-outflow pipe and oil-release stopcock are visible under the right arm of the Kleif carrier (Kleifträger). Both pioneers wear trousers with leather reinforcing patches on the knees.

A shock troop of four Kleif squads (Kleiftruppen) armed with early-model Kleif M.1915. Their gear includes M.1915 Picklehauben with the spikes removed, Mauser C96 pistols, flashlights, M.1915 Gummimasken, water bottles, and assault packs. The igniter holders of the 4.6ft. (1.4m) lances are wrapped in cloth to keep out dirt, and the bulging sacks may be full of "flame balls" or incendiary grenades. Note the bayonet knots; they may be red and blue, which could mean that these are men of the 14th Company of the III. Garde-Pionier-Bataillon.

that was connected to the flamethrower by means of a rubber hose.

The second type of small flamethrower was the *Kleif M.1915*, a weapon that followed the basic layout of the 1910 Fiedler patent in that it had an external propellant tank. Like the *Kleif M.1914*, it featured a separate lance and rubber hose, and it was operated by a four-man *Kleif* squad. This flamethrower was manufactured to the battalion's specifications by a factory in Westphalia. Early and late models were produced.

All small flamethrowers regardless of type had a range of fifty to sixty-six feet. The battalion workshop continually improved the weapons, producing battery flamethrowers that connected two or three large or small flamethrowers to a single lance.

The experimental company of the battalion generated its own ideas and took input from the flamethrower operators in the field. Improvements in the weaponry were made quickly because the workshop was located at headquarters, and technical advancements had high priority. The hands-on experience of the troops was reported directly to the engineers of the research staff, many of whom were firefighters. Prototypes were designed, tested, manufactured, and fielded more rapidly than many present-day armies, partly because office-bound bureaucrats had been entirely eliminated from the process.[13]

Each field company of the 3rd Guard Pioneer Battalion was comprised in part of three combat platoons (*Kampfzüge*); there may have been replacement and ordnance detachments as well. In late 1915 the number of *Grof* per field company was increased from twelve to twenty.

This short, overweight, middle-aged soldier exemplifies the veteran firefighters accepted into the III. Garde-Pionier-Bataillon. He wears the walking-out dress of the Guard Pioneers, including silver-trimmed spiked helmet and vereinfachte Waffenrock, the simplified field jacket mandated on March 3, 1915. Men unfit for combat served as instructors or in the battalion workshops.

Tactics

According to Reddemann, a "technically excellent" weapon, ideal organization, and the fighting spirit of the troops would not bring about the desired results unless the appropriate tactics were applied.[14] Flamethrowers were not suitable for every attack because they could only be used under the right circumstances. Thus it was imperative from the beginning that the flamethrower arm formulate tactics that worked. Every deployment brought new experience and new concepts; the battalion staff collated and improved upon them by talking to the participants and interviewing as many members of the unit as possible.

The tactic used at Malancourt was very simple: "shock" the enemy positions with large flamethrowers installed in intervals of fifty-five yards. This was known as the "stationary attack" (*stehenden Angriff*), and it was successful on only a few occasions. When small flamethrowers were added in order that the operators could leave their own positions and "bring the fear" all the way to the enemy's rear, this became the "combined stationary and pouncing attack" (*vereinten stehenden und springenden Angriff*). Later on the "pouncing attack" (*springenden Angriff*) with small flamethrowers alone was the tactic most often used.

At the training center in Berlin, officers and men were instructed in all three methods of frontal attack. Another tactic was "rolling up" (*Aufrollen*), whereby small flamethrowers were introduced into enemy trenches in flanking attacks, usually in conjunction with hand-grenade throwers.

A fifth tactic was tunneling, used when the enemy trench was more than forty-four yards distant. Long underground tunnels were dug out into No Man's Land, ending in camouflaged vertical shafts in front of the target. Large flamethrowers were moved into the tunnels and placed at the base of the shafts. At zero hour flamethrower operators popped out of the ground and sprayed the enemy at pointblank range. If the tunnel could not be dug far enough because of time constraints, the lance operators were trained to leap into the open and fire the flamethrower on the run, while assistants carried the hose behind. Reddemann claimed that because of the element of surprise, this tactic resulted in far fewer casualties than expected among his men.[15]

On May 15, 1915, the 9th Company of the 3rd Guard Pioneer Battalion was sent to Douai to reinforce Flamethrower Detachment Reddemann; the three remaining companies followed soon after. When the Battalion was fielded, each company received seven two-ton trucks, replacing the automobiles used by the Detachment.

Youngsters identified through other photos as flamethrower pioneers, probably from the III. Garde-Pionier-Bataillon. The square-jawed soldier in the center is outfitted in what appears to be a dark-blue firefighter's overcoat, the collar of which features black "coat panels" (Mantelpatten) with Guard lace.

Flamethrowers in Assault Squads

In the spring of 1915 some German divisions on the western front began deploying flamethrower operators in assault squads (*Sturmtrupps*), units created to overcome French strong points such as shelters and blockhouses hidden in woods. Assault squads were typically comprised of one to three infantry groups and one pioneer group armed with machine guns, trench mortars, and flamethrowers. They received special training behind the front lines and when brought forward were subordinate to infantry company commanders. The personality of the assault-squad leader was considered decisive for achieving success.[16]

It does not appear that the flamethrower personnel in question were members of the 3rd Guard Pioneer Battalion. Reddemann wrote nothing about these missions, and since

Right: Undated carte de visite by E. Petersdorff of Berlin. This flamethrower pioneer from the 16th Company of the III. Garde-Pionier-Bataillon poses for his formal portrait in the M.1895 dark-blue service jacket with plain red shoulder straps and black collar and cuffs piped in red. An M.1897 spiked helmet with a black parade plume (Paradebusch or Haarbusch) sits on the table beside him. The lanyard is a shooting award (Schützen-Abzeichen or Schützenschnuur), and the S98 bayonet displays an all-blue knot.

assault squads were under the direct command of infantry officers, it seems likely that the flamethrower operators and weapons were provided by line-pioneer formations. If so, the flamethrowers were obsolete *Kleif M.1912* that had not been sent back to Berlin.

The Bavarian *Ersatz* Division used assault squads on May 4, May 15, and July 7, 1915, all at unidentified locales. The latter operation began with a seventy-five-minute artillery bombardment, after which the Bavarians overran French positions along a front of almost 2000 yards. While the regular infantry pushed forward all the way to the fourth line of resistance, assault squads reduced the bypassed strong points. The engagement took only twenty-five minutes and cost the Germans few casualties.[17]

An Inauspicious Combat Debut

The 3rd Guard Pioneer Battalion first saw action on May 22, 1915, at Neuville, west of Douai. The 11th Company was ordered to launch a combined stationary and pouncing attack, "shocking" the enemy positions with *Grof* and following up with *Kleif*. Contrary to Reddemann's doctrine, the *Kleif* squads would accompany the infantry across a wide expanse of open ground instead of approaching stealthily under the cover of trenches. Reddemann was troubled by this "entirely new method of insertion," as it seemed ill conceived and a misuse of the flamethrower as a close-combat weapon.[18]

Although the operation was partially successful, the flamethrower troops suffered heavy casualties, sparking a debate within the officer corps over the usefulness of the weapon in frontal assaults. Reddemann rushed back to headquarters and promised that while his new force was not yet sufficiently trained to carry out such a mission, it would devise a way to do so.

As a first step in this process, the battalion adopted the principle that *Kleif* operators would not escort or support the infantry but would instead go in ahead of them as shock troops (*Stosstrupps*), a term coined by Reddemann himself.[19] These highly trained specialists would penetrate deeply into the

Kleif squad armed with a Kleif M.1914. In the center background, the bulky Bernhard Reddemann stands with a notebook. The flamethrower operators are likely from the III. or IV. Garde-Pionier-Bataillon. A disadvantage of the Kleif M.1914 was that the carrier had to support the swiveling oil-outflow pipe with his right hand.

Shock troop of an unknown infantry regiment. The term Stosstrupp was coined by Bernhard Reddemann to describe specially trained units of flamethrower pioneers who attacked ahead of the infantry. The men in this photo are armed with M.1917 stick grenades and the 9mm Lange Pistole 08.

enemy line and either bypass or silence points of resistance such as blockhouses and machine-gun nests. The regular infantry would hold back until the shock troops had broken large holes in the enemy line.

After much deliberation and practice, the battalion developed a tactic for crossing wide expanses of ground – sometimes over 1000 yards – in a "pure" pouncing attack. Reddemann dubbed it "Indian-style Forward Stalking" (*indianermässigen Vorpirschen*).[20] This technique called for the men to approach the target indirectly and as individuals rather than a unified mass. They would describe wide arcs and move forward in short leaps and bounds, staying within hearing distance of each other, constantly varying their intervals and taking cover behind the natural features of the terrain. Specially trained hand-grenade throwers from the battalion would accompany the "forward stalkers" in order to deal with enemy defenses.

It was important that the flamethrower squads hold their fire in order to not betray their presence and to present a harmless-looking, even bizarre spectacle that "the enemy often considers crazy, chaps hopping aimlessly from cover to cover."[21] When they had approached diagonally to within seventy to ninety yards, a designated flamethrower squad released a covering jet (*Deckungsstrahl*), which provided enough smoke and fire to allow the remainder of the group to make the final leap forward and spray the target.

For Indian-style Forward Stalking to succeed, the flamethrower troops had to be covered by machine-gun and trench-mortar or grenade-launcher fire during their entire approach. Such covering and suppressive fire not only forced the enemy to keep his head down, it distracted him from the vulnerable flamethrower squads out in the open. At this point in its development, the flamethrower battalion relied on machine gunners, trench-mortar personnel, and grenade-launcher squads on loan from the infantry. None of the parties were satisfied with this arrangement, however, because infantry commanders were loathe to give up such important assets, and the infantrymen tended to fear the flamethrowers.

Despite the problems, another tactic grew out of the cooperation between flamethrower pioneers and infantrymen. During an assault the machine gunners became part of the forward-stalking shock troops, providing close-range

Above: Kleif operator firing a flame burst by manipulating the lance stopcock. This flamethrower was capable of firing twenty-three one-second bursts with the 0.2in. (6mm) nozzle and ten bursts with the 0.3in. (8mm) nozzle.

Right: Postcard dated June 26, 1915, sent by Pionier Bialecki of the 12th Company, III. Garde-Pionier-Bataillon. The text is a message to Bialecki's daughter in Berlin and reads in part, "Something for your collection, from a different region." Humorously, he addresses his daughter as "Your Reverence" (Hochwohlgeboren). Bialecki's company took part in a flame attack at Côte de Senoux on June 24. Four flamethrower pioneers died in the engagement, indicating heavy fighting.

suppressing fire from the flanks. The grenade-launcher squads would either accompany the shock troops to the objective, or they would lay down covering fire from the jumping-off point. Since the target was "squeezed" between machine guns, grenade launchers, and flamethrowers, this new approach was called the "Pincers Tactic" (*Zangen-taktik*).[22]

According to Reddemann, casualties among flamethrower squads using Indian-style Forward Stalking and the Pincers Tactic were surprisingly light, though he admitted to occasional heavy losses. Steely nerves, physical adroitness, intelligent use of the terrain, quick decisiveness, and "aggressive caution" were important for success, but above all the flamethrower pioneer needed extraordinary courage and contempt for death.

"However, men with such outstanding qualities were, thank God, always present in large numbers among the officers and men of the flamethrower troops," Reddemann wrote.[23]

Successful Large-scale Flamethrower Assaults

General der Infanterie Erich von Falkenhayn, chief of staff of the army, issued the following order on June 11, 1915, about two weeks before Reddemann resumed large-scale flamethrower attacks:

> A secret document concerning instruction for the use of the flamethrower has recently fallen into the enemy's hands again. The loss of such important documents must be avoided under all circumstances. It is therefore repeated that it is strictly forbidden for them to be carried into the front-line trenches.[24]

This memorandum shows that flamethrower training was classified, and the highest levels of the army believed the improved weapon had vast potential. At the end of June the British breached German efforts at secrecy by capturing their first intact portable flamethrower. A cylinder with separate chambers for oil and propellant, this "liquid fire gun" had a range of sixty-six feet and was fitted with universal joints and a nozzle capable of rotation in any direction,[25] all of which identify it as a *Kleif M.1912*. It is possible that the device was captured from a line-pioneer assault squad.

On July 13, 1915, Reddemann personally directed a combined stationary and pouncing attack on the Bolante in the Argonne. Eleven *Grof* and eleven *Kleif* were used by the 11th Company under *Hauptmann* Wolf. Reddemann's clinical observation: "The enemy left the forward trenches screaming."[26] Three positions and many prisoners were taken. On the same day the 9th Company under *Hauptmann* Beck launched another combined stationary and pouncing attack along a front of 2200 yards near St. Hubert in the Argonne.

Late-model Kleif M.1915. Note the white smoke rising from the burning igniter on the lance nozzle. The Kleif squad consisted of an Unteroffizier or Gefreiter in charge, a lance operator (Strahlrohrführer), a Kleif carrier, and an assistant (Hilfsmann).

Nine *Grof* and eleven *Kleif* were employed. Here, too, the enemy evacuated the forward line in a panic, and many prisoners were taken without much resistance.

The most famous large-scale flamethrower operation in this period was carried out on July 30, 1915, against the British Eighth Rifle Brigade at Hooge, about 3 miles east of Ypres. The 9th Company of the 3rd Guard Pioneer Battalion under *Hauptmann* Beck attacked with nine *Grof* and eleven *Kleif* in a combined stationary and pouncing attack. Reddemann's only description of the assault was "After shocking the forward positions, the ones behind were occupied without much resistance. Many prisoners."[27]

The British, however, have written volumes on Hooge, which was their Malancourt, the first time they faced German flamethrowers. A vivid account was provided by poet Colin Mitchell:

> Hooge! More damned than Sodom and more bloody,
> 'Twas there we faced the flames of liquid fire.
> Hooge! That shambles where the flames swept ruddy:
> A spume of heat and hate and omens dire;
> A vision of a concrete hell from whence
> Emerged satanic forms, or so it seemed
> To us who, helpless, saw them hasten hence.
> Scarce understood we if we waked or dreamed.
> "Stand To! Stand To! The Wurtembergers come!"
> Shouting vile English oaths with gutter zest.
> And boastful threats to kill they voice, while some,
> In uniforms of grey and scarlet dressed,
> Wear flame-projectors strapped upon their backs.[28]

The attack took place at 3:25 A.M., adding to its horror.[29] The British first noticed a rain of thick, oily liquid that smelled of

The firing of a Grof M.1912, observed by men from Pionier-Bataillon Nr. 14. This model flamethrower was operated by a squad of five. Nine Grof were used against the British at Hooge on July 30, 1915.

paraffin, the initial spray of the *Grof*.[30] Then there was a loud hiss, and a "bright crimson glare over the crater turned the whole scene red."[31]

For one British soldier the attack began as a splashing sound, followed by the smoky smell of coal tar and a comrade shouting that his forehead had been burned:

> We had no time to notice anything else, for after that preliminary trial the Boches loosened their liquid fire upon us with a vengeance. It came in streams all over the earthworks, while shells containing star lights ignited the black fluid. Sandbags, blankets, top-coats, and anything of the sort that was handy smouldered and then flared. We were choked by the smoke and half scorched by the heat.[32]

After the shock of the nine *Grof* – the stationary part of the assault – the eleven *Kleif* squads followed up in the pounce:

French soldiers testing a captured Grof. The flame attack at Hooge began with the spraying of oil in curved trajectories such as this one.

> Coming across the German trenches were men hunched up under some heavy weights. They were carrying cylinders with nozles *[sic]* like hose-pipes. Suddenly there was a rushing noise like an escape of air from some blast-furnace. Long tongues of flame licked across to the broken ground where the King's Royal Rifles lay. Some of them were set on fire, their clothes burning on them, making them living torches, and in a second or two cinders.[33]

Four Kleif M.1914. Given that no lance operators are present, these Kleif carriers are apparently demonstrating how they perform under the seventy-pound weight of a full flamethrower. The 9th Company of the III. Garde-Pionier-Bataillon used eleven Kleif M.1914 at Hooge.

The British were driven from their foremost trenches but counterattacked throughout the day, winning back all but 500 yards. On August 9 the remaining lost ground was recovered.[34]

It is not clear if flamethrower pioneers were killed when their weapons were struck by bullets. According to one writer, a flamethrower pioneer "exploded like a fat moth caught in a candle-flame,"[35] and a captain of the 2nd Leinsters reported that "a Hun who had his cargo of frightfulness hit by a bullet blew up with a colossal burst,"[36] but the death book of the flamethrower regiment listed no names for July 30, 1915. Such discrepancies occur regularly in accounts of major flamethrower assaults.

A universal observation made in the British reporting on Hooge is that the survivors were utterly enraged. One soldier asserted that "we would have charged cheerfully straight into hell if only thereby we could have got at the enemy."[37] Others leaped to their feet, cursing and firing repeatedly at the German flamethrower operators.[38]

In the ground that the British recaptured on August 9, they found two *Kleif* which were described very accurately in an official dispatch, except that the igniter was labeled a "friction lighter" instead of the percussion-cap system that it actually was.[39] There are no records of flamethrower pioneers being taken prisoner. The Germans may not have survived capture; as a British writer put it, "Warriors who took refuge in poison gas and liquid fire did not seem to the British infantryman to be deserving of mercy."[40]

Early British accounts of the flamethrower generally presented the weapon as an extremely effective, almost supernatural force:

> Where did the Prussian General Staff experiment with Satan's own gear like the flame-projector, before whose coal-tar sheets of fire our men recoiled at Hooge? We lost 500 yards of trenches that day – a position we had held in the face of all other attacks by mortar and battery and bomb. But the aerial-blaze was too much for flesh and blood to bear; this inextinguishable Greek fire from the sky, with its withering heat and hideous slithering roar. Another surprise – each cloud of fire covering an area of 110 feet, beneath which no living thing could survive.[41]

It was only later in the war and afterward that the flamethrower was deemed an abject failure more dangerous to its own operators than its intended victims.

Sturmabteilung Calsow

On March 2, 1915, less than two weeks prior to the establishment of the 3rd Guard Pioneer Battalion, the German

Pioneers of Hannoversches Pionier-Ersatz-Bataillon Nr. 10. On March 2, 1915, this unit provided the men who comprised the 2nd Company of Sturmabteilung Calsow; the 1st Company came from Pionier-Ersatz-Bataillon von Rauch (1. Brandenburgisches) Nr. 3. Later in its development the Sturmabteilung included a flamethrower platoon armed with six small devices.

VIII Army Corps created a pioneer assault detachment (*Sturmabteilung*) under the command of *Major* Calsow of Pioneer Battalion No. 18.[42] It consisted of two companies of assault pioneers and one section armed with twenty 3.7 cm Krupp assault cannons (*Sturmkanone*) fitted with overhead shields. Deployment in June of 1915 on the Loretto front was a disaster because the guns produced a large muzzle flash, attracting enemy counterbattery fire, and the two companies of pioneers – trained to carry steel assault shields – were misused as regular infantry. In two weeks half of the detachment was lost.

In August of 1915 *Major* Calsow was relieved of command, and the Assault Detachment was assigned to Army Detachment Gaede (*Armee-Abteilung Gaede*). The unit would soon undergo a transformation that included arming it with flamethrowers.

Five members of Kurhessische Pionier-Bataillon Nr. 11, the 1st and 2nd Companies of which continued to use small flamethrowers in Poland months after the establishment of the III. Garde-Pionier-Bataillon. The flowers in the tunics indicate that these men are headed for the front.

Kurhessische Pionier-Bataillon Nr. 11

One of the units that continued to deploy the flamethrower in combat after it was officially withdrawn from service in late 1914 was Kurhessian Pioneer Battalion No. 11 (*Kurhessische Pionier-Bataillon Nr. 11*).[43] Even more noteworthy, Pioneer Battalion No. 11 also used the weapon as a poison-gas sprayer.

Based in Hannover-Münden, Pioneer Battalion No. 11 was sent to Poland with the XI Army Corps in late 1914. The battalion's 1st and 2nd Companies used the *Kleif M.1912* extensively during the fighting at Hill 10 in Rawa, a town seventy-six miles southeast of Warsaw. In operating the weapon both offensively and defensively, the men had a relatively high number of casualties, most likely because they had not received adequate training. Bernhard Reddemann and Charles Theune both cited lack of training as a reason for the failure of the flamethrower early in the war.

The first recorded use of flamethrowers by Pioneer Battalion No. 11 was on March 8, 1915.[44] On March 6 the Germans at Rawa observed that the Russian trenches were becoming heavily occupied with infantry, and the artillery fire had intensified. At 3:30 on the morning of March 8, the artillery fire increased to a crescendo. Most of it was concentrated on Hill 10, which at that time was secured by the 8th Company of Infantry Regiment No. 83 (*Infanterie-Regiment von Wittich [3. Kurhessisches] Nr. 83*).

At 4:30 A.M. the Russian infantry attacked in closely packed lines. Part of the assault broke down in front of the German trenches, but at 5:00 A.M. the Russians reached Hill 10 and fell on the 8th Company of Infantry Regiment No. 83. A vicious close combat with sharpened spades and stick grenades raged throughout the trenches. In the midst of the battle, the German infantrymen were rescued by a squad from the 2nd Company of Pioneer Battalion No. 11, which ignited flamethrowers and sprayed the Russians at pointblank range. Later in the morning the Russians retreated, leaving 400 dead and wounded, while Infantry Regiment No. 83 suffered casualties of twenty dead and forty wounded.

When the Russian artillery fire increased on the night of March 7-8, the 1st Company of Pioneer Battalion No. 11 was given the alarm and made available to Infantry Regiment No. 82 (*2. Kurhessisches Infanterie-Regiment Nr. 82*).[45] These pioneers, armed with *Kleif M.1912*, were put in the reserve position at Indomice, further back from Hill 10. The Russian attack began at 5:30 A.M. and concentrated on Hill 10. It was partially repelled by heavy defensive fire from the German infantry and the bombardment from their light and medium trench mortars.

The Russians who assaulted the first German trench on Hill 10 encountered two defensive flamethrower posts under

Officers and men of Pionier-Bataillon Nr. 11 pose on Hill 10 near Rawa, Poland, with soldiers from Infanterie-Regiment von Wittich (3. Kurhessisches) Nr. 83. On March 6, 1915, flamethrower squads from the 2nd Company of Pionier-Bataillion Nr. 11 repelled a Russian assault against this position. The man in the right foreground holds a periscope; behind him sits a light smoothbore trench mortar, either a Lanz or Mauser.

the command of an *Unteroffizier* named Otto. He ordered the flamethrowers ignited, causing a German pioneer to lose an eye. Most of the Russians fled from this unknown weapon. The rest were dealt with by the wave of Infantry Regiment No. 82 counterattacking behind the flamethrowers.

After Hill 10 was back in German hands, a second Russian attack barely made it beyond its own trenches. The only Russians who arrived at the German lines were deserters, frantically racing ahead of their artillery barrage. There were too few Germans to take charge of these men, so they were told to march unaccompanied to Rawa. The Russians happily obliged, relieved to be out of the fight. One German *Unteroffizier* and eight pioneers positioned at the Rawka Bridge had collected approximately 1,000 Russians by the morning of March 8. The prisoners were later brought to the rear.

March 10 dispatches from Petrograd reported that the Germans were using new methods of fighting, "throwing boiling pitch or some other liquid on our infantry."[46] Russian assaults ceased, and on March 11 the 1st Company of Pioneer Battalion No. 11 was pulled out of Rawa. Only one small command stayed to operate the trench mortars and flamethrowers.

Men of the 1st Company of Pionier-Bataillon Nr. 11 with a Kleif M.1912 flamethrower used as a poison-gas sprayer at Rawa on June 6, 1915. The unknown gas killed 600 Russians.

In May of 1915 the 2nd Company of Pioneer Battalion No. 11 was distributed among Infantry Regiment No. 82 and No. 83 in order to develop rest areas northeast of Stolniki. As the weather improved and Russian attacks tapered off, the 2nd Company turned from flame combat to constructing positions for the entire division. On May 18 a *Leutnant* Möhle and two pioneers of the 2nd Company had a serious accident while experimenting with a flamethrower. Möhle succumbed to his severe injuries a few weeks later.[47]

Russian soldier modeling a captured Kleif M.1912. The telescoping lance is in the extended position and has been fitted with the angled nozzle; the igniter holder is empty. This photo has been identified in other sources as a "poison-gas sprayer."

The Flamethrower as a Poison-gas Sprayer

From April 7 to July 17, 1915, the 1st Company of Pioneer Battalion No. 11 engaged the Russians in mine warfare (*Minenkrieg*) at Rawa. One platoon of pioneers was given the task of mining under Hill 10; one platoon was assigned trench mortars and flamethrowers; and one platoon served as assault troops to take the hill itself.[48] The flamethrower used was the *Kleif M.1912*.

On June 1 it was decided that since neither mining nor direct assaults had been successful, poison gas would be tried. *Major* Friedel from Army Command 9, headquartered in Lodz, was sent to organize the attack. Cavalrymen of an unidentified unit were transferred to the sector and trained in the use of flamethrowers as gas sprayers, in accordance with Richard Fielder's 1908 designs.

It is not clear if the devices were to spray liquified gas only, or flame oil mixed with toxic chemicals and ignited. In either case, the flamethrowers required no modification. Charles Theune wrote that water was often sprayed during training in order to save on oil and igniters. These flamethrowers were never again used for combat because there would always be a possibility that moisture would remain and cause firing irregularities at critical moments. Any flamethrower that sprayed water would thereafter be used only for training purposes or as a fire extinguisher.[49]

Chemists and meteorologists made an extensive study of Hill 10 and recommended a new, extraordinarily dangerous gas that was clear as water and harmless in liquid form, becoming deadly only when vaporized. Although the choking agent diphosgene (trichloromethylchloroformate) matches this description in part, it is not harmless in liquid form. In fact no such gas has yet been identified, leading one to wonder if

Stereoview titled "Austrian Asphyxiating Apparatus Captured on Italian Front." According to the printed legend on the back of the card, the Kleif M.1912 pictured is "one of those devilish machines invented by German chemists, to add new horrors to this barbaric war." It is not known how often the Germans and Austrians used flamethrowers to spray poison gas.

Postcard captioned "German military fire brigade in Lida. Oxygen smoke helmet and smoke helmet with bellows." The oxygen helmet on the left – fed by tanks on the operator's back – was worn by pioneer and cavalry flamethrower operators during the poison-gas attack at Rawa.

Army Command 9 downplayed the perils so that the soldiers would be confident enough to carry out their mission. As in the case of all gas attacks, wind direction was critical.

The wind was determined to be favorable on June 6. At 8:20 P.M. the cavalrymen and pioneers donned firefighters' oxygen masks and released the gas from their flamethrowers. Because the masks were equipped with oxygen bottles carried on the operator's back, the flamethrowers were placed on the ground rather than worn. As the gas drifted over the Russian line, the sporadic rifle fire directed at the Germans immediately ceased. A German patrol in oxygen masks later crawled out and found the enemy trenches full of dead and dying. The next day Russian deserters reported that 600 men had been killed by the gas.

During the reconnaissance conducted after the attack, the oxygen mask of one of the German patrol came loose as he crawled across No Man's Land, causing him to instantly lose consciousness. He survived only because a comrade quickly replaced the mask. Since the gas residue remained deadly for hours, it is likely that the pioneers discarded the flamethrowers rather than attempt to clean them.

A June 7 newspaper article painted a grim picture of the Russian situation:

> The reports received state that when the terrible fumes swept down the valleys every living thing suffered. Appalling scenes are described, and it is admitted at headquarters that the Russian operations have been considerably hampered in consequence of the use of the gas.[50]

To date no other accounts of German flamethrowers used as poison-gas sprayers have been found.

CHAPTER FOUR

The Schlayer Gasoline Sprayer

On September 9, 1915, the 3rd Guard Pioneer Battalion launched two assaults in the Vosges Mountains in northeastern France. One was in the area known as the *Schratzmännele*; Reddemann himself directed the combined stationary and pouncing attack and described it in his book:

> Attack of Company Kempf under the Battalion Commander by the *Steinbruch* on the *Schratzmännele* in the Vosges on September 9, 1915, with ten *Grof* and thirteen *Kleif*. After the panicked evacuation of the first positions, the ones behind were taken in close combat with *Kleif*. Many machine guns were silenced. Trenches were rolled up. The ordered objective was greatly exceeded.[1]

The second assault took place in the *Hartmannsweilerkopf*, a rocky, heavily wooded ridge where elite German and French alpine troops clashed. Flamethrower squads from the 9th and 10th Companies of the 3rd Guard Pioneer Battalion carried out the combined stationary and pouncing attack,[2] but Reddemann failed to note the mission. This omission is puzzling given the scale of the operation and the deployment of "gasoline sprayers" used in addition to Reddemann's flamethrowers. The devices were ordered built after artillery bombardments were deemed ineffective.[3]

Opposing front lines at the *Hartmannsweilerkopf* were close together, creating a No Man's Land no wider than thirty-

German trench at the Hartmannsweilerkopf. On September 9, 1915, the III. Garde-Pionier-Bataillon launched an attack in this locale. Five of the flamethrowers used were "gasoline sprayers" designed by Leutnant Schlayer of Kavallerie Kraftwagen-Kolonne 24.

five yards on the summit. Accordingly, *Leutnant der Reserve* Schlayer of Cavalry Motor-transport Column 24 (*Kavallerie Kraftwagen-Kolonne 24*) was appointed on May 13 to design a device that could spray flammable liquid across this short divide. It is not clear why a cavalry motor-transport officer was chosen to design a flamethrower, but the rationale may have been that the central focus of his branch of service was machinery and the combustion of gasoline. In addition, some motor-transport personnel are known to have trained as firefighters, allowing them to become familiar with spraying equipment.

Research into the feasibility of the project was approved by the general staff of the 12th *Landwehr* Division, and the general of pioneers of Army Detachment Gaede agreed to bear the costs of manufacturing.

The resulting construction consisted of one tank that held 69 gallons of gasoline connected to two propellant tanks containing carbon dioxide pressurized to 147 psi. (10 atmospheres). Pressure inside the gasoline tank was reduced to 73.4 psi. (5 atmospheres) so that a range of 115 feet could be achieved. Beginning May 31 two days of trials were carried out at a training field near Westhalten. The observers were high-ranking officers, among them *General der Infantrie* Mengelbier, the commander of the 12th *Landwehr* Division.

Spraying ignited gasoline proved insufficient to burn trenches and blockhouses, and it was also very dangerous for the personnel. A safer and more efficient process was to spray unlit gasoline and ignite it by throwing fire tubes. The months of June and July were dedicated to improving the device and finding the best mixture of gasoline. On August 7, 1915, the Schlayer sprayer was demonstrated to *General* Gaede and the commanding infantry officers of the 12th *Landwehr* Division, and the decision was made to proceed with a flame attack. The target was the first French trench line on the summit of the *Hartmannsweilerkopf.*

On September 8 the Schlayer sprayer was demonstrated to Reddemann, who judged it wanting. He said that the ignition took place too late, and the flame would not be effective against shelters.[4] Nevertheless, preparation for the assault continued, and pioneers of the 1st *Landwehr* Pioneer Company, XIV Army Corps (*1. Landwehr-Pionier-Kompagnie XIV. Armee Korps*) adapted five positions in the foremost German lines where Schlayer's equipment would be installed.

The attack was planned for the late afternoon of September 9. It would be led by two companies of Mecklenburger *Jäger* Battalion No. 14 (*Grossherzoglich Mecklenburgisches Jäger Bataillon Nr. 14*) and pioneers of the 1st *Landwehr* Pioneer Company armed with hand grenades. The pioneers of the 3rd Guard Pioneer Battalion would bring their army-issue flamethrowers (*Heeresflammenwerfern*).[5]

Drivers of Kavallerie Kraftwagen-Kolonne 44. Motor-transport personnel such as these were experienced with machinery and the ignition of gasoline, which may explain why Leutnant Schlayer was asked to design flamethrowers for use at the Hartmannsweilerkopf.

Men of a motor-transport unit training as firefighters. If such training was widespread among motor-transport personnel, Leutnant Schlayer – much in the manner of Reddemann – may have drawn on his familiarity with firefighting equipment to design his gasoline sprayer.

After a one-hour artillery bombardment, the French lines were attacked at three points. One Schlayer sprayer on the southern flank was damaged and did not take part in the action. The remaining four joined Reddemann's flamethrowers in driving the French out of their positions. At the end of the day, the Germans had gained a section of trench ninety-eight yards wide. Three officers and eighty-two men of the French 213th Infantry Regiment were taken prisoner, and three machine guns and two trench mortars were captured. The newly won trench gave the Germans an unobstructed view of the open terrain in front. German losses were ten dead, including one officer and one ensign, and forty-four wounded.[6]

Leutnant Schlayer was also wounded in the attack, but neither the nature nor the extent of his injuries are clear.[7] Despite the Schlayer sprayer being judged a success,[8] it is not known if it was used again. As noted previously, Reddemann never acknowledged the existence of the device. One can only speculate if this was a mere oversight on his part, or if he felt too contemptuous – or threatened – to admit that he had competitors.

The Flamethrower Battalion Grows

By October infantry commanders were making many more requests for flamethrowers. The Supreme Army Command therefore ordered on October 6, 1915, that the 13th and 14th Companies be added to the 3rd Guard Pioneer Battalion, bringing the total number of flamethrower companies to six. This order also decreed that a recruit depot be created. As the demands for flamethrower pioneers kept pouring in, the Supreme Army Command added the 15th and 16th Companies in late December. The battalion now stood at an "inconvenient"

Four members of Vorstoss Trupp Nr. 18, 2. Maschinengewehr-Kompagnie, Grossherzoglich Mecklenburgisches Jäger-Bataillon Nr. 14. Two companies from this unit led the September 9 flamethrower assault at the Hartmannsweilerkopf. Note the leather knees patches, the Guard lace on the collars and cuffs, and the Alpenkorps Edelweiss on the visor cap worn by the man on the right.

Below: This remarkable photo from a newspaper supplement shows a German flamethrower attack against a French position at the Hartmannsweilerkopf. It is quite apparent that the weapon could utterly devastate the morale of the men who faced it.

Grof demonstration. In 1915 the III. Garde-Pionier-Bataillon developed a mode of attack that entailed digging long tunnels and positioning Grof underground in front of French forward positions. On the "Go!" signal, the Grof operators popped out of the earth and unleashed enormous tongues of flame.

strength of eight field companies, one experimental company, one replacement company, one workshop detachment, and one recruit depot.[9]

Total Number of Flamethrower Attacks in 1915

Reddemann wrote almost nothing about the formative year of 1915, other than a straightforward enumeration of the thirty-two flamethrower attacks that six of his companies executed on the Meuse, in the Priesterwalde, the Argonne, Flanders, the Vosges, and the Champagne. These actions were either combined stationary and pouncing attacks with *Grof* and *Kleif*, or they were *Aufrollen*, in which trenches were rolled up with *Kleif* alone. Two of the attacks were not successful.[10]

Other unidentified German flamethrower units fought on the eastern front throughout 1915. A March 28 newspaper article reported that every German infantry company in Poland was being equipped with "liquid fire guns" as rapidly as possible:

> "It is a most devilish device," said a Russian officer.
>
> "It looks like a copper bucket and is swung over the shoulder like a knapsack. A hose is attached. When we charge the Germans wait until we get twenty yards from their lines and then spurt some sort of flaming liquid at us. In one charge last Monday night twenty of our men were burned alive. We drove the Germans from their trenches on Tuesday and recovered the bodies. The flesh from the waist up had been burned off to the bones."[11]

In Suwalki, a town in northeast Poland, an American married to a Pole wrote that during Easter a lonely soldier of the German occupying force dropped by her kitchen, looking for tea and conversation. The front was only five and half miles away. After sharing photos of his wife and children, the German proudly disclosed his forthcoming mission:

> This soldier told me that in two hours time he was going to the trenches to pump fire on the Russians; told how he could make the liquid fire spring sixty-five feet! How it burned all it touched to cinders, spreading on all sides. I had to listen, fascinated by the horror of it!"[12]

Perhaps unknowingly the talkative German provided his shocked listener with the exact maximum range of the *Kleif M.1912*, information vital to Russian intelligence.

On June 15 the Germans used flamethrowers in hand-to-hand combat on the Bzura River,[13] and on September 25 they assaulted the fortress at Dvinsk with poison gas and liquid fire.[14] All of these flame operations were carried out by line-pioneer formations instead of Reddemann's unit.

Allied Confusion About Flamethrowers

By the end of 1915 the Allies had been subjected to several dozen large-scale flamethrower attacks and had captured both the weapons themselves and secret documents relating to their usage. Although military commanders had become more familiar with what was now universally known as "liquid fire," the mass media and general public were still grappling

Newspaper photo of a French soldier modeling a captured late-model Kleif M.1915. The igniter holder has been removed from the lance nozzle. On the right, two more flamethrowers sit on the ground.

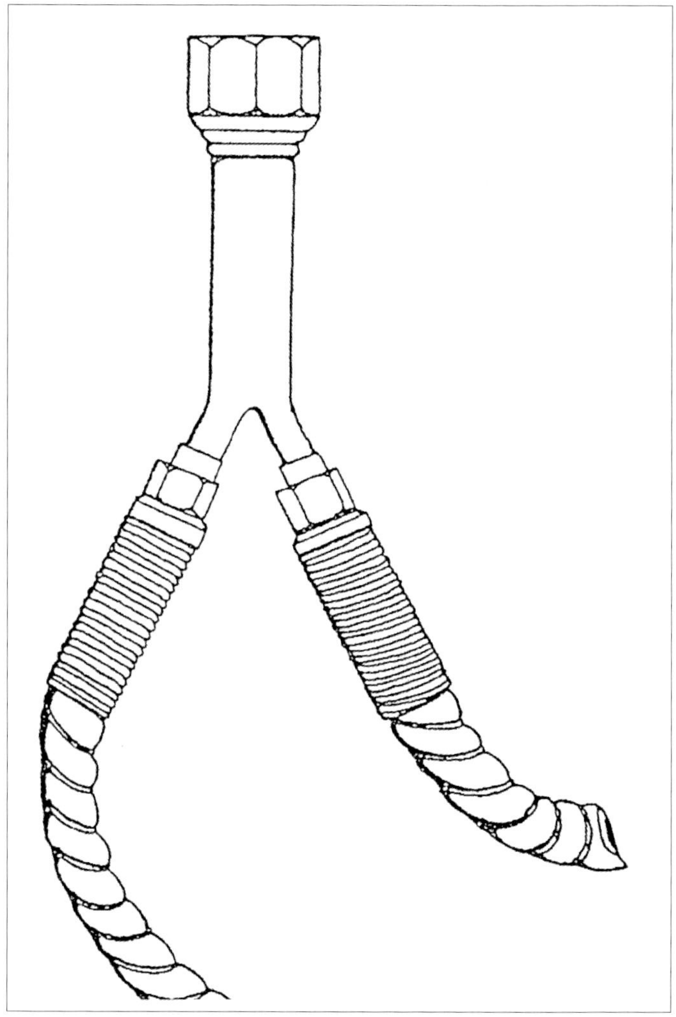

Coupling used on all models of double Kleif to connect the two hoses to the lance. (Conférences de l'Ecole des gaz de combat: Les Lance-flammes. 3ème Conférence. Lance-flammes portatifs étrangers.)

Double Kleif consisting of two late-model Kleif M.1915 connected by a 5ft. hose and a 10ft. hose to a 5ft. (1.5m) large lance. Seven or eight men were required to operate this complicated weapon. It was used in trenches against barricades and to cover the advance of Kleif squads.

with rumor, fantasy, and half-truths, as can be seen in a British magazine article from January of 1916.

It began by claiming that the Germans used honey bees – "winged Huns" – against the British in Africa, a method of attack no less barbaric than the "truly devilish" *Flammenwerfer*.[15] The article went on to ascribe almost apocalyptic powers to the flamethrower, even though the writer mistakenly claimed that multiple lances were supplied with an amount of fuel that would have been exhausted almost immediately:

> Beyond all doubt this instrument of Kultur was used to destroy whole towns in the early German line of march. In a reservoir cylinder is stored the nitrogen which gives the necessary pressure that forces out the oil fuel from the main body of this new arm. This cylinder, about 3 ft. 6 in. high, holds 14 quarts of benzine, and strapped on a man's back it supplies four or five lengths of hose and nozzles, each directed by a pioneer well trained in the devil's own war.[16]

Men were said to simply melt when hit by a blast from the flamethrower, the stocks of their rifles charring with the heat that poured out of the sky, as related by a survivor:

> I thought the world was coming to an end when I beheld an enormous aerial fire-sheet, 20 ft. long and 100 ft. high. I was gaping at this when the flames swooped down. I don't think seas of water would have put out that conflagration. The whole earth appeared in flames. I screamed aloud, as a man might who fell into an ocean of vitriol. Then I ran for it with tunic and trousers uncannily ablaze. But no man has any idea what it's like to face these new blowpipes of Kultur. It's not war, sir. It's scientific flaying and withering[.][17]

Sturmabteilung Rohr

On September 13, 1915, *Hauptmann* Willy Martin Rohr (1877-1930) of the Guard Rifles Battalion (*Garde-Schützen-Bataillon*) was made commander of the Assault Detachment of Army Detachment Gaede (*Sturmabteilung Armee-Abteilung Gaede*).[18] Given a free hand in how to train the unit, he soon requested flamethrowers. War Ministry Order No. 355. 10. 15 A6, dated October 17, 1915, decreed that a flamethrower platoon of one officer and twenty-three men armed with six *Kleif* be assigned to Assault Detachment Rohr (*Sturmabteilung Rohr*).[19] Although an integral part of the Detachment, the flamethrower platoon did not take orders from Rohr or Army Detachment Gaede.[20] Instead, like the 3rd Guard Pioneer Battalion, it was directly subordinate to the Supreme Army Command.

The unit from which the flamethrower operators were transferred cannot be definitively identified. Reddemann wrote nothing about providing men from the 3rd Guard Pioneer Battalion, and *Graf* Eberhard von Schwerin, former adjutant to *Hauptmann* Rohr, reported in his history of the assault formation that the *Kleif* detachment came from "Flamethrower Regiment Pionier Battalion 36" (*Flammenwerfer-Regiment Pionier-Bataillon 36*).[21] By the time a special spiked helmet (*Pickelhaube*) was awarded the *Kleif* platoon in June of 1916, the members were wearing the uniform of the Guard Pioneers.[22] However, it is not at all certain that these men were from Reddemann's battalion.

In describing combat that took place in December of 1915, von Schwerin claimed that the flamethrower troops of the Assault Detachment had never been trained how to cooperate with infantrymen, and they were unable to perform with Rohr's assault pioneers.[23] This criticism would not seem to apply to Reddemann's troops, since the 3rd Guard Pioneer Battalion had already undertaken several successful, large-scale flamethrower assaults in cooperation with the infantry and had produced detailed written instructions on how to do so (see "Instructions for the Employment of Flame Projectors" on page 63).

Another point is that the flamethrower detachment was under the command of *Offizier-Stellvertreter* May,[24] whose name was not included in the list of deputy officers at the end of Reddemann's book. In addition, none of the fourteen noncommissioned officers and men of the Rohr flamethrower section lost during the war were mentioned in the death book of the flamethrower regiment. Instead, the names were recorded in the history of the assault battalion,[25] indicating that the *Kleif* platoon may not have been associated with Reddemann's flamethrower formations.

To add to the confusion, Charles Theune wrote that "the first assault battalion Rohr" was developed as an offshoot of the flamethrower regiment, and the "pioneer shock-troop tactics" of the flame troops were adopted by the emerging assault battalions.[26] While the latter statement may be correct, the flamethrower regiment did not yet exist when Rohr took over command of the Assault Detachment in September of 1915.

Three young assault pioneers (Sturmpioniere) of Sturmbataillon No. 5, a later development of Sturmabteilung Rohr. From October of 1915 this unit included a flamethrower platoon armed with six Kleif. Note the M.1916 steel helmets, grenade bags, M.1917 stick grenades, wire cutters, and slung Kar. 98AZ carbines.

It is possible that the men of Rohr's *Kleif* platoon came not from the nonexistent "Flamethrower Regiment Pioneer Battalion 36," as stated by von Schwerin, but from Pioneer Regiment 36 (*Pionier-Regiment 36*), a poison-gas unit established in May of 1915.[27] These "Stink Pioneers" (*Stinkpioniere*) would not have been trained in flame combat or in how to cooperate with the infantry during assaults. Perhaps Rohr was forced to use gas pioneers because Reddemann refused to supply flamethrower operators. An alternative theory is that in 1915 neither Rohr nor the Supreme Army Command drew a distinction between the two branches of chemical warfare and mistakenly felt that gas pioneers could easily manage flamethrowers. By 1916 the *Kleif* platoon may have been ordered to wear the uniform of the flamethrower pioneers simply as a matter of bureaucratic consistency.

The 3rd Guard Pioneer Battalion and Assault Detachment Rohr worked together on several missions. On October 12, 1915, the 2nd Assault Company of the Assault Detachment attacked French positions in the Vosges at the *Schrätzmannle*.[28] At 5:29 P.M. six *Grof* from the 3rd Guard Pioneer Battalion shocked the French forward trenches. From behind each flamethrower came a squad of assault pioneers assigned a specific section of enemy trench, which it cleared with hand grenades. French artillery and machine guns were dealt with by German counterbattery fire and trench mortars; once the six trench sections were taken, the positions were consolidated by pioneers and infantrymen equipped with sandbags, pickaxes, and shovels. Rohr's flamethrower detachment appears not to have taken part.

Reddemann acknowledged neither this operation nor that of October 15, in which Assault Detachment Rohr struck the French at the *Hartmannsweilerkopf* following a combined stationary and pouncing attack by the 9th Company of the 3rd Guard Pioneer Battalion armed with two *Grof* and six *Kleif*.[29] Again, the Assault Detachment seems not to have deployed its own flamethrowers.

In March of 1916 the Assault Detachment joined the Fifth Army, and on April 1 it became Assault Battalion Rohr (*Sturmbataillon Rohr*). In December of 1916 it was designated Assault Battalion No. 5 (*Sturmbataillon Nr. 5*), amended to Assault Battalion No. 5 (Rohr) (*Sturmbataillon Nr. 5 [Rohr]*) on February 7, 1917.[30]

Young flamethrower pioneer wearing the blouse (Bluse) with light-gray Guard lace and black shoulder straps piped in red, as mandated by the AKO of September 27, 1915. Although the flamethrower operators of Sturmabteilung Rohr were uniformed as Guard Pioneers, they may originally have been members of Pionier-Regiment 36, a poison-gas formation.

Instructions for the Employment of Flame Projectors

From a captured German document dated December 12, 1915:[31]

1. Flame projectors (*Flammenwerfer*) are a new weapon for trench warfare. The 3rd Guard Pioneer Battalion (6 Coys.) has been equipped with them and trained in their use. They are under the command of General Headquarters, and will be placed at the disposal, as a unit or by sections, of particular formations for a particular purpose, when they will, for the time being, be entirely under the orders of the responsible Commander, who, after consulting with the Flame Projector Commander and taking the limitations of the weapon into consideration, will give the tactical orders for the assault. The responsibility for their technical employment rests entirely with the Flame Projector Commander.
2. Each company of the 3rd Guard Pioneer Battalion is equipped with 20 to 22 large flame projectors (range of jet 33-44 yards). They will be built into sapheads, advanced galleries, or the front line position. In addition, each company has 18 small flame projectors (range of jet 16-19 yards). These are easily portable and will be carried on the back.

These excited German officers are photographing a Grof demonstration with their private cameras. The flamethrower lance is barely visible on the far left.

B. Capabilities of Flame Projectors

3. During a flame attack each large flame projector (built in at about 27 yards distance from the enemy's trench), will cover the enemy's foremost trenches with flames on a front of about 55 yards. The enemy in these trenches will either be destroyed or driven off, or if he happens to be in deep dugouts will have his morale so shaken that he will allow himself to be captured without resistance. Machine guns, even if provided with overhead cover or in blockhouses, are put out of action by directing the flames against the loopholes. The flame attack lasts about one minute.

4. The front covered by a company of the 3rd Guard Pioneer Battalion is about 1,100 to 1,640 yards. The effect, physical and moral, of such a flame attack on the enemy is very great.

5. The assault will be made by infantry and pioneers immediately after the flame attack. Detachments with small flame projectors will accompany the assaulting troops in order to overcome any resistance which may be offered by blockhouses, etc., and also to spread the fear of the flames to the enemy's rearward positions. Many successive positions can often be taken by assault at the same time.

6. The small portable flame projectors may also often be employed with advantage in combination with bombers in making progress in the enemy's trenches, and for flank attacks on portions of trench, etc.

Two Guard Pioneers in a Berlin cafe. Their battalion is not identified, but the Gefreiter on the left is seen in another photo as a flamethrower pioneer. He and his companion are uniformed in high-quality, privately purchased M.1910 service jackets of the type worn by officers or enlisted men of elite units.

C. Necessary Conditions for Flame Attacks

7. *For large flame projectors*, trenches, sapheads and galleries must have been pushed forward to within 27 yards at least of the enemy's position at several points, or there must be a

Below: Kleif squad of the III. Garde-Pionier-Bataillon training with an early-model Kleif M.1915. The lance operator perches on the lip of the trench and fires downward while the squad leader and assistant follow behind the carrier. Note the white smoke from the igniter.

Right: Flamethrower pioneers often transported their weapons in horse-drawn carts, which were more efficient than trucks at bringing supplies forward. Accordingly, each field company of flamethrower pioneers was assigned eight grooms and a noncommissioned officer from a train battalion.

prospect that they will be able to approach so near within the next few days.

8. *For small flame projectors*, the portions of trench referred to in para. 6 must be approached under the cover of trenches or saps.

9. In both cases (paras. 7 and 8) an accurate previous reconnaissance of the points at which the flame projectors are to be employed, and of the approaches to them, is absolutely essential. This must be made by the officers of the Flame Projector Battalion. The reconnaissance, transport of the apparatus and other preparations take, as a rule, several days. The building in of the large flame projectors requires 12 hours and can be done without the enemy becoming aware of it.

10. The direction of the wind has very little influence on the effect of a flame attack. A postponement of an attack will become necessary only if there is a very strong head wind.

D. Tactical Employment of the Flame Projector Detachment

11. Flame projectors must be used offensively. It is forbidden to build flame projectors in as defensive weapons in the foremost lines. Small flame projectors may be used, however, to drive off counter-attacks against positions, the capture of which has been facilitated by a flame attack, until such positions have been consolidated. For technical reasons they cease to be effective after about 48 hours. In other special, and quite exceptional, cases when it is proposed to use them defensively, the Commander of the Flame Projector Detachment should be consulted beforehand.

12. Flame attacks proper (*i.e.* sudden attacks with a number of large flame projectors, without any special preparation by artillery and trench mortars) should be the usual method of employment. The assaulting troops (infantry, pioneers, and the small flame projectors) must advance *at once* (*i.e.* 1 minute after the large flame projectors have come into action) and take every advantage of the panic caused in the enemy's ranks by the flame attack, with a view to capturing the 2nd and 3rd Line Positions. For the action of the artillery and trench mortars see para. 35.

Newspaper photo of a captured late-model Kleif M.1915 missing its carrying harness. A second propellant tank has been added to provide the additional pressure needed for curved-trajectory or indirect firing, during which the operator angled the lance upward so that the flame could pass over the parapet of an enemy trench and arc downward to reach the bottom.

13. If the Commander of the Flame Projector Detachment considers it safe to do so, one or more sections of the front to be attacked may be left untouched by the flames, between the areas covered by the individual large flame projectors which have been built in. The length of such sections may be 100 yards or even more.

14. The fact that the enemy is taken by surprise by the flame attack has much to do with making it a complete success. It is, therefore, of the highest importance that the enemy should not obtain information of the arrival of a Flame Projector Detachment in the Division, etc., or of the sector in which it is intended to employ it. It is consequently necessary that the word "*Flammenwerfer*" should never be mentioned during a conversation, when speaking over the telephone or in orders. *A code word is to be used, such as "Neue Minenwerfer" or something similar. The Detachment will not be spoken of as "Flammenwerfer" Company, but as –th Company, 3rd Guard Pioneer Battalion.*

E. General Tactical Instructions

15. When giving orders for an attack in which large flame projectors are to be employed, the following points based on previous experience should be considered:

(i.) Objective

16. Exact instructions must be given *how far* the attack is to be *pushed* under the most favorable conditions. It has happened that our troops, taking advantage of the panic of the enemy, have carried the advance too far, thereby coming under our own artillery barrage.

17. In order to ensure secrecy as much as possible, it is advisable that the intended operation should be denominated by a *code word* (in writing or when using the telephone), such as "*Vortrag*," "*Vorführung*," "*Verhandlung*" (Lecture, production, negotiation).

(ii.) Time of Attack

18. As a rule, half an hour, or on dull days one hour *before sunset* is the most suitable time. Only in exceptional cases, when, in the course of the day, the destruction, by artillery or trench mortars, of the large flame projectors which are built in, appears to be fairly certain, may the attack be carried out in the early morning.

19. It is sometimes advisable that the day and hour should not be mentioned in the orders for the attack, but should temporarily be *kept secret*, and should be referred to as "X" and "Y." In later orders, which will be issued in writing only to Battalion, Artillery, and Group Commanders, and the Commanders of independent Companies, inclusive, the time should then be indicated, for instance, as follows: "X" equals 27th nov. "Y" equals 3.20 p.m.

(iii.) Assaulting Troops

20. The carrying out of the preparations for the attack is often better done if the assault is not made by the troops occupying the trenches, but by a detachment that *has been kept in rest billets*. All troops which up to that time have been in the trenches will then retire to the 2nd Position shortly before the assault, and as soon as the attack by the assaulting party has begun, again move forward into the foremost trenches previously held by them, in order to hold a possible counter-stroke.

Posed photo of infantry advancing in support of a flamethrower attack; note the black smoke in the background. The men wear rolled assault packs (Sturmgepäck) and Pickelhauben with the spikes removed.

21. *The size of the assaulting force must not be too great. The calculation should be one (man?) of the assaulting party to each metre of front. Each party must have a good Second in Command in addition to the Commander.*

22. The individual assaulting columns will be distributed in four successive waves, as follows:

(a) **Assaulting Party**, which advances immediately after the flame attack and occupies the enemy's positions. In this party are included bombers, engineers (for the demolition of obstacles) and small flame projectors.

French illustration dated July 18, 1915, titled "A champion of 'Kultur' provided with a tank of flammable liquid." The flamethrower is a fairly accurate rendering of the Kleif M.1912. (Le Pèlerin.) Courtesy A. Langley.

(b) **Consolidating Party** for the consolidation of the enemy's trenches.

(c) **Communication Trench Construction Party**, to construct communication trenches from the captured trenches to our previous foremost position.

(d) **Carrying Party**, which will take forward material for obstacles, especially knife-rests, sandbags, hand grenades and ammunition.

The attacking parties on the flanks will have *several* bombing parties and Small Flame Projector Detachments attached to them to assist them in clearing the trenches from the flanks.

23. Assaulting Detachments and Consolidating Parties will take up positions in the saps or in the front line trenches; Communication Trench and Carrier Parties will be ready behind them in the communication trenches. The stationing of troops in readiness will of course depend upon the existing system of saps, and will sometimes necessitate previous reconstruction of this system.

24. *The division* of the assaulting columns into these parties is best carried out well behind the front. If no other troops are to be employed except those manning the trenches, it is advisable to relieve them, for a short period at least, from the foremost trenches for the purpose of preparation and organization. The troops will march up to their positions in the line in the order detailed for the assault.

(iv.) Preparations for the Assault

25. Special preparations must be made in order that the assaulting troops can mount the parapet rapidly. *Short ladders* with one pole about 1 metre longer than the other are the most useful means. These should be made previously in the Engineer Parks. One ladder is required for every 3-4 men of the Assaulting Party. When being taken up to the front line they must be carried horizontally. They must not be placed in position in the trenches until the commencement of the flame attack.

26. All necessary *matériel*, such as hand grenades, loophole plates, sandbags, knife-rests, barbed wire, entrenching tools, and light-pistols with ammunition must be kept in readiness either in the communication trench depots or with the assaulting columns.

27. *Communication trenches and approaches* must be divided up and *allotted* to the assaulting columns and reserves. Communication trenches, saps, etc., will be distinctly marked with numbers, letters, or names.

28. Should other troops than those holding the trenches be employed for the assault, their officers and N.C.O.s must carry out a thorough *reconnaissance* of their trenches in the early dawn and during the day. No unusual movement, however, must take place in the trenches and there must be no loud talking.

Flamethrower squad armed with a late-model Kleif M.1915, demonstrating "Indian-style Forward Stalking." The troops in front seem extremely close to the flame jet, which is relatively smokeless due to the use of Yellow oil.

Above: Flamethrower pioneers of an unidentified replacement formation or recruit depot. Despite their youth, most of these soldiers are physically as large as or larger than the two older instructors (Ausbildern) seated in the center of the front row. Flamethrower pioneers tended to be very strong individuals of imposing size.

Below: Late-model Doppelkleif M.1915, which had a continuous firing duration of about twenty-two seconds. In the foreground is a late-model Kleif M.1915 and lance.

29. The advance of the assaulting troops into the front line trenches and the relief of the troops in the trenches must be carried out in *complete silence*. No talking is to be allowed. Unnecessary crowding together should be avoided. *Bayonets* will be fixed behind the lines and not in the front line. Rifles must be carried at the trail as far as possible.

(v.) The Assault in Conjunction with a Flame Attack

30. Charges (long or concentrated), to create gaps in our own *obstacles*, will be exploded by the engineers at the earliest 15 minutes *before* the flame attack, and this work must be completed 10 minutes before the flame attack. It will often be found sufficient if, on the night previous to the attack, the engineers cut the wire which connects the knife-rests in front of the foremost trenches. This must be done without attracting attention, the knife-rests being left in the original position until the troops are ready to attack, *i.e.*, immediately after the flame attack, when the engineers will precede the assaulting force, swinging the knife-rests round lengthways at right angles to the parapet.

Engineers will also hurry forward and make gaps in the *enemy's wire* should these not have been made previously by trench mortars or engineer detachments. Obstacles which are not too strong can very often be easily crossed by the assaulting troops, as after a flame attack the enemy fires very little or not at all.

31. The duration of the *flame attack* is only one minute. The signal for it is given by a siren whistle, or at a given time, watches having been previously synchronized. The *assaulting troops* must be *instructed* that they have nothing to fear from the flames and smoke, nor need they fear that they may themselves be caught by the fire jet, as this is cut off by simply turning a tap previous to their advance. They must understand that they can advance immediately after the cessation of the spray without danger, as small bursts of flame on the ground or in the enemy's trenches will burn out at once, and a little fire on the ground is at once extinguished when trodden upon. It is most important to impress upon the troops that the assault is much facilitated by the use of the flame projector, as it has been proved by experience that the enemy fires very little or not at all after a flame attack.

32. The *assault* is made immediately after the flame attack. The *Assaulting Party* charges, followed closely by the *Consolidating Party*. The small flame projectors allotted to the Assaulting Party attack any machine guns that are still in action, blockhouses that are still being defended, etc., with short spurts of fire. They are at the disposal of the Commander of the Assaulting Party for this purpose.

It is of the highest importance to drive out the enemy simultaneously to a considerable distance on both flanks by means of bombing and flame projector detachments (*see* para. 22), and to construct sandbag barricades at these points. Communication trenches which lead into the captured position must also be cleared for a certain distance and blocked by constructing sandbag barricades about 27 yards forward of the position won.

The action of the *Communication Trench Construction Party* will commence immediately after the nearest enemy position had been taken. Material is brought up as soon as possible by the *Carrier Party*, which will continue to bring up fresh material from the rear as required. Carrier Parties can at times on their return journey also take charge of prisoners as far as the point at which the reserves are situated in rear.

It is especially important to bring up and dig in machine guns immediately.

33. It may be of advantage to order a *password* for our attacking troops, especially if several successive positions are to be taken, and in the twilight of dull days. Words which the enemy would find it difficult to pronounce are particularly suitable, such as "*Schweineschmalz*," "*Stiefelwinsche*," etc.

(vi.) Action of the Artillery and Trench Mortars

34. In a *flame attack pure and simple*, which is generally to be preferred (*see* para. 12), the action of the artillery and trench mortars will not commence until about one minute after the projection of the flames, when the more retired positions, which it is not intended to take, should be shelled. Barrage fire will be opened on the ground behind these positions and on the communication trenches, etc.

35. Should it be impossible, in exceptional circumstances, to dispense with previous *preparation by the artillery and trench mortars*, only the enemy's rear positions and not his foremost position are to be shelled. It does not matter if this results in the enemy pressing forward into the positions nearest to us in order to obtain shelter, thereby reinforcing the garrison. It must, however, always be borne in mind that by artillery and

Pionier Heinrich Borstelmann of the 12th Company, III. Garde-Pionier-Bataillon, in a postcard dated October 28, 1915. His M.1910 service jacket with field-gray shoulder straps piped in red are seen to good advantage. The orthochromatic film has altered the tonal values of his colored bayonet knot; the yellow stem (Stengel or Eichel) appears very dark, while the blue slider (Schieber or Knopf) and crown (Kranz) are much lighter.

22e ANNEE — No 12 | 10 Centimes | 19 Mars 1916

Le Pêle-Mêle

POUR TOUS & PAR TOUS

RAPPROCHEMENT, par M. RADIGUET

— Brigand! quel métier faisais-tu donc dans le civil pour qu'on t'emploie à une pareille besogne?
— Ach! j'étais marchand de coco!

French magazine cover from March 10, 1916. A Poilu asks a German flamethrower operator, "Brigand, what was your civilian job that makes you suited for this work?" The German replies, "Ach! I was a coco merchant." The obscure joke is that in prewar France "coco" was a drink made from coconut milk and licorice, sold on the street by merchants who wore tanks on their backs. Courtesy A. Langley.

trench mortar preparation the enemy is warned of an imminent attack, and is thus enabled to take precautionary measures.

36. In most cases, however, it is advisable to request the *Divisions on the right and left* to open with artillery on the enemy's rear positions behind the front which it is intended to capture. Registration must be carried out so as not to attract attention.

37. As a rule it is advisable to detail a *special Artillery Group* to repulse hostile counter-attacks. Its commander must take up his position with the Commander of the attacking force and must arrange for special telephonic communication.

(vii.) Forces on the Flanks of the Front of Attack

38. The effect of a flame attack is sometimes felt to the right and left of the front which is covered with flame. Our troops which are posted on the flanks of the actual front of an attack can sometimes, therefore, gain ground by a prompt advance in force. It is, consequently, necessary to keep under close observation the enemy's troops on the flanks of the front of attack, and, according to circumstances, either subject them to a heavy fire or attack them as well. Engineer detachments are to be posted in readiness for forming gaps through the obstacles, should this be necessary.

(viii.) Equipment, Ammunition, and Rations

The assaulting troops will wear "assault order." Each man will take his greatcoat, tent square, mess tin, full water bottle, 4 days' rations in his haversack, and, in addition, at least 200 rounds, 2 hand grenades and rifle with fixed bayonet.

The Consolidating Parties are similarly equipped, except that they sling their rifles (bayonets not fixed). Each man will carry a loophole plate, 50 sandbags and heavy entrenching tool,

Communication Trench and Carrier Parties will appear in their usual order of dress. Only the N.C.O.s will carry rifles. The men of the Communication Trench Party will each carry a heavy entrenching tool, 50 sandbags and at least 2 hand grenades.

(ix.) Telephone Communications

40. A number of infantry telephone lines will be laid from the captured position to the rear, immediately after the assault.

41. All lines leading to the Commander of the attacking force are to be used solely for service messages which concern the attack, so that he can bring his personal influence to bear upon every part of the front.

CHAPTER FIVE

Preparations for Verdun

The plan for the Verdun offensive called for the 3rd Guard Pioneer Battalion to provide a flamethrower company for each of the six infantry divisions that would take part. In addition, an attack by two companies armed with large and small flamethrowers was scheduled for the woods of Consenvoye, and a third assault by another company was to take place in the Champagne. Nine companies altogether were required. Since the flamethrower battalion began the year with only eight field companies, a Reserve Company was formed with officers and men from the battalion recruit depot and the Guard Pioneer Replacement Battalion in Berlin.[1]

To meet the army's seemingly endless requests for flamethrowers, the 4th Guard Pioneer Battalion (*IV. Garde-Pionier-Bataillon*) was established in early February.[2] It had its own staff, workshop, and the 1st and 2nd Companies. An expediency that likely annoyed the bureaucrats in Berlin, the unit existed for only two months. Reddemann seemed to go out of his way to avoid mentioning it in his writings.

The enormous scale of the three planned attacks in Verdun, Consenvoye, and the Champagne left Reddemann wanting in *Kleif*. Until January of 1916 each company had been armed with twenty large flamethrowers and eighteen small; for the new year's missions each company was to be provided with fifty-four small flamethrowers. One hundred fifty of these devices were *Kleif M.1915* ordered from the factory in Westphalia. Reddemann sent twelve engineers from his own workshop to assist the factory workers and ensure that the weapons were finished in time. When the flamethrowers were ready, a Guard Pioneer officer and thirty men arrived at the factory under orders to bring back the flamethrowers at any cost. With time running out, the officer decided that a freight train would take too long. Over the protests of railway officials, Reddemann's men stuffed the 150 *Kleif* into the passenger compartments of an express train and made it back to headquarters speedily and in style.

Tripling the number of small flamethrowers required an increase in manpower from 139 men per company to 200. More officers and men of the battalion recruit depot and the Guard Pioneer Replacement Battalion were brought in, along with 360 hand-picked personnel from infantry regiments, who were carefully trained over a period of weeks. Each of the three combat platoons that made up a flamethrower field company were organized into five flame detachments, one machine-gun detachment on loan from the infantry, and one replacement detachment; each flame detachment was armed with two *Kleif*.[3]

The flamethrower troops received new training along with more weaponry and personnel. Previous experience had shown Reddemann that artillery barrages and sheer force of numbers could not completely clear an area. Surviving machine guns caused heavy casualties, particularly when the

Opposite
Top: Men of the 4. Rekruten Depot, Garde-Pionier-Ersatz-Bataillon. In preparation for the Battle of Verdun, a ninth flamethrower company was formed from this unit and the recruit depot of the III. Garde-Pionier-Bataillon. This postcard was sent by Pionier Gerhard, who writes, "Angry faces!!"

Bottom: A flame shock troop (Flammenstosstrup) training with boxlike dummy flamethrowers and hand grenades. These soldiers are uniformed as infantrymen rather than pioneers, indicating that they have not yet graduated from flamethrower school. The snow and mixture of spiked and steel helmets likely date the photo to early 1916, immediately prior to the Battle of Verdun. Courtesy Maurice Sublet.

assault waves were moving across shell-torn ground. Instead of trying to simply hammer the target flat, the attackers were better served by first driving in a number of "steel wedges" in the form of flame shock troops (*Flammenstosstrupps*)[4] consisting of flamethrower squads and infantrymen armed with grenades, rifles, and light machine guns.

This new role for the flamethrower was conceived by the Fifth Army High Command. The 3rd Guard Pioneer Battalion staff helped the Fifth Army prepare an explanatory pamphlet that was distributed to all assault formations. Reddemann himself then made the rounds of the participating divisional staffs to inform them of the new concepts. Finally, flamethrower officers instructed the infantry assault troops in Indian-style Forward Stalking, the method of attacking in wide, indirect arcs.

Men of the 16th Company, III. Garde-Pionier-Bataillon, in an undated postcard sent by Pionier Adam. They display full field kit and obsolete Gew. 88 rifles; note the sawbacked S98/05 bayonets. In his message Pionier Adam apologizes for the quality of the photo but reminds his family that there is a war on. "This is a hole," he writes.

Pamphlet on the Use of Flamethrowers

Pamphlet Ia No. 491, distributed by the Fifth Army High Command, was titled "Use of the Flamethrowers" and dated February 6, 1916:

> A. Organization
>
> 1. Each company in the front line forms a shock troop. It usually remains behind the first swarm line *[Schwarmlinie]* (exception Number 5). Especially courageous and adroit men are now selected from each company and, together with the necessary pioneers, flamethrowers, and machine-gun troops, are immediately trained for their special task.
>
> 2. Each infantry battalion proceeding to the front line receives three flamethrower squads for the shock troops of the foremost companies.
>
> 3. Each shock troop receives a prudent infantry officer as leader and a specially selected deputy (officer or deputy officer).
> Each shock troop consists of:
> (a) sixteen to twenty infantrymen (rifle, three hand grenades each)
> (b) one group of pioneers (axes, hatchets, saws, wire cutters, concentrated and elongated charges)
> Task: Clear the way for the shock troop through the forest, undergrowth, obstacles.
> (c) Flamethrower squad (with reserve apparatus, flame balls, hand grenades)
> Task I: Proceed against blockhouses, machine-gun nests, etc., from general line or immediately together with shock troop.
> Task II: Roll up trenches
> (d) Machine-gun squad
>
> B. Kinds of Procedures
> 4. Rule: as shown in the illustration. The shock troops advance spread out behind the foremost swarm line.
>
> 5. Facing resistance from hostile strong points, etc.
> (a) Swarm line halts and draws fire upon itself from the strong point (use cunning).
> (b) Next, the shock troop thrusts forward (with pioneers, flamethrowers, machine guns) in a spread-out surprise attack on the strong point, etc., launched from the side. One echelon of infantrymen moves forward under cover; the other echelon together with the flamethrowers attacks the strong point from the side or from the rear. Use cover, shell holes when advancing. When appropriate, machine guns can sometimes be set up in shell holes or such along the way. When the shock troop advances to within

approximately 20 meters from the hostile strong point, the flamethrower is activated.
(c) Swarm line penetrates as soon as the fire from the strong point diminishes. Afterwards, the shock troop passes by and continues to penetrate in the same way as the prior unit.

6. It is often necessary for the shock troop to move sideways.

C. Force of Thrust

7. Second echelon overtakes the first echelon according to a certain time frame (also arranged). Third echelon overtakes the second echelon, and so forth.[5]

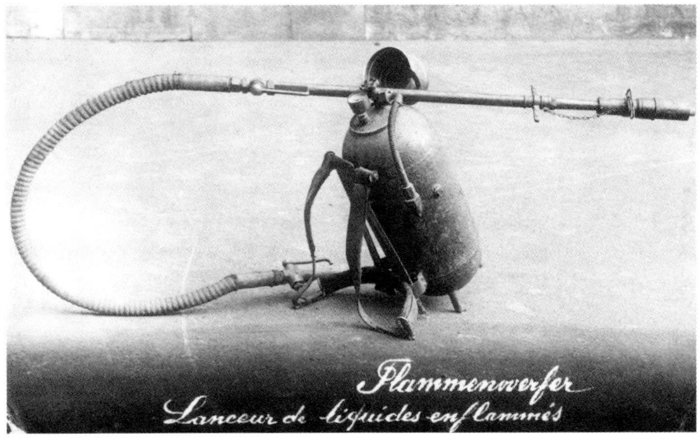

Kleine Flammenwerfer (Kleif) M.1916. The 5ft. rubber hose was sheathed in linen and wrapped in steel wire to prevent kinking; the 3.6ft. (1.1m) lance and shorter, fixed oil-outflow pipe made this flamethrower easier to use in trenches. The protruding knob on the end of the igniter is the detonator, a capsule of fulminate of mercury. Courtesy Maurice Sublet.

Sixty-two infantry battalions provided three companies each for the assault on Verdun; every front-line company formed a shock troop that contained a flamethrower squad with two weapons, one of which would be held in reserve. A total of 372 small flamethrowers were used by shock troops in Verdun.

Enclosure 2 to Divisional Instruction (5th Infantry Division, February 10, 1916), signed by *General der Infanterie* Georg Wichura, described how flamethrowers were dispersed in a specific infantry division:

1. It is necessary to regulate the particulars of the distribution because the troops still lack experience with this new weapon.

2. Twenty-seven small flamethrowers are at the disposal of the Division: ten are available to the Division (from these one as a reserve apparatus) and for the time being seventeen are available to the 10th Infantry Brigade.

Kleif shock troop (Kleifstosstrupp) of the III. or IV. Garde-Pionier-Bataillon. First comes the lead flamethrower squad, armed with a Kleif M.1914. Next are the shock-troop leader and four hand-grenade throwers, all infantrymen. In the background stands the lance operator of the second Kleif squad.

3. Of the seventeen small flamethrowers at the disposal of the 10th Infantry Brigade, one will serve as a reserve apparatus, and the rest are assigned as follows:

to 3rd Batl. 12th Gren. Reg. - three flamethrowers
to 2nd Batl. *Leib* Inf. Reg. - three flamethrowers
to 2nd Batl. 12th Inf. Reg. - two flamethrowers
to 1st Batl. *Leib* Inf. Reg. - three flamethrowers
Two flamethrowers follow (in the shock-troop formation) behind the first wave. Three flamethrowers are at the disposal of the battalion commanders.

4. Six small flamethrowers and one reserve apparatus are moved to the brigade reserve (3rd Batl, *Leib* Inf. Reg.) (In addition to the necessary pioneers and machine guns.)

5. Flamethrowers no longer combat effective are returned to the carrier troop of the 11th Company of the 3rd Guard Pioneer Battalion. They may be returned only on the orders of shock-troop leaders, their deputies, or their weapons-superiors. They separate at this instant from their affiliation [with the division].[6]

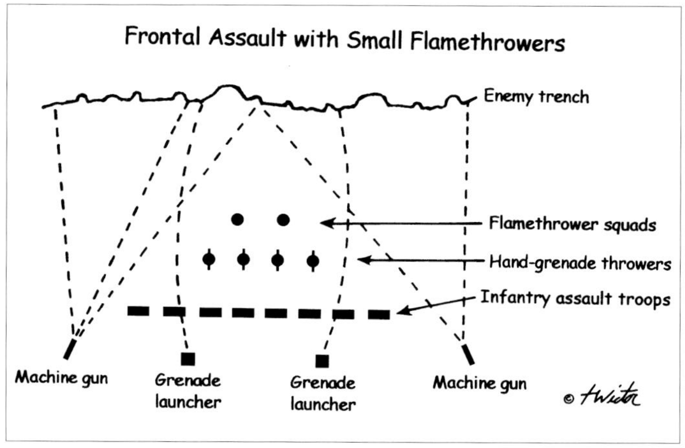

Gefreiter Lu of the 10th Company, III. Garde-Pionier-Bataillon. He has been awarded both classes of Iron Cross, rare for men of his rank. Unfortunately, two lines of text on the back of this postcard have been censored with heavy black ink; one wonders if they are a description of Gefreiter Lu's deeds. His M.1910 service jacket is an expensive privately purchased item with Guard lace of a very dark, non-regulation shade of gray.

Even as preparations for Verdun were being made, other operations were carried out. The first time tunnels were used in a large-scale flame attack was at Maison de Champagne on January 9, 1916. The 14th Company of the 3rd Guard Pioneer Battalion, commanded by *Oberleutnant* Lange, launched a combined stationary and pouncing attack using tunnels on a front of 660 yards. Sixteen *Grof* and twenty *Kleif* were deployed. According to Reddemann, the French were completely surprised and driven out of the trenches. The advancing *Kleif* squads rolled up the rear trenches, overcoming machine-gun nests and dugouts. There were few casualties among the flamethrower troops, and many prisoners were taken.

Another assault took place on the same day near Ripont in the Champagne, where the 9th Company used thirteen *Grof* and sixteen *Kleif* in a combined stationary and pouncing attack along a 440-yard front. The French first line was shocked with *Grof* and the rear trenches were cleared with *Kleif*. Machine guns were silenced and many prisoners were taken.[7]

On February 2 Bernhard Reddemann was promoted to *Major der Landwehr Pioniere*.

The Battle of Verdun

When the Battle of Verdun began on February 21, 1916, nine flamethrower companies were distributed across the western front as follows:

9th Company (*Hauptmann* Kempf) to 21st Infantry Division;
10th Company (*Oberleutnant* Kraensel) to 14th Reserve Division;
11th Company (*Leutnant* Bruckmann) to 5th Infantry Division;
14th Company (*Oberleutnant* Lange) to 6th Infantry Division;
16th Company (*Hauptmann* Sturm) to 13th Reserve Division;
Reserve Company (*Leutnant* Fritsch) to 25th Infantry Division;
12th Company (*Hauptmann* Lewus) and 13th Company (*Oberleutnant* Trage) to 77th Infantry Brigade in Consenvoye Woods;
15th Company (*Leutnant* Müller) in Champagne.[8]

Although not documented by Reddemann, the 1st Company of the 4th Guard Pioneer Battalion also fought in Verdun, losing ten men from April 11 to April 20. The 2nd Company of the 4th Guard Pioneer Battalion took part in the campaign as well; it lost one man in the Chapitre Woods on February 22 and one in the Caillette Woods on March 18.[9]

In his book Reddemann wrote that between February 21 and April 27, ten companies armed with 400 flamethrowers carried out fifty-seven attacks, thirty-three of which he judged to have been successful. His brief notes provide an overview of the many operations:

> Frontal attacks with *Grof* and "forward shocking" with *Kleif* in Consenvoye (12th and 13th Cos.), Caillette Woods (14th Co.), and the woods of Malancourt (12th and 13th Cos.).
>
> Shock troops with *Kleif* assaulting ahead of the infantry in Haumont Woods (10th and 16th Cos.), Caures Woods (9th Co.), Ville (11th Co.), Ville-Beaumont Ravine (Reserve Co.), La Wavrille Works (Reserve Co.), Caurières and Chaume Woods (14th Co.), the heights northwest of Douaumont (9th Co.), west of Malancourt (12th and 13th Cos.), the Dead Man (13th and 14th Cos.), the hedgerows of Hill 304 (12th Co.), Thiaumont Ravine (11th Co.), Froideterre and the village of Fleury (9th Co.).
>
> Woodland battles against blockhouses and other points of resistance in Herbebois (14th Co.), Caures Woods (Reserve Co.), and Chauffour Woods (9th and 11th Cos.).
>
> Rolling up enemy trenches in the Cape of Good Hope (14th Co.), Haumont (10th Co.), south of Fort Douaumont (9th

Photo captioned "Attack on the Haumont Woods 5 P.M. (Verdun)." German assault troops wearing white brassards on their left arms are shown passing through their own barbed-wire cheval-de-frise and crossing the open fields ahead. In the background, a member of the 16th Company, III. Garde-Pionier-Bataillon, runs to the left carrying a Kleif M.1914.

> Co.), the Dead Man (10th, 12th, and 14th Cos.), Albain Woods (9th Co.), Caillette Woods (11th Co.), Hill 304 (13th Co.), Caurette Hill (10th Co.), and Camard Woods (10th Co.).
>
> Street fighting in the villages of Haumont (10th Co.), Samogneux (16th Co.), Douaumont (11th Co.), Vaux (Reserve Co.), Haumont (12th and 13th Cos.), Cumières (10th Co.), and Fleury (13th Co.).

Flame attacks continued on both sides of the Meuse until July of 1916. "What deeds were accomplished here by the officers and men!" Reddemann exulted when describing this period.[10]

Slightly contradicting the number of attacks cited above, the captured German document "Extract from a Report of the Commander of the 3rd and 4th Battalions of Guard Pioneers on the Subject of Recent Flame Fighting," written by Reddemann for the Supreme Army Command, stated that between February 21 and April 4, 1916, fifty-one flame attacks were carried out, forty-one of which were deemed successful. Ten failed either because the flamethrower squads were killed before they could carry out the missions, or because the ground captured by the flamethrowers soon had to be abandoned.[11]

Individual Flamethrower Attacks

On February 21 in the Herbebois Woods, soldiers of the French 51st Division were assaulted by the Germans at dusk. One especially well-defended position was suddenly enveloped in flames shot by squads from the 14th Company of the 3rd Guard Pioneer Battalion, which had crept up unnoticed until they were within range:

> Soon the flamethrower had set fire to even the wattling revetment of the trenches. The defenders, howling in agony, their clothes and hair aflame, fled in disorder. Swiftly the Germans occupied the smouldering position, establishing a machine gun to fire into the backs of the panic-stricken French.[12]

Opposite
Top: Another photo taken at the same time and place, captioned "Assault on the Haumont Woods 21 February, 1916, at 5 P.M., with flamethrowers." In the background, a heavily laden flamethrower squad from the 16th Company, III. Garde-Pionier-Bataillon, advances with an early-model Kleif M.1915.

Bottom: Verdun in early 1916. The men are armed with an obsolete Kleif M.1912, which had been officially withdrawn from service in late 1914. It may have been temporarily reintroduced as a stopgap measure at the beginning of the offensive. The pioneer on the right is equipped with a knapsack-type carrier used to transport igniters and nozzles.

The concentrated charge (geballte Ladung) was made from seven or ten stick-grenade heads wired together. Flamethrower pioneers used concentrated charges against wire obstacles, blockhouses, and tanks.

Two flamethrower operators were killed in this action.[13]

On February 22 the 12th Company under *Hauptmann* Lewus and the 13th Company under *Oberleutnant* Trage launched an "excellent" combined stationary and pouncing attack using fourteen *Grof* and twenty-five *Kleif* in the Consenvoye Woods.[14] Long tunnels were dug toward the French positions, with vertical shafts at the ends. The lance operators leapt out and sprayed the French, driving them out of their trenches. Shock-troop detachments armed with *Kleif* then cleared the blockhouses, machine-gun nests, and dugouts back to the rear positions and took a large number of prisoners.

On February 23 a platoon from the 16th Company under *Vizefeldwebel* Lasch stormed the bridgehead at Samogneux and then the village proper amid furious house-to-house combat. During this engagement, the flamethrower shock troops had to cross more than 100 yards of open ground denuded of trees. To overcome this disadvantage, they sprayed a covering jet of flame toward the French, which created a dense smoke cloud. The flamethrower squads were then able to advance unseen to within striking distance. Illustrating the dangers of putting such information into writing, the secret report describing this technique was captured by the Allies and translated. As a result, the British General Staff wrote that rapid fire should be opened on all clouds of smoke formed by flamethrowers.[15]

In late February the Germans encountered a quarry at Louvemont, where the French occupied a deep cave beneath a plateau. After bombarding the position for forty-eight hours, the Germans advanced onto the plateau and into the quarry,

Grof firing a flame burst. The bright, relatively smokeless jet is likely the result of Yellow oil. Two men handle the lance and two support the hose.

launching a nighttime attack in which they simultaneously dug down through the roof of the cave and assaulted its entrance. French machine-gun fire killed so many that the Germans used the bodies of their dead to build ramparts at the mouth of the cave, the grisly scene illuminated by long jets of liquid fire in red and green. Ultimately the assault failed and the Germans retreated.[16] The flamethrower company remains unidentified.

During the early stages of the Battle of Verdun, an American volunteer ambulance driver saw a pair of German prisoners who stood out in a crowd of thin, raggedy, unhealthy-looking young infantrymen captured by the French:

> A little to the side stood a strange pair, two big men wearing an odd kind of grayish protector and apron over their bodies. Against a near-by wall stood a kind of flattish tank to which a long metallic hose was attached. The French soldiers eyed them with contempt and disgust. I caught the words, "Flame-throwers!"[17]

This "protector" may be the face mask worn by flamethrower troops in 1914. Photographic evidence of an apron has yet to be discovered.

Creation of the *II. Garde-Pionier-Ersatz-Bataillon*

The establishment of the Reserve Company of the 3rd Guard Pioneer Battalion, as well as the two companies of the 4th Guard Pioneer Battalion, syphoned off a large number of men of the Guard Pioneer Replacement Battalion, to the detriment of its parent unit. On February 25, 1916, the War Ministry therefore ordered the founding of a replacement battalion that would specifically provide men for the two flamethrower battalions. It was established in Berlin on March 1 as the 2nd Guard Pioneer Replacement Battalion (*II. Garde-Pionier-Ersatz-Bataillon*).[18]

To create the 2nd Guard Pioneer Replacement Battalion, the Replacement Company of the 3rd Guard Pioneer Battalion was expanded by three additional companies. Soldiers attended flamethrower school before they officially became members of the 2nd Guard Pioneer Replacement Battalion, in order that as replacements they were fully trained flamethrower pioneers ready to be immediately posted.

Exploding Flamethrowers

British and French accounts of German flamethrower assaults invariably claimed that the weapon would explode spectacularly when hit by rifle fire or shrapnel. During the Hooge attack, for example, at least two different writers described such instances, although the death book of the German flamethrower regiment had no entries for July 30, 1915. In the countless actions that comprised the Battle of Verdun, exploding flamethrowers abounded.

Some were seen on the height called the *Mort Homme* in French and *Toter Mann* in German, both of which translate into English as the "Dead Man":

> The terrifying flame-throwers had now largely become suicide weapons, an immediate target the moment they appeared in the open. In horrible fascination French troops watched as the fuel cannisters, punctured by a grenade or shell, turned their bearers into writhing torches; or when, wounded, the German Pioneers spun round to hose their own companions with the hellish liquid.[19]

On March 8 at 10:00 A.M., a platoon of the 11th Company of Posener Infantry Regiment No. 19, accompanied by a flamethrower squad, tried to penetrate the French lines at a position called the *Pfeifenkopf*. A rifle shot caused the

Above: Platoon of the 2nd Replacement Company, II. Garde-Pionier-Ersatz-Bataillon. The older and overweight soldiers in this photo seem more suited for service in the Landsturm. They are almost certainly firefighters recruited not for their fitness but for their experience with flame and spraying equipment. Note the obsolete Gew. 88 rifles, pressed-felt Ersatz Pickelhauben, and M.1910 service jackets with shortened Guard lace on the collar. The chalked signboard reads "With God, for emperor and empire."

Right: French magazine from December 10, 1916. The illustration is captioned "The Angelus, imitation of Millet." It is a parody of L'Angelus, a painting by Jean-François Millet, which shows French peasants in a field momentarily stopping their harvest to pray. The joke here is that Germans piously take time out to pray during a busy day of causing mayhem and destruction with flamethrowers. Courtesy A. Langley.

flamethrower to explode, and the Germans were driven back by a wave of burning oil.[20]

A similar incident occurred in May on the Dead Man, when a flamethrower pioneer took the lead in a German sap, his orders to smoke out the French from their own sap. Before he could ignite his weapon, the French threw a hand grenade that ruptured the oil tank and sent the badly burnt pioneer reeling back. A second flamethrower pioneer went forward to take the place of the wounded man, and this time the mission was successful. When the German infantry saw the large cloud of smoke, they charged forward cheering and routed the French.[21]

There are too many such accounts for all of them to be dismissed as propaganda, exaggeration, or misinformation. The fact remains, however, that Order T.17, signed by *General* Fritz von Below of the First Army in the autumn of 1916, stated unequivocally that flamethrowers did not explode when hit by projectiles.[22] Charles Theune agreed, writing that if a flamethrower were punctured by rifle fire or shell fragments, a cushion of air inside the oil chamber would allow the contents to flow harmlessly out through the holes.[23] Conversely, he also reported that flamethrowers could explode due to leaky couplings or hoses, and he advocated "special caution" when operating in a strong head wind, when using Yellow (smokeless) oil, and when other flamethrowers were firing in close proximity.[24] It therefore seems somewhat optimistic to flatly deny the possibility of flamethrowers exploding when hit by hostile fire.

Final Attack of the 3rd Guard Pioneer Battalion

March 20, 1916, saw the last large-scale flamethrower assault carried out by the 3rd Guard Pioneer Battalion. The 12th Company under *Leutnant* Bock and the 13th Company under *Oberleutnant* Trage launched a combined stationary and pouncing attack in Malancourt Woods, along a front of 875 yards. Eight *Grof* and fifty-five *Kleif* were used, the number of small flamethrowers that armed an entire company. At least 224 flamethrower pioneers were involved in the operation. Many blockhouses and machine-gun nests were silenced, while 3000 prisoners and much war booty were taken.[25]

Above: Men of Pionier-Bataillon Nr. 29 display a captured Schilt Number 2, a semiportable model of French flamethrower with a range of fifty to sixty-six feet. The crew consisted of a gunner who aimed the lance; a "mechanic" who filled the oil tank and fired the weapon by opening the propellant valve; and an igniter-grenadier who attached and lit the fuses or threw incendiary grenades at the target. Twelve Schilt Number 2 were deployed per section, three sections per company, each section covering a front of 108 yards.

Left: In this carte de visite by Otto Hoeffke of Berlin, a pioneer of the 11th Company, Garde-Reserve-Pionier-Regiment, wears his full parade uniform of M.1895 service jacket in dark blue, dove-gray pre-war overcoat, and privately purchased spiked helmet with black horsehair plume. An older man, he is likely a firefighter.

Creation of the Garde-Reserve-Pionier-Regiment

War Ministry Order No. 681. 16. A6, issued on April 20, 1916, called for the Supreme Army Command to establish the Guard Reserve Pioneer Regiment (*Garde-Reserve-Pionier-Regiment*), with *Major der Landwehr* Reddemann as commander.[26] This new formation was created to provide more flamethrower troops and more effectively administrate the two staffs, ten combat companies, reserve company, experimental company, recruit depot, and workshops of the 3rd and 4th Guard Pioneer Battalions.

The 9th through 12th Companies of the 3rd Guard Pioneer Battalion became the 1st through 4th Companies of the First Battalion, Guard Reserve Pioneer Regiment, while the 13th through 16th Companies became the 5th through 8th Companies, Second Battalion. A new staff was formed for the Third Battalion, made up of the 9th and 10th Companies, formerly the 1st and 2nd Companies of the 4th Guard Pioneer Battalion. The regiment also had an experimental company, a recruit depot, and three battalion workshop detachments.

As before, flamethrower troops were directly subordinate to the Supreme Army Command; the regimental staff, Experimental Company, one workshop, and the recruit depot were attached to the Crown Prince's Fifth Army and later Army Group Crown Prince, both of which stayed close to the headquarters of the Supreme Army Command.[27] Flamethrower units returning from combat or standing in reserve were housed in the quarters of the regimental staff. Thus when Reddemann made his monthly written and verbal reports to the Supreme Army Command, he was able to provide information drawn from personal conversations with his staff, combat troops, designers, and engineers.

The Supreme Army Command continued to supply flamethrower troops to army corps or divisions, assigning companies or entire battalions of the regiment on a temporary basis and only for particular engagements. This arrangement was hit upon after a failed attempt to permanently attach flamethrower companies to various army corps, an experiment that resulted in some companies becoming overstressed and worn out while others saw almost no action.[28] In his book Reddemann did not give the date of this venture, but it may have taken place before the regiment was established. Under the new procedure, the corps or divisional staff requisitioned a flamethrower unit from the Supreme Army Command after receiving verbal orders from Reddemann that outlined the upcoming operation.

Flamethrower companies or battalions detached to infantry formations remained subordinate to the Guard Reserve Pioneer Reigment in terms of technical flame tactics. Regarding the particulars of the mission, they answered to the infantry commander to whom they had been detailed. Infantry commanders would refer to printed directives of the Supreme Army Command and consult with Reddemann so that all parties could coordinate the technical limitations of the devices with the objectives of the assault. In this way there were no misunderstandings, and the best possible cooperation between the flamethrower arm and the infantry was assured.

The regimental staff constantly traveled to France and Belgium, taking with them their personal automobiles so that they could quickly reach the front. For larger engagements, an ad hoc regimental battle staff would be formed and sent forward.

Machine-gun crew of Königlich Sächsisches 1. Pionier-Bataillon Nr. 12. Each field company of flamethrower pioneers was equipped with two water-cooled 7.92mm MG08 heavy machine guns. With its sled mount, the weapon weighed 126 pounds. It was fed by 250-round cloth belts and had a maximum range of 4800 yards.

Organization of Flamethrower Companies

Field companies of the Guard Reserve Pioneer Regiment began with three combat platoons each. A combat platoon was comprised of five flamethrower detachments of two *Kleif* squads each, one machine-gun detachment on loan from the infantry, and one replacement detachment. At an unspecified date the field companies were reorganized into five combat platoons and one replacement platoon (*Ergänzungszug*) each. Four combat platoons were each composed of four *Kleif* squads and either a machine-gun or grenade-launcher squad. Two of these platoons also included a squad of hand-grenade throwers. The fifth combat platoon was detached for duty with the emerging assault battalions; it had six *Kleif* squads but lacked hand-grenade throwers and machine-gun or grenade-launcher squads.[29]

Detached platoons were rotated back into the regiment on a regular basis in order to keep their training up to standard. They were subordinate to the regiment in terms of technical and tactical application of their weapons, but were otherwise under the command of the assault battalion. Printed directives issued by the Supreme Army Command spelled out the precise use of flamethrowers in cooperation with the infantry.

Machine Guns in the Regiment

During the attacks on Verdun, flamethrower squads undertaking assaults using Indian-style Forward Stalking or the Pincers Tactic ran into two difficulties: They could not

Opposite
Top: Later in the war, each field company of flamethrower pioneers was armed with five 7.92mm MG08/15 light machine guns. The weapon had a maximum range of 1300 yards and weighed forty-three pounds with full water jacket and 100-round drum (Trommel). Accessories here include three Patronen Kasten 15, each of which held one 250-round belt; one 100-round drum; and the 5.5-pint water can.

Bottom: Graduates of an assault school (Sturmschule) posing with a French Fusil Mitrailleur Modèle 1915 CSRG machine rifle, better known as the Chauchat. Flamethrower pioneers also used the infamous Chauchat, despite its reputation as one of the worst weapons ever produced. The 8mm Chauchat weighed twenty-one pounds with a loaded 20-round magazine and had a firing rate of 250 rounds per minute. Its effective range was about 550 yards.

Right: This grainy image shows the size of the Light Grof M.1916 (Leichtgrof M.1916), the improved version of the large flamethrower. Men who operated the release valves on the fuel and propellant tanks were known as Grof staff (Grofleute). Courtesy Thierry Ehret.

suppress counterattacks, and the preliminary shelling intended to keep the enemy from manning his guns in the trench was simply not effective. Flamethrower troops had been using infantry machine-gun squads, but this arrangement was not satisfactory because infantry commanders were reluctant to part with these valuable assets. Moreover, cooperation between the attached infantry machine gunners and the flamethrower troops was "not always as it should be," to use Reddemann's diplomatic turn of phrase.[30] A flamethrower pioneer put it more succinctly: "The regular infantry were liable to bolt when the flamethrowers were turned on."[31]

To overcome this problem, it was first recommended that only the most courageous and aggressive infantrymen be detailed to flamethrower troops.[32] Later, the regimental staff asked that flamethrower companies be permanently armed with their own MG08 heavy and MG08/15 light machine guns, operated by flamethrower pioneers.[33] In addition, some companies paid their men bonuses for captured French machine guns, even the Mle 1915 CSRG machine rifle, the infamous Chauchat, which flamethrower pioneers hung from the shoulder and fired on the run during the assault.[34]

Improvements of Flamethrowers

One of the main improvements made to the weaponry was that the *Grof* was lightened and reduced in size so that it could be carried by one man when empty and two men when full. The work was credited to the commander of the Experimental Company, *Oberleutnant der Reserve* Lindner. As Reddemann reported, a large number of noncommissioned officers and men of the Experimental Company worked permanently in their factory in France, improving the existing devices and designing new ones. Particular attention was paid to the "egg-shaped" Fiedler portable flamethrowers in an attempt to rectify the "series of deficiencies" that they showed from the beginning.[35]

It is possible – even likely, given the territorial squabbling endemic in military circles – that there was a not-so-friendly rivalry between Richard Fiedler and Bernhard Reddemann. The latter seemed to take special pains to point out all the problems with the weapons he received from the Berlin-based flamethrower entrepreneur. Reddemann claimed that his regiment became fairly independent of Fiedler, due to the acquisition of French steel and the skill of the field workshops in improving what were implied to be faulty designs. Eventually, the regimental factory built its own small flamethrowers and the majority of their fittings, producing what Reddemann said were called "sinister, perfect German flamethrowers" by the French.[36]

This rather self-serving account, however, was contradicted by Charles Theune, who wrote that the flamethrowers manufactured by the regimental workshops "naturally did not have the good qualities and the efficiency of apparatus made in the workshop of the inventor who had had many years experience."[37]

In addition to flamethrowers, the regimental workshops produced their own version of the Grenade Launcher 16 (*Granatwerfer 16*), reducing or eliminating the steel platform and cutting lightening holes in the base plate in order to reduce the weight by about half. This forty-four-pound weapon was

Above: Soldiers of Sturmbataillon Nr. 6, displaying a Granatenwerfer 16. Combat platoons of the flamethrower regiment were armed with grenade launchers to prevent the enemy from manning his machine guns during an assault. The two men on the left hold the weapon itself, while the two on the right carry the steel mounting platform. Note the bags for the finned fragmentation grenades, each of which weighed 4.1 pounds and had a maximum range of 330 yards.

Right: Flamethrower pioneer wearing the wooden carrying frame for the Granatenwerfer 16, developed by the workshops of the Garde-Reserve-Pionier-Regiment. Note the lightening holes cut in the base of the grenade launcher; this and the elimination of the steel platform reduced the weapon's weight by half to forty-four pounds.

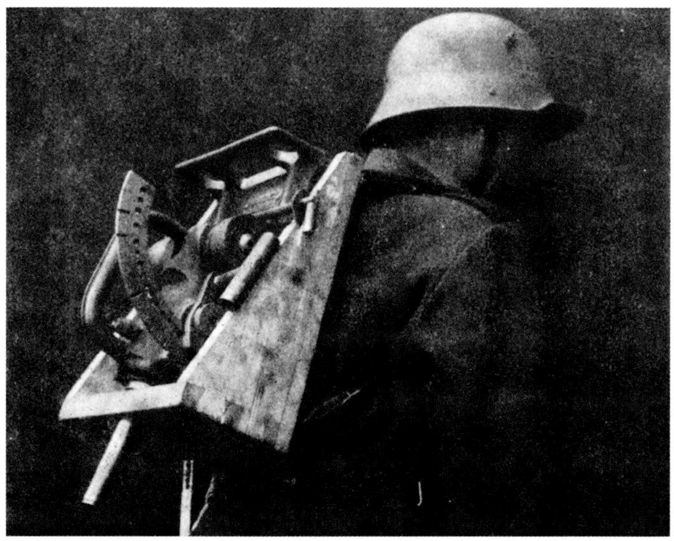

carried in a special wooden frame worn like a knapsack by the pioneer. A second man of the grenade-launcher squad carried twelve grenades in a specially constructed case.[38]

The Explosions at Fort Douaumont

Soon after the flamethrower regiment was established, it was involved in one of the worst catastrophes to hit the German army during the war. On May 8, 1916, a series of explosions devastated the interior of Fort Douaumont at Verdun. The Germans had captured the fort on February 25 and transformed it into an equipment depot and rest station for troops moving forward to the front. Although the exact cause of the explosions has never been determined, most sources agree that flamethrowers played a role.

One speculation is that soldiers carelessly heating coffee or food somehow ignited full flamethrowers stored on the lower floor of the fort, which was where hand grenades and French 155mm shells were also kept.[39] A different version of the accident has a troop of pioneers arriving from the rear, laden with hand grenades, concentrated charges, and flamethrowers. They made a brief stop at the fort just after dawn, piling their weapons at the entrance of a crowded, narrow passageway that they would not have been able to navigate while wearing their equipment. As the pioneers ate a quick breakfast, a passerby knocked a concentrated charge from the pile of weapons and accidentally armed it by stepping on the lanyard. In the hustling crowd, he did not notice. The charge exploded and ruptured the flamethrowers, igniting a river of burning oil that poured into the depths of the fort and reached a stack of abandoned French rifle cartridges and artillery shells.[40]

Whatever the cause, a series of massive explosions rocked the fort, the shock waves traveling the corridors and smashing men together in flattened heaps.[41] The lights blew out and the underground passageways filled with soot and oily black smoke, which forced the survivors to don their gas masks. Even with flashlights, visibility was almost zero. In the confusion an alarm went out that the French were attacking; as the burned and soot-covered survivors of the explosions scrambled up stairs and ladders to the surface, other German soldiers mistook them for French colonial troops, the hated and feared black Africans, their "cruelest enemies."[42] In a final horrific twist, the panicked Germans on the surface threw hand grenades and shot machine guns at the emerging survivors, which may have set off even more stores of shells, grenades, and detonators underground.[43]

A total of 679 German soldiers died in the explosions. Their bodies were walled off in a tomb that after the war became a German national war memorial. Strangely, the death book of the flamethrower regiment listed no names for May 8, 1916, but ten flamethrower pioneers were killed in Verdun on May 7.[44] It is not known if this is a mistake by the regimental historians or if indeed no flamethrower pioneers were killed in the explosions.

Flamethrower Attack on the Dead Man

One of the more successful flamethrower assaults launched by the Guard Reserve Pioneer Regiment in this period took place on May 20, 1916. It was a "pure" pouncing attack on the Dead Man made by the 5th and 6th Companies under the command of Oberleutnant Trage. Sixteen *Kleif* were used in flamethrower shock troops that also included hand-grenade throwers, machine gunners, and possibly grenade-launcher squads. Positions across the entire width of the front were taken to a depth of 1,100 yards. Altogether 1,350 prisoners, four cannons, and sixteen machine guns were captured.[45]

Fort Douaumont photographed on July 31, 1916. Captured by the Germans on February 26, 1916, it was held until retaken by the French on October 24. During that period, it was hit by an estimated 200,000 shells.

Tomb of the 679 German soldiers killed in a series of explosions at Fort Douaumont on May 8, 1916. The cause was not officially determined, but some form of detonation ruptured several flamethrowers stacked in a corridor, which unleashed a river of burning oil that in turn set off a store of hand grenades and artillery shells.

CHAPTER SIX

Charles Theune Conducts an Attack

Oberleutnant Charles Theune, later author of the exhaustive *Strumtruppen und Flammenwerfer*, led a combined stationary and pouncing attack on June 1, 1916.[1] As Reddemann described it:

> The 10th Company under *Oberleutnant* Theune attacked in the Caillette Woods with ten *Grof* and fourteen *Kleif* on a front 300 meters wide. After the shock of the *Grof*, the enemy retreated in panic. The *Kleif* pushed far beyond the objective and went as far as the Chapitre Woods. Altogether 2300 prisoners and twenty-four machine guns taken.[2]

On May 31 the 10th Company was brought into the Bezonvaux Ravine at 7:00 P.M., after which Theune and the commander of Magdeburg Infantry Regiment No. 66 went over the plans for the assault one last time. When darkness fell, Theune moved his company out of the ravine and over the ridge east of Douaumont. Individual flamethrower squads and their weapons were brought forward on June 1 at 2:00 A.M. They entered what Theune called the Trench of the Dead, a heavily damaged communications trench only twenty-eight inches deep, filled with a stinking mixture of bloody bandages, shreds of clothing, body parts, and chloride of lime.

To prevent the large-scale attack they knew was imminent, the French began firing their heaviest-caliber shells at the few German assembly areas, including the Trench of the Dead. German counterbattery fire answered. Caught in the maelstrom of shrapnel and high explosive, the flamethrower squads struggled across the cratered landscape, stooped and groping blindly, making their way toward the Casemate Ravine. The bombardment from both sides increased until it resembled a hurricane that raged throughout the night, severing communications to the rear and preventing the reserves from moving up. Under this onslaught, the morale of the flamethrower pioneers began to ebb.

At 7:30 A.M., two hours before the assault was to start, one of Theune's *Unteroffiziere* reported in a panic that all of the flamethrower pioneers had been killed. Theune raced back to the Trench of the Dead, where he found that five of his large flamethrowers had been destroyed. Although the black flame oil was flowing out over the huddled dead and wounded and a nitrogen propellant tank had exploded, Theune wrote that his *Unteroffizier* had exaggerated; all was not lost, but the troops lacked the will and energy to go forward. Theune reflected on the firmness he was used to receiving from his company, and the personal example that a commander had to set for his men.

When the shelling momentarily let up, Theune ordered his men into two ranks as if they were on the parade ground and marched them forward to their jumping-off points. The five remaining *Grof* were emplaced on the left sector of Infantry Regiment No. 66, at intervals of fifty-five to sixty-six yards, and the twelve *Kleif* squads were positioned between them so that there would be an unbroken front of fire for a width of about 500 yards. Finally, the surviving infantry assault troops – augmented by replacements to make up for the heavy casualties caused by the shelling – assembled on the southern slope of the Casemate Ravine.

Yet another disaster struck when German artillery began dropping high-explosive and gas rounds on their own densely

Genuine combat photo of a flamethrower attack at Thiaumont-Ferme, Verdun. A flamethrower shock troop uses Kleif M.1915 to roll up an enemy trench. In the background, a Kleif carrier rushes forward in a crouch. The blurred object beside the sandbags in the foreground is the propellant tank of another Kleif M.1915, on the back of an unseen flamethrower pioneer.

packed infantry. "The men screamed as if insane with every impact," Theune wrote. "They were not soldiers any more, they were wild men in despair."[3] The flamethrower squads escaped this slaughter because Theune had positioned them in the foremost trenches, often the safest place to be in the unfolding confusion of a mass combined-arms assault.

As the German artillery shaped the battlefield by forcing the French to vacate the Vaux Ravine and take shelter in their front line, Theune decided that the assault would go ahead even though the first wave of infantry had not yet gathered behind his position as planned. At 9:30 the *Grof* were discharged, to Theune's obvious satisfaction:

> The catastrophe of fire broke on the French; a raging sea of fire rolled over those standing thickly crowded in the forward trenches. The enemy saw blazing, jerking stabs of flame coming at him out of enormous clouds of black smoke; he saw no men and no equipment, as if a natural phenomenon of enormous size forced the unknown apparition nearer; that was too much for human beings; human nerves could not endure it.[4]

In the forward trenches the French simply stood, raised their hands, and walked toward the German line, dodging the advancing shock troops and *Kleif* squads. Theune credited the flame shock with stiffening German resolve. Many of the soldiers had never experienced being part of a flamethrower assault; the sizzling flames inspired the Germans to move forward out of the hellish agony of the Casemate Ravine.

Infantry Regiment No. 66 went in as the first wave, and with the help of the *Kleif* squads and shock troops of Assault Battalion Rohr, achieved their objectives without significant casualties. The final contribution of the flamethrowers was the smoking out of concrete bunkers that had withstood hours of the heaviest artillery barrages the Germans could muster.

"With a short jet of flame, all resistance was broken," Theune concluded.[5] Fourteen hundred prisoners including two regimental commanders were taken, along with large amounts

12e Année. N° 128 Le Volume Mensuel 1 fr. net (Etr. 1 fr. 50) 15 Juillet 1916

Je sais tout

DANS CE NUMÉRO :

DU FEU GRÉGEOIS AUX « FLAMENWERFER ».
LE CENTENAIRE DU NAUFRAGE DE LA « MÉDUSE », par PIERRE GIFFARD.
L'ART DE POINTER UN CANON, par le command' GRASSET.
L'HOMME DE DEMAIN, par L. HOULLEVIGUE.
LENOIR ET KELLER, nouvelle, par Frédéric BOUTET.
LA VIE DE GUERRE DES IMPÉRATRICES ET DES REINES, par Louis SCHNEIDER.

PUBLICATIONS PIERRE LAFITTE

Opposite
Top left: French magazine dated July 15, 1916. This illustration is based on patent drawings for the Fiedler M.1910, a weapon that did not see combat. Courtesy A. Langley.

Top right: Sentry wearing Stirnpanzer, steel armor plate that weighed 6.6 pounds and was attached to the steel helmet by the ventilation lugs. Flamethrower pioneers issued Stirnpanzer usually discarded it.

Bottom: Crown Prince Wilhelm observing the demonstration of a Grof. The squad leader (Groftruppführer) uses a makeshift stick fuse (behelfsmässigen Stockzünder) to light the oil because the igniter on the nozzle of the telescoping M.1914 lance has burned out. It is likely that the steel-helmeted Guard officer behind the Crown Prince is Major Bernhard Reddemann. U.S. National Archives 165-GB-3037.

of cannons, machine guns, munitions, and various weapons and booty. Total losses for the 10th Company were three dead, seven wounded, and five gassed.[6]

An infantry officer (left) and a Feldwebel wearing steel Grabenpanzer or Sappenpanzer, which weighed thirty-five pounds. Some sources claim that flamethrower pioneers were issued body armor, but indisputable evidence has yet to be found.

Flamethrower Attack in Flanders

On June 2 the 9th Company under *Oberleutnant* Fritsch assaulted the British positions on the heights of Zillebeke. The Germans attacked with twenty *Kleif* in flame shock troops. According to Reddemann, the flamethrower troops "pushed through the position and broke the fierce resistance of the English." Machine-gun nests were knocked out, trenches were rolled up, and 500 British including a general were captured.[7] Three flamethrower pioneers were killed in the assault.[8]

The Assault on Fort Vaux

Fort Vaux was the smallest of the defensive fortifications at Verdun. It was protected by a wide moat with large, detached concrete installations in the corners. These were the *coffres*, counterscarp or flanking galleries, which were connected to the main body of the fort by underground tunnels. The flanking galleries were armed with cannons and machine guns to engage enemy troops crossing the moat.

German flamethrower squads may have entered Fort Vaux much earlier than is generally accepted, although this cannot be fully corroborated. A report by the 9th Reserve Division, submitted to Army Command 5 on March 19, 1916, stated that on March 8-9 the fort was temporarily occupied by the Germans:

> By order of *Rittmeister* von Scheele and *Leutnant* Baron von Teubern, detachments with pioneers and flamethrowers were sent to clean out the forts. The sections of Reserve Infantry Regiment No. 6 that penetrated into the fort encountered unexpectedly strong resistance, to which they finally succumbed. Nobody returned from the detachments that penetrated into the works. They have either died or have been taken prisoner.[9]

The death book of the Guard Reserve Pioneer Regiment listed one name at Vaux on March 8, two on March 9, and two on March 10.[10] It therefore appears that the first flamethrower attack on Fort Vaux likely took place on March 8, 1916.

On June 2 pioneers climbed on top of the double flanking gallery in the northwest corner of the fort to attack its revolving cannons. The Germans used rope to lower baskets of explosives and bundles of hand grenades that knocked out the guns, then they assaulted the loopholes with incendiary weapons. Although writers have described these devices as flamethrowers fitted with "elbowed"[11] or "specially elongated"[12] tubes, or flamethrowers dropped down with a crankshaft,[13] they were in fact the fire tubes that flamethrowers were supposed to have replaced in 1909:

> But the order for the assault had surprised the pioneers in the same way it had the infantrymen. During the night of June 1 to 2, sections of Pioneer Battalion No.

20 were replaced. It was no longer possible to arrange the dispatching of a unified task force equipped with siege equipment, fire tubes, explosives, etc. What was at hand was sent forward.

Soon after 5:00 in the morning, the first pioneers arrived at the position held by Infantry Regiment No. 158. They brought [Number] "Two" fire tubes with them. *Leutnant der Reserve* Ruberg of the 1st Reserve Company, Pioneer Battalion No. 20, now received the order from Leutnant Rackow to smoke out the [northwestern] gallery. The pioneers crept to the edge of the moat, put the fire tubes on long booms, and poked them into the loopholes of the gallery. Two-meter-long flames hissed into the interior of the casemate. Thick smoke drove the enemy crew from his guns.[14]

It would have been nearly impossible for pioneers to stand on the roof of the flanking gallery and fire a flamethrower downward and into the loopholes, even using the angled nozzle seen on early weapons. However, fire tubes on long guide poles, held in front of the loopholes and ignited with the pull of a lanyard, performed exactly as designed. Before the war flamethrowers had officially replaced fire tubes as a means of assaulting strong points such as flanking galleries, but the fighting at Fort Vaux shows that both weapons were kept in the pioneer arsenal. Ironically, the so-called improvement

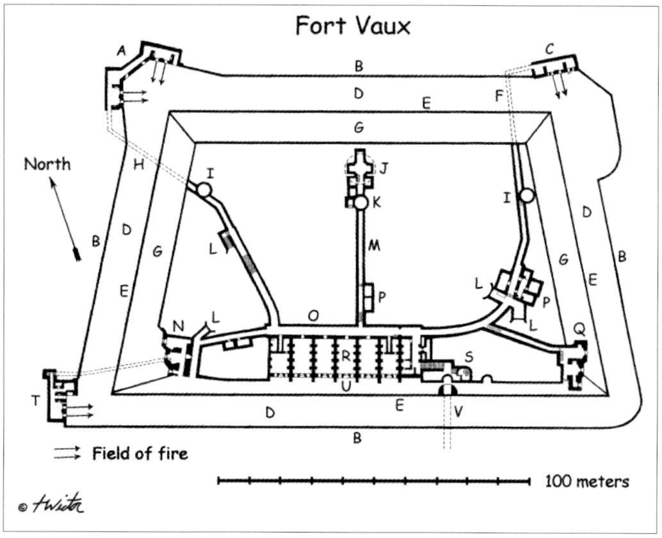

A. Double counterscarp gallery, attacked on June 2 by pioneers positioned on the roof with fire tubes
B. Counterscarp, or outer wall of moat
C. Single counterscarp gallery
D. Moat
E. Scarp, or inner wall of moat
F. Eastern corridor, scene of flamethrower attack on June 4
G. Glacis, or sloping ground
H. Western corridor, scene of flamethrower attack on June 4
I. Armored observation turret
J. 75mm gun turret (destroyed)
K. Armored observation turret in which Colonel Raynal was barricaded
L. Exit to superstructure of fort
M. Corridor to 75mm gun turret
N. Casemate de Bourges or bunker, attacked with fire tubes and then flamethrowers on June 5. This was the final use of flamethrowers inside the fort.
O. Main corridor
P. Magazines
Q. Casemate de Bourges or bunker, reportedly attacked by flamethrowers on June 4; the Germans were said to have been killed and their devices captured by the French
R. Barracks
S. Observatory
T. Single counterscarp gallery
U. Courtyard
V. Entrance tunnel

Pionier H. Faschinski of Pionier-Bataillon Nr. 20. On June 2, 1916, fire-tube squads (Brandröhrentrupps) from this unit assaulted the northwestern double counterscarp gallery of Fort Vaux. Despite assertions from many historians, flamethrowers were not employed in this operation.

over the older method would not have been useful in silencing the flanking galleries.

By the afternoon the Germans had overrun the flanking galleries in the northwest and northeast corners of the moat, and they had established machine-gun positions on the fort's roof. Once inside the galleries, the Germans had access to the western and eastern tunnels. These led into the fort's central corridor, which lay near the barracks and branched off into tunnels connected to the two *casemates de Bourges* or bunkers in the southern corners, as well as the passageway to the commandant's observation turret. It was there that Colonel Sylvain-Eugène Raynal holed up.

At 8:00 P.M. the Germans attacked the French position nearest the fort. A French captain described the experience of facing a nighttime flamethrower assault:

> All of a sudden there is a spurt of flame behind us, with torrents of black and white smoke. It is as though fiery fountains were playing. There can be no doubt about it! They have forced a passage on the right and are directing a liquid fire attack at us.
>
> But now, from the conflagration, red and green flames are rising. What can it be? Ah, it's my store of rockets that is ablaze. At such a moment! Luckily the Boches have been well looked after.[15]

The fire reached the captain's headquarters and threatened to set off a store of hand grenades. A sack of rifle cartridges went off in a series of crackles, and the sandbags lining the trench

Below: The single counterscarp gallery in the northeast corner of Fort Vaux, which the Germans cleared on June 4, 1916, and used as an entryway into the fort.

Right: Chapel in one of the tunnels of Fort Vaux, where the Germans used flamethrowers and fire tubes. Some of the tunnels were thirty-five inches wide by sixty inches tall; the combat often took place in total darkness.

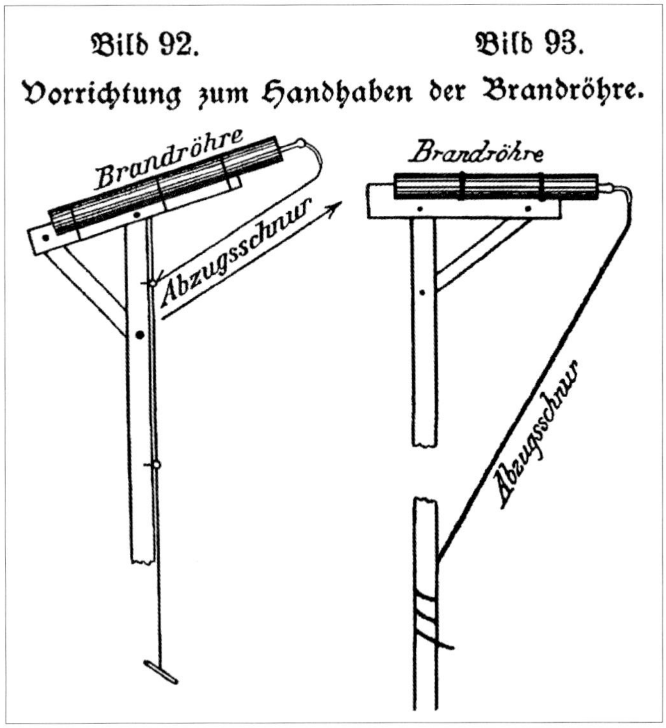

"Devices for handling fire tubes." The fire-tube squads from Pionier-Batallion Nr. 20 climbed onto the roof of the northwestern double counterscarp gallery of Fort Vaux and used these guide poles to lower their weapons to the loopholes. When the fire tubes were in position, the pioneers ignited them by pulling the lanyards. Courtesy Thierry Ehret.

caught fire. After the cases of grenades were cleared away, shovels were used to smother the flames with earth.

Inside the fort the Germans and French fought in the western and eastern tunnels for a day and a half. The French set up sandbag barricades and defended them with machine guns and hand grenades. The Germans used grenades and demolition charges on these barriers, sending waves of assault troops down the two cement corridors that in places were only thirty-five inches wide and sixty inches tall. When a barricade was breached, the combatants engaged in fierce hand-to-hand combat. Much of the fighting took place in pitch darkness filled with suffocating clouds of smoke, cordite fumes, and concrete dust. The Germans requested flamethrowers to clean out the most stubborn pockets of French resistance, but the weapons did not arrive until the morning of June 4.

Despite the many accounts of the participants, it is not possible to recreate an unquestionably accurate narrative of the flamethrower attacks. Time lines are contradictory, as are the descriptions of how and where the devices were used. The chroniclers' nationalities, biases, and ignorance of incendiary weapons are also factors that prevent present-day readers from knowing exactly what happened in the depths of Fort Vaux.

German sources reported that ten *Kleif* squads from the 8th Company of the Guard Reserve Pioneer Regiment arrived from the rear.[16] Four apparatuses were destroyed by artillery fire on the way, leaving six to arrive intact. A *Leutnant* of Pioneer Battalion No. 27 helped the flamethrower pioneers undertake a thorough reconnaissance inside the fort, and then the shock troops entered through the two flanking galleries in the northern corners of the moat.

Flamethrower Attack in the Western Tunnel

In the western tunnel three flamethrower squads under the command of *Offizier-Stellvertreter* Schmidt crept up to the first French barricade, unnoticed by the defenders:

> Three apparatuses simultaneously fling their infernal fire jets through those embrasures into the midday peace of the Frenchmen. Dreadful smoke fills the passageway. Along the walls and the floor, the wooden planking catches fires. In the flickering light of the fire, pioneers of the 27th Battalion proceed, storming up the narrow stairs in order to confront a new barricade. Hand grenades fly at them. From the smoke and flames a machine gun rattles back, its aim true; the attackers escape its fire only by throwing themselves like lightning to the ground and burrowing between the numerous sandbags lying around.[17]

As soon as the machine gun fell silent, the Germans established a breastwork of sandbags. They had taken twenty-seven yards of corridor, including a stairway leading up to the surface. This provided the assault teams with a short, protected connection to German troops on the roof of the fort. The newly won position was strengthened with a second sandbag barricade behind the first:

> Half of the courageous pioneers were wounded, and all were half dead from smoke poisoning when they returned from the combat site with blackened faces and scorched clothing. Sentries of the 39th occupied the new barricades, which the Frenchman in their helpless rage occasionally worked over with machine-gun fire.[18]

In this German account the flamethrower attack took place at 12:30 P.M., the time also given by the French writer Henry Bordeaux. He described the fort filling with a black and acrid smoke that compelled the French to remove the armor plating from the barracks windows in order to get fresh air. As the flamethrower assault continued, the French retreated down the western tunnel into the main corridor and took refuge in the barracks, reluctantly closing the armor-plated windows

Kleif demonstration. The use of such weapons inside the narrow concrete tunnels of Fort Vaux is almost inconceivable. Witnesses reported that flamethrowers panicked the Germans as much as the French.

Double Kleif photographed at Verdun in June of 1916. This example consists of two late-model Kleif M.1915 connected by a 5 ft. hose and a 10ft. hose to a 5ft. (1.5m) large lance. At the feet of the three officers on the right is a late-model Kleif M.1915 connected to a 4ft. (1.2m) small lance with an early self-closing valve; behind is an unseen flamethrower connected to a standard 4ft. small lance. The man marked with an X is General der Infanterie Hermann von François.

again. The Germans tried to blow open the armor using sacks of explosives fitted with delayed-action fuses,[19] but Bordeaux did not state if this action was taken from the inside or outside of the fort. If inside, it means that the Germans made it as far as the main corridor on June 4.

A somewhat different version of the attack was given by Colonel Raynal. He wrote that the flamethrower assault in the western tunnel took place at 8:30 A.M., and it was part of a combined attack that also targeted the barricaded tunnel leading to his observatory:

> Through the openings of our battlements, they launch flames and asphyxiating fumes at us, which spread an unbearable odor and take us by the throat. In the western corridor, the defenders are driven out by the flames and fumes and move into the main corridor. Lieutenant Girard takes over a machine gun and opens fire on the Germans, even as the smoke and fumes seep through the sandbag barricade in front of him. The men return and fire at the Germans for an hour without interruption. Having cleaned the ground in front of the barricade, Girard sends the grenadiers forward. They drive the Germans back into the western corridor.[20]

The battle was fought in complete darkness because the smoke and fumes had extinguished the kerosene lamps. It is not clear from Raynal's account if the Germans used flamethrowers on the barricade leading to his observatory.

Flamethrower Attack in the Eastern Tunnel

According to the Germans, a midday attack was also launched in the eastern tunnel on June 4.[21] A shock troop consisting of men from Pioneer Battalion No. 27 and the 9th Company of Infantry Regiment No. 39 were accompanied by three flamethrower squads from the 8th Company of the Guard Reserve Pioneer Regiment. The shock troop entered the fort from the northeastern flanking gallery and traveled down the

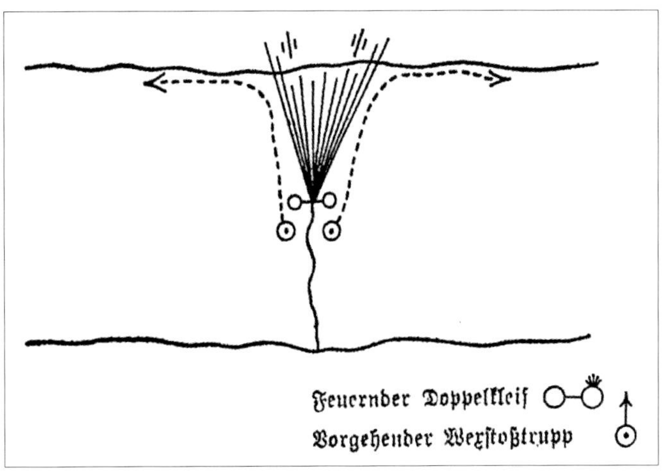

One use for the double Kleif was to lay down covering fire while two small-flamethrower shock troops advanced on either side. (Sturmtruppen und Flammenwerfer.)

Above: Flamethrower squad training with a late-model Kleif M.1915. It is not clear if this weapon was used inside Fort Vaux. Being smaller, it would have been marginally easier to wield in the narrow tunnels than the Kleif M.1916. Courtesy Maurice Sublet.

Below: Single man testing a Kleif M.1917, a flamethrower nearly identical to the M.1916. Both devices were too cumbersome for one man to operate effectively in combat if the other members of the squad were put out of action. U.S. National Archives 165-GB-2944.

tunnel until it reached a stairway of fifty-one concrete steps, at the top of which was a sandbag barricade. Taking the lead, one or more flamethrower squads climbed the stairs and directed their flame jets upward. Rags, sandbags, packs, and pieces of clothing lying around in the stairway caught fire, and thick smoke filled the narrow passageway, nearly overcoming the Germans.

The French continually threw hand grenades that rolled down the stairs and detonated among the attackers, who pushed ahead and left their wounded behind. The Germans were able to breach at least one barricade and force the French back almost to the latrines.[22] Hours after the fires caused by the flamethrowers were extinguished, the smoke continued to pour out of the tunnel. Both the Germans and the French built sandbag barricades to keep out the fumes, and sentries wore their gas masks while on duty.

Raynal claimed that this flamethrower assault took place at 8:30 A.M., the same time as the attack in the western tunnel.[23] He wrote that the defenders were driven back down the eastern tunnel by the flames and asphyxiating smoke, until they put up an airtight sandbag barrier and held fast.

Henry Bordeaux quoted a French survivor of a flamethrower attack in the fort, although the exact location of the action was not described:

> It was then that the Germans, having contrived to blow up a barricade, attacked us with jets of flame and liquid fire. The heat, and the fact that we were taken unawares, caused us to waver for a moment. But Lieutenant Bazy, who was there with his machine-gun, darted forward, and so quick was he, that before we had recovered from our amazement he was standing upright in the middle of the gangway and fighting the Germans single-handed with bombs. The flames came up to his shoes, his left arm was bandaged, being already wounded, but little did he care. As he could not speak, on account of that black acrid smoke, he encouraged us by his example. Accordingly we shook off our stupor and went forward in rotation to stand by his side. At last the flame-throwers were quenched. Despite all their devilish contrivances, their flame-jets, their gases, and their petards, [the Germans] made no advance. It was magnificent. They shouted to us in French: 'Surrender, or you will all be killed,' and we answered by slinging bombs full at their faces.[24]

After this second assault the Germans decided to temporarily refrain from using flamethrowers inside the fort, having deemed the assaults ineffective. The French barricades blocking the corridors would be attacked with hand grenades and machine guns instead. It was only when the fort had fallen that the Germans learned how devastating the June 4 flamethrower attacks had been to French morale. Shouts of "Gas! Masks on!" had echoed down the main corridor, and the closely packed men panicked, some jumping out of the windows of the barracks and landing in the moat below.[25]

The French Capture Flamethrowers

One account of the June 4 attacks claimed that the French killed at least two flamethrower squads at the southwestern *casemate de Bourges*, captured their weapons, and used them to hold off any further German advances into the southern moat.[26]

Raynal told a slightly different story; in his version, the Germans attempted to fire flamethrowers through the loopholes of the southeastern *casemate de Bourges*, not the southwestern. The operators of the "infernal devices"[27] were killed; the French machine gunners seized the flamethrowers and brought them to Raynal, who wrote nothing about using them on the Germans.

The Germans did not mention a flamethrower attack against either of the southern bunkers on June 4, nor did they provide any accounts of pioneers being killed and their weapons taken. In addition, the death book of the Guard Reserve Pioneer Regiment listed no names for June 4 at Vaux. It is possible that the event occurred as Raynal described it, but the Germans simply neglected to report it themselves. Another explanation for the discrepancy is that once again both historians and the participants themselves confused fire tubes for flamethrowers, as is the case of the June 2 assault on the northwestern double flanking gallery.

A Second Flamethrower Mishap

Both Raynal and other writers claimed that on June 5 there was a failed flamethrower assault that did more damage to the Germans than to the French. This was Raynal's "Day of Hell":

> Around five o'clock in the morning, the barricade of the covered passageway close to the casemate de Bourges on the left jumps in a formidable explosion which knocks down a part of the masonry, and the enemy appears

> through the breach thus opened, projecting ignited liquids. Fortunately, the enormous draft which occurs opposes and cancels the action of the flames by rejecting them towards their source of emission. One surprised moment, and then our machine gunners and our grenadiers, led by Bazy and Girard, return and attack with grenade strikes. The enemy moves back.[28]

As the incident was more specifically and dramatically recounted in a later book, a "shattering" explosion blew a "huge breach" in the wall, and German pioneers assaulted it with a flamethrower. "But a freak current of air blew the flame back in their faces."[29]

A German account of this attack reported that the men attacking the passageway to the bunker were five shock troops from Pioneer Battalion No. 15, not the Guard Reserve Pioneer Regiment. They were armed with concentrated charges (*geballte Ladung*) of several grenade heads wired together on one stick handle, and fire tubes instead of flamethrowers.[30] The explosives created only a small hole in the wall of the tunnel; the smoke and flames from the fire tubes were not able to penetrate and did indeed blow back because of the draft. However, there was no mention of flames searing the attackers' faces.

On the roof of the fort, two more shock troops attacked the eastern tunnel. French sentries fired at the pioneers as they ran, but the Germans made it to their objective and ignited the charges. As before only a small breach was blown in the tunnel, and the draft prevented the smoke and flames from the fire tubes from entering. All attempts to enter by blowing holes in the tunnels failed.

French cartoon from 1916. The caption reads, "I say to you, my captain, this good fellow, thinking that it's time to prepare the lamps, has brought his oil." Many French cartoons of the period poke fun at the flamethrower instead of excoriating it. Courtesy A. Langley.

Final Flamethrower Attack Inside Fort Vaux

On June 5 an assault by the 1st Company of Pioneer Battalion No. 15 was launched against the southwestern *casemate de Bourges* at 9:00 A.M. Four flamethrower squads accompanying the shock troop simultaneously sprayed the loopholes of the bunker. The pioneers reported that while smoke penetrated the structures, the flame jets did not, allowing the French to withstand the assault and repel the raiders with hand grenades and machine guns.[31]

According to the Germans, Raynal wrote that the attack – though unsuccessful – caused him more losses because the smoke and dust aggravated the suffering brought about by lack of water. In Raynal's book, however, the incident was described as a failed assault by a single German pioneer

Helmet worn by the flamethrower detachment of Sturmbataillon Rohr, authorized by an AKO of June 6, 1916. An M.1897 Pickelhaube of the Garde-Pionier-Bataillon, the silver eagle-and-star plate was fitted with a small silver-plated death's head identical to the cap badge worn by Braunschweigisches Husaren-Regiment Nr. 17. Courtesy Daniel Griffin.

Postcard sent by Pionier Michaelsen, 2nd Workshop Detachment of the Garde-Reserve-Pionier-Regiment. These mostly middle-aged men are firefighters who have volunteered to be flamethrower pioneers. In what may be a black-humored and deadpan joke, they are posing in front of a fire station wearing the heavy belts of their former occupation. Note the spikeless Garde Pickelhauben and the shooting awards worn by three of the men.

carrying a "case" that emitted intense smoke and noxious fumes after the man was killed by French machine gunners.[32] The device in question was clearly a fire tube rather than a flamethrower.

Neither side reported flamethrower or fire-tube assaults after June 5. Since the weapons had made conditions inside the fort as intolerable for the Germans as they were for the French, the Germans would thereafter rely on the smoke from bursting shells to "make the French miserable."[33] A *Hauptmann* of Pioneer Battalion No. 20 said that in the end, using flamethrowers and fire tubes inside the fort was impossible because the smoke and gases blew back into the passageways occupied by the troops igniting the weapons. Flamethrowers also caused panic among the Germans, so they were sent away.[34]

On June 7 Raynal surrendered the fort.

3rd Battalion of the Flamethrower Regiment

Sources differ on when the 3rd Battalion of the Guard Reserve Pioneer Regiment was established. Reddemann wrote that it was formed in June of 1916, under the command of *Hauptmann* Beck.[35] According to the regimental death book, however, the Guard Reserve Pioneer Regiment had three battalions from its inception on April 20.[36] This unexplained discrepancy is one of many found in the records left by those with firsthand knowledge of the German flamethrower arm.

Regardless of the date it was created, the 3rd Battalion was initially comprised of the 9th and 10th Companies, formerly the 1st and 2nd Companies of the 4th Guard Pioneer Battalion. The 11th and 12th Companies were added on September 26,[37] using officers and men from the recruit depot and the 2nd Guard Pioneer Replacement Battalion. In addition the Fifth Army High Command transferred 500 young infantrymen into the regiment and trained them thoroughly as flamethrower operators.[38]

Total Number of Flamethrower Attacks

There were forty flamethrower assaults in Verdun and on the heights of the Meuse between April 28 and July 10, 1916.[39] The units that fought were as follows:

The 1st Company once; the 2nd Company fourteen times; the 3rd Company three times; the 4th Company five times; the 5th Company six times; the 6th Company three times; the 8th Company five times; the 10th Company twice; and the 5th and 6th Companies together once. Of these forty engagements, twenty-five were judged to have been successful.

Reddemann made no mention of his regiment serving on the eastern front during this period, but at least one newspaper reported that German flamethrower troops fought in Galicia on July 5. According to dispatches from Petrograd, the Russians took 5000 German prisoners when approaching the Koropice and Souhodolsk Rivers.

> In the course of an attack on the village of Vergiki the Germans received our troops with liquid fire.
>
> Owing to their conduct we put all the Germans to the bayonet when we captured the village.[40]

The death book of the flamethrower regiment listed no names of men killed in Poland on July 5. However, one pioneer of the 3rd Company fell at Zlota Gora in Silesia on July 19.[41]

Two NCOs of the 7th Company, Garde-Reserve-Pionier-Regiment, in a postcard sent by Vizefeldwebel Heinrich Freesemann, seated on the left. He writes, "At the front, 1916. The two sergeants with their French magpie called Joffre; Henay, 3 July, 1916." Freesemann's unidentified companion wears the sleeve chevron of an etatsmässige Feldwebel. Although black shoulder straps for pioneers had been mandated on September 21, 1915, both men still have field-gray straps almost six months later. In the background is a Gulaschkanone from the company's field kitchen.

French Reaction to the Flamethrower

The Battle of Verdun saw the flamethrower used more often and in much larger numbers than it had been during the attacks of the previous year. As word of the ghastly siege of Fort Vaux spread among the French population, flamethrowers became symbolic of an inhumanity not seen before. An American volunteer ambulance driver noted this change in a June 10 diary entry:

> Conversation with the private soldiers here furnishes convincing evidence that the Germans lost more than they gained when they resorted to the deadly gas attacks and liquid fire. In the earlier stages of the war, the French peasant Pierre had a sort of good-natured, scornful sympathy for the German peasant Fritz, and occasional true stories filtered from the front of exchanges of friendly words and tobacco between the opposing first-line trenches. At that period, the appeal of "Camarade" stopped many a French bayonet as it was about to sink into a German breast. But that period has passed. It ended with the gas attacks.
>
> "*Plus de camarades*" is an expression we hear everywhere, and the word *Bosche*, expressive merely of contempt, has given place to "*les vaches*" or "*les sales vaches*," which means "cows" in the dictionary, but "dirty beasts" in the argot of the trenches.
>
> Today each French *poilu* is fighting his own war, fighting with a bitter hatred; fighting to kill.[42]

Field companies of the Garde-Reserve-Pionier-Regiment often maintained light trucks such as these "on call" at their barracks. They were kept loaded with large and small flamethrowers as well as assault equipment, so that combat platoons could be deployed instantly.

Flamethrower pioneer firing the 4ft. (1.2m) version of the M.1914 small lance. His left hand grips the lance from above to contain the powerful recoil. In battle the smoke and brightness of flame jets revealed the positions of flamethrower squads, making them vulnerable to enemy fire.

Stern-looking men of the II. Garde-Pionier-Ersatz-Bataillon, ready to be transferred into the flamethrower regiment. All wear new M.1910 service jackets and well-pressed trousers. The decorated Unteroffizier instructor seated in the second row is outfitted in a privately purchased M.1910 service jacket with a high collar and Guard lace of a dark, nonregulation shade of gray. Such uniforms are common in photos of flamethrower pioneers.

Rehearsing a Flame Attack with Assault Infantry

Cooperation between the flamethrower regiment and the infantry expanded dramatically during the Battle of Verdun, requiring intensive training by both arms of service.

To prepare for a specific flame attack, a training facility (*Übungswerk*) was first dug far back from the front lines.[43] When possible it was built as an actual-sized model of the enemy position targeted for attack. Aerial photos were used for this purpose. If there was not enough time, simple trenches alone were dug, the specific objectives laid out with white tape or represented by furrows cut in the earth with a plow.

The entire flame attack – including the participation of the assault infantry and live-firing flamethrowers – was rehearsed at the training facility. Each flamethrower pioneer and infantryman was thoroughly trained in his individual task at the model trench system; he also practiced throwing live hand grenades. Tables were drawn up that specified the number of flamethrowers to be used, the points from which the lance operators would fire the initial flame jets, and the routes to the front line. These were all numbered from the right to the left.

Flamethrower pioneers and infantry assault troops were individually instructed in their line of advance and the connecting trench they were supposed to use to reach their jumping-off point. This was done to prevent the men from giving in to the urge to bunch up. The distances between the jumping-off points and areas of penetration were measured exactly, and the flamethrower pioneers were given clearly drawn sketches of the enemy position. Each flamethrower shock troop was required to know exactly which point it was to penetrate and which task it was to accomplish there. In addition, each flamethrower shock troop was to be familiar with the orders of adjacent shock troops.

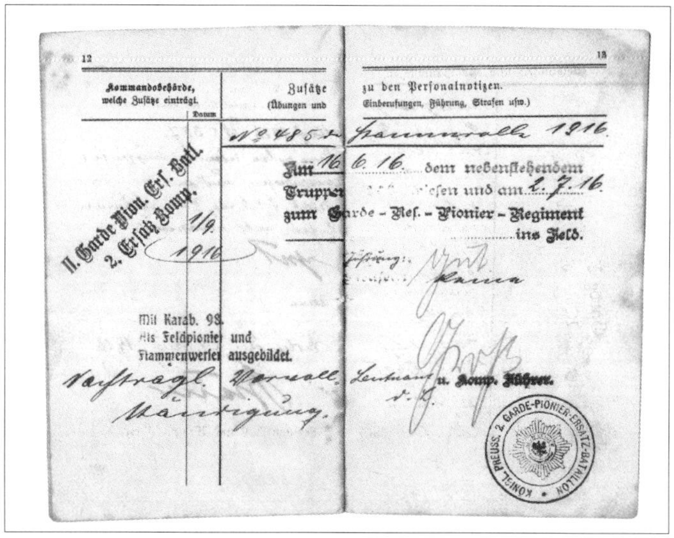

Pages 12 and 13 of the Militärpass of Pionier Franz Hanke. Born in 1896, Hanke was inducted into the Garde-Pionier-Ersatz-Bataillon in October of 1915. He served as a flamethrower operator in the 16th Company, III. Garde-Pionier-Bataillon, before being wounded. Upon his recovery, he was transferred into the 2nd Replacement Company, II. Garde-Pionier-Ersatz-Bataillon and then into the 3rd Company, Garde-Reserve-Pionier-Regiment. He saw combat at the Somme, the Toboly bridgehead, Galicia, Riga, the Jakobstatt bridgehead, Wygoda, and the Chemin des Dames, where he was wounded again in May of 1918. Courtesy Gregg DuBois.

"Wing shock troops" (*Flügelstosstrupps*) secured the flanks, while "flank shock troops" (*Flankenstosstrupps*) secured the trench junctions on the flanks. For a hostile trench system with many junctions, careful preparation and especially thorough practice at the training facility were necessary.

CHAPTER SEVEN

The Battle of the Somme

During the massive British offensive at the Somme, *General der Infanterie* Friedrich Sixt von Armin of the IV Army Corps recommended the extensive use of flamethrowers.[1] His input may have contributed to Reddemann being ordered against his will to deploy his troops defensively.[2]

According to Reddemann, neither his men nor their weapons were suited for a defensive role. Flamethrower pioneers lived for the *Fang*, the abbreviation for "flame attack" (*Flammenangriff*). They had little interest in or aptitude for flame defense (*Flammenverteidigung*), abbreviated *Fert*. Additionally, small flamethrowers used igniters that burned for ninety seconds to two minutes, and they had enough fuel for a continuous firing duration of about twenty seconds, enough for lightning-fast assaults with limited objectives. Flamethrower troops at the Somme would stand in trenches and fire at oncoming waves of the numerically superior enemy. In what amounted to a public prediction on the fate of his men, Reddemann ordered that explosive charges be attached to all flamethrowers deployed defensively so that the weapons could be destroyed when the German positions were inevitably overrun.

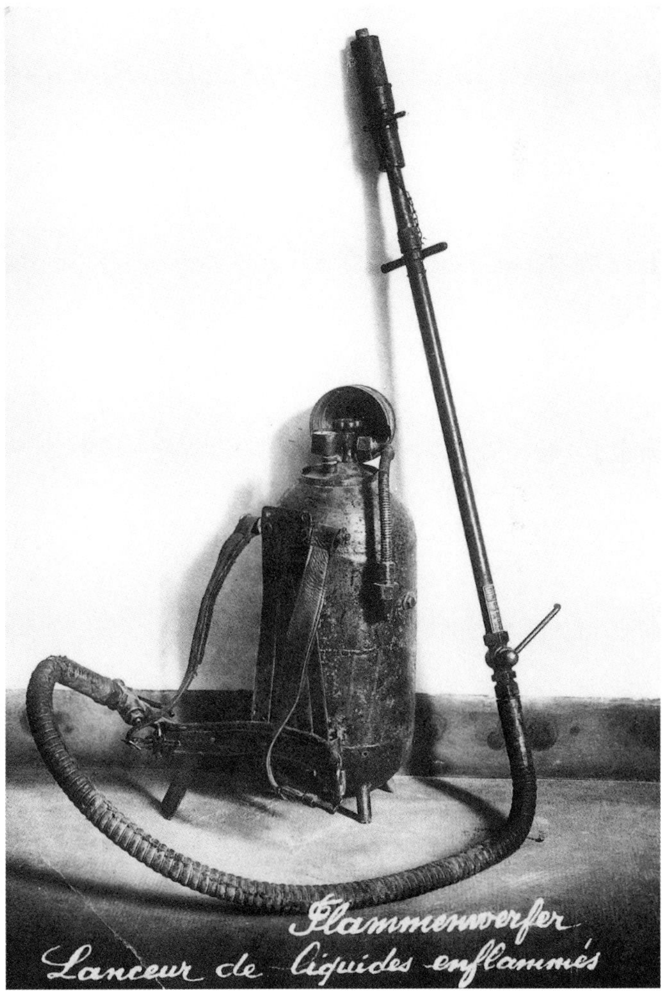

Kleif M.1916. During the Battle of the Somme, Bernhard Reddemann was forced against his will to deploy his men defensively. He therefore ordered that explosive charges be attached to Kleif used in this role, so that the troops could destroy the weapons before their positions were taken. Courtesy Maurice Sublet.

The British Train to Survive Flamethrowers

Prior to the Somme offensive, the British tried to prepare their soldiers for what they would experience during flamethrower attacks. The training appears for the most part to have consisted of having the men occupy mock trenches while captured German flamethrowers were fired over their heads. According to the poet Edmund Blunden, "Gas was loosed over us; we crouched down in the trenches while the roaring heat of the flammenwerfer curled up in black smoke above[.]"[3] The many descriptions of this training are remarkable in that the men were assured that simply ducking down would be enough to save them. They were not told of the curved-trajectory shooting that German flamethrower pioneers used to reach the bottoms of enemy trenches, and nothing was said of shock troops entering the position from the flanks and rolling it up with flamethrowers and grenades. Since the true context of the weapon was not given, the average British soldier may not have known that the initial burst of flame fired at him was a covering jet meant to force his head down so that a shock troop could move in. The British were essentially training their men to do exactly what the Germans wanted them to do.

A typically blasé account of the training was given by a British officer:

> After lunch Jim, Guy and I set out to see a "flammen werfer *[sic]*" demonstration. The machine was captured from the Hun and throws liquid fire about fifteen yards. It is comparatively inocuous *[sic]* to men in trenches as the flame cannot be made to fall, and by crouching at the bottom of the trench you can avoid it altogether and the heat is not excessive. The instrument looks very like a garden water pot with a long nozzle and the flame only lasts two minutes.[4]

Rudyard Kipling wrote that the 1st Battalion of the Irish Guards was subjected to a German air raid while undergoing this sort of training:

> They had been attending a demonstration to prove the harmlessness of a flammenwerfer if only one lay flat on the ground and let the roaring blast hiss over. Ribald men have explained, since, that these demonstrations were more demoralising than the actual machine in action, especially when, as occasionally happened, the nozzle of the flame-shooter carried away and, in the attempts to recontrol the thing, the class, bombed from above and chased by fire below, broke and fled.[5]

Feints and Signaling

At the Somme the Germans would use their flamethrowers not only to attack and defend but to send signals and fool the enemy during feint attacks (*Scheinangriffe*). Flame jets fired upward were more easily seen than rockets or flares during the daytime, especially if the thin, smokeless oil was used.

French Image d'Epinal depicting German flamethrowers engaged in curved-trajectory shooting. British doctrine held that the flame jet had a straight trajectory and could not reach the bottoms of trenches. However, German flamethrower operators could curve the jet and bounce it off the trench walls to fire around corners. Courtesy A. Langley.

The number of flame jets fired would have a specific meaning, such as to halt an artillery barrage or warn of shells falling short.

For feint operations flamethrowers were deployed in conjunction with gas or smoke bombs, machine guns, artillery, and aerial activity.[6] A well-executed feint confused the enemy and left him in doubt as to the actual point to be attacked, which would in turn cause him to distribute his artillery fire. Both large and small flamethrowers were used in these operations. Their smoke and fire made the feints more realistic and diverted the enemy's attention from the intended target.[7]

The British Use Flamethrowers Offensively

As Reddemann prepared to deploy his flamethrowers defensively, the British were fielding their own flamethrowers in an offensive role.[8] The opening of the Battle of the Somme on July 1 was their debut, in the front occupied by the 18th Division, opposite Casino Point and astride the Carnoy-Montauban road. Two "Large Gallery" projectors, inventions of Captain William H. Livens of the Royal Engineers, were employed by the Special Brigade. The Livens flamethrower consisted of five oil tanks connected to a discharge pipe nine inches in diameter. The weapon was almost fifty feet long and weighed two tons when empty. It was emplaced fifteen feet underground in a mine gallery in front of enemy trenches and took six hours for the seven-man crew to assemble. In combat an armored head resembling a submarine periscope cut upward through the earth, and when it broke the surface to a height of one foot, an automatic ignition system lit the jet of oil. The head then traversed ninety degrees from side to side, spraying flame to a range of almost 350 feet. Three shots that consumed ninety-six gallons of oil each could be fired in a four-minute period.

The flamethrowers were fired at 7:15 A.M., fifteen minutes before the British infantry attack. As one writer put it, the "German" had gloried in his own flamethrowers and considered them the triumphant evidence of his superior talent in science:

> While he was in this frame of mind, and rocking under a whirlwind storm of shell, what seemed like a strange display of fireworks played above his trenches. The wet ground then steamed about him, and in splashes and torrents the lava and oil hissed and burnt, surprised and terrified.[9]

This image has been hand captioned "Flammenwerfer (Mittelstrahl)" or "Flamethrower (middle jet)," a stream of flame at full strength rather than at its beginning or end. The term is not found in any of Reddemann or Theune's writings.

At least forty Germans were killed by the massive plumes of flame, but the total number of casualties could not be determined because the trench had been undermined previously and blown up with explosives as the British were crossing No Man's Land.

During the Somme offensive the British also used two-man "Semi-portable" flamethrowers twelve times, without success. Colonel Charles H. Foulkes, the engineer officer in charge of the Special Brigade, concluded that small flamethrowers were unsuitable for the open fighting on the Somme, and the effects of large models were not worth the effort to transport, assemble, and emplace them in their underground saps.[10] It is not known what Reddemann thought of these weapons, but Charles Theune wrote that they "did not appear effectively on any front and belong to the realm of fable."[11]

German Flamethrower Attacks at the Somme

The Germans used flamethrowers forty-four times from July 10, 1916, to February 19, 1917. Assaults took place at Estrées, Thiepval, Monchy au Bois, Longueval, Delville Woods, Goyécourt, Maisonette-Ferme, Pozières, Verman-dovillers, Moquet-Ferme, Fourcaux Woods, Leuze Woods, Halle, Chilly, the woods of Pierre-Vaast, Amboss Woods, and Ablaincourt, among many other places.

Eight companies of the Guard Reserve Pioneer Regiment took part in the battle. The 3rd Company fought seven times; the 4th Company twice; the 6th Company five times; the 7th Company seven times; the 8th Company six times; the 9th Company six times; the 10th Company eight times; and the 11th Company four times.

Conditions were very difficult due to extensive damage to the trenches. Flamethrower troops had to cross wide expanses

The Livens "Large Gallery" flamethrower, used by the British on July 1, 1916, the opening day of the Battle of the Somme. Almost fifty feet long, it had a range of 112 yards. For combat use, it was emplaced in an underground gallery, the nozzle cutting up through the earth to spray the burning oil. British National Archives MUN 5/385/1650/1.

Above: Infantry assault troops and flamethrower pioneers roll up a mock trench. As a Kleif squad sprays a jet on the right, the infantrymen prepare to throw grenades across the open ground separating the traverses. The assault troops' helmets have been painted white as a safety precaution.

Below: Flamethrower pioneers practicing on wood-and-cloth dummies. The lance operator is armed with the 4ft. (1.2m) model of 1914, while the flamethrower on the left has been obliterated by damage to the photo. Courtesy Maurice Sublet.

of open terrain with only shell holes for cover and in the face of stiff resistance. Despite significant casualties among his men, Reddemann claimed that their "spirit of attack" did not slacken. While he did not support the defensive use of his flamethrowers, pointing out that this caused losses among his men that he found exceedingly painful, he acknowledged that the mission helped prevent the British breakthrough.

The flamethrower pioneers frequently held up the enemy assault for short periods; however, the devices were soon emptied. When the waves of British soldiers pressed forward, the Guard Pioneers were wiped out or taken prisoner. In a final act of defiance, most of Reddemann's doomed but determined officers and men managed to blow up their weapons before being killed, wounded, or captured.

Individual Flamethrower Attacks

On July 11 the 16th Welsh encountered a fierce machine-gun and flamethrower defense in Mametz Wood that threw the regiment back slightly. Four days later the 49th Division fought off an attack by shock troops armed with grenades and flamethrowers at the Leipzig Salient of Ovillers. On August 5 the 9th Royal Fusiliers (36 Brigade) were subjected to a grenade and flamethrower attack in Ration Trench at 4:00 A.M. The fusiliers leapt out of the trench on either side and kept the attackers at bay with their rifles and Lewis guns.[12]

One of the attacks highlighted by Reddemann took place on September 10 at Berny. *Unteroffizier* Arp of the 3rd Company was ordered to roll up a barricaded enemy trench during a nighttime attack. He and his flamethrower troop crawled to within five yards of the enemy before firing. The flamethrower pioneers climbed over the barricade, and as they were rolling up the trench, their flames ignited a case of illumination rockets, which exploded and blocked further progress. When Arp and his men climbed out of the trench to make a detour, they were hit by machine-gun fire that killed half of them. The detachment continued forward until the three remaining pioneers were badly wounded. His troop put out of action, *Unteroffizier* Arp carried his men back to the German jumping-off point, making three trips under heavy machine-gun fire. After he had rescued his troop mates, he made two final trips back to the enemy trench to retrieve the flamethrowers, lances, and igniters. He somehow returned unwounded and was awarded the Iron Cross First Class for his bravery. Strangely, the death book of the flamethrower regiment listed no names for September 10 at Berny.

Late-model Kleif M.1915. The Red oil used for training purposes was the cheapest grade available and produced the most smoke. Flamethrowers that fired Red oil had to be thoroughly cleaned afterward.

A notable flame defense was put up by part of the 10th Company on September 17 at Berny-Deniecourt. Under the command of *Leutnant* Lange, the men repeatedly threw back the numerically superior enemy until the position was surrounded, at which point the squads destroyed their flamethrowers. Five *Unteroffiziere* and eighteen pioneers were taken prisoner, while four were badly wounded. Reddemann reported that the rest fought their way out, but the death book of the flamethrower regiment listed five men of the 10th Company as dead or missing at Berny-Deniecourt on September 17 and one dead on September 18.[13] Since the regimental death book was compiled in part from Reddemann's detailed war diaries, the reason for this discrepancy and that of September 10 is not clear.

German Lessons Learned at the Somme

The document "Experiences of the IV. German Corps in the Battle of the Somme During July, 1916," authored by *General der Infanterie* Friedrich Sixt von Armin, called for more flamethrowers and suggested how they may be better used:[14]

> The employment of small *Flammenwerfer* in wooded country which is full of obstacles, and in which there is no extended view, suffers, in an attack with a distant objective, under the disadvantage of the heavy weight of the apparatus. It is better to use the *Flammenwerfer* from a well prepared assaulting position and against well

defined, close objectives which have been previously reconnoitred.[15]

Reddemann had come to these precise conclusions as early as 1915; one can only wonder if he had tried to explain the proper use of flamethrowers to von Armin before the battle but had been ignored.

In January of 1917 *General der Infanterie* Fritz von Bülow, commander of the First Army, wrote about the usefulness of the flamethrower at the Somme:

> The attachment of "*Flammenwerfer*" to the assault troops is especially desirable when methodical counter-attacks are to be carried out. Consequently, one of the "*Flammenwerfer*" battalions allotted to the [First] Army was combined with an Assault School, and, by means of small detachments, trained those divisions which were behind the front, waiting to act as reliefs, in the technical use of "*Flammenwerfer*."[16]

Presumably von Bülow meant that the infantrymen were trained not how to use the devices themselves but how to assault in conjunction with flamethrower pioneers.

Stereoview hand captioned "With the Bavarian assault battalion. Flamethrower attack on enemy machine-gun nest." Two flamethrower squads simultaneously fire on a concrete pillbox from opposite directions, covering the advance of troops from Sturmbataillon Nr. 6 or 15.

Flamethrower attack at night. Note the overwhelming size of the flames in comparison to the barbed-wire posts. German flamethrower pioneers regularly undertook nocturnal operations; the terror inspired in the enemy was considerable.

Jäger- (Sturm-) Bataillon Nr. 3

In April of 1916 four *Jäger* battalions were to be converted to assault battalions modeled on Assault Battalion Rohr. The two-month training course took place at Beauville. Although three of the *Jäger* battalions were ultimately withdrawn from the program and sent to the Rumanian front instead, Brandenburger *Jäger* Battalion No. 3 (*Brandenburgerisches Jäger-Bataillon Nr. 3*) became *Jäger* (Assault) Battalion No. 3 (*Jäger- [Sturm-] Bataillon Nr. 3*) on July 8, 1916, after 500 officers, NCOs, and men considered physically unfit for shock-troop duty were replaced by younger soldiers.[17]

The new battalion was composed of four assault companies, one machine-gun company, one trench-mortar company furnished with eight light weapons, one infantry-gun battery equipped with six small field pieces captured from the Russians, and one flamethrower platoon (*Flammenwerferzug*) armed with six *Kleif M.1916*. The flamethrower personnel were transferred into the new assault battalion from the 2nd Guard Pioneer Replacement Battalion. On July 25 the flamethrower platoon was strengthened with an additional officer and twenty-five NCOs and men from the 2nd Guard Pioneer Replacement Battalion.[18] This increase in manpower was apparently accompanied by a corresponding increase in the number of flamethrowers, but details are lacking.

Although the flamethrower platoon of *Jäger* (Assault) Battalion No. 3 was an integral part of the unit from its beginning, the flamethrower operators themselves remained members of the Guard Reserve Pioneer Regiment. They wore the Guard Pioneer uniform, and when they were killed in action their names were recorded in the regimental death book, unlike the flamethrower operators of Assault Battalion Rohr. Additionally, the flamethrower platoon of *Jäger* (Assault) Battalion No. 3 took its orders directly from Reddemann and the Supreme Army Command.

More infantry assault battalions were formed from December of 1916, utilizing flamethrower platoons from the Guard Reserve Pioneer Regiment. These platoons were not permanently attached to individual assault battalions; instead, they were regularly rotated back into the regiment in order to keep their training level high. The flamethrower platoon of *Jäger* (Assault) Battalion No. 3 was subject to this rotation as well.

Flamethrower Attack in Verdun

As the Battle of the Somme ground on, fighting continued in Verdun, where a dramatic flamethrower attack was described by a French captain named Michel.[19] On the morning of July 11, after an all-night artillery barrage, he was preparing to eat his breakfast when he saw torrents of flame suddenly spray onto the men of his front-line trench. He sprang to his feet and alerted his reserve section as Germans armed with flamethrowers poured out of foxholes only thirty yards in front of his position. In the midst of the black smoke, French and German soldiers fought hand-to-hand, lobbing grenades and bayoneting each other. French officers fired their pistols into the advancing crowds of Germans, and jets of flame erupted continuously.

Overhead, stick-handled German grenades and French "lemon" grenades crossed in arcs. German riflemen fired on the run, while Bavarian alpine *Jäger* leapt over the charred corpses of *Poilu*. The *Jäger* approached in a dense column along a front 110 yards wide extending back over 160 yards, preceded by flamethrowers spraying the last pockets of resistance. On the sides of this steel-helmeted crowd, German

Jäger Karl Egger, of Brandenburgerisches Jäger-Bataillon Nr. 3. On July 8, 1916, Jäger-Bataillon Nr. 3 was transformed into Jäger- (Sturm-) Bataillon Nr. 3, which included flamethrower operators from the II. Garde-Pionier-Ersatz-Bataillon. While most of the new unit retained the gray-green Jäger uniform seen here, flamethrower personnel were outfitted as Guard Pioneers.

Postcard captioned "During a flamethrower attack on the western front: The colossal length of the flame jet itself and the wall of smoke towering over it." The flamethrower is a Grof with a telescoping lance; the actual setting is a training ground, not the western front.

In this wartime German magazine illustration, the artist has mistakenly given the flamethrower troops infantry uniforms with the number 7 on their shoulder straps. The Kleif M.1915 are being used to engage in curved-trajectory shooting. In the center, a lance operator adjusts a pair of goggles.

light machine gunners fired from the hip. As the *Jäger* closed in, Captain Michel ordered his reserve section to form a square around him.

Survivors of the French 10th and 11th Companies whirled around Michel's square, mixed with German grenadiers wearing gas masks that made them resemble bestial figures from the Apocalypse. Taking heavy losses from Michel's men, the Germans sent an assault company into the ravine. This force, accompanied by two flamethrower squads, advanced so quickly it seemed to be running a race, undeterred by continuous French rifle and pistol fire.

Michel was informed that his machine guns had jammed and most of their crews had been killed, leaving him with no way to halt the German advance. Men fell around him as he emptied his pistol. Suddenly his position was encircled, the *Jäger* stopping only twenty paces away. The French fixed their bayonets as a German officer flanked by two flamethrower squads cautiously stepped forward. His pistol was trained on Michel, and the flamethrower operators kept their hands on the levers of their lances:

> "Mister Officer," the enemy leader shouts at me in French. "Surrender. You are surrounded."
>
> I nervously grit my teeth, slacken my arm suddenly, and discharge my pistol at my adversary. He collapses, firing into the air. The flamethrower is about to operate. I empty my clip at the figure and his tank. A gigantic flame spouts from the barrel, exploding toward me and burning the right sleeve of my jacket.[20]

Somehow Michel survived the gout of flame and continued to fight. He threw away his empty pistol and picked up rifles and grenades from the fallen, shouting encouragement to his men until he was severely wounded by a grenade and captured.

Five flamethrower pioneers from the 1st Company and three from the 5th Company of the Guard Reserve Pioneer Regiment were killed in Verdun on July 11, 1916.[21] None were officers.

The Conferment of the Death's Head Sleeve Badge

On July 28, 1916, the Guard Reserve Pioneer Regiment received a death's head (*Totenkopf*) sleeve badge, given to commemorate the unit's 150th flamethrower attack. The emblem was announced in a letter to the regiment written by Crown Prince Wilhelm:

> His Majesty the Kaiser and King has, at my recommendation, decreed that the Guard Reserve Pioneer Regiment, which has been developed under my eyes, should wear during the war on the left sleeve of its uniform an insignia in the form of a death's head. In recognition of its outstanding achievements I wish to congratulate the flame projector regiment on the award of this insignia.
>
> Always placed into action in the most difficult places, both officers and men everywhere brought their arm into play both effectively and quickly, and became one of the most fearful opponents in close combat the French had.
>
> I am convinced that the outer insignia of the young arm will always be an exhortation to continue to develop in the spirit of death-defying joy of combat.[22]

With the conferment of the sleeve badge, the men of the regiment became known as the Death's Head Pioneers (*Totenkopf-Pioniere*). The death's head was a symbol of great prestige in the German military, dating back centuries. It was worn by *Leib* Hussar Regiment No. 1 (*1 Leib-Husaren Regiment Nr. 1*), the Crown Prince's former unit; *Leib* Hussar Regiment No. 2 (*2 Leib-Husaren-Regiment "Königin Viktoria von Preussen" Nr. 2*); Brunswicker Hussar Regiment No. 17 (*Braunschweigisches Husaren-Regiment Nr. 17*); and Brunswicker Infantry Regiment No. 92 (*Braunschweigisches Infanterie-Regiment Nr. 92*.) The "Prussian" version was a rounded, three-quarter view facing left, while the "Brunswick" was a slimmer, almost piratical design that faced forward. During the First World War, the flamethrower detachment of Assault Battalion Rohr and the Guard Reserve Pioneer Regiment were the only units to be awarded death's-head insignia.

The Crown Prince and the Flamethrower Regiment

It is not surprising that the Crown Prince would ask his father the Kaiser to award the death's head badge to the flamethrower regiment. When Flamethrower Detachment Reddemann first took to the field, many unit commanders were skeptical of the new and still unknown weapon. Only the Crown Prince – commander of the Fifth Army – immediately grasped the flamethrower's potential. He allowed its first combat trial to be conducted in his sector at Malancourt on February 26, 1915, and from that point on he took a personal interest in both the unit and the technical development of the weaponry.

According to Reddemann, the Crown Prince had a close, cordial relationship with the flamethrower pioneers. He

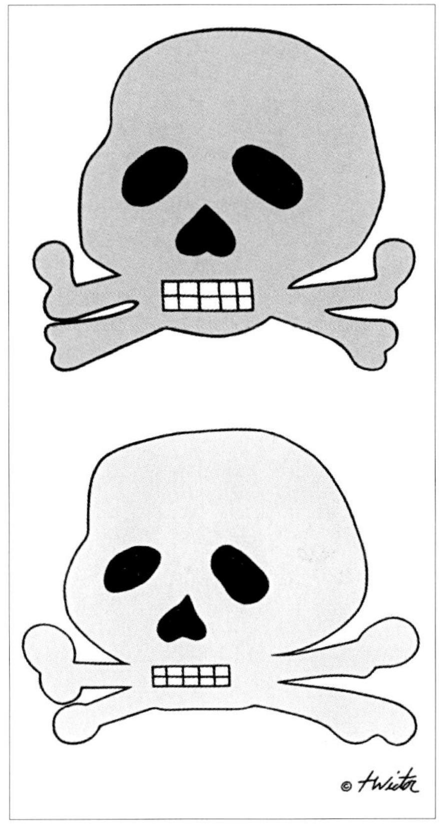

Above: Photo taken during the Allied War Exposition held in Chicago, Illinois, from September 1 to 21, 1918. An American doughboy shows off the busby (Pelzmütze) of 1 Leib-Husaren Regiment Nr. 1. This death's head was the model for the sleeve badge awarded to the Garde-Reserve-Pionier-Regiment on July 28, 1916.

Right: The death's head sleeve badge, traced from photographs. The top image represents the most common pattern, while the bottom is an officially sanctioned variation. For enlisted men the badge was cut from medium-gray cloth; for officers it was embroidered in silver bullion. Both versions had eye and nose holes in black velvet and ten teeth embroidered in white and black thread. The emblems were mounted on field-gray ovals of no fixed size. It is likely that the bottom version is the officers' badge.

asked to have all innovations demonstrated to him, and he often gave Reddemann useful advice, although the nature of these contributions is not known. Such was the level of his involvement that on March 27, 1917, he said to Reddemann, "I have collaborated in the development of the flamethrower. Under my eyes and with my cooperation you have developed yourselves to what you are now! That is a bond that continually binds me to my Death's Head Pioneers!"[23]

Reddemann credited the Crown Prince with changing the minds of other high-ranking commanders. They soon recognized the value of flamethrowers and began requesting them. The Crown Prince would often personally summon Reddemann and point out important positions lost to the enemy, as was the case of the "Soldered Joint" in the Champagne. "You and your brave fellows must repair this damage as soon as possible!" said Wilhelm, after which flamethrowers were sent in with the infantry and the ground recaptured by the Germans.[24]

The Crown Prince held the Death's Head Pioneers in such esteem that he called them his Body Guard (*Leibgarde*), on whom he could always rely. His personal affection for them manifested itself in his frequent presence on the training grounds and his inspection of companies recently returned from heavy fighting. He apparently encouraged informality – as Reddemann put it, "He himself maintained a cordial and simple kind of manner with the individual men whom he had known for a long time, allowing them to give him personal

German soldiers at a cafe, including an Unteroffizier of the Garde-Reserve-Pionier-Regiment on the right. They have been drinking wine or brandy from tankards, which would explain their glazed expressions. The flamethrower pioneer is a twice-decorated veteran wearing an M.1910 service jacket with the light-gray Guard lace mandated for the M.1915 blouse. His gray death's head sleeve badge is seen to good advantage.

reports on the battles and inquiring with great sympathy about their families in the homeland."[25]

The image of the Crown Prince as a foppish, ineffectual dilettante is somewhat refuted by Reddemann's assertion that his battle-hardened flamethrower pioneers could not thank Wilhelm enough for his respect, his support, his personal affection, and the faith he had in them from the beginning. Reddemann went so far as to use the seemingly un-Prussian word "love" to describe the Crown Prince's feelings for the Death's Head Pioneers.

The Kaiser Meets a Flamethrower Pioneer

The 2nd Company of the Guard Reserve Pioneer Regiment was billeted in Stenay-sur-Meuse, near the headquarters of the Fifth Army. Crown Prince Wilhelm would often visit the men to chat and hand out cigarettes. One day the Kaiser arrived with his son to review the company:

> As he walked down the row of soldiers, he stopped in front of one very young pioneer and asked, "Well, my boy, have you burned up many Frenchmen lately?" The flustered soldier, having never spoken to the emperor, stammered, "No, your Majesty. They usually run away when we turn on the flamethrowers." The Kaiser scowled and continued his inspection without another word. When he was out of earshot, the sergeant came over and chewed out the youngster: "Idiot! The Kaiser doesn't want to hear about Frenchmen running away. He wants to hear about Frenchmen fighting bravely to defend their positions and being burned to a crisp!" The Kaiser's entourage constantly fed him gory war stories, and he was clearly hoping for another. He especially liked the men's name for the flamethrower: the "frog toaster."[26]

If Wilhelm had ever opposed arming his men with flamethrowers, as alleged by American newspapers, he had certainly changed his mind by this stage of the war.

Mass Flamethrower Attack at Skrobova

In late 1916 the German 5th Reserve Division was ordered to take an extensive Russian trench system at Skrobova. Located on a hillside north of Baranowitschi, the target area was about 4,400 yards wide and 1,100 yards deep and had withstood several assaults by the Austrians. Reddemann described the positions as fortresslike strong points, blockhouses, and flanking installations of concrete, "climbing up one behind the other," bristling with machine guns and served by as many as one hundred soldiers per site.[27] After Reddemann personally reconnoitered the system, he decided that none of the tactics he had developed for frontal attacks would work. He had to try something new, something more audacious, an approach he christened the "Knife Tactic" (*Messertaktik*).

Kaiser Wilhelm II (1859-1941) inspecting an infantry unit as the Crown Prince stands diffidently on the right. The Kaiser – not known for his sense of humor – may be smiling at something said by the soldier in front of him. Wilhelm enjoyed hearing gory war stories, particularly from flamethrower pioneers.

First, Reddemann made a verbal report to the Supreme Army Command and received permission from *General der Infanterie* Erich Ludendorff to use four companies of the Guard Reserve Pioneer Regiment, which he would command himself. The assault would be a combined stationary and pouncing attack with *Grof* and *Kleif*, the latter being used to pierce the Russian trench system ahead of six infantry battalions advancing abreast. In preparation for the attack, the Russian positions would be subjected to an artillery and trench-mortar barrage, and particular trenches would be "shocked" with twenty-four *Grof* secretly positioned in the German line a few days before.

The real innovation was the deployment of flame shock troops (*Flammenstosstrupps*). A flame shock troop was composed of six *Kleif* troops, each of which contained two *Kleif* squads. Rounding out each flame shock troop were a hand-grenade squad from the flamethrower regiment and several infantry groups under the command of flamethrower officers and deputy officers.

Reddemann described the flame shock troops as "snakelike,"[28] indicating long, thin formations. They were to

Above: Kleif squad and infantry assault troops rolling up a mock trench. The flamethrower pioneers wear white helmets, while the grenadiers have cloth helmet covers with what appear to be the painted number 9. Note the over-the-shoulder firing stance used by the lance operator to arc the flame into the next traverse. The flamethrower is a Kleif M.1917, recognizable by the round orientation plaque. (Le Miroir.)

Below: Kleif shock troop advancing through barbed wire during a training exercise armed with two Kleif M.1917 and 4.6ft. (1.4m) small lances. At Skrobova, each flame shock troop was composed of twelve Kleif squads, one hand-grenade squad, and several infantry groups. Courtesy Antonio Rossetto.

sprint across 330 to 550 yards of open ground, moving side by side 220 to 330 yards apart and striking the Russian lines perpendicularly. Their speed and momentum, as well as their single-file formation, would allow them to pierce the Russian line and cut it into "still-twitching pieces"[29] by destroying every point of resistance in front and to the sides with flamethrowers, hand grenades, and machine guns. The specific routes they would take were precisely determined beforehand, based on large aerial photos that the men studied carefully.

As the flame shock troops punched through the Russian lines and raced up the enemy communication trenches to take the heights, flamethrower and hand-grenade squads would turn to the sides and suppress the heavy flanking fire that was expected. These shutting-down (*schliessenden*) units would screen infantry shock troops that followed 55 to 110 yards behind the flame shock troops. Two *Kleif* squads were placed in the interval between each flame shock troop and infantry shock troop to neutralize any remaining or developing points of resistance. After the infantry shock troops poured through the holes in the Russian line, the six battalions of regular infantry would follow in four waves. Twelve flame shock troops would execute the frontal Knife attack, followed by twenty-four *Kleif* squads. Four flame shock troops would take

Euler two-seater equipped with camera and radio for infantry-contact patrols. The curved guide tube for the radio antenna is visible on the underside; the antenna itself is weighted on the end so that it can be reeled out in flight. During the mass flamethrower attack at Skrobova on November 9, 1916, airborne intelligence officers controlled the battle by radioing observations back to headquarters and dropping fresh orders in message streamers to the troops below.

Below: Assault troops of Württemburgisches Landsturm-Infanterie-Bataillon Eßlingen (XIII/18). Note the crate of twenty-five egg grenades (Eierhandgranaten) leaning against a spool of barbed wire. The smaller egg grenade was not as powerful as the stick grenade, but being lighter it could be thrown further. Flamethrower pioneers were equipped with both types of grenades.

important objectives on the left wing and be held in reserve by Reddemann; thus a total of 216 *Kleif* would be used.[30]

The operation was rehearsed for a week in a mockup of the Russian trench system built behind the German lines. On November 9, 1916, German artillery and trench mortars unleashed a four-hour barrage, near the end of which the twenty-four *Grof* in five separate groups shocked their targets. While the artillery barrage and *Grof* assault continued, the twelve flame shock troops left their jumping-off points, crossed No Man's Land, and bored into the Russian line. On the left wing, two more flame shock troops drove forward under the cover of smoke and fire. Behind these forces, the infantry shock troops advanced, each preceded by two *Kleif* squads. The four waves of regular infantry brought up the rear.

From his headquarters Reddemann kept track of the battle through airborne intelligence officers in observation aircraft equipped with two-way radios. They reported on the progress of individual flame shock troops and dropped message streamers containing fresh orders to the troops on the ground, allowing Reddemann to save his reserves for the toughest points of resistance.

One such example was a concrete fortification on a commanding height occupied by a garrison of more than 100. Given the code name "Stronghold" (*Feste*), it was armed with dozens of machine guns that swept the glacis in front and threatened to halt the entire advance. Since the reinforced concrete withstood direct hits by artillery and heavy mortars, the decision was made to attack the fortress with Flame Shock Troops 5 and 6, one of which was commanded by *Leutnant* Fredenhagen. During the ensuing frontal assault, Fredenhagen and a number of his men were killed, but the flame shock troops persevered in an "exceedingly death-defying fashion."[31] Despite the rain of bullets, they moved in close enough to spray their weapons through the firing loopholes of the Stronghold, which persuaded the Russians to surrender.

After an hour the entire Russian trench system had been taken. Russian casualties were considerable, according to Reddemann, although he gave no numbers. In addition, forty-nine officers and 3,380 men were captured, along with many machine guns, trench mortars, and other material. The flamethrower pioneers suffered sixty-nine casualties, including two officers and fourteen NCOs and men dead. Reddemann described these numbers as high in comparison with those of the infantry, a view shared by divisional commander

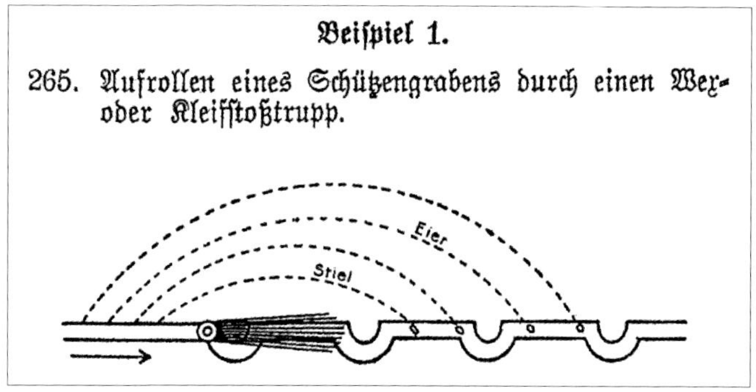

Rolling up a trench with a small-flamethrower shock troop. The flamethrower is sprayed across the open ground between traverses while the hand-grenade throwers behind use egg and stick grenades to drive out the enemy. (Sturmtruppen und Flammenwerfer.)

Generalleutnant der Infanterie von Woyrsch. "Of decisive importance was the participation of the flame shock troops in the attack," he wrote:

> These troops, who for three days had worked to move up during the artillery-fire preparation on the enemy positions, went forward with the greatest bravery... The success of the flamethrower units was certainly bought through considerable casualties that were much higher than among the infantry, for whom they had cleared the way for victory... A carefully selected and excellently organized and led elite unit.[32]

The Knife Tactic Used on the Western Front

"The art of the flamethrower assault," as Reddemann called it, had to be constantly adapted due to changes in position warfare on the western front.[33] The elastic defense used by the enemy in the featureless, shell-cratered landscape required that the regiment modify its shock-troop tactic. Flame shock troops were from this point split into two echelons, the second

Right: Some of the 3500 Russian prisoners captured at Skrobova on November 9, 1916. They are guarded by men of Infanterie-Regiment Nr. 410, one of whom has a French needle bayonet attached to his rifle.

Men of the 7th Company, Garde-Reserve-Pionier-Regiment, stationed in the French village of Grugies in Picardy, 1915-1916. Note the drawing of the death's head. This postcard was sent on December 8, 1916, by Füsilier R. Schubert, who is seated in the right front. He writes that his health is good and he has been assigned to the 1st Replacement Battalion of Niederrheinisches Füsilier-Regiment Nr. 39. Schubert was apparently an infantryman who was wounded, declared unfit for flamethrower duty, and returned to the replacement battalion of his original unit.

moving from cover to cover behind the first and eventually overtaking and relieving it. In addition, trenches and occupied lines of shell holes were rolled up from the inside using much heavier firepower.

There were also more mass flamethrower assaults in which the individual squads ran at the enemy side by side in intervals of five to ten yards, under continuous jets of flame fired over their heads by *Grof*. Upon breaking through, these flamethrower squads would keep the enemy at bay until the infantry shock troops arrived. Then the flamethrower squads would either go in ahead of the infantry as shock troops, or they would advance with them as flame accompanying squads (*Flammenbegleittrupps*). The objective was to both impact the enemy's morale and distract his attention from the infantry shock troops.

This new form of assault was usually made against the most critical strong points, such as command blockhouses and machine-gun nests. Proper execution required that the flamethrower squads utilize blind spots for breaking through laterally in what Reddemann called "surprise flanking thrusts"; once inside the enemy line, the squads would then turn against the actual objective. For the tactic to work, the opposing trenches had to be relatively close. If not, there had to be enough cover for the flamethrower squads to approach undetected to within 90 to 110 yards.

CHAPTER EIGHT

Flame Battles from January to June 1917

In 1917 the Guard Reserve Pioneer Regiment fought a total of 169 engagements on the western and eastern fronts, twenty-four of which were unsuccessful. The following individual attacks were highlighted by Bernhard Reddemann. He described them as single companies and detached platoons being thrown in here and there in brief strikes at flash points along the broken front lines.[1]

January 3 - Three flame shock troops of the 4th Company under the command of *Vizefeldwebel* Kamm crossed the frozen Duna River northwest of nearby Dunaberg, completely surprising the enemy, rolling up trenches, and taking the island of Glandon. Forty prisoners were captured.

One of the participants was *Unteroffizier* Rudolf Falk of Reserve Pioneer Company 80, who together with twenty-three other pioneers from his unit accompanied the 1st Battalion of Reserve Infantry Regiment No. 259. Falk's section of the assault force included twelve batteries of forty-three field pieces, fourteen heavy machine guns, six medium trench mortars, and six small flamethrowers. The operation was rehearsed several times on an exercise ground, the final sessions using live ammunition. Three of the flamethrowers failed during the rehearsals, leaving only three for the actual assault. Wooden carriages were built to transport the flamethrower squads over the frozen river.

When the assault was in progress, Falk suddenly heard a strange sound over the noise of the two working flamethrowers, the machine guns, and the artillery barrage. In the heat of battle, the men of the 1st Company of Reserve Infantry Regiment No. 259 had spontaneously begun singing "O Germany, High in Honors!" ("*O Deutschland, hoch in Ehren!*") Falk wrote that the moment would not be forgotten by the survivors of the mission.[2]

January 23 - The 3rd and 7th Companies of the Guard Reserve Pioneer Regiment under *Hauptmann* Beck launched a frontal attack to retake positions in the dunes on either side of the Aa River north of Mitau. Thirty-four *Kleif* were used. In spite of the great cold and the boggy terrain, enemy positions 5.6 miles wide and 1.2 miles deep were taken. Trenches were rolled up, blockhouses were taken, and 3,000 prisoners were captured.

February 6 - West of Parroy in French Lorraine, the 5th Company under *Unteroffizier* Asperger crept across almost 900 yards of open terrain and rolled up enemy trenches. Machine guns were silenced and many prisoners were taken. In this action the flamethrower troops wore "snow coats" (*Schneemänteln*) or white camouflage suits.

February 12 - The 8th Company under *Hauptmann* Sturm attacked Italian positions on Hill 1050 at Paralovo in Macedonia. Four *Grof* and eighteen *Kleif* were used in a combined stationary and pouncing attack. Trenches were rolled up and machine guns were silenced. Enemy trenches and encampments behind them were taken. Many prisoners and much war material were captured.

February 15 - The 6th Company under *Leutnant* Krauss struck positions between Jahn-Petit Bois and Maison de Champagne south of Ripont. Twenty-four *Kleif* were used on a front of 2,800 yards, which was taken to a depth of almost 900 yards.

Above: Postcard sent by flamethrower pioneer Rudolf Friedrich on June 25, 1916, when he was still a member of Pionier-Ersatz-Bataillon Nr. 17. Friedrich is the smiling, round-faced young man lying in the front on the left. The photo was taken at a hospital in Thorn, where Friedrich was recuperating from an undisclosed wound or illness.

Below: In this image from September 2, 1916, Pionier Friedrich now belongs to the 3rd Replacement Company, II. Garde-Pionier-Ersatz-Bataillon. He is in the center of the front row, lying on his right side and looking remarkably aged. The men are equipped with uncovered Pickelhauben, full packs, and Kar. 98AZ carbines. They will not be awarded the death's head sleeve badge until they are transferred into the flamethrower regiment.

Trenches were rolled up, machine guns were silenced, and 900 prisoners were taken.

March 18 - The 2nd Company under *Oberleutnant* Kraensel attacked on the eastern slope of Hill 304. Ten flame shock troops achieved a frontal breakthrough, rolled up trenches, and took out blockhouses and machine-gun nests. A total of 400 prisoners were taken.

March 28 - The 5th and 6th Companies under *Oberleutnant* Trage and *Leutnant* Haertel carried out a frontal attack on Hill 185 and Maison de Champagne south of Ripont. Flamethrower troops broke into enemy positions, rolled up trenches, smoked out cellars and dugouts, and silenced machine-gun nests. They pushed far beyond the original objective and took 300 prisoners.

April 4 - The 11th Company under *Leutnant* Hornung assaulted a position south of Berry au Bac on the Aisne, using twenty *Kleif*. They crossed 330 yards of open terrain under an intense artillery barrage and broke into the enemy line, rolling up trenches, smoking out cellars and dugouts, and silencing machine guns and other points of resistance. The entire village of Le Soldat was taken, as well as 843 prisoners. Much military material was captured.

April 15 - Part of the 11th Company under *Leutnant* Hornung successfully advanced across 2,200 yards of open terrain in

Postcard described on the back as "Flamethrower squad: Unteroffizier Pfeifer and Pioniere Wrek, Somerschlag, and Friedrich." The flamethrower is the Kleif M.1917, and the M.1916 lance is armed with an igniter. All four men wear cloth helmet covers and carry P08 pistols; three also have two M.1917 stick grenades each. Only Friedrich, standing on the left, displays the death's head sleeve badge on his M.1910 service jacket. He survived the war and became a chef in Frankfurt.

front of the Siegfried Line to attack the villages of Demicourt and Boversies in Artois. Twenty *Kleif* were used. Many prisoners were taken.

May 8 - A platoon of the 11th Company under *Leutnant* Rackles carried out an assault on the village of Fresnoy in Artois. After successful house-to-house combat, the village was taken.

June 27 - A platoon of the 12th Company under *Leutnant* Pütz carried out a reconnaissance in force northwest of Hulloch in Artois. One *Grof* and twelve *Kleif* were used in a combined stationary and pouncing attack, after which trenches were rolled up.

Flamethrower Attack on Toboly

On April 3 the 3rd, 4th, and 7th Companies under Battalion Commander *Hauptmann* Beck conducted a successful attack on the Toboly bridgehead northwest of Kowel in Russia. Following a heavy artillery bombardment of five hours and 45 minutes, ten flame shock troops using sixty-four *Kleif* penetrated 1,600 to 3,300 yards across a front of 4,400 yards. During their advance, they stayed fifty-five yards behind a rolling barrage of shrapnel, high explosive, and gas shells that suppressed the Russian artillery, while box barrages prevented both reinforcements from moving in and the bridgehead defenders from retreating in an orderly fashion.[3] Ten thousand prisoners, fifteen cannons, and much war material were captured. One pioneer of the 3rd Company and one *Gefreiter* of the 7th Company were killed in action.[4]

Postcard hand captioned "Flamethrower in action at Toboly in the war-year 1917." A Kleif squad trains in the background as infantry hand-grenade throwers stand ready. The soldier in the right center slips his grenade bags over his head.

One of the ways in which the flamethrower regiment improved its mobility during large operations such as the assault on Toboly was to field half-*Kleif* squads (*Halbkleiftrupps*). These were flamethrower squads armed with *Kleif* that were only half filled with oil. Although half-*Kleif* squads were "exceptionally fast," the tradeoff was that the lightened flamethrowers fired a drastically reduced number of flame bursts.[5]

An *Oberstleutnant* Mayernitz, staff officer in several army corps and armies, wrote after the war that the flamethrowers had allowed the Germans to completely overrun the Russians at Toboly:

> Service in the flame projector units during the war required initiative of a high degree. Officers, as well as men, often were employed in very small units, so that they frequently had to make decisions and act on their own initiative in difficult situations. Consequently great demands were placed upon their intelligence and energy, their knowledge of tactics and their military training. For this reason only picked officers and men were admitted to the flame projector units, only those who had already shown themselves to be fearless and death-defying.[6]

Austro-German Cooperation on Flamethrowers

As noted previously, the flamethrowers and lances adopted by the Austro-Hungarian army were based on Fiedler designs patented in 1910. The Germans also provided the Austrians with flamethrower instructors, but precise information about this arrangement is vague.

The Austrian flamethrower operator was designated a sapper (*Sappeur*) rather than a pioneer. He learned his trade from the Imperial and Royal Special Sapper Formation (*k.u.k. Sappeur-Spezial-Formation*), a training and replacement company of the Replacement Battalion for Special Weapons (*Ersatzbataillon für besondere Kampfmittel*) based in Krems, on the Danube river in northern Austria. In 1915 the first squads of flamethrower sappers were assigned to the pioneer platoons of infantry battalions. They were armed with the *50l M. 15 Flammenwerfer*, a thirteen-gallon device which was carried into battle as an offensive weapon without infantry support, resulting in a high casualty rate among the operators. Flamethrower troops were thereafter used in a defensive role, and the *50l M. 15 Flammenwerfer* was reclassified as a static weapon.[7]

With the introduction of the large flamethrower (*grosse 200l M. 15 Flammenwerfer*) and the small flamethrower (*kleine 22l M. 15 Flammenwerfer*), the thirteen-gallon model became the medium flamethrower (*mittlere 50l M.15 Flammenwerfer*). By 1916 flamethrower platoons (*Flammenwerferzüge*) of sixty-four men armed with all three sizes of weapon had been organized. They were made available to infantry commanders to reinforce specific areas of the front line deemed vulnerable to attack. Depending on the mission, flamethrower platoons were armed with two large, four medium, and eight small flamethrowers, or four large and eight small flamethrowers. Each large device was served by one NCO and four enlisted men, while each medium and small flamethrower was served by one NCO and two enlisted men. The personnel of a flamethrower squad could be doubled, depending on the conditions of the operation.[8]

Although the Austro-Hungarian army designated the flamethrower primarily a defensive weapon, it could be used offensively if circumstances warranted. One method was the stationary attack in which emplaced flamethrowers were used to drive the enemy from his trench.[9] Another was the combined stationary and pouncing attack, a "shock" of large flamethrowers followed by an assault of small-flamethrower squads. The Austrians learned these techniques from the Germans, but they did not use Reddemann's terms to describe them.

Austrian flamethrower platoons were deployed as unified bodies in order to avoid splintering the flame effect; individual apparatuses were assigned only in special cases. When flamethrower platoons were installed in front-line trenches, the large and medium devices were distributed at distances that corresponded approximately to the weapons' spraying width.

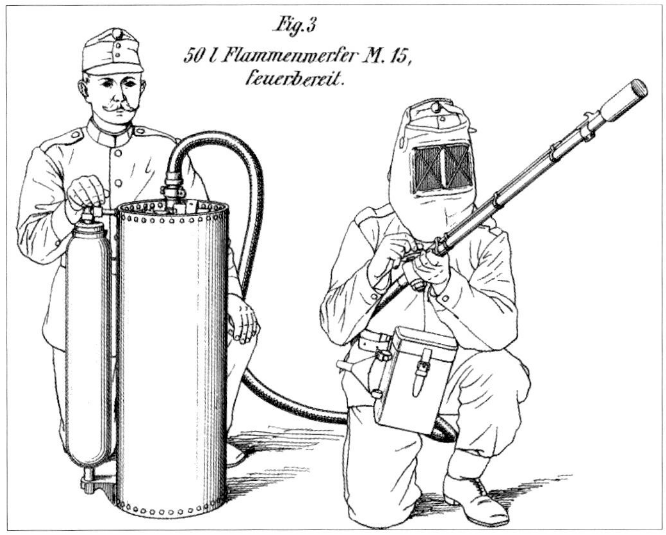

50l Flammenwerfer M. 15, the first flamethrower of the Austro-Hungarian army. It held 13.2 gallons of oil for a continuous duration of fifteen seconds and a range of approximately ninety-eight feet. The flame shooter (Flammenschütze) wears an asbestos face mask with wire-reinforced glass vision ports; the assistant opens the release valve on the pressure tank, following which the flame shooter will open the fuel-release stopcock on the lance, simultaneously activating the igniter. (Anleitung für Flammenwerfer.)

Zur frommen Erinnerung im Gebete

an den ehrengeachteten Jüngling

Josef Dengg,

geb. in Aderns am 2. Dezember 1891.

Derselbe diente b. der Flammenwerfer-Abteilung des 1. Tirol.-Kaiserj.-Reg.

Am 14. Februar 1916 zog er in das Feld und erlitt am 16. Juli 1916 in Südtirol den Heldentod für Gott, Kaiser und Vaterland. Er liegt auf dem Ortsfriedhofe in Isera bei Rovereid begraben.

Gott gebe der jungen Heldenseele die ewige Ruhe!

Stets wandeln auf dem Pfad der Tugend,
In Wort und Tat ein ganzer Christ,
Im wahren Frohsinn heit'rer Jugend,
Gabst freudig Gott, was Gottes ist.

Im Kriege erst der Pflicht obliegend,
Ein Held du ja geworden bist.
Der gab, ob sterbend oder siegend,
Dem Kaiser, was des Kaisers ist.

Als Helden schmückt dich nun zum Lohne
Dort, wo die ew'ge Freude wohnt,
In hehrer Pracht die Himmelskrone
Beim Lamme, daß zur Rechten thront.

Das ist's, was süßen Trost uns spendet
In uns'rem kummervollen Leid,
Daß Kampf und Schmerz nun hat geendet.
Für dich die ganze Ewigkeit.

Barmherzigster Jesus, gib ihm die ewige Ruhe!
(7 Jahre und 7 Quadragenen Ablaß.)

Alles für Dich, heiligstes Herz Jesu!
300 Tage Ablaß jedesmal.

Heiliger Josef! Muster und Vorbild der Verehrung des göttlichen Herzens Jesu, bitte für uns!
(100 Tage Ablaß einmal täglich.)

Druck von Fel. Rauch, Innsbruck.

Austrian death card memorializing Josef Dengg of the Flamethrower Detachment, 1. Tiroler-Kaiserjäger-Regiment. Born on December 2, 1891, he "suffered a hero's death for God, Emperor, and Fatherland" on July 16, 1916. Austro-Hungarian flamethrower sappers had high casualty rates.

Unlike the German versions, Austro-Hungarian flamethrowers carried a high risk of accidental combustion. The large flamethrower was built into the position in such a way that in the case of a fire the entire trench did not have to be vacated. It was inserted deeply into the breastworks, between heavy

Above: Austrian flamethrower squad training with a mittlere 50l M. 15a Flammenwerfer, the improved model of the 50l M. 15. The flame shooter climbing the hill and the assistant operating the flamethrower wear asbestos overcoats. Note the German soldier in a round field cap standing second from the right; he is almost certainly an instructor from the Garde-Reserve-Pionier-Regiment.

Right: Flame shooter and assistant aim the lance of an Austrian grosse 200l M. 15 Flammenwerfer. They are stationed in a separate bunker from the flamethrower in order to prevent accidental ignition of the oil tank. The assistant supports the hose and holds the lanyard attached to the igniter on the lance nozzle. (Anleitung für Flammenwerfer.)

earthen weirs set apart from troop shelters and ammunition-storage bunkers. The medium and small flamethrowers were often used lying on their sides and covered with earth, indicating that these weapons were as dangerous to operate as the large model.

Hoses thirty-three feet long were provided with the large flamethrower so that the oil tank could be placed at some distance from the lance operator's station. This was to prevent the "flame shooter" (*Flammenschütze*) from becoming distracted during combat and spraying the tank, which could ignite its contents. If the tank were ruptured by enemy grenades or demolition charges, substantial losses could be suffered by the flamethrower platoon.

For engaging live targets, the oil was ignited upon leaving the lance; for setting alight inanimate objects such as barricades, barbed-wire posts, bridges, and other structures, the target was first sprayed with unlit oil and the jet was then ignited. At the end of 1915 the Austrian flame lance was fitted with a wick holder (*Dochträger*) over the nozzle, around which a paraffin-soaked length of fuse was wrapped. This wick burned long enough that multiple shots could be fired.

Grosse 200l M. 15 Flammenwerfer, emplaced apart from the lance. Note the propellant tank on the left, filled with nitrogen. The squad member on the right controls the flow of oil by turning the large valve on the top of the tank. (Anleitung für Flammenwerfer.)

During this period it was recommended that flamethrowers be used offensively only when the opposing trenches were about sixty paces apart. If the distance between trenches was greater than the range of the flamethrowers, saps or tunnels were to be dug. The thick cloud of black smoke was also used as cover for attacking infantry.

In 1916 the pioneer platoon of each infantry battalion was expanded into a "technical company." This new unit was composed mainly of sappers equipped with searchlights, trench mortars, and hand grenades. Photographic evidence shows that technical companies were also armed with small flamethrowers, either the *kleine 22l M. 15 Flammenwerfer* or the *kleine 15l M. 16 Flammenwerfer*, also known as the *Sturmtruppen-Flammenwerfer M. 16*.

Around the same time that small flamethrowers became available, the Austrians formed their first assault battalions, loosely based on the German model. An Army Assault Battalion (*Armeesturmbataillon*) consisted of four infantry companies, each of which had two nine-man Assault Patrols (*Sturmpatrouillen*); one or two machine-gun companies; one mountain-artillery battery with four guns; one infantry-gun battery with four pieces; one trench-mortar platoon with four grenade launchers and four medium trench mortars; one flamethrower platoon with six portable devices; and one construction company.[10]

May of 1917 saw a massive reorganization of the Austro-Hungarian Army that included shifting most engineering duties to the sappers and relegating the pioneers to bridging activities.[11] In addition, all flamethrower sappers not already attached to assault battalions were integrated into four companies (*Flammenwerferkompanien*), numbers 1 through 4. Two were assigned to the Special Sapper Formation in Krems; one was sent to Parje to provide flame troops for the southwestern front; and the last was ordered to Huszt to supply flamethrower sappers for the northeastern front.[12]

In June of 1917 the Army Assault Battalions were transformed into Divisional Assault Battalions (*Divisionsturmbataillone*). Every infantry division would now have an assault battalion consisting of one assault company from each regiment in the division; one machine-gun company; one infantry-gun battery; one sapper platoon; one ordnance platoon; one flamethrower platoon; and one telephone detachment.[13]

Yet another sweeping change came about in September of 1917, when the four flamethrower companies were amalgamated into Sapper Battalion No. 61 (*Sappeurbataillon Nr. 61*), which like the Guard Reserve Pioneer Regiment was directly subordinate to Supreme Army Headquarters. During the Battle of Caporetto (October 12-November 24, 1917), it was noted that local infantry commanders did not know what to do with flamethrower operators. Since these specialized troops were sappers, many were put to work building trenches instead of engaging in flame warfare.[14]

On the few occasions that flamethrower squads were correctly employed, they performed most efficiently when paired with the nine-man Assault Patrols. In early 1918 the four companies of Sapper Battalion No. 61 were therefore ordered to report to the following Divisional Assault Battalions:

1st Flamethrower Company to Assault Battalion No. 55, I Corps;
2nd Flamethrower Company to Assault Battalion No. 27, XXVI Corps;

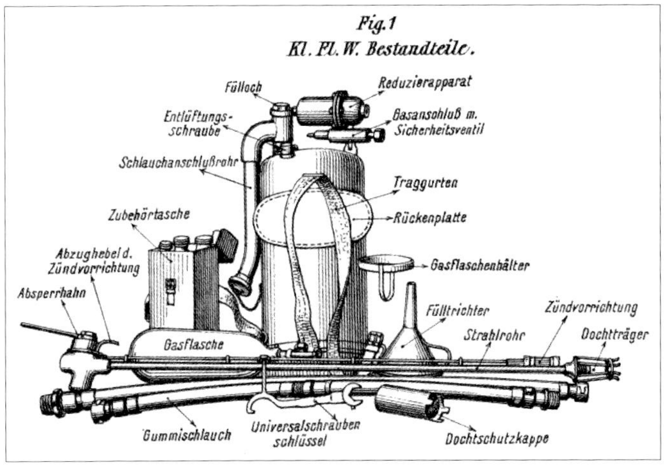

Kleine 22l M. 15 Flammenwerfer, the first portable Austrian flamethrower. It held six gallons of oil for a continuous duration of fifteen seconds and had a range of eighty-two feet. The lance was capable of firing multiple shots through the use of a wick. (Anleitung für Flammenwerfer.)

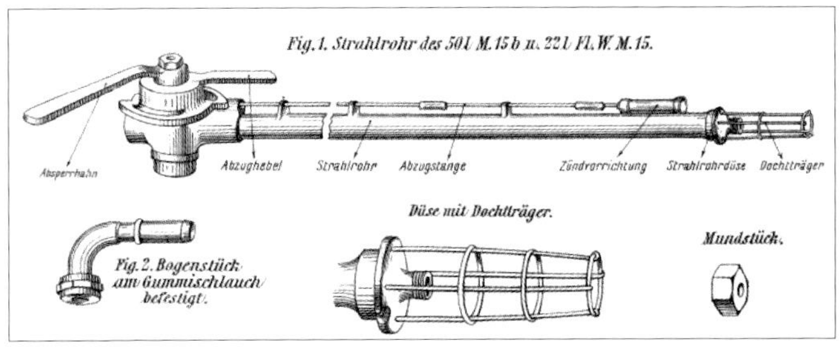

Austrian flamethrower lance. The shutting-off tap (Absperrhahn) controls the flow of oil, while the trigger lever (Abzughebel) activates the igniter (Zündvorrichtung) by pulling the trigger rod (Abzugstange). Note the nozzle (Düse) with wick holder (Dochtträger); the mouthpiece (Mundstück) had a diameter of either 0.16in. (4mm) or 0.2in. (6mm). (Anleitung für Flammenwerfer.)

3rd Flamethrower Company to Assault Battalion No. 6, III Corps;
4th Flamethrower Company to Assault Battalion No. 18, VI Corps.[15]

The individual flamethrower companies would be under the control of the respective corps commands, which could transfer them to other assault battalions within the corps but were not allowed to split them up without authorization from the Supreme Army Headquarters.[16]

Duties of the four flamethrower companies included taking part in assaults, training new recruits, training officers in flame operations, and maintaining and repairing the weapons of flamethrower platoons attached to other divisional assault battalions. Austro-Hungarian tactical doctrine called for flamethrowers to be assigned to the second and third wave of the assault force and to be used mainly for mopping up trenches already overrun by the infantry. Frontal attacks against emplacements such as machine-gun nests were avoided.[17]

Due to its offensive role, Sapper Battalion No. 61 became informally known as Special Assault Battalion No. 61 (*Spezial-Sturmbataillon Nr. 61*). By the spring of 1918 there were seventy-five flamethrower platoons attached to the infantry assault battalions; a flamethrower platoon had six *kleine 15l M. 16 Flammenwerfern* operated by three squads armed with two devices each.[18] German flamethrower instructors continued to work with their Austro-Hungarian colleagues until the end of the war, particularly at large training camps such as those at the Galician towns of Rohatyn, Hucisco-Olesci, Buczacz, and Olesky-Olasko.

The Battle of Bullecourt

On May 3, 1917, fourteen British, Canadian, and Australian divisions attacked the Hindenburg Line during the Battle of Arras.[19] At Bullecourt the Australian 5th and 6th Brigades broke through to the second German line amidst furious hand-to-hand fighting. They passed through a narrow sap dug by engineers and moved down the trenches, bombing their way with hand grenades that had been supplied in massive quantities. By the end of the day, they had advanced over 1,100 yards.

The Germans began their counterattacks on May 4. In one such operation, a shock troop accompanied by flamethrowers struck at a trench held by the 1st Battalion of the Australian Imperial Force (A.I.F.). The assault was repelled by a Captain Somerset, who leapt out of his trench and hurled hand grenades, killing five of the attackers.[20] According to the death book of the Guard Reserve Pioneer Regiment, three flamethrower pioneers from the 10th Company died at Bullecourt on May 4.[21]

German counterattacks continued with "waves of men bearing flame-throwers, debouched from Bullecourt and

Austro-Hungarian assault platoon (Sturmzug). On the back of this postcard, a handwritten caption in Czech reads, "Our assault troops, with mortars and machine guns. They are the first who go against the enemy." Four different types of mortars – including a pneumatic model – are present, as well as a British Vickers .303 heavy machine gun, a Danish 8mm Madsen light machine gun, and an Italian 9mm Villar Perosa submachine gun. On the right is a half-seen kleine 22l M. 15 Flammenwerfer, and on the left a grosse 200l M. 15 Flammenwerfer.

Quéant, after fierce artillery preparations."[22] The Australians were surrounded and fired on from all directions. On the morning of May 6, the Germans managed to reach the lone Australian sap used to bring up reinforcements and supplies, assaulting it with two flamethrowers. While one shock troop advanced down a communication trench from the north, steadily throwing grenades ahead of it, another used grappling hooks to drag away a barbed-wire barrier in Old German Line No. 1 (O.G.1). The obstruction cleared, the two flamethrower squads launched a flank attack on an Australian bombing-post:

> It was still dark. The lurid flare, dense smoke, and loud roar of the flame-throwers produced a formidable effect, and, the trench having been previously battered into a mere shallow depression, these instruments were more than usually dangerous. At the same time, the men working them were more than usually exposed.[23]

Austrian kleine 15l M. 16 Flammenwerfer, also called the Sturmtruppen-Flammenwerfer M. 16, modeled by a French soldier. It held four gallons of oil and was operated by a flame shooter and an assistant. Note the prominent reducer valve on top of the oil tank and the twin handles of the lance.

The Australian bombers withdrew, and the Germans brought light machine gunners and more hand-grenade throwers forward into the craters on either side of the trench. They were now so close that the foremost Australian Stokes mortar could not reach them, so the crew retreated, throwing mortar shells by hand along with grenades. A second Stokes mortar opened fire on the Germans, who continued to advance. One flamethrower squad led; the hand-grenade throwers followed; and the second flamethrower squad brought up the rear. The shock troops flung egg and stick grenades that exploded ahead of the flame bursts.

A Lieutenant MacNeil of the 3rd Light Trench Mortar Battery ordered his men to retreat and remained alone at his post to keep the shock troops away from the trench junction:

Austrian assault patrol (Sturmpatrouille) with three kleine 15l M. 16 Flammenwerfern and their two-man squads. Equipment includes M.1916 Berndorfer helmets, M.1916 Austrian steel helmets, the Mannlicher M95 8mm Short Rifle "Stutzen," 8mm Roth Steyr M.1907 automatic pistols, M.1915 gas masks, and two different types of Austrian stick grenades. The wire wick holders around the flamethrower nozzles are bare, indicating that the weapons are empty. Courtesy Antonio Rossetto.

> He was standing in a crevice off O.G.1 when the leading flame-thrower came round the bend full into sight. With the flame roaring past, MacNeil flung a bomb at the bearer and killed him. The second flame-thrower was still active, but at this critical moment MacNeil was joined by Captain Newland of the 12th [Battalion], whose company had held the flank sector. With a box of bombs, they held up the second flammenwerfer, while the two mortars got clear, withdrawing down O.G.1 to come into action again from the Central road.[24]

Newland was wounded, but after MacNeil killed the second flamethrower operator, the Australians rallied and pushed the Germans back. It was in this action that Corporal George Julian "Snowy" Howell of the 1st Battalion won the Victoria Cross for climbing up on the parapet of his trench and fighting off a shock troop with grenades, rifle fire, and bayonet.[25]

Offizier-Stellvertreter Wilhelm Hilger and *Unteroffizier* Wilhelm Ladendorf, both of the 12th Company of the Guard Reserve Pioneer Regiment, were killed in action at Bullecourt on May 6.[26] The presence of a deputy officer, the Australian observation that the Germans used incendiary grenades,[27] and the description of how the flamethrower troops advanced through the trenches indicates that this was a *Kleif* shock troop (*Kleifstosstrupp*) consisting of two *Kleif* squads, four hand-grenade throwers, and two shock-troop leaders. When rolling up a trench the men kept two yards apart, and if the first flamethrower squad ran out of oil or were put out of action, the second moved up to take its place.[28]

Assault Battalion No. 5 (Rohr) Attacks Hill 304

On June 29, 1917, Assault Battalion No. 5 (Rohr) spearheaded an attack on Hill 304 in Verdun. Rohr's 1st Assault Company was strengthened with elements of the battalion's extensive assets, including shock troops from the 2nd Assault Company, a machine-gun platoon, a howitzer platoon, "a number" of trench-mortar squads, and the flamethrower platoon.[29]

Opposite
Top: Pioneers of the 4th Company, Garde-Reserve-Pionier-Regiment, in Upper Alsace during the winter of 1917. Two flame shock troops consisting of four Kleif squads, eight hand-grenade throwers, and two squad leaders pose with infantrymen of Sturmbataillon Nr. 16. The flamethrowers are the Kleif M.1917, connected to 4.6ft. (1.4m) lances with igniters in place. All of the pioneers are equipped with P08 pistols and gas masks in metal carriers. Courtesy Maurice Sublet.

Bottom: Undated photo of men from the 1st Replacement Company, II. Garde-Pionier-Ersatz-Bataillon. Their age range of late teens to mid-forties is typical for flamethrower pioneers. The young man standing third from left in the back row appears in the next photo as a member of the Garde-Reserve-Pionier-Regiment.

According to American newspapers, the assault battalion began the operation with three weeks of daily rehearsals behind the German lines, exercises photographed by French aviators.[30] The attack focused on a salient 1,800 yards wide, held for some inexplicable reason by only forty dismounted dragoons of the 24th Regiment.[31] On the afternoon of June 29 the position was subjected to the most intensive artillery bombardment the French had ever experienced. At 6:30 P.M. the German shock troops raced forward, led by three flamethrower squads advancing at intervals of twenty paces. Behind the flamethrowers were three squads of hand-grenade throwers, then came regular infantry carrying spades and rifles with fixed bayonets. The consolidating troops were next, followed by purveying squads loaded down with grenades, ammunition, and sandbags.[32]

The French dragoons used their rifles, a light machine gun, and hand grenades to repulse the first wave of shock troops.

Carte de visite produced by Atelier Ideal of Hamburg. This very young flamethrower pioneer in M.1915 blouse and rakishly cocked M.1910 service cap belongs to the 11th Company of the Garde-Reserve-Pionier-Regiment. As in many such photos, he has been posed to display his crisp death's head sleeve badge to its best advantage.

In the midst of the fighting, a dragoon named Leduc was buried to the waist by the explosion of a Bangalore torpedo set off in the barbed-wire entanglements. Though partially immobilized, he fought off two attempts by the Germans to take him prisoner, throwing grenades until he was rescued. Their frontal assault checked, the Germans launched a flank attack on the trench. The French responded by stationing teams of five at each traverse, two men kneeling on the parapet and the rest crouched in the trench, passing up grenades for their comrades to hurl at the attackers.

Three and a half hours of fierce hand-to-hand fighting resulted, as the German flamethrower and hand-grenade squads pushed the French 200 yards down the trench. When the dragoons reached the mouth of a communication trench leading to the rear, they dug in for a last stand.[33] Half of them had been killed or wounded. At this point the German attack faltered, allowing the French survivors to mount a counterattack with grenades. The German shock troops vacated the trench, and the French were able to retake all the ground they had lost.

American newspapers reported that this assault cost the Germans two entire companies of shock troops.[34] The history of Assault Battalion No. 5 (Rohr), however, listed eight dead from the 1st Assault Company, two missing from the 2nd Assault Company, and one missing from the flamethrower platoon, for a much more realistic total of eleven.[35] In addition, three flamethrower pioneers of the 2nd Company of the Guard Reserve Pioneer Regiment were killed in action or went missing at Hill 304 on June 29.[36] Reddemann made no mention of this operation; it is worth repeating that earlier in his book he also neglected to describe missions that his men undertook with Assault Detachment Rohr in 1915. A reasonable supposition is that Reddemann may not have liked sharing the spotlight with those he considered competitors.

Exaggerated Allied claims of German casualties were fairly common, particularly in regard to flamethrower operators. As one writer described the July 14 fighting on the heights of Cerny and Craonne: "Scores of Germans using flame-projectors were killed[.]"[37] Not surprisingly, the death book of the Guard Reserve Pioneer Regiment did not concur. It listed only *Pionier* Otto Lange of the 10th Company, who died in hospital in nearby Laon on July 14.[38] Allied reports of scores or dozens of flamethrower operators dying in a single action were never corroborated by the regimental death book. The greatest single-day loss was sixteen, incurred during the fighting at Skrobova on November 9, 1916.[39] A former

Austro-German training camp at Hucisco-Olesci, Galicia, photographed by a German officer in June of 1917. A mixture of Austrians and Germans from Landwehr-Infanterie-Regiment Nr. 99 go through their paces on the mock battlefield or "model-garden" (Modellgarten). Training in flamethrowers also took place at this camp.

flamethrower pioneer said that Reddemann kept casualties low by refusing to squander his men pointlessly. An operation in which three or four flamethrower pioneers died was viewed by the regiment as a "catastrophe."[40]

German Flamethrower Training Course

Duty roster for brief training in flamethrower service over eighteen training days (three weeks).[41]

First Week

Monday: Day 1

8:00-9:00 A.M. - General instruction in flamethrowers. Historical.

9:30-11:00 A.M. - Technical training in the small flamethrower.

2:30-4:00 P.M. - Individual technical training in the small flamethrower.

Tuesday: Day 2

8:00-9:00 A.M. - Instruction in the tactical use of the small flamethrower.

9:30-11:00 A.M. - Individual technical training in the small flamethrower and live firing.

2:30-4:00 P.M. - Individual technical training in the small flamethrower.

Wednesday: Day 3

8:00-9:00 A.M. - Instruction in the tactical use of the medium flamethrower.

9:30-11:00 A.M. - Technical training in the medium flamethrower.

2:30-4:00 P.M. - Individual technical training in the medium flamethrower.

Thursday: Day 4

8:00-9:00 A.M. - Instruction in the tactical use of the large flamethrower.

9:30-11:00 A.M. - Technical training in the medium flamethrower, double medium flamethrower, and live firing.

2:30-4:00 P.M. - Individual technical training in the medium flamethrower.

Friday: Day 5

8:00-9:00 A.M. - Instruction in the simultaneous tactical use of small, medium, and large flamethrowers during the unified flame attack.

German flamethrower squad rolls up a mock trench at Hucisco-Olesci. The men wear colored bands around their helmets, identifying them as either the "Red" or "Blue" team. This photo and the previous were taken during an Austrian assault course (k.u.k. Sturm-Kursus) attended by men from Landwehr-Infanterie-Regiment Nr. 99.

9:30-11:00 A.M. - Technical training in the large flamethrower and live firing.

2:30-4:00 P.M. - Individual technical training in the large flamethrower, double large flamethrower, and multiple large flamethrower.

Saturday: Day 6

8:00-9:00 A.M. - Instruction. Recapitulation of previously taken subjects.

9:30-11:00 A.M. - Recapitulation of individual technical training in small, medium, and large flamethrowers.

2:00-3:00 P.M. - Cleaning the apparatuses.

Second Week

Monday: Day 7

8:00-9:00 A.M. - Instruction. Technical specifications of small, medium, and large flamethrowers in comparison of weight, contents capacity, and so forth.

9:30-11:00 A.M. - Shock-troop practice for the small-flamethrower shock troop and medium-flamethrower shock troop.

2:30-4:00 P.M. - Individual technical training in hand-grenade throwing in support of flamethrower shock troops.

Tuesday: Day 8

8:00-9:00 A.M. - Instruction. Preparing the flame attack.

9:30-11:00 A.M. - Rolling up a trench with a flamethrower shock troop and hand-grenade throwers.

Above: Second photo of the same pioneers, a few seconds after firing the flamethrower. The wincing indicates a substantial amount of heat and fumes blowing back from the lance. Courtesy Maurice Sublet.

Below: Flamethrower pioneers training with a Kleif M.1917. Most of the men wear white or gray cotton drill uniforms (Drillichanzug) and jackboots. Courtesy Thierry Ehret.

Flamethrower platoon attached to an assault battalion. Patched and rumpled uniforms are very much in evidence, as are the older pioneers – former firefighters – common to the flamethrower service. The rustic trellis on the front porch of the barracks behind the men contains the letters FL and W, an abbreviation for Flammenwerfer. This photo was probably taken at the billet of the assault battalion, where the flamethrower platoon was housed in separate quarters.

2:30-4:00 P.M. - Rolling up a trench with a flamethrower shock troop and hand-grenade throwers.

Wednesday: Day 9

8:00-9:00 A.M. - Instruction. The flame attack.

9:30-11:00 A.M. - Rolling up a trench with live-firing flamethrowers, machine guns, practice hand grenades, Example 1.

2:30-4:00 P.M. - Individual training with grenade launchers in support of a flamethrower shock troop.

Thursday: Day 10

8:00-9:00 A.M. - Instruction. After the flame attack.

9:30-11:00 A.M. - Assault on an enemy blockhouse with a flamethrower shock troop, machine guns, grenade launchers, hand-grenade throwers, Example 4.

2:30-4:00 P.M. - The same as during the morning, with live-firing flamethrowers and practice ammunition for hand grenades and grenade launchers.

7:00 P.M. - Night exercise. Patrol assault on a hostile post. Opponents represented by straw mannequins.

Friday: Day 11

8:00-9:00 A.M. - Instruction. Reconnaissance in force.

9:30-11:00 A.M. - Overcoming an enemy barricade in a communication trench using the double medium flamethrower and a small-flamethrower shock troop, Example 2.

2:30-4:00 P.M. - The same as in the morning, with live-firing flamethrowers.

Saturday: Day 12

8:00-9:00 A.M. - Instruction. Weapons and equipment of the flamethrower pioneers.

9:30-11:00 A.M. - Assault on sap heads in the enemy position using the double medium flamethrower and a small-flamethrower shock troop with live-firing apparatuses, Example 3.

2:00-3:00 P.M. - Cleaning the apparatuses.

Third Week

Monday: Day 13
8:00-9:00 A.M. - Instruction. Simulated attack.
9:30-11:00 A.M. - Emplacing and assembling the large flamethrower by transportation troops with large-flamethrower carts. Bringing back the devices.
2:30-4:00 P.M. - The same as in the morning.

Tuesday: Day 14
8:00-9:00 A.M. - Instruction. Flamethrower defense, antitank defense.
9:30 11:00 A.M. - Flame attack; live firing of the large flamethrower.
2:30-4:00 P.M. - Advance of the lance operator equipped with a long hose attached to the large flamethrower during flame shock.

Wednesday: Day 15
8:00-9:00 A.M. - Instruction. The flamethrower in street fighting; flame signals; flame obstacles; flame bombs; the flamethrower as a burning tool, and so on.
9:30-11:00 A.M. - Frontal assault by a small-flamethrower shock troop under covering fire of large flamethrowers, Example 7.
2:30-4:00 P.M. - The same as in the morning, with live-firing apparatuses.

Thursday: Day 16
8:00-9:00 A.M. - Instruction. Cautionary measures and noteworthy measures for the flamethrower service. The auxiliary weapons of flamethrowers (machine guns, hand grenades, grenade launchers).
9:30-11:00 A.M. - Infantry attack with flamethrower shock troops, Example 5.
2:30-4:00 P.M. - Infantry attack with flamethrower shock troops, Example 6.
7:00 P.M. - Night exercise. Assault on an enemy reinforced-concrete dugout by a reinforced small-flamethrower shock troop, and blowing up a reinforced-concrete dugout with a hand-carried explosive charge.

This somewhat overage Hauptmann of the Garde-Reserve-Pionier-Regiment wears a privately purchased M.1910 service jacket decorated with both classes of Iron Cross. His death's head sleeve badge is of the rarely seen second pattern, which may have been the officers' version embroidered in silver bullion. There were only seven Hauptleute in the regiment: Koch, Fritsch, Beck, Kempf, Lewus, Sturm, and Walter. Courtesy Maurice Sublet.

Friday: Day 17

8:00-9:00 A.M. - Instruction. The arrangement and equipment of a flamethrower company in the field. The tactical attachment of the flamethrower company.

9:30-11:00 A.M. - Attack with flamethrowers in summarized groupings, Example 9.

2:00-3:00 P.M. - The same as in the morning, with live-firing apparatuses.

Saturday: Day 18

8:00-9:00 A.M. - Instruction. Recapitulation of previously taken subjects.

9:30-11:00 A.M. - Concluding exercises with small, medium, and large flame throwers.

2:00-3:00 P.M. - Cleaning the apparatuses.

CHAPTER NINE

Turkish Flamethrower Troops

On January 9, 1916, the Turkish 19th and 20th Infantry Divisions were combined to form the XV Corps, which was ordered to the eastern front in July. By Ottoman standards the 30,000-man corps was well trained and very well armed with forty-eight field pieces of various calibers, eight trench mortars, and thirty captured Russian machine guns; eight German machine-gun detachments were added when the Turks arrived in Galicia in August. The XV Corps was assigned to Army South and given a seventeen-mile sector on the west bank of the Zlotalipa River, where it endured months of extremely heavy fighting.[1]

In January of 1917 the Turks formed divisional assault companies that included one *Kleif* shock troop, although it is not known if this apparently unique flamethrower contingent saw combat. Since Army South provided the XV Corps with only two flamethrowers,[2] it is possible that the Turkish *Kleif* shock troop was created for training and demonstration purposes. Its personnel may have come from the 3rd Company of the 3rd Engineer Battalion (19th Division) or the 4th Company of the 4th Engineer Battalion (20th Division).

Only one photograph of the Turkish *Kleif* shock troop has surfaced, taken in the spring or summer of 1917 at a large training camp near Rohatyn in Galicia. Known today as Rogatin, this Ukrainian town is located forty-three miles southeast of Lvov. Courses at the Rohatyn camp included extensive flamethrower training for the German, Austro-Hungarian, and Turkish assault troops deployed to the eastern front.

The Germans gave the Turks a wartime total of thirty flamethrowers, model and dates of receipt unknown.[3] According to General Sir Ian Hamilton, the Turks had flamethrowers during the Gallipoli campaign of March 1915 to January 1916 but did not use them,[4] leading members of the East Lancashire Regiment to speak of the chivalrous, "clean-fighting Turk" who refused German offers of poison gas as well.[5] Both infantry divisions of the XV Corps – one of which formed the *Kleif* shock troop – were veterans of Gallipoli; they seemed to have changed their minds about incendiary weapons in late 1916 or early 1917.

From June 29 to July 7, 1917, the Battle of Brczany in Sector Rohatyn was fought by the German 4th *Ersatz* Division, the 15th and 75th Reserve Divisions, elements of the 241st Infantry Division, Assault Battalion No. 8, the Austro-Hungarian XXV Corps, the Ottoman XV Corps, and the 4th Company of the Guard Reserve Pioneer Regiment. Russian attacks tapered off after July 11, and the XV Corps returned to Turkey in August. No further information about Turkish flamethrower troops has been discovered.

Unternehmen Strandfest

On June 20, 1917, the British XV Corps took over French positions in Flanders near Nieuport and Lombartzyde, moving into a bridgehead on the eastern bank of the Yser Canal. This changeover was part of the preparations for the Third Battle of Ypres, more commonly called Passchendaele. The British plan was for the troops in Nieuport to link up with an amphibious invasion force that would land on the Belgian coast.

On the left flank of the bridgehead was a narrow belt of sand dunes about 1,400 yards wide. In order to strengthen this position, four Australian tunneling companies were brought in.[6] They began offensive mining toward the German lines,

Extremely rare image of a Turkish Kleif shock troop training at Rohatyn. It consists of two four-man Kleif squads, four hand-grenade throwers, and a shock-troop leader. The soldiers are equipped with the Kleif M.1917 and the first model of Turkish steel helmet, essentially a German helmet with the brim cut off. Note the rolled assault packs, slung rifles, and shortened pioneer shovels. At least two of the helmets are camouflaged in broad vertical bands of color.

The soldier peering from the leftmost edge of this trench at Rohatyn is a Turk wearing a cut-down M.1917 steel helmet. He may be an officer attached to a German Kleif squad to observe their training methods.

Above: Turkish honor guard reviewed by Kaiser Wilhelm II on October 17, 1917, during the German emperor's third and final visit to Turkey. The other dignitaries include Sultan Muhammad V and Kemal Mustapha Bey. Note the cut-down German steel helmets and Gew. 98 rifles; the Germans also supplied the Turks with thirty flamethrowers, model unknown. The second man from the left is wearing his helmet backward, probably because he had never seen one before he was ordered to put it on.

Below: Sailors of the Marinekorps Sturmabteilung. This unit attacked Nieuport with five shock troops accompanied by flamethrower squads from the Garde-Reserve-Pionier-Regiment. The officer standing on the left is armed with a P04 Luger, while the man lying on his side in the right front displays the arm chevron of an Able Seaman (Matrosen-Gefreiten). All wear field-gray M.1915 blouses.

built subways and dugouts, and sank wells for drinking water. The bridgehead was connected to the western bank of the canal by three wooden pontoon bridges, the only way reinforcements and supplies could be brought in.

While the British were preparing for their large-scale offensive, the Germans were devising a preemptive strike against the bridgehead, a plan dubbed Operation Beach Party (*Unternehmen Strandfest*). A second, smaller mission within *Strandfest* was Operation Section Dunes (*Unternehmen Abschnitt Dünen*).[7] The attacks were to be carried out by the Naval Corps Flanders (*Marinekorps Flandern*), which would provide Naval Infantry Regiment No. 1 and No. 2 (*Marine-Infanterie-Regiment Nr. 1* and *Nr. 2*) and the 400-man Assault Detachment (*Sturmabteilung*).

It is not clear how many flamethrower pioneers took part in Strandfest. According to the war diary of the Naval Corps Assault Detachment, five officers, nine NCOs, and sixty-three enlisted men from the 6th Company of the Guard Reserve Pioneer Regiment were assigned to the unit on July 3. They served as both flamethrower operators and field pioneers. Bernhard Reddemann, however, wrote that the entire 6th and 12th Companies – some 400 men – participated.[8] However many were involved, the Death's Head Pioneers provided shock troops for the Naval Corps Assault Detachment and flame accompanying squads for Naval Infantry Regiment No. 1 and No. 2.

Operation Beach Party called for the Naval Corps Assault Detachment to open the way for the naval infantry regiments, which would attack from the east on a front 2 miles wide and about 1000 yards deep. The Assault Detachment supplied five shock troops of twenty-five to forty-five men each; it is not known how many flamethrowers were attached to these formations. On July 4 and 5 an unspecified number of shock troops trained with the 3rd Battalion of Naval Infantry Regiment No. 2 for the smaller Operation Section Dunes, the precise objective of which is not described. The next day this training was repeated with the participation of flamethrowers. Also on July 6 the Germans began shelling the Nieuport sector in preparation for the assault.

Strandfest was launched on July 10. Reddemann devoted one paragraph to it:

> The 6th and 12th Companies under Battalion Commander *Hauptmann* Koch carried out a frontal attack on positions in the dunes and reclaimed land at Lombartzyde in Flanders. Four *Grof* and twenty-six small flamethrowers in shock troops were used on a front 2,500 meters wide. Enemy positions were penetrated, trenches rolled up, machine-guns silenced, and blockhouses and large company dugouts smoked out. The flamethrower troops advanced 800 to 1,000 meters deep, capturing 1,300 prisoners and much war material.[9]

It began at 5:30 A.M. with a sustained barrage from coastal batteries, howitzers, and heavy mortars. Aircraft dropped bombs and strafed relentlessly at low levels. Mustard gas –

Flame accompanying squad (Flammenbegleittrupp) armed with a Kleif M.1917 prepares to advance with the infantry. At Nieuport the Death's Head Pioneers served as both flame accompanying squads and shock troops. U.S. National Archives 165-GB-3074.

which the Germans called Yellow Cross – was used for the first time. The British positions were pulverized and all three of the pontoon bridges were destroyed, isolating the bridgehead on the eastern bank of the Yser. At 7:51 P.M. the German sailors advanced in a crescent formation between the ebb-tide sands in the west and the Lombartzyde position in the east.[10] The use of the four *Grof* would indicate that a combined stationary and pouncing attack took place, a "shock" immediately prior to the infantry moving in.

In the dunes on the far-left flank, the two battalions comprising the British 2nd Brigade, 1st Division, were virtually wiped out. Survivors took shelter in the dugouts and subways, but the Germans dropped hand grenades down the ventilation shafts and fired flamethrowers into the entrances.[11]

Shock Troop 1 of the Naval Corps Assault Detachment reported that since the British soldiers in two underground shelters refused an "energetic request" to emerge, they were killed with flamethrowers. Likewise, flamethrowers were sprayed at British machine-gun positions before they could fire a shot, whereupon the burning crews fell out on the ground. In the case of Shock Troop 4, however, some of the flamethrowers were damaged during the assault, and the rest were quickly emptied.[12]

Sapper James O'Connell of the 2nd Australian Tunneling Company was in an underground subway when the infantry attack commenced:

> The Germans threw a bomb down the entrance which killed one man and severely tore the tunneler's hand. Another German squirted the jet of a flammenwerfer down the stair and burnt him seriously. The German passed on and was killed at the canal bank by a fragment of one of the shells of his own field guns.[13]

As in many other accounts by Allied military personnel, the flamethrower was described as a one-man weapon. If this report is accurate, the device in question was the *Wechselapparat M.1917*, abbreviated *Wex*, a ring-shaped flamethrower that was served by a four-man squad consisting of an *Unteroffizier* or *Gefreiter* in charge, a lance operator, a *Wex* carrier (*Wexträger*), and an assistant. In the event that the three other men of the squad were incapacitated, the *Wex* carrier could operate the flamethrower by himself.[14] The *Kleif*, on the other hand, could not be operated by the carrier alone.[15]

Burned on the face, Sapper O'Connell gathered up several grenades and threw them one by one at his attackers as he made his way to the canal. At the river's edge he was

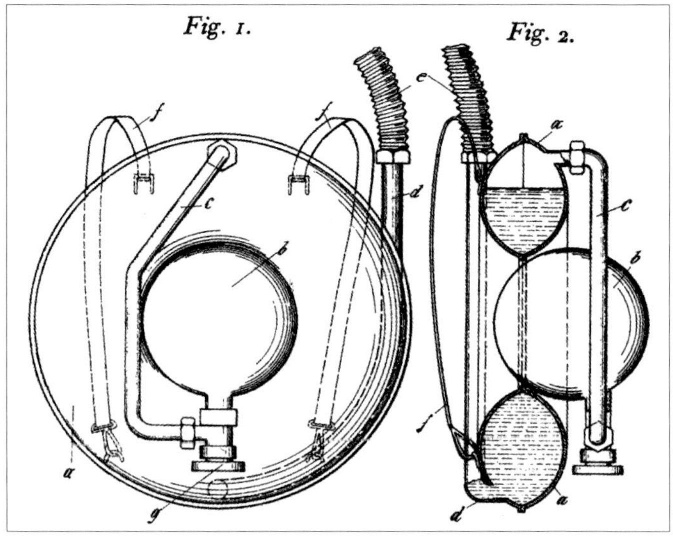

Patent for ring-shaped flamethrower, filed by Hanseatische Apparatebau-Gesellschaft on August 15, 1916. The Wechselapparat (Wex) M.1917 produced by the Garde-Reserve-Pionier-Regiment may have been based on this device. (German patent No. 307605.)

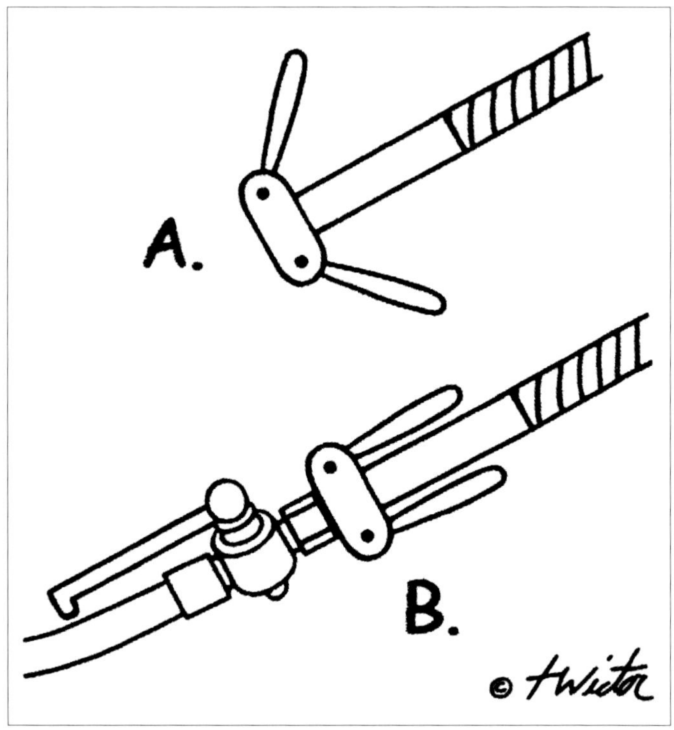

Quick-release hose coupling used with Wex: (A) unlocked, (B) locked. Originally Wex squads were to be armed with three flamethrowers and one lance; the empty flamethrowers could be quickly exchanged for full ones, hence the name "Interchangeable Apparatus" (Wechselapparat). The plan proved too difficult to execute in combat.

The Wex M.1917 and 4.6ft. (1.4m) M.1914 small lance. Although fielded with the same four-man squad as the Kleif, this flamethrower could be operated by the Wex carrier alone, in the event that the three other members of the squad were put out of action.

again wounded, this time in the head, by either a bullet or a shell fragment. He fell into the canal, pulled himself out, and took shelter in a dugout, where he was bandaged by a British officer. O'Connell then jumped back into the canal and swam to the western bank and safety. As he crawled out, he heard a cry for help from the canal; returning to the water, he found a struggling comrade and dragged him to shore. For this action, Sapper O'Connell was awarded the Distinguished Conduct Medal.[16]

The fighting lasted until 8:30 P.M. When it was over, the Germans occupied a front on the bridgehead 1,400 yards wide and 600 yards deep. Only four officers and sixty-four men of the British 2nd Brigade had managed to escape this position and swim across to the western bank of the Yser. South of Lombartzyde the Germans were driven back by a counterattack, but *Strandfest* was deemed "a great and magnificent success" by Ludendorff.[17] One *Unteroffizier* and two pioneers of the 6th Company of the Guard Reserve Pioneer Regiment were killed. The next day, the company lost an additional *Leutnant der Landwehr* and a pioneer.[18] No deaths for either day were recorded for the 12th Company.

A French late-model Schilt No. 3 modified by the Germans, then captured by the British in 1917. The nozzle on the rigid lance has been given a bend of several degrees and fitted with an igniter holder. To operate this primitive weapon, an assistant simply opened the valve on the bottom of the propellant tank, pressurizing and firing the oil simultaneously.

Individual Flamethrower Attacks on the Western Front

July 11 - A platoon of the 10th Company under *Leutnant* Riis launched a surprise pouncing attack east of Monchy le Preux.[19] Breakthrough was achieved with six flame shock troops deployed in a flanking maneuver simultaneously with the frontal attack. Trenches rolled were up, and the positions were sealed off.

July 25 - A platoon of the 10th Company under *Leutnant* Schmidt II *[Author's note: There were so many Schmidts in the German army that they were often numbered.]* carried out a flanking pouncing attack against the forward trenches east of Monchy le Preux. Following the breakthrough of flame

shock troops from the north and south, the enemy was unable to resist a frontal attack by infantry. Trenches were quickly rolled up and sealed, and many prisoners were taken.

August 21 - A nighttime flamethrower attack against a British bombing post at Epehy was foiled single-handedly by twenty-year-old Second Lieutenant Harry Falconer Parsons of the 14th (Service) Battalion, the Gloustershire Regiment. The British grenade throwers were forced back by the flamethrowers, but Parsons remained by himself and threw grenades even though he was severely burned. He held up the attack long enough for a bombing party to be organized, which prevented the Germans from gaining entry into the trench. Parsons later died of his injuries and was awarded the Victoria Cross.[20] Since Reddemann did not mention this attack and the regimental death book contained no names for the date, the flamethrower company involved remains unidentified.

August 24 - The 12th Company under *Hauptmann* Walter carried out a frontal pouncing attack in cratered terrain at the Herenthage Estates in Flanders, using sixteen *Kleif*. After breakthrough, trenches were rolled up and blockhouses and machine guns were silenced. A vigorous enemy counterattack was defeated with the cooperation of the flamethrowers. Many prisoners were taken. Reddemann did not point out that ten flamethrower pioneers were killed in this action, one of the heaviest single-day losses suffered by the regiment.[21]

October 29 - A platoon of the 2nd Company launched a flanking pouncing attack on the Vaux-Cross Hill at Verdun, going in ahead of the infantry. After the platoon achieved breakthrough into enemy positions from the side, trenches were rolled up, machine guns silenced, and underground bunkers smoked out. Despite fierce enemy resistance, 200 prisoners were taken.

December 5 - The 6th Company under *Leutnant* Reinfeldt carried out a frontal pouncing attack with shock troops west and south of Moeuvres in Artois, using thirty-two *Kleif*. Trenches were rolled up and sealed off on a front 1.2 miles wide. Resistance was quickly broken by *Kleif*, and the objective of the day was exceeded. Many prisoners were taken.

December 12 - The 2nd Company under *Leutnant* Zachow and *Offizier-Stellvertreter* Sausner carried out a large reconnaissance in force with two infantry battalions south of Ornes at Verdun, using fourteen *Kleif*. Trenches were rolled

Hand-pulled carts used to transport Leichtgrof M.1916 to the front line. Empty Grof could be carried by one man wearing a knapsack harness, while two men were required to haul the weapon when it was full. Courtesy Thierry Ehret.

up, machine guns and other points of resistance silenced, dugouts smoked out. The men returned from the mission in eight minutes with eighty-five prisoners.

December 30 - The 6th Company under *Leutnant* Ruhig captured a British position over 1,300 yards wide and 440 yards deep south of Marcoing, using sixteen *Kleif* and working with infantry shock troops. After breakthrough was achieved, trenches were rolled up and machine guns were silenced. Despite very stubborn resistance, 250 prisoners were taken.

Individual Flamethrower Attacks in Russia and Galicia

July 19 - The 3rd Company under *Leutnant* Bruckmann seized hilltop positions at Zlota Gora and Wertepy on the Strypa River in Galicia.[22] Using twenty-one *Kleif*, the troops broke through despite a heavy artillery barrage and fierce resistance, penetrating to a depth of 1,100 yards across a front of 2,200 yards. Trenches were rolled up and machine guns were silenced. Three hundred prisoners and much war material were captured.

September 1-4 - The 3rd and 7th Companies under Battalion Commander *Hauptmann* Beck attacked at Riga with eighty-four *Kleif*. After the Germans were ferried across the Dvina River in wooden pontoon boats, breakthrough was achieved by flamethrower shock troops using the Knife Tactic, advancing in long, snakelike formations behind a rolling barrage. Machine guns were silenced and dugouts and farm

houses were captured. Eight thousand prisoners, 180 cannons, 200 machine guns, and much war material were captured.

September 21 - The 3rd and 7th Companies under Battalion Commander *Hauptmann* Beck made a frontal attack on the bridgehead of Jakobstadt on the Duna River. Flame shock troops using 101 *Kleif* broke through despite strong resistance, silencing machine-gun nests and rifle positions. Four thousand prisoners, fifty-five cannons, and much war material were captured.

Above: Photo taken during the Battle of Riga, September 1-6, 1917. Infantry assault troops are crossing the Dvina River in wooden boats of the type used to build pontoon bridges. In the background, an artillery bombardment hammers the Üxküll Peninsula. The group of soldiers on the right includes a Kleif squad, the flamethrower reflecting the sunlight in a vertical band.

Below: Unteroffiziere of the 3rd and 7th Companies, Garde-Reserve-Pionier-Regiment, in a postcard sent from Vilna, Lithuania, on November 27, 1917. These two companies engaged the Russians near Riga, Latvia, from September 1 to November 12. Standing on the far right is Vizefeldwebel Heinrich Freesemann of the 7th Company, who served on the western front in 1916. The flag behind the men is a trophy with a Cyrillic inscription that reads "United Socialists Horse Army."

November 12 - The 3rd and 7th Companies under Battalion Commander *Hauptmann* Beck attacked Skrobova-Bach southeast of Goroditsche. Flame shock troops armed with sixty-four *Kleif* broke through across a front of 2,400 yards, overcoming machine-gun nests, rolling up trenches, and capturing 250 prisoners.

The Battle for Hill 70

On August 15, 1917, the 2nd and 3rd Brigades of the 1st Canadian Division took Hill 70, a low rise 1.5 miles north of Lens. The hope was that if the height were occupied, the Germans would be forced to evacuate the town. On August 16 the 2nd Canadian Battalion moved forward to relieve the 3rd Brigade, the same day that the Germans counterattacked with waves of infantry from the 4th Guard Division that were annihilated by British and Canadian artillery and machine-gun fire.[23] The 2nd Canadian Battalion arrived on the 17th and settled in, only to be hit by a violent German assault the next evening. It began with a bombardment of gas shells, followed by a "remarkable" number of flamethrower squads screened by a high-explosive barrage:

> Behind the men carrying on their backs lifebuoys full of petrol, which they pumped out alight from nozzles they held in their hands, there rushed some ten thousand of the best storm troops that Ludendorff could spare from the Ypres battlefield. The scheme completely failed. The Canadian riflemen and machine-gunners most gallantly stood to battle when the flame fell on them. They shot at the distant end of the flame-jets, brought all the flame-throwers down, and then maintained such a machine-gun and musketry barrage that the German shock troops could not move and live through it.[24]

As at Nieuport, the flamethrower was the *Wex*, which held 2.9 gallons of oil for a laden weight of fifty-five pounds, as compared to the 4.2-gallon *Kleif*, which weighed sixty-eight pounds. The lance was identical to that used on the *Kleif*, but the hose was fitted with a friction coupler that allowed the lance to be attached to a new flamethrower in a matter of seconds. In 1928 Reddemann wrote to the American head of the Chemical Warfare Service, describing how flamethrower pioneers performed with the lightweight *Wex*:

> As they were not hampered to a greater extent by their flame projectors than an ordinary infantryman by his equipment, they were able to run fast, throw themselves down on the ground, take to cover, jump forward, etc.
>
> This fact also demonstrates that the flame projector troops were able as a whole to take part in the offensive, and that the movements of the individuals were in no way "hampered," that they were very well able to advance or retreat.[25]

Undated portrait of a muscular, deeply suntanned flamethrower pioneer. His neat M.1910 service jacket is adorned with black M.1915 shoulder straps piped in red; gray death's-head sleeve badge on oval backing cut from field-gray cloth; and a ribbon for the Iron Cross, Second Class. The white guard lace is glaringly bright and clean, possibly indicating that this is a "ceremonial" tunic brought out for formal occasions such as photo sittings. Flamethrower pioneers kept a second uniform for training and combat; this "work outfit" often lacked the sleeve badge.

A slightly different time frame for the August 18 flamethrower attack was given in the history of the 2nd Canadian Battalion:

> The first of a series of assaults was delivered about 4.45 a.m. Preceded by peculiarly equipped men, whose armament appeared to consist of tanks and lengths of hose, the German infantry stormed across No Man's Land. As

> their barrage lifted from the new front line, they rained a hail of bombs against the defenders. In the half-light of the morning, the enemy offered themselves as excellent targets for the Battalion's Lewis Gunners, while their tendency to crowd in on each other resulted in themselves suffering from the Battalion bomb-throwers.[26]

From this description, it appears that the flamethrower operators did not apply the extensive training they had received in the Indian-style Forward Stalking that called for them to advance in small, spread-out groups, utilizing cover such as shell holes. They also neglected to fire covering jets to obscure their movements. Both Reddemann and Charles Theune provided several instances in which the Death's Head Pioneers used both Indian-style Forward Stalking and covering jets to cross hundreds of yards of open ground without suffering undue casualties, which reportedly did not happen at Hill 70:

> The purpose of the curiously equipped assailants was soon made manifest, when, still at a measurable distance from Hugo Trench, a stream of flame spurted from the nozzles they were carrying. With it the enemy sought to sweep the parapet. The Battalion had heard of flame-throwers and pamphlets had been written about them; but this was the first time they had ever been up against them. On No. 4 Company's front the defenders declined to be subjected to a roasting of this sort. Sergeant R.C. Allday disposed effectively of the operator of one machine, wounding him. The German obviously did not like his role, for he surrendered, and, together with his equipment, he was conveyed to Battalion Headquarters.[27]

For the men of the Canadian 3rd and 4th Companies, the threat came more from German grenadiers than flamethrowers. Despite the heavy fire they were taking, the Germans kept coming, throwing their egg grenades with deadly accuracy. Unlike the flamethrower operators, they tried to survive by dodging from shell hole to shell hole:

> In the centre of the line, at the junction of Nos. 2 and 3 Companies more flame-throwers attempted to ply their peculiar art, followed by more bombers. A bitter fight was waged close to where Humbug Alley branched off from the front line. The scorching flame swept the trench and the operator of the contrivance clambered over the parapet to continue his work. There, however, he was encountered by Lieut. Hugh Smith who grappled with him and after a violent tussle disposed of him. The flame-throwing device eventually arrived at Battalion Headquarters for examination.[28]

This account indicates that a single man operated each *Wex*, apparently because the three other members of the squad had been killed or wounded.

On August 19 at around 1:00 A.M. the Germans launched a flamethrower attack on Cité St. Emile south of Hill 70, while simultaneously thrusting from the north at Hugo Wood and from the east along the entire front. These assaults failed, forcing the Germans to draw back in the "flaming, thundering, poisoned darkness of the summer night."[29] All in all the Germans made between sixteen and twenty-one counterattacks, none of which succeeded.

Chicken-wire screens such as these were used to instruct flamethrower pioneers how to throw hand grenades in high arcs. Company commanders often sponsored grenade-throwing competitions with prizes for the winner.

Flamethrower squads practicing an assault on a mock trench. The three men on the right each train to operate the Wex singly. Note the instructors running alongside, no doubt shouting orders.

Above: This Kleif squad demonstrates the advantage of the German two-man flamethrower in trench fighting: Because of the long hose, the operator can raise his arms high enough to fire across the open ground and reach targets in the next traverse without exposing himself. He can also hold the lance around corners.

Below: The oil fired by this small flamethrower appears to ignite several feet beyond the nozzle of the lance. It may be that the operator is spraying unlit oil on an ignition source off camera, which causes the flames to race backward along the stream.

Despite multiple Allied reports of heavy casualties among German flamethrower operators at Hill 70, the death book of the Guard Reserve Pioneer Regiment listed no names for August 16-18, 1917. Even if the men had been attached to assault battalions during this operation, they would have been noted as killed in action. There is no satisfactory explanation for this discrepancy. Clearly the chroniclers of one side or the other were mistaken. Given the scale and importance of this particular attack, it is remarkable to find such a disagreement among the participants.

Flamethrower Attack at Passchendaele

British author Guy Chapman of the Royal Fusiliers, London Regiment, described a German flamethrower raid that took place on an October morning during the Third Battle of Ypres. The setting was a marshy, shell-pocked moonscape choked with corpses; a thick ground fog hid the attackers. Following a ten-minute barrage laid down by by trench mortars, a wave of fire approached the British:

> The enemy were attacking under cover of *flammenwerfer*, hose pipes leading to petrol-tanks carried on the backs of men. When their nozzles were lighted, they threw out a roaring, hissing flame twenty to thirty feet long, swelling at the end to a whirling oily rose, six feet in diameter. Under the protection of these hideous weapons, the enemy surrounded the advance pill-box, stormed it and killed the garrison.[30]

The Germans tried to consolidate the pillbox, but the British counterattacked. Two officers took a few enlisted men to carry hand grenades for them and bombed their way inside, killing most of the Germans and capturing six. Groaning British survivors of the flamethrower attack were brought back, their hair singed, their faces burnt black, and their lips hideously swollen and red. They were bandaged and sent to the rear. Of the 353 men with whom Chapman had started, a third had been killed or wounded; No. 2 Company, which had borne the brunt of the flamethrower attack, was reduced to seventeen.[31] The 12th Company of the Guard Reserve Pioneer Regiment lost two men in Flanders on October 1 and one each on October 3 and 4.[32]

Late-war carte de visite by Otto Hoeffke of Berlin. This Gefreiter of the Garde-Reserve-Pionier-Regiment wears the field-gray M.1915 peacetime jacket (Friedensrock) with red piping and black collar and cuffs, mandated by the AKO of September 21, 1915. His death's head sleeve badge is of the second pattern, more commonly worn by officers. It has been temporarily attached to his sleeve with two straight pins. The prewar greatcoat has black shoulder straps piped in red, while the spiked helmet is a privately purchased item. Note the ribbon for what may be the General Service Award issued by the Grand Duchy of Hesse-Darmstadt.

Individual Flamethrower Attacks in South Tirol and Galicia

October 17 - The detached platoon of *Leutnant* Jahns attacked Italian trenches on Mount Piano at Schluderbach in the Dolomites.[33] A steep ravine fifty-five yards deep separated the opposing positions; the Austrians had not been able to advance because Italian machine guns swept the slope on the near side of the depression. Platoon Jahns slid with its flamethrowers down the snow-covered mountainside, moving so quickly that the enemy did not see them. The platoon then climbed up out of the ravine to within ten feet of the Italians and opened fire in a surprise attack, silencing a machine-gun position on the precipice and rolling up the trenches.

October 18 - The detached platoon of *Leutnant* Hübner took part in a large-scale nighttime reconnaissance in force on Monte Solgi Bianchi in Italy. Using twelve *Kleif* on a front of 330 yards, Platoon Hübner achieved breakthrough, rolled up trenches, and smoked the enemy out of dugouts and caves. A total of 300 prisoners were taken.

November 16 - The detached platoon of *Leutnant* Hübner launched a surprise attack against positions on Mount Cornella and the village of Quero on the Piave River. The platoon crossed almost 700 yards of open terrain under covering fire from artillery and captured the village, taking 585 prisoners.

November 22 - The detached platoon of *Leutnant* Hübner made a surprise attack on Mount Tomba southwest of Quero on the Piave River. The platoon climbed almost 200 yards up the mountainside and completely surprised the Italians, who put up a fierce resistance. Breakthrough was achieved; trenches were rolled up; and machine guns were silenced. A total of 835 prisoners, four mountain cannon, and forty machine guns were captured.

Although more attacks were carried out on the Italian front, Reddemann wrote that it was not possible to describe them individually. This period was characterized by the use of single flame shock troops that often had to cross up to 1,100 yards of open terrain and engage in arduous mountain warfare. The physical destruction of the battlefield, due to the pounding of heavy-caliber shells, prevented the flamethrower regiment from deploying its emplaced *Grof* as often as in the past. Consequently, large flamethrowers were put into action just ten times on the Italian front in 1917, once with twenty such devices. To make up for this deficit, increased numbers of small flamethrowers were deployed, up to 101 in one operation.

One Death's Head Pioneer who served in Italy was left with a disdain for the fighting abilities of friend and foe alike. Because of what he described as the incompetence and suicidal bravado of the Italians versus the plain incompetence of the Austrians, he dubbed the Italian front the "Clown Apocalypse."[34]

These unidentified assault troops may have been photographed on the Italian front during the Battle of Caporetto (October 24 - November 12, 1917). On the left is an attached flamethrower half-platoon (Halbzug) from the Garde-Reserve-Pionier-Regiment.

Kleif squad demonstrating its weapon to a crowd of Austrians. The handwritten caption on the back reads "Flammenwerfer (Anfangstrahl)" or "Flamethrower (beginning jet)," meaning an initial burst of flame.

Germans Attack Their Own Flamethrower Operators?

An American newspaper article dated October 31, 1917, described an incident that – if true – illustrates the deep resentment some German infantrymen had for the Death's Head Pioneers. According to a letter written by a British officer and reported by the Associated Press, an unidentified Liverpool regiment captured a group of Germans during an assault on a strong point. These prisoners made a pretense of launching a counterattack against the British, but in reality they only wanted to escape their own officers and surrender. A second, genuine German counterattack was organized to recover the prisoners from the British-held trenches. The prisoners panicked and begged the British to save them. As the unnamed letter writer related, the second counterattack contained several flamethrower squads:

> "Fortunately, we were alert and charged at once, capturing the whole liquid fire outfit. There ensued a terrible row between the earlier prisoners and the men we had taken with the liquid fire outfit. The first prisoners wanted to kill the liquid fire men. We had our hands full getting them all back."[35]

Neither Reddemann nor Charles Theune discussed the possibility that the average German infantryman might hold a grudge against assault formations such as the Death's Head Pioneers, units that wore distinctive uniforms and badges, were romanticized by the home press, lived in comfortable billets behind the lines, and were given double rations. Assault units also departed the sector after their missions, leaving the regular infantry to suffer the Allied artillery barrage that usually followed. Men taken prisoner could very well have become enraged at the idea of being dragged back into the war by what they perceived as a pampered elite.

***Jäger* (Assault) Battalion No. 3 at Cambrai**

On November 19, 1917, prior to the German counterattack at Cambrai, the flamethrower platoon of *Jäger* (Assault) Battalion No. 3 was inserted in a feint operation with Infantry Regiment No. 418 opposite Malakoff-Ferme.[36] As part of the hurried preparations for the subsequent counterattack, the assault battalion was then divided: The 1st Assault Company along with two flamethrower squads and the 2nd Machine-gun Company were attached to the 34th Infantry Division, and the 2nd Assault Company with two flamethrower squads was attached to the 28th Infantry Division. The 28th Division assaulted the environs of Banteux, while the 34th Division attacked south of the village.

The 1st Assault Company provided the 34th Division with three assault squads and two light machine-gun squads attached to the 3rd Battalion of Infantry Regiment No. 67; two assault squads and two light machine-gun squads attached to the 2nd Battalion of Infantry Regiment No. 67; and three assault squads attached to the 2nd Battalion of Infantry Regiment No. 25. Two assault squads under the assault-company commander remained behind at the center of Infantry Regiment No. 67. The disposition of the two flamethrower squads is not clear, but they were sent forward with the assault squads.

After an exhausting march throughout the night of November 29, the infantry and *Jäger* assault troops reached their jumping-off points at dawn. An enormous artillery barrage began at 8:50; the assault was launched an hour later, supported by "an extraordinary number" of aircraft flying low strafing runs.[37] The assault troops followed behind the first wave of infantry, with orders to deal with points of resistance and thereafter act on their own initiative. Attacking in the form of triangular wedges, the assault troops quickly overcame the first and second British lines. The *Jäger* fought at the forward points of the triangles, while at the sides and bases the infantry engaged in further close combat, cleaning out the trenches and gullies. Soon the two *Jäger* assault squads kept in reserve were brought up to engage the British. The attack achieved a forward depth of three to four miles past Villers-Guislain, into the area of Gouzeaucourt and nearly reaching the road to Epehy.

The operation was deemed successful, and the 1st Assault Company of *Jäger* (Assault) Battalion No. 3 was slowly pulled out. On its march to the rear, it cleared the remaining British shelters of resistance. Several hundred prisoners were taken, and numerous cannons, machine guns, and rifles were captured, much of which were then used on the British. The *Jäger* assault troops were said to have contributed substantially to the success of the operation, due in part to the role played by the flamethrowers. Seventeen *Jäger* of the 1st Assault Company were killed in action, and twenty-six were wounded.

The flamethrower operators who fought at Banteux were members of the 10th Company of the Guard Reserve Pioneer Regiment.[38] *Offizier-Stellvertreter* Hermann Müller was killed, and an *Unteroffizier* and a pioneer were wounded.

Simultaneously with the attack by the 1st Assault Company, the 2nd Assault Company of *Jäger* (Assault) Battalion No. 3 was tasked to lead Baden *Leib* Grenadier Regiment No. 109 through two British trench systems. Together with some specially assigned infantry groups, the assault company would go in ahead of the grenadiers and take the British first and second positions to a depth of over 1800 yards. For this mission, the 2nd Assault Company assembled ad hoc units called *Blocks*, commanded by *Leutnants* or *Vizefeldwebeln*. There were two assault blocks (*Sturmblocks*) and one security block (*Sicherungsblock*), each of which would attack in three waves.

Assault Block Right was composed of four assault squads, two light machine-gun squads, two grenade-launcher squads, and one flamethrower squad. Assault Block Left had three assault squads, two light machine-gun squads, one grenade-launcher squad, and one flamethrower squad. Three assault squads comprised the Security Block. The three blocks attacked three different trench systems, all of which were furiously defended. After repeated assaults, the British were finally driven from their positions, opening a passage for the regular infantry. Total losses for the assault company were nine dead and twenty-eight wounded.

Assault trooper of Jäger- (Sturm-) Bataillon Nr. 3. This unit used flamethrowers extensively at Cambrai in November of 1917. Note the Kar. 98AZ, P08 pistol, and gray-green M.1910 service jacket.

Although no flamethrower pioneers were reported killed in this specific operation, the death book of the flamethrower regiment listed three pioneers dead and one missing for November 30 in Cambrai.[39] All were from the 12th Company instead of the 10th, which seems to indicate that they were lost in a different mission than the two carried out by *Jäger*

Combat platoon of the Garde-Reserve-Pionier-Regiment, specifically organized for attachment to an assault battalion. It is composed of one Vizefeldwebel, six four-man Kleif squads, and one orderly. Note the two Kleif M.1917 and 4ft. (1.2m) lances. Oddly, the Vizefeldwebel with the walking stick wears an M.1915 blouse with a death's head sleeve badge but no Guard lace. For the counterattack at Cambrai, Jäger- (Sturm-) Bataillon Nr. 3 assigned flamethrower pioneers to ad hoc units called Blocks.

A shock unit (Stosseinheit) practicing a combined stationary and pouncing attack in the snow. On the left, several Grof lay down a huge wall of smoke and flame to "shock" the enemy as infantry and Wex squads leap out of foxholes. At Cambrai the Germans used artillery and aircraft instead of large flamethrowers, but the effect was the same. U.S. National Archives 165-GB-6756.

(Assault) Battalion No. 3. It is not likely that men from two different companies of the Guard Reserve Pioneer Regiment comprised the single flamethrower platoon of the assault battalion.

The organization and weaponry of the assault blocks was very similar to Reddemann's flame shock troops, used a year before at Skrobova in Russia. Cambrai marked the first time that the infiltration tactics often attributed to *General der Infanterie* Oskar von Hutier were used on the western front, yet Reddemann neglected to comment on this dramatically successful German counterattack. Only five flamethrower pioneers died or went missing and two were wounded in a battle that cost both sides approximately 45,000 men.[40]

CHAPTER TEN

Flame Battles on the Western Front

January 1 to March 20, 1918

As Ludendorff planned the great spring offensive called Operation Michael or the Kaiser's Battle (*Kaiserschlacht*), intelligence about the enemy became crucial. The Germans had to both identify the divisions that opposed them and determine their fighting capabilities. Of the forty-nine flamethrower deployments during this period, thirty-nine were therefore reconnaissance in force.[1] Nine flamethrower companies were inserted in Artois, French Lorraine, Verdun, the Vosges, the Argonne, the Champagne, Flanders, and the Aisne. Seventeen of these forty-nine attacks were not successful.

Individual Flamethrower Attacks

January 25 - Flamethrower squads of the 2nd Company commanded by *Vizefeldwebel* Neumann crossed more than 160 yards of open terrain under heavy fire at Avocourt. They reached the enemy positions, rolled up trenches, silenced blockhouses and other strong points, and took prisoners, all in a very short time.

March 1 - A platoon of the 12th Company under *Offizier-Stellvertreter* Scharow attacked the Wetterrecke south of Ripont in the Champagne. Using twelve *Wex* across a front of over 1,500 yards, the platoon penetrated to a depth of 440 yards. Trenches were rolled up, machine guns were silenced, and many prisoners were taken.

March 1 - A platoon of the 1st Company under *Leutnant* Hennebold launched a reconnaissance in force against American positions at Remières Woods northeast of Seicheprey in French Lorraine. Using ten *Wex* in shock troops, the platoon broke into the enemy line, rolled up trenches, and breached barricades.

March 1 - A platoon of the 11th Company under *Leutnant* Dierks "struck in a grand manner" during a patrol at Fort de la Pompelle in the Champagne. Using ten *Wex* and two grenade launchers in shock troops, the platoon broke through, rolled up trenches, silenced machine guns, and took prisoners.

March 7 - While on patrol, a platoon of the 11th Company under *Leutnant* Hoffmann attacked south of Berry au Bac in the Champagne, crossing open terrain into the enemy positions. Trenches were rolled up, machine guns were silenced, and prisoners were taken.

The 21st Canadian Battalion Repels a Flamethrower Attack

At dawn on the morning of March 4, German shock troops raided a trench at Lens, in the 2nd Canadian Division Front.[2] The 21st Canadian Battalion was first bombarded by the heaviest artillery barrage of the winter, then the position was hit by four shock troops of thirty to forty men each, advancing under the cover of flame jets from several *Wex* squads.

The Canadians vigorously resisted. Parties of German shock troops were mowed down when they advanced through a culvert and scaled a railway embankment at the southern flank

Above: Men of the Experimental Company, Garde-Reserve-Pionier-Regiment, celebrating Christmas in their workshop. Although almost all of the Guard lace is the short, white version mandated by the AKO of March 3, 1915, the extravagantly mustached man seated on the right displays the long prewar lace on his M.1915 blouse, a very unusual combination. The rack on the left is hung with Kar. 98AZ carbines and a belt displaying a bayonet knot of unidentified colors.

Below: Undated postcard showing many of the same pioneers as in the previous photo; the sign reads "Room 7." The men smoke, sweep, read, and play the accordion or cards, while the scowling pioneer seated in the foreground pours himself a glass of rum. Note the chaotic mixture of tunics, shoulder-strap colors, and styles of Guard lace. True uniformity in the regiment was never achieved.

of the trench, exposing themselves to heavy Lewis-gun and rifle fire. On the left flank, about seventy-five Germans pushed through the front line and advanced along a communication trench, preceded by a flamethrower squad. As they worked their way toward Company Headquarters, they tossed stick grenades into the dugouts they passed.

A Canadian counterattack ejected the Germans from the trench and forced them to flee into No Man's Land, leaving their dead and wounded. Some of the prisoners taken were from Reserve Infantry Regiment No. 55, who told their captors that the shock troops belonged to an unidentified assault battalion. Three wounded shock troopers brought in from No Man's Land gave up valuable information to the Intelligence Staff. Losses among the Canadians were three officers wounded, three other ranks killed, and ninety-eight other ranks wounded.

Although at least forty Germans were reported killed in the assault, the death book of the Guard Reserve Pioneer Regiment listed only *Pionier* Otto Schmidt of the 10th Company for March 4 at Lens.[3]

Flamethrowers Against Tanks

The advent of the tank naturally spawned antitank tactics. Charles Theune wrote that small flamethrowers were very suitable for antitank missions. They would spray the tank only from the front, where experience had shown the Germans that the hatches, pistol ports, and vision slits could not be closed tightly enough to keep out the burning oil.[4] The closer the flamethrower was to the tank, the greater the destructive effect; an ideal range was 11-16 yards.

On February 12, 1918, at the Beuville training ground of Assault Battalion No. 5 (Rohr), Bernhard Reddemann volunteered to sit inside a captured British Mark IV tank that was sprayed with a flamethrower. His reason for undertaking this potentially deadly experiment was that he wanted to see for himself how effective the weapon would be. As soon

Postcard captioned "Our assault troops during a gas attack. The advance of the flamethrowers." The posed nature of the photo is given away by the fact that this seven-member unit falls well short of the twelve-man Wex shock troop, which would include four hand-grenade throwers in addition to the two Wex squads and the Unteroffizier on the right. There are also no igniters in the lances.

as the flamethrower was ignited, Reddemann and the other occupants hastily abandoned the vehicle because the oxygen inside was immediately burned up and the tank's oil supply caught fire.[5]

According to Charles Theune, "When defending against tanks and undertaking flame defense, the daring spirit of attack generally remains the best guarantee for the success of the flamethrower. The flame attack is the best flame defense."[6]

Preparations for the Kaiser's Battle: March Companies

Reddemann wrote that flamethrowers had to be deployed in large numbers if they were to play a decisive role in the Kaiser's Battle. To meet the requirements of this new kind of position warfare, the regiment underwent a fundamental reorganization.[7] When flamethrower squads broke through the enemy positions and continued advancing with the infantry, they would have to take with them a minimum amount of supplies in order to retain combat effectiveness. Each man would need a greatcoat, a groundsheet, and three days' provisions, while the flamethrower squad itself would require a supply of flame oil, nitrogen, igniters, and reserve flamethrowers, all following closely behind.

For this reason, the twelve field companies of the regiment were reorganized as March Companies (*Marsch-Kompagnien*), each composed of three March Platoons (*Marsch-Züge*) and one Ordnance Platoon (*Gerät-Zug*).

Wex squads practicing an assault on a captured British Mark IV tank. British tanks were vulnerable to frontal flame attacks, where the burning oil could seep through the vision ports and hatches. Bernhard Reddemann once volunteered to experience a flamethrower attack from inside a captured Mark IV, which he quickly abandoned when the oxygen was almost immediately burnt up. Imperial War Museum Q.43463.

Below: A flamethrower pioneer opens the propellant-release valve on a Doppelgrof M.1916 while a Wex carrier prepares to go over the top. Behind them a Grof squad sprays unlit oil onto a burning patch of ground to enlarge the intimidating wall of black smoke. Courtesy Maurice Sublet.

Each March Platoon consisted of a combat platoon (*Kampfzug*), a replacement troop (*Ersatztrupp*), and a maintenance section (*Gefechtstross*). The combat platoon was composed of four *Wex* squads (*Wextrupps*), one machine-gun squad, and one grenade-launcher squad; each *Wex* squad was

Infantry assault troops accompanied by Wex squads. The two men second and third from the right advance together with one Wex, while the soldier on the right carries both flamethrower and lance by himself. Regulations called for Wex carriers to march with the lance at right shoulder arms so that they could spring instantly into action.

armed with two flamethrowers and reinforced with extra men. If necessary, the personnel of the grenade-launcher squad could be equipped as a fifth *Wex* squad armed with two reserve devices, bringing the total number of flamethrowers in the platoon to ten.

The replacement troop of each March Platoon was equipped with two-wheeled horse-drawn carts. On the march, these vehicles advanced behind the combat platoons, loaded with weapons and small reserves of equipment and flame oil. Every member of the combat platoon carried his own marching pack; when the combat platoon was about to be inserted, or if the replacement troop had to be left behind because of heavy enemy fire or because the advance was somehow blocked, the flamethrower squads left their packs on the carts of the replacement troop and retrieved their flamethrowers, machine guns, and grenade launchers.

Following the three replacement troops of the March Company were three trucks, one for each combat platoon. These vehicles were manned by the maintenance sections and carried fuel oil, nitrogen, igniters, and reserve equipment. The remaining men of each combat platoon marched near their replacement troop and maintenance section. When circumstances warranted, the maintenance section and replacement troop refilled the empty devices and returned them to the combat platoon.

Behind the three March Platoons advancing with the infantry regiment was the company Ordnance Platoon. It consisted of trucks carrying additional fuel oil, nitrogen, igniters, reserve devices, aerial grenades, and hand grenades. The maintenance sections of the three combat platoons replenished their supplies from the company Ordnance Platoon; men of the regimental Experimental Company (*Versuchs-Kompagnie*) also rode with the Ordnance Platoon. They undertook minor repair work on the equipment so that it would not have to be returned to the regimental workshops in the rear.

For longer advances with more frequent insertions, the March Companies were brought up by three battalion truck columns. These columns were resupplied from the three flamethrower depots set up in the sector covered by each battalion, and the three depots were replenished from the two permanent regimental pioneer parks at Nouzon and Avesnes (later St. Quentin) respectively.

Breakthrough Battles on the Western Front

March 21 to July 17

Ludendorff launched five offensives on the western front between March 21 and July 17. Although these failed operations cost the Germans their best assault troops and devastated their morale, one would never know from reading Bernhard Reddemann's history of the Guard Reserve Pioneer Regiment. The irrepressible Prince of Hades referred to the offensives as the Breakthrough Battles (*Durchbruchsschlachten*), omitting all reference to their outcome. His writing was nearly incandescent with optimism:

> The special joy of attack pulsed through all, down to the last man, as they went into these battles. The prospect

Above: Members of the Experimental Company of the Garde-Reserve-Pionier-Regiment testing a Kleif M.1917. The Kleif carrier wears thick leather kneepads and lacks both Guard lace and a death's head sleeve badge; he also appears to have an all-green Jäger bayonet knot. The 4.6ft. (1.4m) small lance has yet to be armed with the igniter, which the pioneer furthest to the right holds in his right hand.

Below: Grof squad armed with a 5ft. (1.5m) large lance covers the advance of a Wex squad. For his dual role as replacement and grenadier, the Wex assistant bringing up the rear is equipped with two grenade sacks. Courtesy Thierry Ehret.

> of the coming of a final victory and the end of the war appeared for all to see. The advance of the flamethrowers in all of the different combat sectors during these battles was once again excellent. Resolute in the face of death, the men stormed forward with the infantry.[8]

At the start of Operation Michael, the 1st, 6th, 8th, 9th, 10th, 11th, and 12th March Companies were inserted on the western front. Each was equipped with thirty *Wex* flamethrowers, three light machine guns, and three grenade launchers to divide up among its three March Platoons. The seven March Companies were transferred to attack divisions (*Angriffsdivisionen*) that distributed them by platoon to their infantry regiments. There was a total of twenty-one flamethrower platoons for the forty-two attack divisions of the Second, Seventeenth, and Eighteenth Armies. As later breakthroughs were attempted in other sectors on the western front, the March Companies were shifted around. Beginning on May 27 the 3rd, 5th, and 7th March Companies were also brought into the western front for single engagements.[9]

The task organization for *Jäger* (Assault) Battalion No. 3 on March 21, 1918, is an example of how flamethrowers were distributed among attack divisions. The 1st Assault Company was assigned to the 79th Reserve Infantry Division, bringing with it two infantry guns and one platoon from the 1st March Company of the Guard Reserve Pioneer Regiment, armed with ten *Wex*. Similarly the 4th Assault Company was sent to the 18th Infantry Division; its assets consisted of two light mortars, two infantry guns, one machine-gun company, and one platoon from the 1st March Company of the Guard Reserve Pioneer Regiment, armed with ten *Wex*. The 3rd Assault Company was assigned to the 50th Reserve Infantry Division with two light mortars, two infantry guns, one machine-gun company, and the assault battalion's own flamethrower platoon, which had seven *Wex*. Thus *Jäger* (Assault) Battalion No. 3 went into battle with a total of twenty-seven small flamethrowers.[10]

In his history Reddemann listed 105 attacks on the western front from March 21 to July 17, of which only six were not successful. Illustrating his meticulous record keeping is his summation of the actions in Battle Sector Arras-St. Quentin-La Fère from March 21 to April 4, in which the following March Companies were engaged:

> The 1st March Company with Infantry Regiment No. 31 and No. 86 at Hargicourt (two attacks).
>
> The 6th March Company with Reserve Infantry Regiment No. 80 and No. 87, and Infantry Regiment No. 115 and No. 117 at La Vacquerie, Hargicourt, and Villeret (three attacks).
>
> The 8th March Company with Reserve Infantry Regiment No. 104 and No. 107 at Boursies and Demicourt (four attacks).
>
> The 9th March Company with Infantry Regiment No. 128 and No. 463, and Bavarian Infantry Regiment No. 1 at the village of Urvillers between St. Quentin and Grugies; and between Itancourt and Urvillers. Later with Infantry Regiment No. 463 and Bavarian Infantry Regiment No. 24 at the villages of Roye sur Matz, Boulogne la Graffe, and Rollet (five attacks).
>
> The 10th March Company with Infantry Regiment No. 41, No. 452, and No. 453 northwest of Bullecourt and at the villages of Bullecourt, Croisilles, and Ecoust. Later with Infantry Regiment No. 28 and No. 63 at Monchy le Preux (five attacks).
>
> The 11th March Company with Infantry Regiment No. 53, No. 158, and No. 211 between St. Quentin and Savy and at the village of Roupy (three attacks).
>
> The 12th March Company with Infantry Regiment No. 352 and No. 426 at Holnon Woods and at Fayet. Later with Reserve Infantry Regiment No. 242 at village of Mailly-Raineval (four attacks).
>
> In addition, detached flamethrower platoons from the 6th, 9th, and 10th March Companies fought with assault battalions at Gricourt and at the villages of Channy, Grivesnes, and St. Gobain (four attacks).
>
> Of these thirty attacks, two were unsuccessful.[11]

Three Leutnants of the Garde-Reserve-Pionier-Regiment in their billet, enjoying tea with bread and jam. The men in the center and on the right wear their death's head badges on the cuffs of their sleeves, in the position prescribed for enlisted men. It could be that these are former noncommissioned officers only recently promoted. Courtesy Thierry Ehret.

The Changeable Fighting of the Breakthrough Battles

During this period the staffs of the three flamethrower battalions stayed close to the front in order to more easily supervise and instruct the March Companies in tactics and technical matters. Another reason the staffs wanted to be on hand was to consult with the various armies' divisional and regimental headquarters regarding replenishment of supplies such as fuel oil. The flamethrower regiment's tactical operations staff also went forward with the headquarters of the many army corps.[12]

From March 21 to July 17 the Death's Head Pioneers generally served either as shock troops that spearheaded frontal attacks to break through the enemy line, or as flame accompanying squads that escorted the infantry, mopped up, and were sent against specific points of resistance as the need arose. According to Reddemann, the platoons used a great number of flamethrowers against a wide variety of tenaciously defended targets. The men would begin the day with trench fighting that in short order might evolve into street fighting, then house-to-house fighting, then fighting in tunnels, woods, caves, mine galleries, barracks, blockhouses, bunkers, or dugouts.

The fighting of March 21 embodied what Reddemann called his regiment's "magnificent achievements":

> Platoon of the 8th March Company under *Leutnant* Reicherdt engaged in trench and village fighting at Louvervall and Doignies.
>
> Platoon of the 6th March Company under *Leutnant* Müller engaged in trench fighting at Villeret.
>
> Platoon of the 6th March Company under *Leutnant* Böttcher engaged in trench and house-to-house fighting at Hargicourt.
>
> Two platoons of the 9th March Company under *Leutnant* Saeckel and *Offizier-Stellvertreter* Sommerfeld silenced machine-gun nests and smoked out dugouts south of St. Quentin.
>
> Platoon of the 9th March Company under *Leutnant* Springmeyer engaged in trench fighting south of St. Quentin during which it smoked out cellars and dugouts.
>
> Platoon of the 9th March Company under *Leutnant* Terjung engaged in trench fighting north of St. Quentin during which it silenced machine-gun nests and smoked out dugouts.
>
> Platoon of the 10th March Company under *Leutnant* Werther engaged in trench and village fighting at Ecoust.

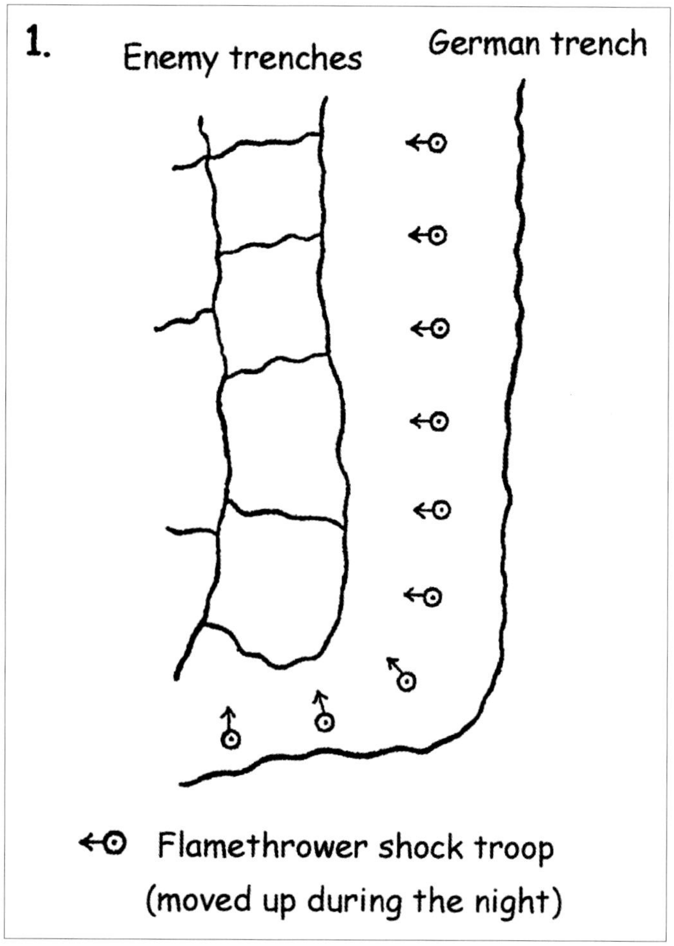

> Platoon of the 10th March Company under *Leutnant* Hermann Schmidt engaged in village fighting at Bullecourt-Croisilles during which it silenced machine-gun nests and smoked out blockhouses.
>
> Platoon of the 11th March Company under *Leutnant* Hoffmann engaged in trench and village fighting on the St. Quentin-Savy Road.[13]

Flamethrower Attack at Croisilles

Reddemann cited one action as the model of what he called the even more courageous way that the men of the flamethrower regiment discharged their duties during the breakthrough battles.[14]

On March 21 the advancing Germans encountered a British machine-gun post east of Croisilles, in a sector that had been heavily shelled and mostly evacuated. Almost impervious in their concrete pillbox, the British put up a remarkably stiff resistance with seven strongly built-in weapons. Since artillery could not destroy the position, infantry assault troops were sent against it, but each attempt was repulsed with heavy

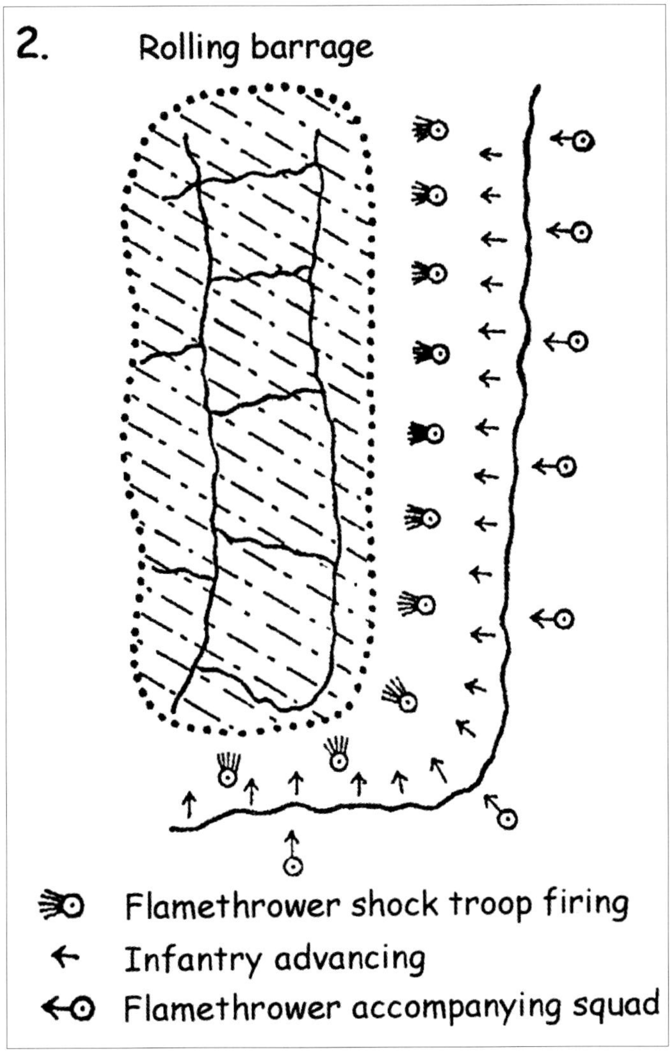

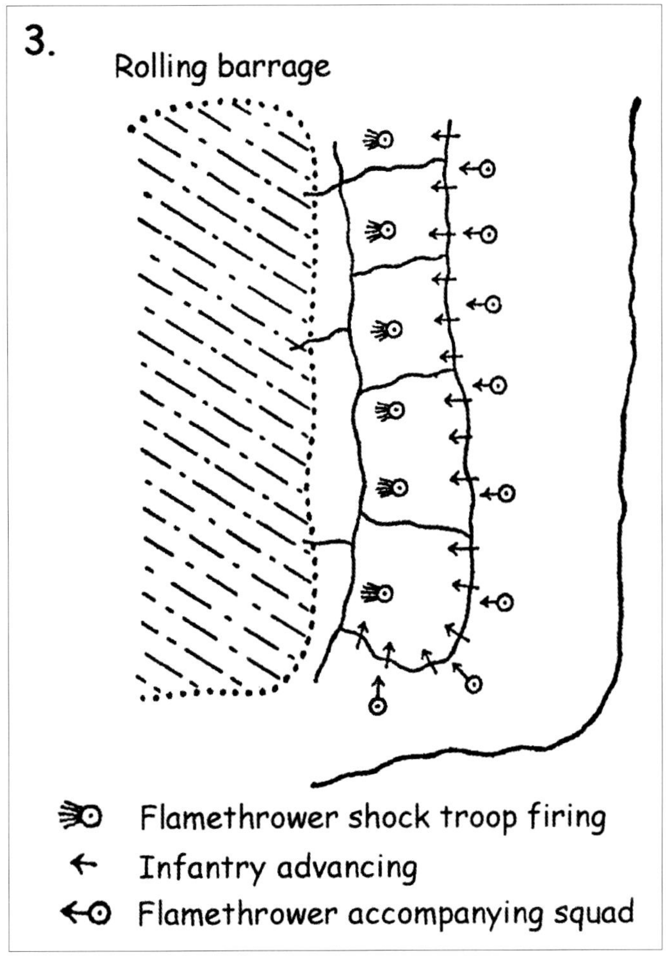

casualties to the Germans. One of the infantry battalions had attached to it a flamethrower half-platoon (*Halbzug*) from the 10th March Company of the Guard Reserve Pioneer Regiment, armed with six small flamethrowers and under the command of *Unteroffizier* Grund. This unit was given the order to silence the machine-gun nest, which lay more than 1,000 yards ahead.

Unteroffizier Grund divided his half-platoon into two flame shock troops of ten men and three flamethrowers each. They immediately launched into Indian-style Forward Stalking in wide arcs, while the infantry assault troops concealed themselves and tried to distract the British machine-gun position with heavy fire. The two flamethrower shock troops were able to advance for a short distance in a shallow communication ditch, then they had to cross open terrain individually, sprinting from cover to cover. They came under machine-gun fire from a tank on their left; instead of retreating, they turned and attacked the tank. Two flamethrower pioneers were killed, but the rest slowly approached the tank diagonally in a flanking maneuver until they were close enough to fire two streams through a pistol port, which silenced the machine gun.

The bright jets of burning oil apparently alerted the garrison of the British machine-gun position because several weapons opened fire, killing one member of the right-hand shock troop and wounding another. The survivors were pinned down in a shell hole while *Unteroffizier* Grund and the other shock troop crept up on the machine-gun post from the left. As Grund's troop reached a battered section of trench behind the position, they were spotted and fired upon by British infantry. The Germans responded with a flame jet, killing the riflemen. Grund's shock troop then sprayed a covering jet, which allowed one or more flamethrower squads to approach the machine-gun post and fire through the loopholes.

"One could hear the enemy screaming and moaning loudly," noted Reddemann. "They ran out of the exits wailing painfully with arms held high, some of them burned."[15]

Three British officers, seventy-two men, and seven machine guns were captured by nine flamethrower pioneers. More importantly, a stubborn obstacle was removed from the German advance. For his bravery *Unteroffizier* Grund was promoted to *Vizefeldwebel*.

Flamethrowers Used to Kill British Prisoners?

Reddemann wrote that on March 28 a platoon of the 10th March Company under *Leutnant* Schade engaged in trench fighting at Monchy le Preux, during which it silenced machine-gun nests and smoked out dugouts. He did not report the taking of prisoners, but this action was the subject of a postwar newspaper article claiming that the Germans at Monchy used flamethrowers to kill unarmed British soldiers who had already surrendered.

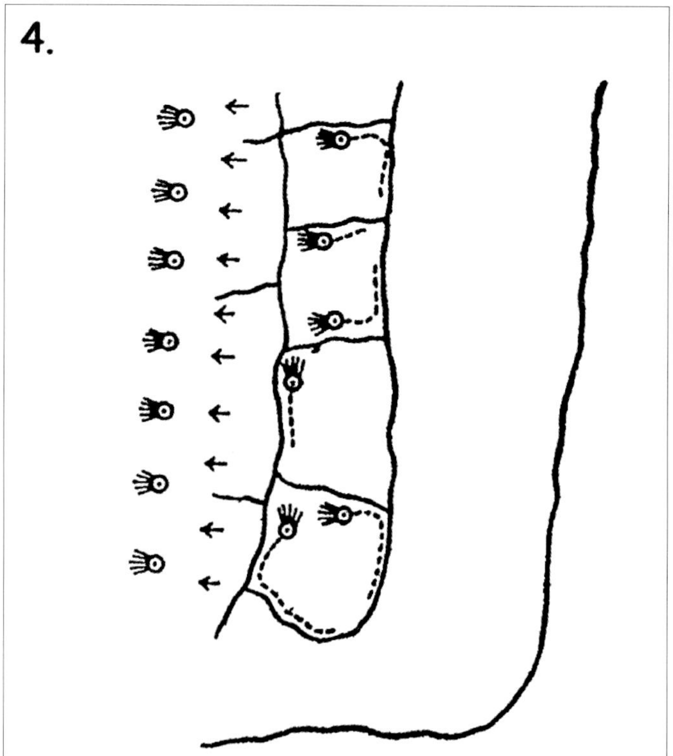

Flamethrower accompanying squads mop up last pockets of resistance.

Titled "Huns' Torture of Prisoners," the article quoted from affidavits by soldiers of the Royal Highlanders, who testified at an official government inquiry.[16] Three separate instances of British prisoners killed by flamethrowers on March 28 were presented. In the first, one officer and fifteen men, ten of them wounded, were lined up in their trench. A German officer and two men appeared; one of the men was ordered by the officer to spray the British prisoners with liquid fire, which he did for six or seven minutes. The witness testified that he and some of his companions escaped by running down a communication trench, climbing over the top, and making it back to the British lines.

Another private described how he and other prisoners were marched down a trench into an open-air emplacement. Tightly packed inside this enclosure, the British watched two Germans approach. One was an officer armed with a revolver, and the other had a cylinder on his back with a flexible pipe

Father-and-son portrait. The older man is a Wachmeister of Train-Bataillon Nr. 76, while his teenage son is a pioneer of Sturmbataillon Nr. 5 (Rohr). His sleeve badge of a white-metal crown above a W on a field-gray cloth oval was adopted unofficially by the battalion on February 18, 1918. An argument can be made that the flamethrower regiment was the more elite of the two units since the Kaiser personally bestowed its sleeve badge at the behest of the Crown Prince. Courtesy Maurice Sublet.

This group of officers from several branches of service includes a pilot in the center and a young Leutnant of the Garde-Reserve-Pionier-Regiment standing second from right. The flamethrower pioneer wears a privately purchased M.1915 blouse with high collar, Iron Cross First Class, and gray enlisted man's death's head badge above the cuff. Courtesy Thierry Ehret.

attached to it. This man sprayed hissing flame onto the British soldiers nearest to the entrance, who shrieked, writhed, and fell to the ground. His coat and tunic ablaze, the witness scrambled up the slope of the emplacement and got away.

In the third instance a soldier described how a wounded British officer, four wounded men, and three unwounded including himself were standing in an old trench when they were accosted by two Germans. One sprayed them with liquid fire, and the other brandished a revolver and ordered them to the German line. Three of the Britons managed to escape and reach their own positions, but the remaining five were never heard from again. The witness was burned on his right ear and both hands.

Almost ninety years later these anonymous statements can be neither proved nor disproved. One must ask if it is likely that flamethrower pioneers would expend their limited and difficult to replace supply of igniters and oil to kill harmless prisoners during a firefight. Furthermore, the witness in the first case claimed that the flamethrower was ignited for six or seven minutes, yet no apparatus in the German arsenal had such a duration.

It is also entirely possible that events occurred exactly as the witnesses testified, in which case Reddemann's men were guilty of committing inexcusable war crimes.

Review of the Breakthrough Battles

According to Reddemann, the reorganization of the flamethrower regiment into March Companies and March Platoons generally withstood the test of actual battle conditions. It showed that in a war of movement flamethrowers were successful in bringing down casualties among the infantry and quickly reducing exceptionally strong points of resistance. Reddemann also claimed that after initial inevitable problems related to the physical movement of combatants, the resupplying of his regiment with its needed chemical agents worked "faultlessly." So too did the integration of the flamethrower into the framework of infantry attack.

As a result, the flamethrower troops could look back with pride and satisfaction on the great breakthrough battles in the west, wrote their commander. They had especially distinguished themselves through their successes.[17]

Battles on Other Fronts, March 21 to July 17

During this period the remaining companies and the platoons attached to assault battalions took part in forty-nine flame combats on other fronts. Nine of these attacks were not successful.[18]

Thirty-seven of these actions were reconnaissance in force; of the remaining twelve, Reddemann singled out two.

On May 3 two platoons of the 9th Company under *Offizier-Stellvertreter* Sommerfeld and *Vizefeldwebel* Gmilkowsky assaulted Oise den Mont Renard near Pont Evèque. Armed with twelve *Wex*, they penetrated the enemy line and engaged in trench fighting, rolling up trenches and capturing buildings. Many prisoners were taken.

On May 27 all three platoons of the 6th Company under *Leutnants* Grosse and Schmidt and *Vizefeldwebel* Wosniak made a frontal pouncing attack southeast of Dickebusch-See in Flanders. Armed with twenty-four *Wex*, they penetrated the enemy line, rolled up trenches, silenced machine-gun nests, and took out points of resistance.

Flamethrower squad rolling up a mock trench with a Kleif M.1917. The effectiveness of flamethrowers in such a confined space can well be imagined. During training light-colored cloth helmet covers were worn for visibility rather than camouflage.

Flamethrowers and the German A7V Tank

The A7V tank (*Sturmpanzerkraftwagen*), of which only twenty examples were built, was produced in both "male" and "female" versions. Armament of the male A7V was one 57mm Belgian Maxim-Nordenfeldt cannon in the bow and six 7.62mm MG08 machine guns, two mounted in each side and the stern. The female version lacked the 57mm cannon and was designed to be armed with two small flamethrowers along with the six machine guns. Originally the flamethrowers were to be fired from inside the tank, a concept later abandoned in favor of having the vehicle simply carry the devices so that they could be used by the dismounted crew. Ultimately neither arrangement came to fruition.

As late as September 29, 1917, the War Ministry decreed that the armament of female A7Vs would include two flamethrowers,[19] but early trials with the new tank had already convinced the Motor Transportation Inspection Service (*Verkehrsteknische Prüfungs-Kommision*) that the idea was too complicated and dangerous, requiring specially trained engineers to operate the weapons.[20] Thus War Ministry orders written subsequent to September 29 stipulated only machine guns as armament for the female A7Vs. An unpublished typewritten study from 1932 reported that by late November of 1917, "Trials and reflections led to the decision not to carry flamethrowers inside the tanks. However, they might be held in readiness at certain designated locations in order to support assault troops in attacking tanks, especially in cases were field guns and mortars could not effectively work."[21]

In January of 1918 the Supreme Army Command sent Assault Tank Detachment No. 1 (*Sturmpanzerkraftwagen-Abteilung Nr. 1*) to Sedan for training. Crown Prince Wilhelm observed a demonstration of the Detachment's five A7Vs and suggested to the Supreme Army Command that the unit be sent to Beuville so that the crews could be trained by Assault Battalion No. 5 (Rohr). At the end of the month the new tank detachment therefore attended a six-week course that taught the crews how to function as shock troops when dismounted from their vehicles. They learned how to clear trenches with grenades and fire captured enemy machine guns, and the engineers and pioneers among them were taught how to use flamethrowers to roll up enemy positions.[22]

The training paid off on March 21, when Assault Tank Detachment No. 1 saw action in St. Quentin. Tanks 501 and 506 launched a flanking attack on a British position that was pinning down the German advance with its heavy machine-gun fire, mortars, and rifle grenades. The tanks were accompanied

Front de la Somme. — Tank allemand capturé.

Captured German A7V tank, only twenty of which were built. The "female" version of this eighteen-man vehicle was initially intended to carry two small flamethrowers, but the idea was rejected as too complicated and dangerous. Instead, the crew was trained to dismount and use flamethrowers pre-positioned by infantry assault troops.

Postcard showing a Kleif M.1917 painted in a camouflage pattern. The handwritten message on the back reads, "Dear parents and sister! I send you a card with a dangerous killing machine. It is a flamethrower. There is loud smoke and fire that come out from the front. If there is a spark you are lost beyond rescue. Everything else is fine. Goodbye. Best wishes from your son Karl." One wonders what sort of reaction Karl's family had on reading these words. Note that the assistant behind the lance operator is covering his left ear with his palm.

by the 1st Battalion of Infantry Regiment No. 28, the 2nd and 5th Assault Companies and 2nd Machine-gun Company of Assault Battalion No. 5 (Rohr), and a flamethrower platoon of the 9th Company of the Guard Reserve Pioneer Regiment. After the tanks successfully enfiladed the position with machine-gun and cannon fire,[23] the dismounted crews of the disabled Tanks 505 and 507 fought as shock troops, using hand grenades and flamethrowers to roll up the trenches from the flank.[24] The position was completely overrun and the British fled. Thirteen machine guns and much equipment were captured. Since the tanks did not carry flamethrowers, one has to wonder where the crews obtained them.

Strangely, the death book of the flamethrower regiment listed one name for March 21, 1918, at St. Quentin, but he was a member of the 11th Company.[25] All other sources state that the flamethrower platoon fighting at St. Quentin was from the 9th Company. It is possible that the pioneer, Ignatz Rogowski, had been transferred to the 9th Company but the paperwork had not yet been completed when he was killed.

Americans Experience Flamethrower Attacks

As Reddemann's breakthrough battles went on, the newly arrived Americans found out for themselves what their allies had faced since 1915. One of the first instances in which the doughboys were attacked with flamethrowers took place on March 8, in a sector northeast of Toul.[26] Described by a journalist as "the last remaining exhibit of the enemy's chamber of horrors to be tried on the Americans," the flamethrower reportedly made little impression on its intended targets, who "refused to be horrified or even scared" and blazed away with their rifles and machine guns.[27] The German shock troops were also targeted by a nearby American patrol, the members of which easily picked out the flamethrower operators behind the bright light of their flame jets.

Under fire by both the patrol in No Man's Land and the men in the trench, the Germans cut short their attack and fled. In their haste they discarded four complete *Wex* flamethrowers, two of the lances still burning and two having yet to be ignited.[28] No significant damage was done to the American position by the flames, aside from the scorching of some woodwork. Four *Wex* could mean that the raiders were a shock unit for rolling up a trench (*Stosseinheit in Form zum Aufrollen eines Schutzengrabens*) consisting of two *Wex* shock troops, two light machine-gun squads, one grenade-launcher squad, and one infantry squad.

The flamethrowers lay in No Man's Land for three days; the Americans tried several times to recover them but were prevented by German machine-gun fire. Eventually, a lieutenant and three men succeeded in bringing the devices in.[29] All of the flamethrowers had been punctured by bullets, and one was spattered with blood. Two were taken back to headquarters for examination.

In April doughboys moving into Picardy learned the value of flamethrowers from the French. *Poilus* came to the training grounds with Schilt No. 3 *bis*, apparatuses that resembled fire extinguishers, with a hose and nozzle connected to the side under the soldier's armpit. These engineers were attached to the American battalion assaulting Cantigny because the French wanted German prisoners for interrogation. They explained to the Americans that for bringing Germans out of

Above: American soldiers of the 18th Infantry Regiment displaying four Wex captured during a trench raid on March 6, 1918, at Menil-la-Tour, France. The lances all appear to be the 1917 model, two of which are missing the nozzle and/or igniter holder. U.S. National Archives 111-SC-8399. Below: Rear view of the same doughboys wearing their captured Wex. Note the wire support stand on the bottom of each ring-shaped oil tank. U.S. National Archives 111-SC-8400.

cellars with their hands up, there was nothing like a little spurt of flaming oil:

> The Doughboys of the 28th Regiment knew of these devices – six weeks before, in the sleet at Seicheprey, some untried buddies had been burned to death by German *Flammenwerfers* which suddenly appeared on the parapets during a brisk enemy raid.[30]

As mentioned previously, the flamethrower pioneers who launched that particular attack were a platoon of the 1st March Company. Their mission was a reconnaissance in force, for which they armed themselves with ten *Wex*. According to Reddemann the platoon formed shock troops that broke into the American line, rolled up trenches, and breached barricades.

Jean GrosJean, a doughboy of the 307th Infantry Regiment, recorded another flamethrower attack in his diary.

> In the early morning of June 24, Jerry pulled a raid on the first battalion at Neuville, killing and wounding some of our men. Our enemy here was the famous Prussian Guards. They used liquid fire most cruelly; burning to death 9 men from Company 'D.' The fire was so intense that it bent the men's rifles.[31]

The flamethrower pioneers in question were likely from the 11th Company. None were reported to have been killed.

On July 2 twenty-two men from B Company, 127th Infantry Regiment, were garrisoned at Post 54-a on the Rhône-Rhine Canal. Here the two sides were about 500 yards apart, in low and swampy terrain. At 3:00 A.M. the Americans heard the sound of metal against metal in No Man's Land, possibly pliers cutting through wire. A private named Murphy hurled a grenade:

> When the grenade burst there were startled exclamations and then night was like day lighted by three 50-foot tongues of searing, roaring flame which leaped out of the dark and licked hungrily at the listening post. Murphy had surprised a group of raiders out there equipped with three portable flammenwerfer or liquid flame throwers.[32]

According to German records, the raiders were men from *Landwehr* Infantry Regiment No. 382, accompanied by two, not three, *Wex* squads from Assault Battalion No. 16.[33] Private

Carte de visite by Otto Hoeffke of Berlin. This young flamethrower pioneer of the 11th Company, Garde-Reserve-Pionier-Regiment, poses in his full parade uniform consisting of M.1895 service jacket in dark blue, privately purchased spiked helmet, and light-gray overcoat. The edge of the overcoat has been pushed back to expose the death's head badge, which flamethrower pioneers were not authorized to wear on the blue tunic.

Murphy ducked under the flame jets and avoided injury. The Americans fired their rifles at the illuminated Germans, who replied with stick grenades and pistol shots. As the flames continued roaring into the post, one American launched a rifle grenade at the huddle of Germans and scored a direct hit. The flamethrowers died out and the pistol shots and shower of stick grenades ceased. Taking stock, the Americans found that only two of their number had been wounded.

Soon a shaking voice began moaning in German from No Man's Land, "Dear American brothers, I've been left behind. Help me! I'm in a lot of pain. I've been wounded."[34] The Americans listened for an hour, too wary to respond. Dawn revealed two dead Germans, two wounded, and a blood

Ohňomety.

trail from a trench raider who had escaped. The wounded were brought in and treated; one was an officer who in his agony complained that he had survived four years of war without a scratch, and now he had been badly hurt by a "bunch of greenhorns." Assault Battalion No. 16 reported one flamethrower pioneer killed and one wounded.[35] The dead flamethrower operator, *Pionier* Willy Uhde, belonged to the 4th Company of the Guard Reserve Pioneer Regiment.[36]

Still new to the war, the Americans struggled to collect accurate information about German flamethrowers and flame tactics. A pamphlet published by the Historical Section of the U.S. Army General Staff stated that the Germans were armed with "Wix[sic]" flamethrowers that were useful in combat against villages. The flamethrowers preceded the assault troops; when resistance was encountered, the flamethrower operators were to lie down and let the assault troops go forward to throw grenades.[37]

Although taken from German documents, this description does not comport with Reddemann's view of the flamethrower as a weapon of aggressive offense. Indeed, nowhere did the Prince of Hades recommend that his "dear little gray lads"[38] lie down and allow others to do their fighting for them.

Opposite

Top: Kaiser Wilhelm II and General der Infanterie Oskar von Hutier (1857-1934), Commander of the 8th Army, inspecting assault troops in late 1918. The soldiers in the front rank belong to various infantry and pioneer units. They are armed with 9mm Bergmann MP18/I submachine guns slung over their right shoulders. The man second from the left, directly behind the Kaiser's standard bearer, is a pioneer of the Garde-Reserve-Pionier-Regiment, identified by his black shoulder straps, Guard lace, and death's head sleeve badge. It is not known if flamethrower pioneers used submachine guns in combat.

Bottom: Flamethrower section of the 39th 'Vysocansky' Regiment, 6th Czech Division, Czech Legion. These specialists were trained by the Italian Arditi, who were themselves inspired by German and Austrian assault troops. The flamethrowers are Schilt No. 3 bis OFC, modified French devices. Personal weapons consist of Austrian Mannlicher M95 8mm Short Rifle "Stutzen" and trench daggers. On their upper left arms, the men wear the Italian flamethrower qualification badge, a black winged dragon puffing out red flames, its body wrapped around a silver staff above a silver Savoy knot.

CHAPTER ELEVEN

August of 1918

From July 17 to the end of August, the March Companies and the platoons attached to the assault battalions fought nineteen times. After August 12 there were no more large-scale flamethrower operations, as the German army was essentially in retreat. Reddemann characterized the actions from mid-August to the end of the war as counterattacks against the pursuing enemy, small frontal or flanking attacks, the taking out of individual machine-gun nests, reconnaissance in force, and feints designed to draw enemy artillery fire away from other targets.[1] For the latter mission, the flamethrower troops were ordered to go out and fire their weapons in such a way

Ten Unteroffiziere of the Garde-Reserve-Pionier-Regiment, three of whom have been awarded the Iron Cross, First Class. At least two of the men wear their "work clothes" – uniforms lacking the prestigious death's head sleeve badge. The date and place of this image is not known.

that they would be seen and immediately shelled, another task for which the men would be required to draw on their "death-defying joy of combat."

Flamethrowers on the Vesle

Even in retreat the Germans were able to inflict appalling casualties on the fresh, numerically superior Americans, as shown by the fighting in Fismette, a suburb of Fismes separated from the town by the Vesle River. When the Americans moved into Fismes on August 3, the Germans withdrew their largest artillery to the Aisne, 5 miles to the north of the city:

> Lighter field pieces in great numbers crowned the high ground near the Vesle, and machine guns held their usual prominent place in the German scheme. Once more they brought their flame projectors into play, using them in this instance at what is believed to have been the greatest distance they tried to operate these weapons during the war. They accomplished little with the "flamenwerfer," however.[2]

As Reddemann had long since declared the flamethrower strictly a close-combat weapon, firing it from great distances makes little sense. A possible explanation is that the Americans witnessed flame signals and mistook them for a raid.

For most of August the Americans and Germans in Fismette engaged in horrific house-to-house fighting amidst endless shelling, mustard-gas attacks, and sniper and machine-gun fire from the surrounding hills. Lieutenant Hervey Allen of the 111th Infantry Regiment, 28th Division, was evacuated after four days. In his memoir he described a flamethrower assault of August 14:

> Suddenly along the top of the hill there was a puff, a rolling cloud of smoke, and then a great burst of dirty, yellow flame. By its glare I could see Gerald standing halfway up the hill with his pistol drawn. It was the Flammenwerfer, the flame throwers; the men along the crest curled up like leaves to save themselves as the flame and smoke rolled over them. There was another flash between the houses. One of the men stood up, turning around outlined against the flame – "Oh! my God! he cried. "Oh! God!"[3]

Flamethrower platoons from the 9th Company of the Guard Reserve Pioneer Regiment fought at Fismette. Two pioneers

American soldiers modeling a captured Wex and an M.1917 small lance, which differed from the M.1916 in that the igniter fork was attached to a hinged flap, eliminating the need for a retaining chain. This lance has not been fitted with an igniter, and the wire stand on the bottom of the ring-shaped Wex has been bent outward. U.S. National Archives 111-SC-29489.

were killed on August 12, and one was killed in Fismes on August 22.[4]

On August 17 the Americans preempted a flamethrower attack in Ville Savoye, another town on the Vesle. Lieutenant MacDougall of E Company, 308th Infantry Regiment, captured the first German prisoner – a "blonde German youth" – credited to the 77th Division:

> Catching a glimpse of a crouching form, and with no time to draw my pistol I grabbed and pulled a very much terrorized Boche down the side of the cut to the railroad tracks below, assisted by Sergeant Powers. The Division's first prisoner was taken and proved to be the leader of a combat patrol of eight men, some of the number carrying tanks of liquid fire. They retreated when they heard the startling cry of their leader. I recall his wanting to know when he would be shot. After being assured he had twenty minutes to live, he attempted to bribe us by giving valuable information concerning the enemy positions as far as he knew.[5]

The German was stripped of his weapon and equipment, including four "potato masher" hand grenades. He was escorted to Regimental Headquarters and interrogated, his story corroborating the regimental intelligence report. The prisoner's unit was not disclosed in this account, but since his eight-man patrol was armed with multiple flamethrowers, it is likely that he was a Death's Head Pioneer leading a reinforced *Wex* squad.

In late August the German 29th Division organized two major attacks on the American 77th Division on the Vesle.[6] The first, called either Operation America (*Unternehmen Amerika*) or Operation Border Guard (*Unternehmen Grenzschutz*), was launched on August 22. A *Hauptmann* Petersson led ten shock troops composed of men from the 1st Battalion of Baden Infantry Regiment No. 112, the 9th and 10th Companies of Baden Infantry Regiment No. 113, the 1st Company of Pioneer Battalion No. 14, and six flamethrower squads from the 9th Company of the Guard Reserve Pioneer Regiment.

The goal of Operation America/Border Guard was to destroy bridges over the Vesle. Six of the ten shock troops were accompanied by one flamethrower squad each. The result of the mission was two officers and thirty-one men of the American 308th Infantry Regiment captured. One German report stated that the flamethrowers could not be easily moved through obstructed areas, perhaps indicating that they were *Kleif* instead of the smaller *Wex*. In addition, they "partly sprayed their oil too early and provided only a very limited support for the infantry."[7]

I and K Companies of the 308th Infantry Regiment suffered heavy casualties during the fighting in and around Ville Savoye on August 21 and 22. The German assault came after a heavy barrage of high-explosive shells; fierce close-quarter fighting followed:

> Company I, as was later learned from prisoners, was attacked by four companies of Baden troops accompanied by a detachment of pioneers with flame-throwers. These flamenwerfer[sic] did considerable damage, though it is supposed that all belonging to this command were killed by the men of I Company with the exception of those who were burned to death by their own hands through getting the nozzles of their machines entangled in the heavy underbrush of the swamp.[8]

In the American view, the flamethrowers were very effective, even though some Death's Head Pioneers were alleged to have been killed by their own carelessness.

Company K was also engaged by flamethrowers. A jet of liquid fire penetrated the shelter housing Company Headquarters; Private Edwin T. Van Duzer, a member of a combat-liason team, was severely burned on the face and

Double Kleif photographed at Verdun in 1918. This example consists of two Kleif M.1917 attached by a 5ft. hose and a 10ft. hose to a 5ft. (1.5m) large lance. The double Kleif seems an almost nightmarishly awkward weapon in that it forced a crowd of seven men to move together as one. Courtesy Maurice Sublet.

Right: Two well-groomed young pioneers, possibly brothers. The flamethrower operator on the right has been awarded a silver or gold wound badge, and although he is an enlisted man, his death's head badge is worn above the cuff of his M.1915 blouse in the position usually reserved for officers and Offizier-Stellvertretere. Photographic evidence shows that this was a relatively common practice, the significance of which is not known. One speculation is that the higher position was used by the members of the flamethrower platoon of Sturmbataillon Nr. 5 (Rohr) to differentiate themselves from Reddemann's men. Courtesy Ronny Pobucky.

Below: Flamethrower squad training with a Kleif M.1917 and 4.6ft. (1.4m) small lance. The lance operator wears oil-stained grenade bags and an early steel helmet with a square-dip visor. He is spraying fluid onto the ground in front of him; this and the lack of an igniter indicate that the flamethrower is likely filled with water. U.S. National Archives 165-GB-7270.

body. There are two different versions of what happened next. One writer claimed that the burning Van Duzer was thrown into a pool of water by a comrade. After the flames had been extinguished, Van Duzer made his way through the woods to Company Headquarters, even though only two paragraphs earlier in the same account he was reported to have been burned *at* Company Headquarters.[9]

His location notwithstanding, the wounded man – hatless and coatless, face blistered – informed his captain that I Company still held the line. After being heavily bandaged, Van Duzer started for the aid station but soon returned with the news that a dozen "Dutchmen" were in the woods behind the headquarters building. He then accompanied five men into the woods to show them where he'd seen the enemy. When a German-speaking member of the party called for the soldiers to surrender, a young "Boche" appeared and asked if they would be killed:

Undated photo of officers from the flamethrower regiment, including Bernhard Reddemann in the center, beneath the clock. They are identified only by name, not seating position. Present are Hauptmann Beck and Leutnants Hevelke, Meyer, Hoffmann, and Baruthio. Note the silver death's head sleeve badge, undress "small jacket" (kleiner Rock), and smock (Litewka) worn by the three men on the right.

> He was assured that Americans don't kill prisoners, and disclosed the fact that several of his comrades were in the woods. They were found and marched to the railroad track in their favorite "Kamerad" attitude, led by a sergeant-major, who disclosed the fact that the attack had been made by a battalion, with orders to drive the American outposts beyond the Vesle River before 4:45 A.M. It was a regular raiding party, equipped with light machine guns, hand grenades and flame-throwers. All the prisoners had been told that capture by the Americans meant instant death, and in their gratitude at being spared, they turned out their pockets, furnishing an abundance of souvenirs, among which was a large package of British cigarettes.[10]

German morale must have been at rock bottom for a *Wex* or *Kleif* shock troop armed with flamethrowers, grenades, and machine guns to surrender to six Americans without a fight and immediately disclose their orders. Bernhard Reddemann would not have been pleased.

Private Van Duzer later received the Distinguished Service Cross, something the previous writer neglected to mention. The text of the citation gave a significantly different version of what he did on August 22:

> For extraordinary heroism in action near Ville Savoye, France, August 22, 1918. He was a member of a combat liaison group which was attacked by liquid fire. Although severely burned, he alone charged the flame thrower and put him out of action, after which he reassembled his men and continued on duty until relieved.[11]

The 9th Company of the Guard Reserve Pioneer Regiment provided the flamethrower operators for this assault, but the regimental death book recorded no names for August 22. Seven flamethrower pioneers from the 4th Company died in

Above: Kleif M.1917, which was used until the end of the war. When surprise and mobility were necessary, flamethrower squads often went into combat wearing field caps and leaving behind their packs, belts, bayonets, and ammunition pouches. For personal protection, they carried unholstered pistols in their jacket pockets.

Below: Possibly a reinforced flamethrower shock troop (verstärkter Flammenwerferstosstrupp) consisting of three small-flamethrower squads, two NCOs as shock-troop leaders, and six hand-grenade throwers. They pose with an officer, the young man in the center who has been awarded the Iron Cross First Class. The P08 pistols, respirators, and flower-decorated French army caps worn by four of the men place this photo on the western front, perhaps immediately after an engagement.

Courcelles on August 23,[12] which was clearly a separate event. Once again there is no satisfactory explanation for this major discrepancy between the combatants' accounts of the same action.

The second major assault organized by the German 29th Infantry Division was launched on August 27.[13] This was Operation Baden (*Unternehmen Baden*). A *Major* Grohe commanded thirteen shock troops composed of men from the 1st Battalion of Baden Infantry Regiment No. 113, the 3rd Battalion of Baden Infantry Regiment No. 142, and flamethrower pioneers from the 9th Company of the Guard Reserve Pioneer Regiment. Eight of the thirteen shock troops were accompanied by one flamethrower squad each. The goal of Operation Baden was to take Fismette, which the Germans accomplished on August 28. Three officers and 254 men from the American forces were captured, mostly from the 307th Infantry Regiment. In addition, the two companies of the 112th Infantry Regiment holding Fismette lost 165 of their 206 men.

Three flamethrower pioneers and one *Unteroffizier* were killed in Fismette on August 27.[14]

Italian Leaflet Dropped to the Austrians

As the morale of the Central Powers' fighting forces plummeted, the Allies stepped up their propaganda. One German-language Italian leaflet, dropped to the Austrians in 1918, was a map titled "Number 330: A Graphic View of the Gains of the Big Entente Offensive in France from 9 August to September." It pictured the opposing battle lines and showed the gains that the French had made during the dates mentioned. The text consisted of two sentences:

> The material results of the Entente offensive of July 15 to August 31. In this offensive the Allies captured 128,000 German prisoners of war; 2,674 officers; 2,069 artillery pieces; 1,734 flamethrowers; 13,783 machine guns; and an extensive amount of ammunition, equipment, and other material.

These figures must be viewed with caution because if they were accurate, it would mean that in six weeks the Allies captured twice the total number of flamethrowers held by the twelve combat companies of the Guard Reserve Pioneer Regiment.

The handwritten message on the back of this postcard identifies these four soldiers as attendees of flamethrower school. They are uniformed in the M.1915 blouse, and two have black wound badges authorized in March of 1918. The seated Sergeant wears a small metal death's head on his left cuff; this is a cap badge from 1 Leib-Husaren Regiment Nr. 1. Flamethrower pioneers did not receive their official sleeve badge until they were transferred into the Garde-Reserve-Pionier-Regiment. Courtesy Maurice Sublet.

Americans Awarded for Courage Facing Liquid Fire

The following men were awarded the Distinguished Service Cross of the United States for actions taken while being subjected to flamethrower attacks.

Corporal Van Horton, Company E, 366th Infantry Regiment. For extraordinary heroism in action near Lesseau, France, September 4, 1918:

> During a hostile attack, preceded by a heavy minenwerfer barrage, involving the entire front of the battalion, the combat group to which this courageous soldier belonged was attacked by about twenty of the enemy, using liquid fire. The sergeant in charge of the group and four other men having been killed, Corporal Horton fearlessly rushed to receive the attack and the persistency with which he fought resulted in stopping the attack and driving back the enemy.[15]

Late-war photo of Pionier L. Schulze. He wears his death's head sleeve badge above the cuff of his simplified M.1910 field jacket, which could mean that he is a member of the flamethrower platoon of Sturmbataillon Nr. 5 (Rohr). Note the light-gray cloth strip (Mützenverdeckband) camouflaging the black band of the field cap, mandated on March 29, 1915. Despite the AKO of September 21, 1915, Schulze's uniform still displays outdated white Guard lace and field-gray shoulder straps.

This undated carte de visite of an older enlisted man serving in the Garde-Reserve-Pionier-Regiment was taken by Atelier Gebr. Barasch in Königsburg. The new M.1915 blouse with green collar, black shoulder straps, light-gray Guard lace, and death's head sleeve badge together represent the ideal appearance of the flamethrower pioneer late in the war.

Private Joe Williams, Company E, 366th Infantry Regiment. For extraordinary heroism in action near Lesseau, France, September 4, 1918:

> Private Williams was a member of a combat group which was attacked by twenty of an enemy raiding party, advancing under heavy barrage and using liquid fire. The sergeant in charge of the group was killed and several others, including Private Williams, were wounded. Nevertheless, this soldier with three others fearlessly resisted the enemy until they were driven off.[16]

Second Lieutenant John C. Duffy, Company F, 53rd Infantry Regiment. For extraordinary heroism in action near Landersbach, Alsace, October 4, 1918:

> During an attack by a German raiding party of about 300 men he took command of a post where the five men manning it had been killed or wounded by liquid fire. By his coolness and fearless exposure of himself he was able to hold the post with a small reinforcement. After the raid he removed some twenty grenades which had become dangerously hot, due to the fire, and were about to explode.[17]

The Aerial Flamethrower

There exists at least one eyewitness account of Germans firing flamethrowers from low-flying aircraft. This undated narrative is credited to Frank Washington, rank unknown, of B Company, 371st Infantry Regiment. A native of Edgefield, South Carolina, Washington was wounded in the arm by an

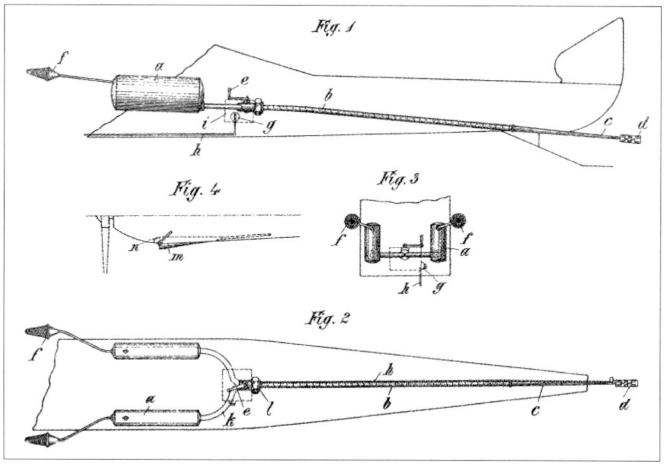

Patent for the Bunge Aircraft Flamethrower: (a) fuel container; (b) hose; (c) lance; (d) electric fuse; (e) supply cock; (f) compressed-air funnel; (g) fuse-control switch; (h) electrical fuse-control line connected to magneto; (i) insulated covering; (k) main fuel line; (l) hose connector; (m) funnel; (n) hood. At least one eyewitness account exists of such a flamethrower used in combat.

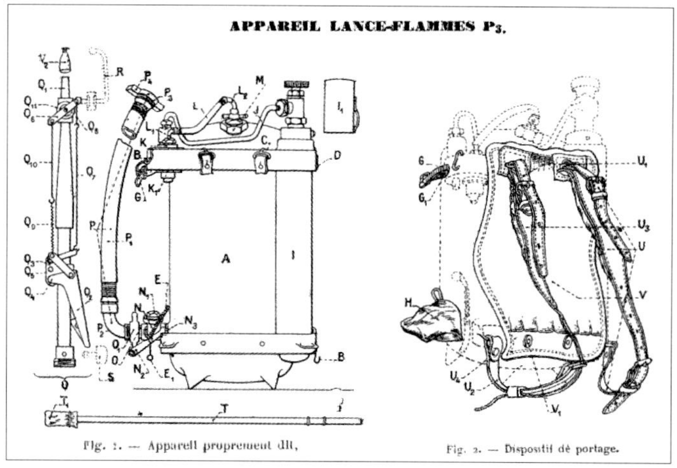

French P3 flamethrower, which was tested for suitability as an aircraft-mounted weapon. It held 3.7 gallons of oil, weighed fifty-three pounds, and had a range of ninety-two feet. The tests were not successful.

explosive bullet in the Champagne, and then he was strafed by German flame-planes:

> It was all bad, but the worst came when the German airplanes flew low and sprayed the wounded with liquid fire. There is no way of putting out that liquid flame, and no one can help you, because the fire spreads so quickly. It is bad enough to be helpless out there, without water or friends, but to have a hellfiend fly over and just squirt torture at you – well, the Indians or the savages of Africa were not much worse. They were not so bad, in fact, for they were savages – while the Germans are supposed to be civilized.
>
> A Hun plane flew over when I was wounded, but believe me, when I saw that fire coming I sure did some lively hopping around. There wasn't going to be any broiled Washington if I could help it. But some of the mortally wounded were burned to death. Those Huns should be made to pay for that sort of thing. It ain't fighting; it's concentrated hell! But we had to attend to their wounded, and one of our officers saw that we did it.[18]

On the face of it, the gripping story seems preposterous, just another "frightful Hun" propaganda tale. However, a design for an aircraft-mounted flamethrower has indeed been found in the German patent office.

Patent No.325694 was filed by Robert and Richard Bunge on February 15, 1918. The layout of the Bunge Aircraft Flamethrower called for two oil tanks to be mounted inside the fuselage of a two-seater, the lance protruding from beneath the tail and positioned to fire backward as the ship made a low strafing run in the manner of the "J" class of armored aircraft used for close-air support.

According to the Bunge patent, the flame gunner in the rear cockpit first opened forward-facing air funnels attached to the flamethrower oil tanks, allowing the aircraft's speed to pressurize the oil to a low level. The fuse-control switch on a small dashboard was turned to the setting "One," igniting the fuse with an electrical spark, and the supply cock was opened to spray a stream of pressurized oil out behind the aircraft. The entire load of oil could be delivered at once, or individual bursts could be fired by controlling the supply cock and reigniting the electric fuse using the dashboard switch.

As absurd as it seems, it therefore appears that the Germans actually did field an aerial flamethrower. Other than the eyewitness account and patent, more information is presently lacking. It is unknown if Death's Head Pioneers operated the system, or if members of the Army Air Service (*Luftstreitkräfte*) were trained in the capacity of flame gunner. From the near-total lack of documentation, one can assume that the weapon was not widely used.

It should be noted that a *Leutnant* Jünger of Assault Battalion No. 16 conducted unsuccessful experiments with Flying Detachment 223 (*Flieger-Abteilung 223*) on the feasibility of mounting flamethrowers in combat aircraft,[19] and the idea was also explored by the French, who described it in an incomprehensible postwar report:

The question of using aircraft provided with flamethrowers in order to set fire to enemy aviation hangers was studied. Tests were carried out at the Belgian aerodrome of Juvisy (May 1918), by trying out the P3 [flamethrower] on planes parked on the ground with the propeller spinning. A P3 apparatus was placed exactly on the extension of the axis of the propeller (maximum wind): the jets ignited irregularly because oil was thrown onto the fuse, resulting in poor ignition and failures. The experiment was redone, fitting a sort of cone between the fuel tap and the support of the fuse and including the fuse; a hole bored in the base plate allowed the lighting of the fuse. The ignition took place without failures; the range of the jet was approximately twenty-five meters. However, there was a rather strong spray, and the apparatus was drained quickly.[20]

German Pioneer Companies Receive Flamethrowers

War Ministry Order No. 1672. 18. G. A6, dated September 28, 1918, decreed that all pioneer companies on the western front would receive six portable flamethrowers each,[21] the number of devices that armed a platoon. Those pioneer companies attached to the infantry divisions would be equipped first. As the initial installment the companies were given two flamethrowers each, to be used by a "special unit" under the command of an officer. It is not known whether they were to be deployed offensively or defensively. The Guard Reserve Pioneer Regiment was not affected by this order. It retained its function as a combat formation that undertook difficult missions, a training school for the army, and the authority responsible for the further development of the weapon.

The Lost Battalion

Arguably the most famous flamethrower attacks of the First World War were launched against the American unit known as the Lost Battalion, a mixed formation from the 77th Division that included companies of the 307th and 308th Infantry Regiments and the 306th Machine Gun Battalion, some 554 men in total. As in the case of other major flame assaults, the opposing sides presented accounts that cannot be reconciled.

Men of the Garde-Reserve-Pionier-Regiment pose with line pioneers who are undergoing flamethrower training. Note the wooden mockup of a French FT-17 tank. A War Ministry order of September 29, 1918, decreed that each pioneer company on the Western Front would receive six Wex and form a flamethrower platoon commanded by an officer. Two Wex with M.1918 lances sit in front of the men; the Death's Head Pioneer on the far right and the pioneer third from the left hold igniters in their hands. Most of the line pioneers wear camouflaged helmets and rolled assault packs.

Above: A second photo of the same training ground. Two Wex squads combine the sprays of their weapons to form a single enormous jet. In the background sits the wooden FT-17 mockup. The spectator standing fifth from the right, hands in pockets, is a small boy in knee pants; his presence at a dangerous live-fire flamethrower exercise is inexplicable.

Right: Pioneer of the 2nd Company, Garde-Reserve-Pionier-Regiment, in a carte de visite taken in Berlin. Judging by his youth and the newness of his M.1915 blouse and M.1910 service cap, he is likely a new recruit. He has also adopted the stance of the proud flamethrower pioneer, left hand cocked on hip to display the death's head sleeve badge. Courtesy Gregg DuBois.

What is not in dispute is that the Americans were cut off from the rest of their division in the Argonne and subjected to a siege from October 2 to October 7, 1918. Under the command of Major Charles Whittlesey, the Lost Battalion – low on food, water, and ammunition – was surrounded and attacked unremittingly by the Germans, who assaulted the position with machine guns, snipers, grenades, mortars, and artillery. Since none of these worked, shock troops armed with flamethrowers were sent in on October 6:

> There were sudden shouts and a man came charging down the hill to Whittlesey. "Liquid fire!" he shouted.
>
> "Liquid hell!" retorted the Major. "Get back there where you belong." Everybody could hear him.
>
> A long pennon of sissing, smoky black slashed through the leaves and among the brown trunks, a hundred feet or more, its drops shedding into little fiery pools whenever they touched anything – liquid fire sure enough, the most dreaded, though actually one of the least dangerous German methods of attack. All around on the flank where it had come men were swearing and sobbing, letting off their guns blindly in a kind of wild fury over this final barbarity. Another slash of it and another, half a dozen of them, and arching above it the potato mashers with their violent shock.[22]

An American shot the large German sergeant running behind the flamethrowers, hitting him between the eyes. On the right flank doughboys with Chauchat machine rifles mowed down the flamethrower operators, bringing the attack to a sudden halt.

Infantry assault troops training late in the war. Hidden among the trenches and shrubbery is at least one Wex squad. The legendary Lost Battalion of the American Expeditionary Force endured multiple assaults on similar terrain, October 2-7, 1918.

The report of Reserve Infantry Regiment No. 254 to the 76th Reserve Division Headquarters, signed by *Hauptmann* von Sybel, summed up the day's action as a long attack with the support of hand grenades and flamethrowers that won some ground from the *Amerikanernest*. Two light machine guns and one heavy were captured, along with nine badly wounded prisoners who were not expected to live.[23]

The flamethrower attack had created a break in Whittlesey's line that was quickly repaired. Only two Americans had been killed, but the liquid fire had impacted the doughboys' morale. Soldiers whispered to each other in dread, reflecting the growing irresoluteness in the mental state of the command.

On October 7 the Germans captured an American and told him that a new battalion of shock troops would arrive in the afternoon, bringing with them enough flamethrowers to burn off the entire side of the hill. The American soldier returned to Whittlesey with a letter from the German commanding officer, which contained an appeal to the major's humanity:

> The Major glanced from letter to messenger. Then passed the note back to McMurty, who read through it, then handed it to Holderman, who had just joined them. The three officers looked at each other, and as though by a common impulse all grinned – that appeal to "human sentiments" from the man who had been directing flame-thrower attacks against them.[24]

Whittlesey refused to reply to the surrender demand. An intense German attack followed in the afternoon, the heaviest that the Americans had yet experienced. The doughboys defiantly shouted obscenities, including the German word *Windbetreben*, which supposedly meant the noise made by a horse with diarrhea. Shock troops armed with flamethrowers were again used; on the right flank, a Chauchat gunner fired on them pointblank, "kindling the *Flammenwerfer* men into human torches."[25]

Ultimately, the Germans were unable to dislodge the Americans, who were rescued by their division on the night of October 7. Only 194 of the original 554 were able to walk out unassisted.

The German units that fought the Lost Battalion were Reserve Infantry Regiment No. 254, a battalion of dismounted Uhlans, *Landwehr* Infantry Regiment No. 122, Pioneer Battalion No. 376, and Pioneer Companies 76 and 77.[26] Assault Battalion No. 2 also provided two NCOs, a sixteen-man shock troop, eight rifle grenadiers, and fifteen flamethrower operators armed with five portable devices, model unknown.[27]

Losses to the shock troop were two dead and one wounded. The Americans reported several flamethrower operators killed in both assaults, but the death book of the Guard Reserve Pioneer Regiment listed no names for October 6 or 7. Flamethrower pioneers attached to assault battalions remained members of the flamethrower regiment; as stated previously, they were regularly rotated back into the regiment for training.

There is no simple explanation for why the flamethrower regiment acknowledged no deaths for October 6 or 7, 1918. The attacks obviously took place, and it is unlikely that the men of the Lost Battalion lied or were mistaken. It could be that the German regimental historians were careless, or perhaps the flamethrower operators were not actually members of the Guard Reserve Pioneer Regiment. Another possibility is that the emphatic failure of the attacks led the Germans to simply pretend that they never happened. Since most records pertaining to the flamethrower regiment were destroyed during the Second World War, the truth may never be known.

Two very young members of Sturmbataillon Nr. 2, which carried out flamethrower attacks on the Lost Battalion October 6 and 7, 1918. For the mission the assault battalion provided two NCOs, a sixteen-man shock troop, eight rifle grenadiers, and fifteen flamethrower operators armed with five small devices.

Below: Flamethrower squad armed with a Kleif M.1917 and the 4ft. (1.2m) small lance firing a covering jet, used to screen the advance of assault troops. The Kleif carrier and lance operator both wear large sacks on their belts for carrying spare igniters.

Distribution of Flamethrower Companies October 1918

Near the end of the war, the component parts of the flamethrower regiment were distributed as follows:[28]

Units	*Army Groups and Armies*
Regimental Staff	Army Group Imperial Crown Prince
Experimental Company	
Recruit Depot	
1st Workshop Detachment	
Staff of 1st Battalion	Army Group Crown Prince Rupprecht of Bavaria
Staff of 2nd Battalion	Army Group Boehn, then Army Group Imperial Crown Prince
2nd Workshop Detachment	
Staff of 3rd Battalion	Army Group Albrecht von Württemberg
3rd Workshop Detachment	
1st Company	Sixth Army
2nd Company	Second Army, then Eighteenth Army
3rd Company	Seventh Army, then Third Army
4th Company	Seventeenth Army
5th Company	Fourth Army
6th Company	Second Army
7th Company	Fifth Army
8th Company	Seventh Army
9th Company	Seventh Army
10th Company	Army Detachment A, then Nineteenth Army
11th Company	First Army
12th Company	Army Detachment B

The End of Hostilities

The signing of the Armistice on November 11, 1918, was not welcomed by Bernhard Reddemann:

> And then came the bitter end of the campaign! Undefeated and crowned with glory, the divisions walked the retreat back to the homeland. With them came the battalions and companies of the regiment that had been dispersed among other units, performing their final missions. Before they left France and Belgium, they destroyed as many of their flamethrowers as possible to keep them from falling into the hands of the enemies. They assembled in Berlin, where the regiment was disbanded.[29]

Reddemann gave no date for the disbanding, but the last name entered in the regimental death book was *Pionier* Gustav Hüttmann, 2nd Guard Pioneer Replacement Battalion, who was killed in Berlin on January 1, 1919.[30] It would follow that the regiment ceased to exist sometime afterward.

Total number of Flamethrower Deployments 1915-1918

A total of 653 flamethrower attacks were carried out by Flamethrower Detachment Reddemann, the 3rd and 4th Guard Pioneer Battalions, and the Guard Reserve Pioneer Regiment during the war:[31]

Year	*attacks*	*successful*	*unsuccessful*
1915	32	30	2
1916	158	124	34
1917	169	145	24
1918	294	236	5
In total	653	535	118

Eighty-two percent of these attacks were considered successful. Reddemann wrote that the number of insertions made was the absolute maximum possible with the flamethrower troops available to him. In order to have carried out more missions, he would have needed more than twelve combat companies.

Twenty attacks were carried out with large flamethrowers alone or battery devices made up of two or more small flamethrowers. Large flamethrowers or battery devices were used in conjunction with small flamethrowers on 101 occasions. The remaining 525 attacks involved the use of small flamethrowers only.

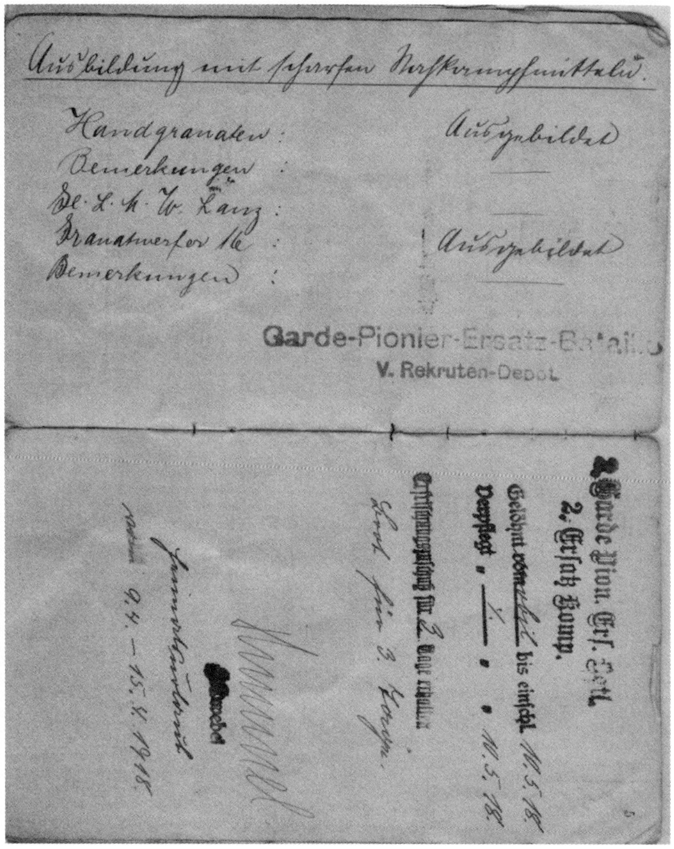
Ausbildung mit schweren Nahkampfmitteln.
Handgranaten: Ausgebildet
Bemerkungen:
Gr. L. M. W. Lanz:
Granatwerfer 16: Ausgebildet
Bemerkungen:
Garde-Pionier-Ersatz-Bataillon
V. Rekruten-Depot

2. Garde Pion. Ers. Batl.
2. Ersatz Komp.

Right: Soldbuch of Pionier Karl Elsemann. Born in Hamburg on September 8, 1899, he joined the 5th Recruit Depot, Garde-Pionier-Ersatz-Bataillon, on June 19, 1917. These pages document his training in close-combat means (Nahkampfmittel) such as hand grenades and the Granatenwerfer 16. On October 5, 1918, Elsemann was transferred to the 2nd Replacement Company of the II. Garde-Pionier-Ersatz-Bataillon; by the end of October he belonged to the 6th Company of the Garde-Reserve-Pionier-Regiment. He saw no combat during the war.

Below: Flamethrower pioneers posing with two Wex, a Kleif M.1917, and two M.1917 small lances with igniters. The dark band around the igniters is the adhesive tape that secured a protective metal cover over the primer. Before firing, the tape and cover were removed. The young pioneer reclining on the right is holding an inert stick grenade with a drilled head, while the man reclining on the left wears an M.1915 blouse converted from an M.1910 service jacket.

Casualties of the Flamethrower Pioneers

According to Reddemann, casualties among his flamethrower pioneers were often considerable. For example, during the first three weeks of the Battle of Verdun, the eight flamethrower companies involved lost two company commanders, nine platoon commanders, and 464 NCOs and men through death, wounding, or disease. These figures translate to thirty-five percent of company and platoon commanders and thirty-seven percent of enlisted men. The 9th Company of the 3rd Guard Pioneer Battalion in particular lost fifty-six percent of its personnel.[32]

Infantrymen attending a flamethrower demonstration. The weapons are, from the right, a Kleif M.1914, a late-model Kleif M.1915, a Wex M.1917 (partially obscured by a propellant tank), and two Kleif M.1917. Several igniters lie on top of the metal oil container next to the Kleif M.1917 on the left. A modified Granatenwerfer 16 in its wooden carrying case sits on the far left, between its cut-down base plate and a wooden box of aerial grenades.

Although casualties could be as high as twenty percent, the training in utilizing the terrain as cover, as well as the spirit of the men themselves, generally kept the attrition rate much lower than expected.

The regimental death book provided a thorough accounting of flamethrower pioneers who were killed in action, went missing, or died from disease during the war.[33]

Units	*Officers and Deputy Officers*	*NCOs*	*Gefreitere and Pioneers*	*Total*
Headquarters Staff	-	-	-	-
Experimental Company	-	-	2	2
Recruit Depot	-	-	3	3
Staff 1st Battalion	1	-	1	2
Staff 2nd Battalion	-	-	-	-
2nd Workshop Detachment	-	1	-	1
Staff 3rd Battalion	-	-	-	-
2nd Guard Pioneer Replacement Battalion	1	1	23	25
1st Company	3	6	82	91
2nd Company	-	5	50	55
3rd Company	2	9	65	76
4th Company	3	11	58	72
5th Company	-	8	70	78
6th Company	2	11	70	83

7th Company	3	6	50	59
8th Company	2	11	73	86
9th Company	-	9	55	64
10th Company	3	10	67	80
11th Company	1	9	43	53
12th Company	2	7	46	55
Reserve Company, 3rd Guard Pioneer Battalion	-	2	3	5
In total	**23**	**106**	**761**	**890**

Four men of the Replacement Company, 3rd Guard Pioneer Battalion, were included in the tally for the 2nd Guard Pioneer Replacement Battalion. Flamethrower replacements were killed in accidents at training grounds in Berlin, Tempelhof, Mariendorf, Muskau, and Dernbach.

The story of the Death's Head Pioneers did not end with the Armistice. They had one final mission, which they would undertake dispersed and without the leadership of Bernhard Reddemann.

A rather unhappy-looking flamethrower pioneer late in the war, equipped with an M.1916 steel helmet, bread bag, respirator, S98/05 bayonet, and P08 pistol. The shabbiness of his uniform is likely due to the years of Allied economic blockade. Courtesy Ronny Pobucky.

CHAPTER TWELVE

Postwar Time Line

Prior to the armistice German Communist revolutionaries formed Workers' and Sailors' Councils (*Räte*, singular *Rat*), followed soon after by Soldiers' Councils. They took control of cities and set up their own governments hostile to the old order. The Kaiser abdicated on November 9, the same day that the German Republic was proclaimed by the German Socialist Party (SPD). A few hours later the German Socialist Republic was declared by the Spartacus League (*Spartakusbund*), a rival leftist party dedicated to world revolution.

On November 10 the SPD joined with the Independent German Socialist Party (USPD) to form a six-man Provisional Government called the "Council of People's Commissioners" (*Volksbeauftragte*). Challenging the new government was the Council's movement (*Räterbewung*), made up of more than 10,000 Workers', Soldiers', and Sailors' Councils all over Germany. Since the imperial army had essentially disintegrated, the Supreme Army Command ordered its subordinate commands to raise new units of volunteers whose loyalty was unquestionable. These formations became the *Freikorps*.

The year ended in chaos and looting, while the socialist Congress of Soldiers' Councils competed with the Supreme Army Command for power over the armed forces. In January of 1919 the Spartacus League officially changed its name to the German Communist Party (KPD) and seized large sections of Berlin. The Provisional Government responded by legalizing the *Freikorps* and sending them in. They reclaimed the city after heavy fighting that saw the use of tanks, artillery, trench mortars, and flamethrowers. Following elections, the victorious SPD moved the seat of the government from

Vorläufiger
Ausweis.
Dem
Pionier Fritz Pusch
der 1. Komp. des
Garde-Res.-Pion.-Regts.
wurde unterm 23. 12. 18
durch das Generalkommando
des Gardekorps
das
Eiserne Kreuz II. Kl.
verliehen.

Certificate declaring that Pionier Fritz Pusch of the 1st Company, Garde-Reserve-Pionier-Regiment, was awarded the Iron Cross Second Class on December 28, 1918, more than six weeks after the Armistice. The regiment was disbanded in early 1919, replaced by a Reichswehr flamethrower battalion. Courtesy www.gmic.co.uk.

Berlin to Weimar. *Freikorps* units went on to defeat German Communists at home, engage the Russian Red Army and indigenous forces in the Baltic, and hold back the Poles in Upper Silesia.

On March 6, 1919, the National Assembly created the Provisional German Defense Force (*Vorläufige Reichswehr*), the land componant of which was the Provisional German Army (*Vorläufige Reichsheer*) of about fifty brigades. Many of the larger *Freikorps* were integrated into the new army as brigades, regiments, or battalions, while smaller organizations were combined and absorbed piecemeal.

The Provisional German Army had a strength of about 400,000 including *Freikorps* formations. On September 30 it was replaced by an entirely new Transitional Army (*Übergangsheer*), which consisted of thirty brigades. The Treaty of Versailles, signed on June 28, 1919, limited Germany to standing army of 100,000 men with no general staff. After the terms of the "*Diktat*" came into effect on January 10, 1920, banned weapons such as flamethrowers were ordered turned over to the Allies. The pared-down military, designated the *Reichswehr*, was officially formed on January 1, 1921; the army (*Reichsheer*) was composed of two group commands, seven infantry divisions, and three cavalry divisions.

"The Freedom Movement in Berlin": Communist revolutionaries display their firepower on November 9, 1918, two days before the Armistice. The Spartacists used flamethrowers during the postwar fighting, but not as profusely or effectively as government and Freikorps troops.

Member of Freikorps Hülsen, which had a flamethrower platoon. He wears the unit's oak-leaf collar badges and a cuff title that reads "Armored Train" (Eisenbahn Panzerzug). The death's head sleeve badge is the insignia of the Kommand der Kampfwagenabteilungen or Kokampf, a Freikorps unit equipped with armored vehicles. Historians have often confused this sleeve badge with that of the Death's Head Pioneers.

Flamethrowers and Revolution

On November 9, 1918, the day he abdicated, Kaiser Wilhelm proposed to *Feldmarschall* Paul von Hindenburg and *Generalquartiermeister* Wilhelm Groener that the spreading rebellion in German cities be quelled by picked troops armed with the most modern weapons, including smoke grenades, gas, bombers, and flamethrowers. Groener replied that it was impossible, as the troops to do it could not be found. "Sire, you no longer have an Army," he told the disbelieving emperor.[1]

Charles Theune wrote that during times of street fighting due to political unrest, flamethrowers proved useful in making an impression on the morale of the rebels. Generally, the loud command "Flamethrower, prepare to fire!" or a vertical jet of fire in the air were enough to persuade a crowd to leave. Flamethrowers precluded negotiations or the need to use firearms, which in turn prevented bloodshed. For street fighting, medium and large flamethrowers were best left on vehicles such as troop-carrying trucks, cargo trucks, or armored cars.[2]

According to Bernhard Reddemann, a small detachment of flamethrower pioneers remained in the Peacetime Army (*Friedensheer*) after the disbanding of the Guard Reserve

Pioneer Regiment. This unit took part in the fighting against the Spartacists in Berlin, most prominently the assault on the *Vorwärts* newspaper building on January 11, 1919. While the *Freikorps Potsdam* is generally identified as the unit that deployed flamethrowers during this operation, Reddemann credited his unnamed detachment of former Death's Head Pioneers. Whichever group it was, the Prince of Hades was quick to point out that according to an official report, "the success of the government troops was owed 'not least to the all-suppressing fight of the flamethrowers.'"[3]

Reddemann noted that flamethrowers were also repeatedly and successfully used to defend the borders after the war. A *Reichswehr* flamethrower company was formed from the detachment in order to suppress rebellions and disturbances, but this unit was later disbanded because of the "disgraceful" Treaty of Versailles. In total, Reddemann devoted only three paragraphs of his book to the postwar period.

Charles Theune continued his pattern of slightly opposing Reddemann's version of events by stating that after November 9, 1918, the flamethrower regiment was reduced first to a single battalion and then to one company. As part of the *Reichswehr*, this formation helped suppress riots and unrest. It existed until the summer of 1920, when it was disarmed by the Allies. "Our weapons had to be handed over to our enemies," Theune wrote. "Our opponent demanded the flamethrower apparatuses with particular emphasis! We flamethrower pioneers and assault troops know why!"[4]

In addition to the two successive *Reichswehr* flamethrower units, several of the new pioneer battalions – such as *Reichswehr-Pionier-Bataillon 10* and *19* – were armed with flamethrowers.[5] Some of them kept their weapons years after they were banned by the Versailles Treaty. Since each of the *Reichswehr* Brigades had an engineer battalion with two companies, there may have been many more army flamethrower units than the two that Reddemann and Charles Theune described. Detailed information about such formations is lacking.

This natty former Death's Head Pioneer displays the shoulder straps of an Oberleutnant, but his wartime sleeve badge is the gray enlisted man's version. A handwritten message on the back of the photo describes him as a "Noske-Gardist," a derogatory term for government forces used by Spartacists and their sympathizers. Note the Iron Cross First Class and gold wound badge.

Very young Freikorpskämpfer of the Deutsche Schutzdivision, identified by the collar badge of a silver sword inside a wreath. His unit was armed with twenty-five flamethrowers. He is lightly equipped as a shock trooper, with Kar. 98AZ carbine, a single M.1909 ammunition pouch, and a bayonet.

Flamethrower Pioneers Remove Sleeve Badge

Immediately after the cessation of hostilities, former flamethrower pioneers were required to remove the death's head sleeve badge. The original letter from the Crown Prince, dated July 28, 1916, authorized the men of the Guard Reserve Pioneer Regiment to wear the badge "during the war."[6] This would seem to classify the emblem as an official award rather than a mere decoration, with limitations on how it was to be displayed. Photos of flamethrower pioneers in the immediate postwar period show that many did indeed remove their badges, often replacing them with generic skull-and-crossbones patches to denote their former membership in the elite Guard Reserve Pioneer Regiment.

Men of the veterans' association of the flamethrower regiment wore a silver death's head – possibly a metal lapel pin – on their civilian coats.[7] Such a pin can be seen in photos of firefighters who had served in the Guard Reserve Pioneer Regiment.

Unteroffizier of Minenwerfer Detachment Heuschkel, which began with a flamethrower platoon that was reduced to a single troop. He wears the unit's arm badge of a death's head at the top of a wreathed oval with the letters MWH; he also displays collar badges of the Garde-Kavallerie-Schützen-Division and a generic white death's head on his cuff, indicating that he is a veteran of the Garde-Reserve-Pionier-Regiment.

Freikorps Units with Flamethrower Sections

On December 27, 1918, Gustav Noske, the governor of Kiel, was made Reich Minister of Defense and Supreme Commander of the Armed Forces. In this capacity he was given carte blanche to crush the socialist revolution.[8] For the Spartacists and their sympathizers, government troops and the *Freikorps* were therefore known as the Noske Guard (*Noske-Garde*).

As early as November of 1918, *Freikorps* units began forming all over Germany, usually coalescing around a single charismatic leader. Advertisements were taken out in newspapers such as the *Berliner Tageblatt*, *Vorwärts*, and the *Vossische Zeitung*:

VOLUNTEERS!
From the West – March to the East!
FLAME-THROWER PERSONNEL
Enlist in the Flame-thrower section of
THE LUETTWITZ CORPS
Immediate pay plus 5 marks daily bonus.
Free food and equipment.[9]

One of the first large-scale *Freikorps* was founded on December 14, 1918, by *General* Ludwig Maercker, commander of the 214th Infantry Division. His *Freiwilligen Landesjägerkorps* was the model for many other *Freikorps*. Each company had its own machine-gun and trench-mortar sections; light and heavy artillery, armored cars, aircraft, and flamethrowers were added as the occasion demanded. Maercker deployed his men in small, self-sufficient units that used wartime shock-troop tactics to crush isolated pockets of resistance throughout Germany.[10]

Another unit, *III. Marine Brigade Löwenfeld*, was established by *Fregattenkapitän* Wilfried von Löwenfeld and consisted mainly of naval personnel. One famous member was U-boat hero Lothar Arnauld de la Perière, who led the assault battalion. Löwenfeld claimed that his *Freikorps* was the strongest in Germany. It had 8,000 infantrymen and pioneers armed with artillery of four calibers, trench mortars, flamethrowers, armored vehicles, tanks, aircraft, and trucks. "We could handle every demand of war," said Löwenfeld.[11]

The following list of *Freikorps* units known to have had flamethrowers is by no means exhaustive.[12] However, it provides a good overview of major formations. It is not likely that all flamethrowers were operated by former Death's Head Pioneers. Many of Bernhard Reddemann's men did engage in combat during this period, but they may also have trained others to use the weapons.

Well-known photo of government-loyal soldiers taken in Berlin during the general strike of March 1919. The Ehrhardt armored car is surrounded by a Wex shock troop commanded by the Unteroffizier on the far right, a former Death's Head Pioneer whose collar insignia identifies him as a member of Generalkommando Lüttwitz. Note the visorless "Turkish" steel helmets and the spare igniter in the right tunic pocket of the lance operator.

Berliner Freischützenkorps

Also known as *Freischützen-Regiment Berlin*. Served as the volunteer military arm of the police during Berlin uprisings of 1919. Unknown number of flamethrowers.

Detachment Gerstenberg

Special task force composed of elements of *II. Marine-Brigade Ehrhardt* and *3. Landesschützen-Brigade*; used for the pacification of Bremen in February of 1919. Flamethrower platoon from *Minenwerfer Detachment Heuschkel*.

Deutsche Schutzdivision

Founded in December of 1918; fought in Berlin. Became *Reichswehr-Brigade 25*. Twenty-five flamethrowers.

Eiserne Division

Founded on December 5, 1918; fought in the Baltic. Dissolved in 1920 for taking part in Kapp Putsch. One flamethrower platoon.

Freikorps von Brandis

Founded in January of 1919 by *Hauptmann* Cordt von Brandis, hero of Douaumont. Fought in Baltic. Unknown number of flamethrowers.

Freikorps Hülsen

Founded December 26, 1918; fought in Berlin and Leipzig. Became *Reichswehr-Brigade 3*. Flamethrower platoon.

Freikorps von Lützow

Founded January 18, 1919; fought in Baltic, Munich. Became part of *30. Jäger-Bataillon* of the *Reichswehr*. Flamethrower platoon.

Freikorps Potsdam

Founded January 15, 1919; fought in Berlin. Absorbed into *Freikorps Hülsen*. At least two flamethrowers.

MÖBEL-FABRIK
PATZENHOFER
Berliner Straßenkämpfe März 1919.
6595
Flammenwerfer.

Freiwillige Sturmabteilung Rossbach

Founded in November of 1918; fought in Baltic, Ruhr, and Silesia. Became *37. Jäger-Bataillon* of Provisional *Reichswehr*. Was formally dissolved in January of 1920 but continued as an underground paramilitary force until 1933. Four to six small flamethrowers.

Opposite

Top left: A second photo of the same Unteroffizier from the previous page. He retains his black wartime shoulder straps but has removed the Guard lace from his collar. On his left sleeve he wears a white Prussian-style death's head as a replacement for his official badge.

Top right: Trumpeter of Freiwilligen Regiment Reinhard. This unit contained a flamethrower platoon; the sleeve badge consists of a metal disk with a large R above 1919, surrounded by a wreath.

Bottom: Postcard captioned "Berlin street fighting, March 1919: Flamethrower." Freikorps or Reichswehr flamethrower shock troop armed with late-model Wex, the M.1918 small lance, Kar. 98AZ carbines, and M.1917 stick grenades. Note the M.1918 helmets with cutouts in the rim. On the far left, the Wex carrier is equipped with a large sack of igniters on his hip.

Below: Postcard captioned "Machine guns in position against Lichtenberg." The officer in the center wears the beribboned-wreath collar badge of the Freiwilligen Landesschützenkorps, a Freikorps equipped with an unknown number of flamethrowers.

Freiwilligen Landesjägerkorps

Founded on December 13, 1918; fought in Berlin, Weimar, Halle, Magdeburg, Brunswick, Dresden, Leipzig and against the Poles in Upper Silesia. Became *Reichswehr-Brigade 16*. One flamethrower with each infantry company for a total of fifteen in January of 1919.

Freiwilligen Landeschützenkorps

Founded on January 3, 1919; fought in Berlin, Hamburg, Magdeburg, and Bremen. Became *Reichswehr-Brigade 4*. As *Detachment Reichswehr-Brigade 4*, part of *Korps Lettow* task force created to pacify Hamburg, used unknown number of flamethrowers in combat.

Freiwilligen Regiment Reinhard

Founded in January of 1919; fought in Berlin and against the Poles in Upper Silesia. Became part of *Reichswehr-Brigade 15*. Flamethrower platoon in engineer detachment.

Garde-Kavallerie-Schützen-Division

Founded in January of 1919; fought in Berlin, disbanded and absorbed into various *Reichswehr* units. Flamethrower platoon attached from *Minenwerfer Detachment Heuschkel*; also had

three *Kavallerie-Schützenkommandos* equivalent to infantry brigades, two of which had flamethrower platoons.

Gruppe Division Münster
Unit created to reinforce *Reichswehr-Brigaden 7* and *31*; fought in Ruhr in April of 1921. Further Information lacking. Flamethrower platoon from 1st Company, *Reichswehr* Pioneer Battalion 10.

Kavallerie-Schützenkommando 14
One of three brigade-sized units of *Garde-Kavallerie-Schützen-Division*; fought in Munich in May, 1919. Flamethrower platoon, probably attached from *Minenwerfer Detachment Heuschkel*.

II. Marine Brigade Ehrhardt
Founded February of 1919; fought in Berlin, Oldendurg-Ostfriesland, and Munich. Dissolved in 1920. Flamethrower platoon.

III. Marine Brigade von Löwenfeld
Founded in December of 1918; fought in Berlin. Dissolved in June of 1920. Six flamethrowers in Assault Battalion Arnauld de la Perière and six flamethrowers in marine engineer battalion.

Minenwerfer Detachment Heuschkel
Founded in January 1919 by *Hauptmann* Heuschkel of Pioneer Battalion No. 29; fought in Bremen in February and Berlin in March of 1919. Originally had a flamethrower platoon, but by March of 1919 had reduced its flamethrower section to a single troop.

45. Reserve-Division
Wartime formation renamed *Brigade Nord-Litauen* on March 26, 1919; fought in Baltic. Become *Reichswehr-Brigade 43*. Flamethrower troop in Engineer Company Böttcher, formed from elements of *Reserve-Pionier-Kompagnie 45*.

Youngster of III. Marine Brigade Löwenfeld, a naval unit that had a total of twelve flamethrowers. This soldier is armed with a Gew. 98 and two M.1917 stick grenades. His collar badge is an anchor on a beribboned wreath.

Flamethrower Deployments by *Freikorps* and the *Reichswehr*

During the first week of January, 1919, Spartacist forces began massing in Berlin. On January 8 *Freikorps* troops with machine guns were posted on top of the Brandenburg Gate and adjoining buildings. Soldiers in government offices were equipped with flamethrowers after Chancellor Friedrich Ebert resolved that instead of negotiating with the revolutionaries he would suppress them with "frightfulness."[13] On January 9 the Communists attacked.

Several *Freikorps* units entered central Berlin on January 10. They targeted the Spartacists who had taken over Newspaper Row, where the offices of the major dailies were located. After very heavy fighting the revolutionaries were driven from the government printing office and the barracks of the Guard Pioneer Battalion on Köpernickerstrasse. The chancellor's palace on Wilhelmstrasse – the seat of the

Above: A Wex squad of the Berliner Freischützenkorps, the volunteer military wing of the postwar Berlin police, in an undated postcard captioned "Street fighting in Berlin: flamethrower." The weapon is the late-model Wex, while the lance is the M.1918. Note the peakless "Turkish" helmets. On his left sleeve, the lance operator displays the two white bars of an Unteroffizier.

Right: The Vorwärts newspaper building in Berlin, which Freikorps Potsdam assaulted with flamethrowers and trench mortars on January 11, 1919. In this photo of the aftermath, a flamethrower pioneer wearing full imperial uniform stands in the center, his hands in his pockets. His Guard lace, black shoulder straps, and death's head sleeve badge are clearly visible.

government – was converted into an armed camp, the spacious reception hall filled with soldiers bearing rifles, hand grenades, and flamethrowers.[14]

The battle for Newspaper Row continued without resolution until the *Freikorps* brought in artillery, heavy mortars, and flamethrowers. On January 11 the *Vorwärts* building was assaulted by *Freikorps Potsdam*:

> Only with the help of a flamethrower was the board fence [behind the building] set on fire and the way cleared for the shock troop. Under the fire of the heavy machine guns of the Guard *Jäger* from the Reichs Patent Office, and because of the corrosive smoke clouds of the flamethrower and the strong effect of the artillery fire from the Belle-Alliance-Platz, the Vorwärts garrison now retreated to the rear. Nearly simultaneously with the shock troops of the 1st Guard Regiment, the Guard *Jäger* penetrated into the Vorwärts building with hand grenades. The forward-storming troops encountered only isolated, weak resistance. Everywhere the dead and wounded lay

about. With raised hands the remainder of the defenders pushed into the clear. Some fanatics tried to set the remaining provisions and clothing on fire, which was rapidly put out by the alert fire brigade.[15]

According to a flamethrower pioneer who participated in the attack, he and his *Wex* squad had been recruited into *Freikorps Potsdam* by Bernhard Reddemann. On the day of the assault, this pioneer and his team entered the rear of the building and called out, "Yoo-hoo! We have flamethrowers!" The Spartacists inside had barricaded themselves behind rolls of highly flammable newsprint, so they very sensibly gave up.[16]

While claiming that the Ebert government used poison gas on the insurgents during this uprising, some news agencies stated that flamethrowers had been issued but not actually fired.[17] Others reported the opposite:

Every weapon and method employed in the world war was used by the Ebert government in its battles with the Spartacides in Berlin. Barbed wire entanglements were constructed at many of the principal street crossings and across public squares, liquid fire was used effectively, artillery and machine guns were stationed all over the city and trenches were dug across the streets were the fighting was hottest.[18]

A general strike was declared in Leipzig on February 27, after which a 3,000-man force of the *Freiwilligen Landesjägerkorps* and the Peacetime Army entered Halle by armored train. These troops attacked with machine guns, artillery, and flamethrowers, but they still took three days to defeat the meagerly armed strikers. Twenty-four were killed and sixty-seven wounded.[19]

Shipboard photo of men from Freiwilligen Landesjägerkorps, a formation armed with fifteen flamethrowers. Its collar badges were silver oak leaves with an acorn. The Unteroffizier second from the left has been awarded the Iron Cross First Class and two gold wound badges, indicating ten or more wounds.

Postcard captioned "Street fighting in Berlin during the general strike. Flamethrower." These Freikorps fighters wear white cotton drill jackets, either to ward off the cold or as a form of identification. The M.1918 small lance, 5ft. hose, and late-model Wex are seen to good advantage. Personal arms include a Gew. 98 and M.1917 stick grenade for the lance operator and a Navy or Artillery Luger, M.1917 stick grenade, and S98/05 bayonet for the Wex carrier.

On March 3 the KPD and USPD called a general strike in Berlin and again tried to take the city. The government responded by declaring martial law and arming the *Freikorps* and Peacetime Army with "the whole gamut of war devices."[20] Newspapers in Europe and the United States made much of the government's use of flamethrowers during the street fighting. "Fight Bolsheviki with Liquid Fire" was the caption of one much-reproduced photo of a *Wex* shock troop.[21] Another well-known image of a *Wex* squad carried the caption "Hun Frightfulness Ready for Use on Home Folks." The legend read in part, "Hun frightfulness has reacted on the home folks and rebellion is fought with the same ruthless instruments that were invented for the conquest of the world."[22]

A March 8 newspaper account with the subtitle "Street Battle Desperate and Bombs and Flame Throwers Are Used in Struggle" drew a vivid picture of the ferocious combat that wracked the capital for a week, killing thousands. By now the Provisional *Reichswehr* had joined the *Freikorps* in putting down the revolutionaries:

> Describing the fighting in Berlin on Thursday night a dispatch to the Exchange Telegraph Company from Copenhagen says that during the whole night there were sounds of heavy detonations of cannons and explosions in the district where fighting was taking place. Flame throwers and trench weapons of all kinds were employed in the struggle, which was particularly violent around the police headquarters which the Spartacans made desperate efforts to capture.[23]

In Munich the communist Bavarian Councils' Republic (*Bayerische Räterrepublik*) was declared on April 7. Noske sent some 30,000 *Freikorps* troops arrayed in several task forces to assault the city from all sides on May 1. During the two-day battle, flamethrowers saw action several times:

> Firing broke out, but the Red guards, finding themselves outgunned, soon scurried for cover behind the newspaper kiosks on the nearby Stachius Square. Here

Above: Sicherheitspolizei in a postcard sent from Munich on May 8, 1919. The Security Police were armed with flamethrowers, but the number of weapons distributed per unit is not known. These officers crew a 77mm Feldkanone.

> they received reinforcements and held out in a hail of bullets. Eventually the Whites, using a flame-thrower set the kiosks alight and the Red guardists retreated towards the Palace of Justice. They continued to offer spirited resistance from this massive building; when after artillery bombardment the Palace of Justice fell to the Whites some red guardists escaped to the Mathäser beerhall which in turn became a battlefield.[24]

Although the flamethrower-armed *Freikorps* unit was not identified, it may have been *Kavallerie-Schützenkommando 14* of the *Garde-Kavallerie-Schützen-Division*. The vast Mathäserbräu was the headquarters of the communist workers' council that ruled Munich. Once the revolutionaries had retreated inside, the building was assaulted by an unknown *Freikorps* pioneer company that burnt it to the ground with flamethrowers.[25] The fighting continued into the evening, the *Freikorps* reducing the last points of resistance with flamethrowers and artillery.

Right: Freikorpskämpfer wearing the collar insignia of two units: The hunting horn is that of Freikorps Lützow, while the wreathed helmet on the Garde star over oak leaves is the badge of the Garde-Kavallerie-Schützen-Division. Each formation had its own flamethrower platoon. The Garde-Kavallerie-Schützen-Division also included three Kavallerie-Schutzen-Kommandos, two of which were armed with flamethrowers.

On July 22 in Berlin, three large, open-air demonstrations of communists and their sympathizers turned into antigovernment marches. One group made its way down Unter den Linden onto Wilhemstrasse, intending to demonstrate in front of Noske's offices. It was stopped by soldiers under a huge sign that read, "Halt! Whomever comes further will be shot!" The leaders tried to argue, but when a government officer snapped, "Prepare to fire!" the demonstrators headed back down Unter Den Linden. Before they reached the Brandenburg Gate, two truckloads of troops dismounted, placed machine guns in the roadway, and advanced with flamethrowers. The crowd turned into New Wilhemstrasse, where more government troops broke it into small groups that were dispersed into side streets.[26]

The Abolition of Flamethrowers and Their Illegal Use

Article 171 of the Treaty of Versailles stated that the use, manufacture, and importation of asphyxiating, poisonous, or other gases and all analogous liquids, materials, or devices were prohibited in Germany, as were materials specially intended for the manufacture, storage, and use of these products or devices.[27] Flamethrowers were considered "analogous devices" and thus banned. To oversee the disarmament of Germany, the Inter-Allied Control Commission was instituted in 1919. On January 5, 1920, five days before the terms of the Treaty came into effect, the German Transitional Army reported a remaining stock of 3,500 flamethrowers that were slated for destruction.[28]

Despite the ban, German soldiers continued to deploy the weapon. On January 14 a mob of 40,000 factory workers and shopkeepers attacked the *Reichstag* in Berlin. In response, police and *Freikorps* troops opened fire. "Noske showed his teeth to the radicals," a journalist wrote, ordering his men to turn machine guns and flamethrowers on the crowd.[29] The fighting reached the very steps of the *Reichstag* and was said to resemble an engagement on the western front as the Noske Guard launched assaults from behind barbed-wire entanglements and sandbag parapets. Twenty-two protesters were killed and many more wounded.

During the failed Kapp Putsch of March 12-18, 1920, the *II. Marine Brigade Ehrhardt* displayed its flamethrowers when it entered Berlin to overthrow the Ebert government for accepting the Versailles "Dictate." Once the Ehrhardt Brigade had retreated, government-loyal troops assembled in front of the chancellory on Wilhelmstrasse, "all carrying hand grenades: several squads trundled machine guns and flame throwers."[30]

Wex carrier with the sleeve badge of Reichswehr-Brigade 15. Note the cloth helmet and flamethrower covers and the makeshift stick fuse made from kerosene-soaked rags tied to the end of a board. This man also wears a Brunswick-style death's head on his sleeve as a replacement for the wartime badge. Courtesy Thierry Ehret.

On March 19, *Reichswehr-Brigade 19* left the Leipzig town hall to assault strikers headquartered at the city's historic das Volkshaus. Traveling in armored cars and equipped with flamethrowers operated by *Reichswehr-Pionier-Bataillon 19*, the Brigade lost seven men and suffered twenty wounded along the way. It shelled the union headquarters until the strikers surrendered, then it set the building ablaze. Eleven workers were killed or wounded.[31]

As mentioned previously the *Reichswehr* flamethrower company identified by Reddemann and Charles Theune retained its weapons until the summer, and the revolutionaries also kept flamethrowers in their arsenals. After the Kapp Putsch, the Socialist Defense Committee (*Sozialistische Verteidigungskomitee*) of the town of Köpenick created a citizens' militia to defend against the marauding and vengeful Ehrhardt Brigade. It had approximately 1,000 men armed with fifteen light machine guns, ten heavy machine guns, 1,050 carbines, 100 pistols, two trench mortars, and two flamethrowers. However, the force agreed to lay down its arms in compliance with the martial law declared after the putsch. The Ehrhardt Brigade thus entered the city unopposed, rounded up the militia leaders, and shot them after summary trials.[32]

As a response to the Kapp Putsch the Red Army of the Ruhr (*Roten Ruhr Armee*) was formed on March 13. Numbering 50,000 and armed with large numbers of flamethrowers and French 75mm field pieces,[33] it defeated local police, *Freikorps*, and *Reichswehr* units over the next several days. On the night of March 19, government-loyal troops armed with flamethrowers and machine guns were sent to the Ruhr from Stuttgart.[34] This force was likely *Reichswehr-Brigade 13*, deployed as part of Division Haas; if so, the flamethrower operators were from *Reichswehr-Pionier-Bataillon 13* or *313*.

A truce was negotiated on March 24, during which both sides built up their forces. On April 3 the *Freikorps* launched a major offensive in the Ruhr. Three task forces used wartime assault-troop tactics to defeat the numerically superior Communists after five days of savage fighting. An April 8 newspaper article described a raid near the end of the operation:

Above: Assault troops of II. Marine Brigade Ehrhardt, which contained a flamethrower platoon. The silver sleeve badge consisted of a rope oval surrounding a Viking ship on waves above the word "EHRHARDT" and oak leaves. These fighters also wear collar badges of the Garde-Kavallerie-Schützen-Division. Note that the man on the right is armed with an MP18/I submachine gun.

Below: A 76mm light trench mortar squad of Freikorps von Brandis. Many former Death's Head Pioneers joined this unit because of the high regard in which they held its founder, Hauptmann Cordt von Brandis. These veterans of Grenadier-Regiment Köning Friedrich der Goße (3. Ostpreußisches) Nr. 4 wear the Freikorps von Brandis insignia of an elk's antler over the Guard lace on their collars.

Men of the Eiserne Division, which had a flamethrower platoon. These mostly teenage fighters are adorned with the unit's Prussian death's head cap and/or sleeve badge in at least four different styles. Note the MG08 machine guns, stick grenades, and heavy mortar shell.

Troops of Freiwillige Sturmabteilung Rossbach wearing their sleeve badge of an elk skull and St. Andrew's cross above a black, white, and red chevron; and the collar badge of the Grenzschutztruppen des 17. (Westpreuss.) Armeekorps, a silver fir tree with crossed swords over the torn-out roots. Weapons include MG08 and MG08/15 machine guns. The unit also had a total of four to six small flamethrowers.

> *Reichswehr* (German government troops) used flame throwers against the Reds when they entered Dusseldorf yesterday, causing scores of casualties, according to information received at the headquarters of the American Army of Occupation today. The government troops entered Dusseldorf to "clean up" the town and a short but bloody battle ensued.[35]

Various paramilitary groups also kept their flamethrowers after the devices were officially banned. The Security Police (*Sicherheitspolizei*) was one such force, as reported by an American journalist in May of 1920:

> But what is this *Sicherheitspolizei*? It is a body of trained soldiers, each in full uniform, with a loaded rifle and fixed bayonet on his shoulder, an ammunition belt about his waist, a hand-grenade stuck in his belt, and a flame thrower hanging at his back. He is extremely useful for killing people, and extremely useless for anything else.[36]

On August 7, 1920, the *Reichstag* passed the National Disarmament Law (*Entwaffnungsgesetz*), which took effect on August 11. As a result, civilians were required to turn over all military weapons in their possession. By the end of the year the authorities had collected more than 18,000 machine guns; 1,680 submachine guns; 2.2 million rifles and carbines; 85,000 hand grenades; and 932 cannon, trench mortars, and flamethrowers.[37]

Some *Freikorps* formations such as *Gruppe Division Münster* were openly armed with flamethrowers well into 1921, but for the most part the manufacture and use of the illegal weapons simply went underground. The *Freikorps* were virtually banned by the National Disarmament Law, putting hundreds of thousands of able-bodied men out of work. To both provide these individuals with a livelihood and circumvent

Undated postwar photo purporting to show telegraph linesmen employed by the Berlin postal service. However, the individuals standing second from the left and third from the right are former flamethrower pioneers. Their presence, along with the field-gray uniforms and the men's obvious physical fitness, suggests that this is actually a cell of the Black Reichswehr (schwarze Reichswehr), possibly even a clandestine flamethrower shock troop.

This photo of a Reichswehr Wex shock troop has the cryptic handwritten message "In memory of the wonderful days at Oberhausen," which may date it to the Ruhr campaign of March 15 to April 8, 1920. Three of the fighters wear the hussar Attila; ten are armed with Kar. 98AZ carbines, while the Feldwebel in the center carries an American M.1911 .45 caliber automatic pistol. Another unusual detail is that the M.1918 small lance on the left is fitted with the early-model self-closing valve. Note the departure bouquets tucked into the Wex and the Attila of the kneeling hussar.

Captioned "Street Fighting in Berlin, during which the fighters move forward on the double," this photo has also been identified as having been taken during a Spartacist air raid. To the left of the street sign, a Wex squad advances with the crowd of soldiers.

the limitations of the hated Dictate, the Black *Reichswehr* (*schwarze Reichswehr*) was created. This clandestine network of paramilitary organizations afforded job opportunities and military training for an underground force much larger than 100,000 men. There is no doubt that some of these groups trained with flamethrowers.

While the Germans were busy flouting Allied-imposed limits on military manpower, they were also working around restrictions placed on armaments. A total of 1,072 flamethrowers was eventually turned over to the Inter-Allied Control Commission,[38] but the weapons continued to be manufactured in defiance of the Treaty. According to a British observer, German authorities said that flamethrowers were needed to spray insecticide.[39] This clearly tongue-in-cheek rationale had a basis in fact, as Richard Fielder's early designs and the *Kleif M.1912* had been dual-use flamethrowers and poison-gas sprayers.

As late as 1923, three years after they were abolished, flamethrowers were still being passed around in secret. Telegrams sent by the protofascist political party *Deutschvölkische Freiheitspartei* included the term "Minimax" as a code word for "flamethrower."[40] Not coincidentally, Minimax was a company that had manufactured flamethrowers during the war, as a subcontractor of the *Fiedler Flammenapparate Gesellschaft*. It was also a leading manufacturer of firefighting equipment, which is why Bernhard Reddemann joined the firm after the war. Like so many other German veterans, he may also have become involved in ultranationalist politics, possibly even Nazism.

CHAPTER THIRTEEN

The Legacy of the Flamethrower

During the war the Allies minimized the effectiveness of the flamethrower by giving demonstrations and publishing books such as *Tanks, Gas, Bombing, Liquid Fire* (1917), which expressed the approved view of the weapon:

> The smoke is very dense and black, the flames are a yellowish red, and there is great roaring noise. The moral effect is liable to be great unless men are instructed in the limitations of the instrument.
>
> The heat developed by the flames is great, but all the burning takes place in the air, and the jet cannot be directed downward owing to the upward current of air caused by the heat. A man crouching down on the firing step or just inside a dug-out, should be quite safe from the flames, while any non-inflammable overhead cover gives perfect protection.[1]

These two short paragraphs were the only mention of flamethrowers in the entire book, despite liquid fire being featured in the title. Nothing was said about smokeless oil, curved-trajectory firing, covering jets, combined stationary and pouncing attacks, flamethrower shock troops, rolling up trenches, the Pincers Tactic, the Knife Tactic, Indian-style Forward Stalking, or tunneling. Writers from Allied countries almost totally ignored the science of flame warfare; instead, the flamethrower was usually presented as a failed terror weapon and nothing more. By denigrating flamethrowers in general, Allied military leaders – particularly the commanders of chemical-warfare units – were able to rationalize their own relatively lackluster efforts in the field.

An example of the confusion about German flamethrowers that persists to the present day, this 1918 stereoview is titled "Liquid Fire Gun Captured from the Germans in the Somme by Our Troops." In reality, the weapon is an MG08 machine gun clad in barrel armor and mounted on a two-wheeled cart.

A passage from another book published in 1917 neatly summed up what the Allies wanted their troops and the general public to believe:

> The flame looked like a big gas-jet as it came towards one, and the natural instinct was to jump back and get out of the way, for even a man who was getting used to shell and bullet did not like the prospect of being roasted alive. But the devilish weapon was not effective. Its range was very limited, and the men who manipulated it were usually shot or bombed.[2]

The heads of the British and American chemical-warfare sections were particularly dismissive of the flamethrower. Colonel Charles H. Foulkes, commander of the British Special

Brigade, wrote less than 300 words about the German version of the weapon in his memoirs. His description of an attack on September 21, 1918, stated that "German bombers advanced behind a screen of flammenwerfer, but the latter were only capable of emitting smoke and flame to a distance of about ten feet, and the party was wiped out by our Lewis gunners."[3] As is often the case, the death book of the Guard Reserve Pioneer Regiment listed no names for the date. In addition the notion that the flamethrowers had a range of only ten feet is simply nonsensical.

It is possible that for this mission the German assault troops used fire tubes, which had a range of about seven feet. As an expert in chemical warfare, Foulkes should have known the difference between these weapons and flamethrowers. However, like so many Allied commanders, he was clearly not familiar with fire tubes, and he was apparently not even aware of his ignorance.

Colonel Amos A. Fries, chief of the American Chemical Warfare Service, wrote that the flamethrower was one of the greatest failures of the many promising weapons tried out on a large scale during the war, and the Guard Reserve Pioneer Regiment was a punishment formation composed entirely of men convicted of offenses in other units. These wretched souls were transferred temporarily or permanently into the flamethrower regiment and forced under penalty of death to carry out their dangerous work.[4] Fries's assertions provoked Bernhard Reddemann to write him a comprehensive letter in 1928, which is discussed on page 211.

Flamethrowers as Weapons of Savages

Not content to declare flamethrower ineffective, the Allies also pronounced them the height of barbarity. In 1915 an anonymous British writer claimed that the Germans used flamethrowers to kill wounded Englishmen lying on the ground, proof that the Germans had "done everything that the most degraded creatures in human shape could do, with the sole exception that they had refrained from cannibalism."[5] According to an American pamphlet from 1917, the use of flamethrowers and poison gas had fastened "everlasting odium" to the German army, leading the British to pronounce the Germans dirty fighters, a name which would stick forever.[6]

Since the use of flamethrowers was a well-documented act of "frightfulness" emphasized in anti-German propaganda, the Allies could not have openly described their own incendiary-weapons programs without exposing themselves to the same charges of war crimes that they leveled at the Germans.

This device is a French pneumatic mortar, not a flamethrower. The soldier on the left holds the protective leather end cap for the barrel in his left hand, and the propellant tank and feed lines are visible in the foreground.

Austrian flamethrower misidentified in several sources as an "acid sprayer." Instead, it is an early-model kleine 22l M. 15 Flammenwerfer.

Reddemann himself addressed the issue of barbarity in the final pages of his book. His tone and choice of words are revealing:

> Not only our enemies in the World War but also weak sisters and old maids in the homeland believed

> at that time that the flamethrower should be denounced as an "inhuman" weapon. However, it was not at all inhuman and was indeed perhaps more humane than many other weapons used in wars because its main effect was the moral shock it produced in our enemies, which was so great that they scarcely ever attempted physical resistance. Moreover, it remains worthy of note that our enemies nevertheless brought forth such alleged "inhuman" weapons themselves only a few months after the German flamethrower unit was introduced.[7]

This passage explains how Reddemann the firefighter – a man dedicated to saving people from fire – could enthusiastically transform himself into the Prince of Hades. Despite his conviction that the weapon was in fact humane, the conventional wisdom remains that the flamethrower was both barbaric and supremely inefficient, a notion that resulted in part from reports such as the following.

The Myth of the Mass Exploding Flamethrowers

One of the ways that the German flamethrower was demystified and denigrated was through the spreading of what in present-day terminology would be called urban legends. In an article that appeared in the April 16, 1916, edition of the *New York Times*, titled "3,000 Germans Perish in a Sea of Fire," an anonymous Special Correspondent narrated the action in the first person. The catastrophe he described is said to have taken place on April 12, 1916, at Caurettes Wood in Verdun.

The most stirring element of the story was the heroic French artillery observers who volunteered to stay behind in the trenches after the bulk of the defenders had retreated. At dawn on April 12 the observers reported a large German advance. They telephoned the batteries in the rear, telling them to redouble the bombardment of the German front-line positions and the abandoned French trenches, which the Germans believed were still occupied. Suffering severe casualties, the Germans pushed forward, deploying "the most recent trench-storming device," flamethrowers operated by squads of four:

Postwar French magazine titled The German Booby Traps. German soldiers grin savagely as they plant an exploding spiked helmet to kill Allied souvenir hunters, while in the background, a comrade armed with a flamethrower hoses down a nearby house. The flamethrower is thus defined as a weapon of sadists.

> The grayness of the dawn was illuminated by sheets of green and red flame, and black oily clouds rolled along the valley toward the river like smoke from a burning "gusher."
>
> Suddenly the air was filled with shrill whistling as shells of the 75s were hurled against the attackers. Thanks to the devoted sentinels dying at their posts in the sea of fire, the range was exact, and the exploding

Left: Classic Allied vision of the World War I German flamethrower attack. Suicidal flamethrower operators clad in body armor and armed with spurious one-man weapons charge at entrenched British troops, only to die pointlessly.

Despite assurances from modern-day historians, Guard Pioneers laden with seventy-pound flamethrowers were able to keep pace with lightly equipped infantrymen, as shown in this photo. Like firefighters, flamethrower pioneers possessed great physical strength and endurance. U.S. National Archives 165-GB-2954.

German postcard captioned "German flamethrower shooting the stinging flames; forward-assaulting German shock troops." The flamethrower squad is barely visible on the right.

> melinite shattered the charging columns. An appalling scene followed. The shells had burst or overthrown the fire containers, and the Germans were seen running wildly amid the flames, which overwhelmed hundreds of wounded and disabled.
>
> In this confusion the French charged with the bayonet, despite the furnace heat and fumes produced by the red-hot containers lying in all directions. The enemy offered little resistance. It was like a slaughter of frenzied beasts. The mitrailleuse corps pressed close on their comrades' heels, placing weapons in what vantage points had escaped the fire and showering a leaden hail upon the main body of Germans retreating up Corbeaux Hill.[8]

The Germans were routed; of the 5,000-man brigade only 500 made it back to their lines in safety. Hundreds were wounded or captured and 3,000 were killed, the majority charred out of human semblance. Five of the French artillery observers survived with burns, but one later died.

This spectacular article reported an event that almost certainly never happened. The death book of the Guard Reserve Pioneer Regiment contained only one Verdun entry for April 12 and five for April 11.[9] If there were enough exploding flamethrowers to kill 3,000 German soldiers, dozens of flamethrower pioneers would have died as well. More tellingly, at least two more versions of this story exist, one British and one French.

The British account was found in an article with a nearly identical title "Caught in a Sea of Fire," in the September 16, 1916, edition of *The War Illustrated*. This time the story was told in the first person by a British observer in a tree overlooking the German positions at Poziéres Ridge. As before, he had a field telephone. Nothing happened for about an hour, and then Germans emerged from their trenches and advanced on the British positions with flamethrowers. As in the *Times* article, there was an empty trench that the Germans attacked because they mistakenly believed it was still occupied:

> Well, the German soldiers advanced till they were within ten yards of this trench; then they halted and I could see them getting ready to squirt. They must have been working under orders, for with appalling suddenness

The same card reproduced by an American company and captioned "Gas Attack." It may have been sold in the immediate postwar period, by which time the effort to eradicate the flamethrower from public consciousness had already begun.

> a score of white and yellow jets of fire darted up into the air, to fall plumb into the deserted trench.[10]

The observer was told to come down out of his tree and take cover, which he did as the artillery barrage began:

> I got a dim idea of what hell must be like. Our gunners had the range to an inch, and they simply poured shells over. Shrapnel shells burst about thirty yards ahead, and you could hear the leaden balls shrieking as they tore onwards; lyddite tinged the burning liquid a dull yellow, and asphyxiated every man within forty yards.
>
> The Germans broke and ran as the shells struck their Flammenwerfer, but it was impossible to escape. The ground was a sea of fire, with the blazing stuff spurting up in fountains where the shells struck and burst. The Germans were simply living torches, dying horribly. One chap didn't even attempt to run – I believe he was too paralysed with fear. He spun round slowly like a top, his clothes all aflame, till he fell into a pool of fire. Others rolled along the ground, squirming and screaming in mortal agony. I thought that they'd have had a quick death, but, in spite of the guns booming, the shells bursting, and the crackle of rifle fire on both flanks, you could hear those horrible screams.
>
> When our guns lifted a bit, we saw that behind the curtain of flame and smoke a German regiment had been advancing in close order, evidently intending to attack us as soon as the fire was extinct. But the sight had shocked them horribly, and they broke and ran as soon as our machine-guns on the flank opened fire, taking cover in the woods. The machine-guns sprayed them with bullets all the way, and lots of them rolled over, dead and wounded.[11]

The British version contained the same elements as the *Times* account: observer(s), trench which the Germans did not know was empty, artillery barrage, exploding flamethrowers, slaughter with machine guns, and panicked German retreat.

A third version of this event was titled "The Nemesis of Flame," found in the 1920 book *Deeds of Heroism and Daring*. This time the action took place on the Somme, narrated in the first person by a French observer left behind after his unit is pulled back. As in the British account, he was up in a tree with a telephone, watching as the Germans prepare to attack an abandoned trench. For an hour, nothing happened:

A typewritten message in English on the back of this postcard reads, "Some say this is cloud gas, others that it is liquid fire. I am not sure but think the latter myself. All the gas I ever came in contact with came over in shells and I never saw any liquid fire." Even combat veterans had trouble distinguishing between gas and flame.

> "Suddenly a group of about forty Boches crept from the wood, rapidly followed by the best part of a company. I telephoned: 'Enemy advancing led by a detachment of flamenwerfer,' for I had recognized the devilish apparatus carried by the foremost group. When the latter were about eighty feet from the empty trench, they halted in a hollow just below the rise of ground, and then, with appalling suddenness, a dozen jets of white and yellow flames darted up to fall plumb into the trench.
>
> "A few moments later I had a glimpse of what hell must be like. Our gunners had the range to an inch, and a torrent of shells burst right among the flame-throwers, exploding the containers. Great sheets of flame shot up, one jet from a container just grazing me, burning my clothes so that my ribs were scorched rather badly. But it was impossible to escape. The ground was a sea of fire. In the midst of it the Germans, like living torches, were dying horribly. One man spun round like a top, not even trying to run away, until he fell in a pool of flame. Others rolled on the ground, but the blazing liquid ran over them everywhere, and I could smell the sickening odor of burning flesh.
>
> "I don't think any of the fire-throwers escaped. Their screams, heard despite the cannonade and rifle fire, seemed to continue terribly long. The company behind them was panic-stricken. As the smoke lifted, I saw them moving back to the wood, and our mitreilleuse did severe execution, spreading added slaughter over that scene of horror."[12]

Famously miscaptioned postcard put out by the Chicago Daily News. These French sapeurs lance-flammes are demonstrating Schilt No. 3 bis flamethrowers to Americans from the 30th Engineer (Gas and Flame) Regiment. Confusion over gas and incendiary weapons was rampant in the civilian press.

The heroic, badly burned French observers of the *Times* story had merged with the lone British soldier in the tree to become a lone, badly burned Frenchman in a tree, and the wording of the latter two stories was nearly identical. It seems clear that the myth in all its forms was designed to reassure readers that flamethrowers were suicidally worthless, and the Germans were incompetent and cowardly. Thousands of such stories over the years have had their effect, to the extent that many historians no longer know fact from fiction.

Reddemann on the Effectiveness of Flamethrowers

Reddemann believed that spirit and will were more important requisites for victory than skill and weaponry. The Death's Head Pioneers became famous in the military for their "flamethrower spirit" (*Flammenwerfer-Geist*), which was constantly reinforced by the higher ranks in the regiment. The "death-scorning joy of battle" pushed the men forward to perform their heroic deeds and kept them from losing heart even in the most serious situations.[13]

The flamethrower spirit as defined by Reddemann was a combination of uncompromising will to achieve victory, faith in the weapon, knowledge of prior success, and pride in the Death's Head Regiment. Enthusiasm and cheerfulness were maintained through the joy that came from performing one's duty and engaging in combat that brought honor to the regiment. According to Reddemann, "When the poet said, 'Joy is the mother of all virtues,' one must add 'and deeds.'"[14] Flamethrower spirit born out of joy pushed the men to carry out what Reddemann described as their heroic deeds. It prodded them to new heights of courage and self-sacrifice, allowing them to achieve new victories in spite of sometimes heavy casualties.

Reddemann concluded that the greatest effect of the flamethrower was on the morale of the enemy. Even the most stouthearted man could not withstand hissing, luminous streams of fire. They made him feel powerless, involuntarily fleeing the gruesome corpses of his comrades killed by fire.

An equally important effect of the flamethrower was to lift the spirits of the attacking German infantry. Reddemann gave several testimonials, such as that of the commander of the 45th Reserve Division, who stated that whenever flamethrowers were inserted they successfully assisted in attacks, and they

Above: German cigarette card from the 1920s, depicting an assault with large and small flamethrowers; note the Wex squad in the lower left. Such cards were among the most widely distributed images of weaponry available to the general public.

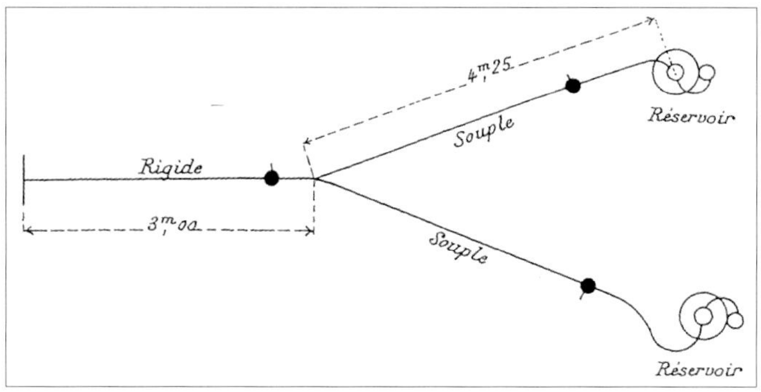

Right: Drawing of a double Kleif, taken from a secret French government manual. The lance is said to be 9.8ft. (3m) long, while the hoses are 14ft. (4.25m). These figures are wildly inaccurate, despite appearing in an official document put out by French military intelligence. (Conférences de l'Ecole des gaz de combat: Les Lance-flammes. 3ème Conférence. Lance-flammes portatifs étrangers.)

had a very favorable effect on the morale of German infantry. The flamethrower pioneers set a courageous example and served as an awakening jolt for the infantry, according to regimental and battalion commanders. Reddemann was not surprised that during the breakthrough battles of 1918 many infantry commanders resisted having their attached flamethrower platoons transferred to other sectors. They would gladly have kept the Death's Head Pioneers with their units on a permanent basis.

Charles Theune on the Effectiveness of Flamethrowers

The former commander of the 10th Company of the Guard Reserve Pioneer Regiment, author of *Sturmtruppen und Flammenwerfer*, regretted that there had been only one flamethrower regiment of twelve companies. Since one company was almost always resting with the Regimental Staff and the others were weakened by their constant assignment to assault battalions and armies on extensive fronts, fresh fighting forces were not always available available for larger operations. There were usually so many requests for flamethrowers that the regiment could not meet them. Theune believed that the failure to create more than one flamethrower regiment cost Germany dearly. A lack of money and raw materials prevented the army from developing the weapon to its full potential, which in the postwar period Germany's former enemies certainly did themselves.[15]

Theune also stated that the success of flamethrower troops in the war could not be attributed to the technical development of the apparatus alone, but was owed principally to the spirit of the officers and men. Like any other close-range weapon in the field, the flamethrower owed its effectiveness to the daring with which operators used it.

The flamethrower regiment depended on young replacements who loved their work and their country. "Iron energy, proud self-confidence and high moral worth on the part of leaders and men, together with scrupulous obedience to the assault orders, were required to open the assault before the mass of the Infantry."[16]

In April of 1921 Theune wrote to the military attaché of the American embassy in the Hague, the Netherlands, offering to sell to the United States secret patents of an improved model of flamethrower. He apparently passed himself off as the inventor of the first flamethrower,[17] but he was turned down by Amos A. Fries without explanation.[18] As discussed below, it was likely due to Fries's abject loathing of flamethrowers.

Bernhard Reddemann Confronts Amos A. Fries

In a letter dated February 29, 1928, addressed to the military attaché at the American embassy in Berlin, Bernhard Reddemann challenged eight specific distortions he found in the book *Chemical Warfare*, cowritten by Amos A. Fries and Clarence J. West.[19] Reddemann filled his very long missive with facts, dates, and examples intended to refute what he said was clearly secondhand information that had deceived the authors. He concluded his letter with several testimonials by German military commanders who vouched for the effectiveness of the flamethrower and the bravery and professionalism of its operators.

Unfortunately for Reddemann, Fries was apparently a man with a deep-seated, nearly pathological antipathy toward flamethrowers. He had made the very strange statement in his book that "In the Chemical Warfare Service it has been the habit for a long while not to mention the flame thrower at all, unless questions were asked about it."[20] Additionally, Fries did indeed lack personal knowledge of German flamethrowers, as shown by his underestimation of their ranges by as much as

Below: The caption notwithstanding, this much-published photo is almost certainly an assault rather than a retreat. Note the shovels and grenade bags, as well as the Wex carrier in the right foreground.

Right: A closer view of the Wex carrier. The lance is fitted with a live igniter, which would almost certainly not be the case if this were a panicked withdrawal. This flamethrower operator is likely part of a Wexbegleittrupp or Wex accompanying squad.

fifty percent,[21] and the repeated claim that the Guard Reserve Pioneer Regiment was made up of condemned men who the army could not be bothered to shoot. Instead, they were given flamethrowers and sent over the top to their deaths.[22] As Reddemann noted, Fries seemed to have based his pronouncements on garbled hearsay rather than hard military intelligence.

Rather than respond to Reddemann personally, Fries directed the Military Attaché in Berlin to thank "Dr. Redemann *[sic]*" for his interest and inform him that there was no record of the Germans ever having attacked American troops with flamethrowers during the war, and all of the world's armies had subsequently discarded the weapon as worthless.[23] Both assertions are not only false, the first is utterly inexplicable. As a high-ranking American military official, Fries had surely heard of Fismette and the Lost Battalion. However, he seems to have been a man blinded to facts and not interested in informing himself. He and Reddemann shared no more correspondence.

The Germans Confirm the Effectiveness of Flamethrowers

One of the more compelling examples of the effectiveness of flamethrowers is found in "Extract from a Report of the Commander of the Third and Fourth Guard Pioneer Battalions, on the Recent Flame Fighting," dated April 20, 1916:

> The moral effect of the flame jets has been considerable. A large number of the enemy have surrendered before the flame jet reached them, often even before the smoke cloud came close to them. During the engagements at Samogneux and Haumont, the flamethrower troops ran out of igniters but continued to spray unlit fuel oil. This was enough to persuade the occupants of the enemy houses to surrender.[24]

The 45th Reserve Division reported that hand grenades did not always force the British from their shelters, but one stream of flame into the dugout entrance encouraged the occupants to hurl themselves out. Flamethrowers were also much better than hand grenades at silencing machine-gun nests because they took less time and cost fewer casualties.[25]

Generalleutnant Meyernitz, staff officer of several army corps and armies, wrote one of the testimonials that Reddemann sent to Fries:

> As a means of combat the effects of the flame projector in the cases which came under my observation were fearful and decisive. The first impression produced upon our enemies was paralysing. The fact that the flame projectors were brought into action by surprise on all fronts of combat, generally only for certain definite combat operations, resulted in their being used in a majority of cases against an enemy who did not yet know them and who was defenseless against them. *But troops which were already acquainted with the flame projector frequently ran away, instead of turning to fight.*[26]

Well-known image often used to illustrate the mistaken belief that large German flamethrowers were lit by hand. In fact, the squad leader on the left is wielding a makeshift stick fuse because the igniter is spent. Since the lance operator has a spare igniter tucked into the right pocket of his M.1915 blouse, it is likely that the stick fuse is for the benefit of the photographer. In the background, a Wex squad stands ready. U.S. National Archives 165-GB-3553.

UFA photo of German soldiers captioned "Attack with small flamethrowers." The figure at the bottom of the trench in the center appears to be armed with a captured French P4 flamethrower. The lance – visible at the operator's waist – may be the 1916 model, the self-closing valve of which was copied by the Germans. This is likely a propaganda or postwar image.

PORTABLE APPARATUS FOR PROJECTING FLAMES.
A, carbonic acid; G, gas; P, gasoline; R, valve; I, igniter for lighting the inflammable liquid; J, flame.

Artist's impression of a German flamethrower operator, based on Richard Fiedler's patent drawings. No such weapon was actually used by the Germans during the war. (The Literary Digest.)

Another testimonial by *General* Baron von Ziegesar, a divisional commander in the war, stated that the expectations placed on the flamethrower pioneers were very high due to the results promised by Reddemann. After the successful assault on Hill 1050 on February 12, 1917, von Ziegesar became "confident that no task could be too difficult for us and the Death's Head Pioneers to accomplish in cooperation."[27]

Probably the best argument that Reddemann and a *General* von Lossberg made is that if the flamethrower were actually such an ineffective weapon, the Allies would not have outlawed it with the Versailles Treaty.[28]

The Allies Confirm the Effectiveness Flamethrowers

The 1923 book *The Riddle of the Rhine* attempted to correct the "mistaken notion that the flame projector was a negligible quantity."[29] While the writer dismissed large, nonportable flamethrowers, he argued that the small versions were very efficient, allowing the Germans to gain local successes on many occasions when used in surprise attacks. He also pointed out something generally ignored by detractors of the flamethrower: The French adopted the weapon and used it extensively. In fact, the French had seven flamethrower companies (*Compagnies Schilt*) named after Captain Victor Alexandre Joseph Schilt of the Parisian Firefighting Sapper Regiment (*Régiment des Sapeurs Pompiers de Paris*). Schilt was the godfather of the French flamethrower; his career in many ways mirrored that of Reddemann.

A typical French flamethrower attack was described in a postwar series of lectures:

> On September 22, 1915, the Schilt Company took part in an attack on the German first lines in the sector known as the "*Poche*" (the pocket), to the west of Perthes-les-Hurlus, with the 22nd Infantry Regiment. The mission was very clearly defined: To move with the first wave into the first lines of the enemy's trenches, and there, while the infantry was moving toward the second line, to clean out the trenches by applying the flame projectors to the underground shelters, in a word, completely cleaning out this sector.
>
> Results: 180 prisoners, 13 of whom were more or less seriously burned.[30]

The proof that the Allies recognized the effectiveness of the flamethrower, despite all their protestations to the contrary, is found in the 1918 book *Tactics and Duties for Trench Fighting*, by Georges Bertrand and Oscar N. Solbert. Bertrand was a captain of the *Chasseurs Alpins*; his lectures on trench fighting caught the attention of Major Oscar N. Solbert, U.S. Army Corps of Engineers, who was stationed at the Fort Sheridan Training Camp in Illinois. Solbert wrote to the War Department on October 26, 1917, asking for permission to publish Bertrand's lectures. Since the book was approved by the Adjutant General of the War Department on October 31, 1917, the following appears to have been the officially held viewpoint on flamethrowers:

> The enemy may make an assault with a special detachment of liquid fire operators in the first line. The object of these operators is to throw jets of liquid fire on the occupants of the first line to allow the assaulting columns to penetrate into the position without losses. The only means of combating such an attack is to evaluate the part of the trenches against which the liquid fire is directed, and move by the flanks. Machine guns and automatic rifles should be established to bring flanking fire to bear against the detachment of liquid fire operators. *It is impossible to withstand a liquid fire attack if the operators succeed in coming within sixty yards before the garrison can man its parapets*. [Emphasis added.][31]

Opposite
Top: This still from a postwar French film crudely recreates a German flamethrower and hand-grenade attack on the Dead Man, March 15, 1916; the flamethrower is the late-model Kleif M.1915. The scene resembles a desperate banzai charge more than an attack by German shock troops. None of the soldiers carry side arms or grenade bags, and all wear Pickelhauben with the spikes in place.

Bottom: In this second still from the same film, the third member of the Kleif squad is carrying the flamethrower hose, as prescribed by erroneous Allied intelligence reports. In reality, the man is only getting in the way of his two squad mates.

Above: Another famous image, this one adding to the general public's confusion through its caption: "Our French comrades sending out gas flames against the German trenches." The weapon is the Schilt No. 3.

The Legacy of the Guard Reserve Pioneer Regiment

The Treaty of Versailles reduced the *Reichswehr* to 100,000 men. To preserve the heritage of the Kaiser's army, each of the new formations had a Traditions Unit (*Traditionstruppe* or *Traditionstruppenteil*) that oversaw a "tradition room" where historical items from particular imperial battalions or regiments were stored. The Traditions Unit would also host meetings of veterans of the old organizations.

At an unknown date the 1st Company of (Prussian) Pioneer Battalion No. 3 (*[Preusisches] Pionier-Bataillon Nr. 3*), garrisoned in Küstrin, became the Traditions Unit of the Guard Pioneer Battalion and the Guard Reserve Pioneer Regiment. *Generalmajor* Haenichen, president of the German Pioneers Association, tried to have the 1st Company awarded the death's head sleeve badge as a tribute to the flamethrower regiment, but he was told by the defense minister that this would not be possible.[32]

The Former Members of the Guard Reserve Pioneer Regiment (Flamethrowers) (*ehemaligen Angehörigen des Garde-Reserve-Pionier-Regiments [Flammenwerfer]*) was established on October 5, 1928.[33] By 1931 it had 200 members. On August 9, 1931, a memorial for the Guard Reserve Pioneer Regiment was dedicated at the New Evangelical Garrison Church in Berlin. Rather than a "pompous monument," it was a wooden cabinet that held a copy of the regimental death book listing the names of the 890 fallen.[34] On top of the cabinet was an oval wooden plaque with a carved relief of a dying flamethrower pioneer sitting slumped over, his helmet at his feet. Behind him, two more flamethrower pioneers fired a *Grof*.

Crown Prince Wilhelm, "the old patron and friend of the flamethrower troops,"[35] attended the dedication ceremony and laid the first wreath at the foot of the cabinet. Reddemann gave a long speech that contained a somewhat eccentric exhortation: "Our flame jets of war defeated many! Our flame jets of peace, i.e. our joy for work, our vitality, and not least our unity, will still lead us to victories!"[36] The memorial cabinet remained in the church until it was moved to a Munich pioneer school during the 1980s. Its current whereabouts are unknown.

Undated photo of a pioneer of the Reichswehr formation (Preussisches) Pionier-Bataillon Nr. 3, the 1st Company of which was the "Traditions Unit" (Traditionstrupp) of the Garde-Pionier-Bataillon and Garde-Reserve-Pionier-Regiment. A retired pioneer general unsuccessfully lobbied for this to unit to wear the death's head sleeve badge.

Reddemann Disappears from History

Like the memorial cabinet, much of the information about German flamethrowers of the First World War has vanished. The records of the Guard Reserve Pioneer Regiment were lost when the German national archives were bombed during World War II. While Richard Fiedler and his flamethrower company simply faded away, Bernhard Reddemann left a few traces. In 1928 he was the Technical Director of Minimax A.G. in Berlin, as shown by his correspondence with Amos A. Fries. Minimax produced firefighting equipment and had manufactured flamethrowers during the war, but the documentation on Reddemann's time at the company shared the same fate as the records of the Death's Head Pioneers. All that remains in the files is the fact that he published the firefighting journal *Fire and Water* (*Feuer und Wasser*) until 1930. In the late 1920s he also patented several firefighting inventions, including fire-extinguisher nozzles and devices for introducing foam into tanks of flammable liquids. He died at Klotzsche, near Leipzig, on January 12, 1938, at the age of sixty-nine.[37]

In 1934 an article titled "Flamethrowers to the Front" ("*Flammenwerfer vor die Front*") was published in the Nazi periodical *Der S.A.-Mann*, under the byline *Major a.D.Pg. Dr*. Reddemann. Although it is not known if the Prince of Hades joined Adolf Hitler's party, he very likely did. He was an ardent nationalist and military veteran embittered by the Armistice and the Treaty of Versailles, factors that together make it almost a certainty that he would be drawn to Nazism. It is also possible that the article was reprinted from another source.

Full of drama, exclamation marks, and ellipses, "Flamethrowers to the Front" described a flamethrower attack by the Death's Head Pioneers, who moved forward at the behest of brave officers shouting, "Let's go, children!" Reddemann obviously longed for the action-packed days of his command, when he was leader of the most elite unit in the Imperial German Army:

Postcard captioned "German Pioneer and Transportation Troops' Day, Munich, July 19, 1925." In the center of the photo, a robust and clean-shaven Bernhard Reddemann marches along, his right arm swinging high. He wears the walking-out uniform of a Prussian fire official, complete with spiked helmet and sword. It is unclear why he is not dressed as a Guard Pioneer.

The handwritten caption on the back of this postcard reads "Fire Station 7, Leipzig, 1935." On their left breasts, seven of these firefighters wear silver death's head pins, indicating their service in the flamethrower regiment.

Run further on the road! Shots slam from the house on the left. The bullets strike between those assaulting. A small white cloud sprays up each time a bullet tears a large hole in the finery of the opposite house... The foremost men leap across the road toward the house. Some sink before they reach the cover of its wall.

A few flame pioneers fall as well. The circular apparatus, which the individuals carry on their backs, is perforated by bullets. The black flame oil runs from it onto the pavement beside the red blood. Here the entry door. Strong butt strokes destroy it. A long fire jet into the hall. Thick smoke. It rises upward inside the house. They've only just been shot, but already fearful cries come from the windows... A few Germans stay to bring the victims out.

Again flamethrowers must help here and there. There a jet in a cellar window, there against shooters in the upper floors. The small fights for the individual houses takes a lot of time. Meanwhile, the courageous infantry second lieutenant and a section of his magnificent people unconcernedly and inexorably penetrate forward into still-occupied parts of buildings on the village main road, while the others remain behind to search and clean the rest of the houses.

The last resistance is broken. The village is taken.[38]

CHAPTER FOURTEEN

German Flamethrower Data

grosse Flammenwerfer (Grof) M.1912

The large static flamethrower was the end result of work done by Richard Fiedler and the Pioneer Experimental Company from 1908 to 1912. It was served by a five-man squad consisting of an *Unteroffizier* or *Gefreiter* in charge, a lance operator (*Strahlrohrführer*), an assistant (*Hilfsmann*) to support the hose, and two *Grof* staff (*Grofleute*) to open the propellant and oil valves. Based on a "gas sprayer" used in fire fighting, it had separate oil and propellant tanks, following the basic layout of the Fiedler portable flamethrower. Primary sources differ on the weapon's oil capacity; Reddemann consistently gave it as twenty-six gallons,[1] while files in the German national archives put it at forty-five gallons.[2] The firing duration was forty-five seconds,[3] and the range was 115-130 feet.[4] Photos indicate that the propellant was stored in two exterior tanks.

grosse Flammenwerfer (Grof) M.1916

Also known as the "light *Grof*" (*Leichtgrof*), this improved version of the large flamethrower was introduced in late 1916, the result of work done by the commander of the Guard Reserve Pioneer Regiment research company, *Oberleutnant der Reserve* Lindner.[5] Smaller and lighter than the initial design, the *Grof M.1916* is the version that appears in most photos. It had a welded steel oil tank that held twenty-six gallons, which made it portable by one man when empty and by two when full. The external propellant tank provided a pressure of 221 psi. (15 atm.).

The *Grof M.1916* had a range of 131 feet and a duration of forty-five seconds.[6] As before, it was fired by a five-man crew. Many modern sources claim that it was lit with burning twigs, but the lance was in reality fitted with an automatic igniter that allowed for multiple shots, as were all German flamethrower lances of the First World War. The burning twigs were used only as improvised igniters.

Two or three twenty-six-gallon *Grof* oil tanks could be linked, providing 70 or 120 seconds of firing time respectively. Up to six 16.4-foot *Grof* hoses could also be connected to create a hose ninety-eight feet in length. Such long hoses did not affect the weapon's performance.

For curved-trajectory or indirect firing, the *Grof* staff charged the oil tank to 29-44 psi. (2-3 atm.), while the operator elevated the lance and opened the ball valve halfway, creating an arc of flame that had a range of 50-66 feet and a duration of ninety seconds.

kleine Flammenwerfer (Kleif) M.1912

The *Kleif M.1912* was the first production-model portable flamethrower developed jointly by the Pioneer Experimental Company and the *Fiedler-Flammenapparate Gesellschaft*. It was a welded steel cylinder 23.6 inches tall with a diameter of 9.8 inches; the propellant was housed in an internal chamber at the top of the oil tank. The oil capacity of 4.2 gallons gave the weapon a laden weight of seventy-one pounds.[7] Carbon dioxide or nitrogen were usually used as the propellant, although deoxygentated air – compressed air mixed with carbon dioxide – was initially tried as well. Regardless of the gas used, the propellant chamber was filled to 338 psi. (23 atm.), which pressurized the oil to 265 psi (18 atm.) when the weapon was armed. The carrying harness lacked a waist belt so that the carrier could instantly divest himself of the flamethrower if the weapon ignited from leakage or from being punctured by enemy fire.

A rigid telescoping lance was attached to the right side of the tank by means of a swiveling connection. The lance could be lowered to a horizontal attitude but not beyond because it collided with the metal waist support. Either an angled or a straight nozzle could be used, both of which were fitted with the early igniter holder. The flamethrower was filled though a curved tube on the left side, while the propellant chamber was filled through a threaded opening on the top. A threaded screw-on cover protected the pressure gauge and propellant filler cap.

Two men were required to fire the weapon. An operator aimed the lance, while an assistant stood beside him and turned a disc-shaped valve that pressurized the oil through an internal feed line. The assistant then opened a block valve on the lance; the pressurized oil rushed into the lance, automatically extending it to its full length and activating the igniter. To contain the powerful recoil, the operator wore a leather lance sling around his right shoulder.

The igniter featured a deep groove around its wooden base. Spring-loaded clips inside the igniter holder fit into this groove to lock the igniter in place during firing. To eject the spent igniter, the operator pulled the igniter holder back along the nozzle, which compressed an internal spring that unlocked the clips. A second spring then ejected the igniter. To fit a new igniter, the operator again pulled the holder back along the nozzle to open the spring-loaded clips. The igniter was inserted and the holder released, allowing the clips to snap into the groove at the base of the igniter.

According to at least one report, the *Kleif M.1912* had an optimum range of about sixty feet.[8] The angled nozzle may have been used when the weapon was deployed defensively from trenches. In 1912 this model of flamethrower was assigned to the siege trains (*Belagerungstrains*) of pioneer regiments, the section which assaulted fortresses. Upon mobilization many if not all pioneer formations were trained in the use of the *Kleif M.1912*. By late 1914 it was mostly withdrawn from service except for on the eastern front, where it was also used as a poison-gas sprayer.

kleine Flammenwerfer (Kleif) M.1914

The *Kleif M.1914* was converted from the *Kleif M.1912* by replacing the telescoping lance on the right side with a swiveling outflow pipe fitted with a oil-release stopcock, to which was attached a rubber hose and lance. It was served by a four-man squad consisting of an *Unteroffizier* or *Gefreiter*, a lance operator, a *Kleif* carrier (*Kleifträger*), and an assistant who also served as replacement and grenadier.

Arming the weapon required three steps. First, the assistant turned a disc-shaped valve on the lower right side of the flamethrower, releasing the propellant into the oil through an internal feed line. Second, the tank carrier opened the stopcock on the end of the outflow pipe, which released oil into the hose. Third, the lance operator quickly opened and shut the lance stopcock, releasing the air from the hose. After all connections were checked to ensure that they were not leaking, the igniter was placed in the holder on the end of the lance; when the lance operator opened the stopcock fully, the igniter was activated.

The *Kleif M.1914* had a range of 50-60 feet[9] and a duration of fifteen seconds with the 0.2-inch (6mm) nozzle; internal pressure of the propellant tank was 338 psi. (23 atm.), which pressurized the oil to 265 psi. (18 atm.) when the weapon was armed.

kleine Flammenwerfer (Kleif) M.1915, early model

This model flamethrower was built in a factory in Westphalia, to the specifications of the 3rd Guard Pioneer Battalion. Closer in layout to the original Fiedler design, it had a welded steel oil tank eighteen inches tall by ten inches in diameter, with a capacity of five gallons. The external propellant tank attached to the back of the oil tank was sixteen inches tall and five inches in diameter. Together the flamethrower and carrying harness had a laden weight of seventy pounds.[10]

As in the case of the *Kleif M.1914*, a four-man squad operated the *Kleif M.1915*. To arm the weapon, the assistant opened a needle valve on the top of the propellant tank, which was pressurized to 338 psi. (23 atm.); the propellant passed through the external feed line and pressurized the oil to 265 psi. (18 atm.) The oil then entered a rigid outflow pipe attached to the shoulder harness and filled the rubber outflow hose that hung in front of the tank carrier. After the tank carrier opened the stopcock on the outflow hose, filling the lance hose, the lance operator expelled the air by quickly opening and shutting the lance stopcock. All connections were checked for leakage, and the igniter was placed in the holder on the lance nozzle.

When the lance operator opened the stopcock fully, the igniter was activated.

This flamethrower had a range of eighty-three feet with the 0.2-inch (6mm) nozzle; a duration of forty-five seconds is given in the French source referenced above, but the actual figure is more likely 20 to 25 seconds.

kleine Flammenwerfer (Kleif) M.1915, late model

This improvement of the *Kleif M.1915* appears to have been fielded in early 1916. The dimensions were identical to those of the earlier model; the main differences were that the rubber outflow hose was replaced by a rigid steel outflow pipe attached by a bracket to the right side of the oil tank, and a protective metal cover was provided for the pressure gauge on the propellant tank.

Arming and firing the weapon was the same process as that of the earlier model.

The late-model *Kleif M.1915* likely had a similar range and duration as the early model. However, the improved weapon was sometimes fitted with a second propellant tank that supplied the additional pressure necessary for curved-trajectory or indirect fire. This flamethrower was still in use as late as April of 1917.

kleine Flammenwerfer (Kleif) M.1916

Externally the *Kleif M.1916* was almost identical to the *Kleif M.1914*, with the same dimensions and oil capacity. The main changes were as follows:

A.) The disc-shaped propellant-release valve on the right side of the flamethrower was replaced with a needle valve on the top of the weapon.

B.) The swiveling outflow pipe on the right side of the flamethrower was replaced with a shorter, curved pipe that was fixed in place.

C.) The internal propellant feed line was replaced with an external line which ran from the propellant valve on top of the tank to the oil-filling tube on the left side. This change was carried out in order to simplify manufacture and repair. According to a postwar French report, the internal propellant feed lines of the *Kleif M.1912* and *M.1914* were impossible to reach in the event of damage or blockage.[11]

D.) A hinged cover replaced the screw-on cover on the top of the flamethrower.

The *Kleif M.1916* was operated by a four-man squad and weighed sixty-eight pounds when full. It had a range of seventy-two feet and a duration of twenty-five seconds with the 0.2-inch (6mm) nozzle, and a range of 105 feet and a duration of twelve seconds with the 0.3-inch (8mm) nozzle. The propellant chamber was filled to 338 psi. (23 atm.), which pressurized the oil to 265 psi. (18 atm.) when the weapon was armed.[12]

To arm and fire the *Kleif M.1916*, the assistant opened the pressurization valve on top of the flamethrower, and the tank carrier fully opened his stopcock, releasing oil into the hose. The lance operator quickly opened and shut the lance stopcock, which emptied the hose of air. After all connections were checked for tightness, the igniter was placed in the holder over the lance nozzle. The igniter was activated when the lance operator fully opened his stopcock.

mittlere Flammenwerfer (Kleif) M.1917

The *Kleif M.1917* was a modification of the *M.1916* that eliminated most of the shortcomings of the former. Major differences were that the oil-filling tube on the left side of the flamethrower was enlarged, and the external propellant feed line was moved from the left side to the right. This allowed it to enter the oil reservoir through a new opening positioned so that the line lay against the surface of the tank, making it less vulnerable to damage incurred during training, transportation, or combat.

Dimensions, performance data, and arming/firing procedures appear to be identical to those of the *Kleif M.1916*. The introduction of the *Wex* (see below) in 1917 as the new "small flamethrower" (*kleine Flammenwerfer*) meant that the former small flamethrower became the "medium flamethrower" (*mittlere Flammenwerfer*). Somewhat confusingly, however, the abbreviation for this model flamethrower remained *Kleif*. It was also known as the "improved small flamethrower" (*verbesserte kleine Flammenwerfer*). Examples were still being manufactured in 1918.

The double *Kleif* (*Doppelkleif*) that utilized the medium flamethrower had a capacity of 8.4 gallons, a range of 100-116 feet, and a duration of twenty-two seconds with the 0.4-inch (11mm) nozzle.[13]

Wechselapparat (Wex) M.1917

This flamethrower was designed and built by engineers in the workshops of the Guard Reserve Pioneer Battalion.[14] It was readily distinguishable from other models in that it was comprised of a ring-shaped oil tank with a spherical propellant container in its center, both in welded steel. "*Wex*" was an abbreviation for "interchangeable apparatus" (*Wechselapparat*); the original plan was for a *Wex* squad to be armed with three flamethrowers and only one lance and hose. The threaded hex coupling on the hose was replaced with a quick-release friction connector that allowed empty flamethrowers to be exchanged for full ones without the use of wrenches. Since the process was difficult to carry out under combat conditions, the *Wex* was ultimately fielded as a single device equipped with one lance and hose and served by the same four-man squad as the *Kleif*.[15] The *Wex* appears to have seen its first combat use in early May of 1917.[16]

The oil capacity of 2.9 gallons gave the *Wex* a laden weight of fifty-five pounds. It had a range of eighty-two feet and a duration of twenty seconds with the 0.2-inch (6mm) nozzle, and a range of ninety-eight feet and a duration of nine seconds with the 0.3-inch (8mm) nozzle. Propellant pressure was 338 psi. (23 atm.), which brought the oil to 265 psi. (18 atm.) when the weapon was armed.[17] The oil ring was filled through a cap on the top, while the propellant sphere was filled through an opening on its underside.

To arm and fire the flamethrower, the carrier reached behind him with his left hand and opened the pressurization valve; he then opened his stopcock to release oil into the hose. The lance operator quickly opened and shut his lance to empty the hose of air, after which the igniter was placed in the holder over the lance nozzle. When the lance operator fully opened his stopcock, the igniter was activated.

Being smaller and lighter, the apparatus could be fired by the *Wex* carrier (*Wexträger*) alone, in the event that the squad *Unteroffizier* or *Gefreiter*, lance operator, and assistant were wounded or killed. Many Allied reports showed that *Wex* carriers often continued flamethrower attacks by themselves, despite the difficulty of handling the lance and the stiff five-foot hose.

Battery models of the *Wex* were not used because neither the the range of the jet nor the duration were appreciably increased compared to those of a single *Wex*.

As mentioned above, the *Wex* became the new "small flamethrower," while the *Kleif* became the "medium flamethrower."

Field-manufactured and Other Flamethrowers

Although the *Fiedler-Flammenapparate Gesellschaft* and subcontractors such as Minimax A.G., Selke GmbH, and *Siegler Flammenwerfer Gesellschaft* provided most of the weapons used by the Guard Reserve Pioneer Regiment, there was an element of competition between Richard Fiedler and Bernhard Reddemann. The latter wanted to keep the flamethrower regiment as independent as possible, so he authorized the regiment's workshop to copy Fiedler's designs and create their own. Not much is known about these in-house flamethrowers, but the field-manufactured copies of Fiedler's weapons were by most accounts inferior to the originals. The major shortcomings were that oil tanks were unable to maintain the required pressure, and the Fielder valves and igniters could not be duplicated.

There is also evidence that the Germans modified captured French Schilt No. 3 flamethrowers and used them in combat, although not extensively.

Lances

The Pioneer Experimental Company improved the original Fiedler flamethrower by developing lances capable of firing multiple shots. The basic German flamethrower lance had a steel jet tube (*Strahlrohr*), a brass stopcock and handle, and a brass nozzle. The nozzle was threaded to the jet tube and tightened or loosened by turning the hex nut cast into its base. In 1916 the jet tube of the small lance was fitted with a handled coupling that aided nozzle replacement by creating a firmer grip for the operator. The nozzle of the large flamethrower was 0.4 inch (11mm) in diameter; portable flamethrowers could be fitted with nozzles in diameters of either 0.2 inch (6mm) or 0.3 inch (8mm).[18] The larger-diameter nozzles were painted with a red stripe for easy identification; they increased the range at the cost of duration.

A funnel-shaped brass igniter holder (*Zünderhalter*) was attached over the lance nozzle. (For a description of the early-model igniter holder, see the *Kleif M.1912* above.) After 1914 the igniter holder was fitted with an internal spring and a retaining fork attached to a short length of chain. To arm the post-1914 lance, the operator pushed a cylindrical igniter into the igniter holder, compressing the spring, and inserted the two-pronged retaining fork that fit into a groove in the base of the igniter. The tension from the compressed spring held the igniter tightly against the fork. To fire the lance, the operator opened the stopcock, releasing a rush of pressurized oil that activated the igniter. When the igniter was spent, the operator removed the retaining fork, and the spring in the igniter holder ejected the empty shell.

In 1917 a new igniter holder was introduced. It featured a hinged flap that incorporated the two-pronged retaining fork, thus eliminating the flimsy chain and reducing the process of expelling the spent igniter to one movement.

Most lances had a simple stopcock or ball valve which was opened with a faucetlike handle; however, two models of self-closing gate valve were developed to prevent a wounded or killed operator from spinning and accidentally spraying his comrades.[19] A second benefit of both self-closing valves was that they reduced recoil and thereby improved accuracy.

The early-model self-closing valve was a thick, pedal-shaped bar attached to a spring housing at the base of the lance. The operator lifted the bar into the "open" position for firing; when the bar was released, it was pulled back into the closed position by the tension in the coiled spring.

The late-model self-closing valve was a copy of a French design used on the Schilt No. 3 *bis* flamethrower. To fire the lance the operator squeezed the grip in the manner of releasing an automobile brake handle of the day. The internal spring caused the valve to close when the grip was released.

A.) 5-foot (1.5m) large lance (*grosse Strahlrohr*) - Weighed 15.4 pounds[20] and was used with both the large flamethrower and the double *Kleif*. The M.1914 had an igniter fork attached by a short length of chain, while the M.1917 had a hinged flap that incorporated the igniter fork.

B.) Telescoping large lance (*grosse Strahlrohr*) - Retracted length of 4.5 feet (1.35m); extended length of 5.7 feet (1.75m).[21] It is unclear if the lance was extended by hand prior to firing or if the act of firing automatically extended the lance, as was the case of the *Kleif M.1912*. The M.1914 had an igniter fork attached by a short length of chain; the M.1917 had a hinged flap that incorporated the igniter fork.

C.) 4.6-foot (1.4m) small lance (*kleine Strahlrohr*) M.1914 - Fitted with an igniter fork attached to igniter holder by short length of chain.

D.) 4-foot (1.2m) small lance (*kleine Strahlrohr*) M.1914 - 7.7 pounds in weight.[22] Igniter fork attached by short length of chain. Identical to 4.6-foot small lance except in length.

E.) 3.6-foot (1.1m) small lance (*kleine Strahlrohr*) M.1916 - Shortened in order to make it easier to use in trenches. Jet tube fitted with handled coupling to give operator a better grip when changing nozzles. Igniter fork attached by short length of chain.

F.) 3.6-foot (1.1m) small lance (*kleine Strahlrohr*) M.1917 - Identical to M.1916 small lance except that the igniter fork was held in the nozzle by a hinged flap, and the hose coupling was simplified.

G.) 3.3-foot (1m) small lance (*kleine Strahlrohr*) M.1918 - 5.5 pounds in weight.[23] Similar to the small lance M.1917, with a shortened nozzle.

Colors of Flamethrowers and Lances

Flamethrowers and lances were factory painted in shades of field gray that ranged from greenish to almost black. During winter the troops applied a water-soluble whitewash. The top half of the *Kleif* was sometimes painted brown or white to match the surrounding terrain, providing concealment when the flamethrower protruded from foxholes or trenches.

Late-model *Kleif* and *Wex* were often painted in camouflage of at least three distinct patterns. The first was similar to the regulation camouflage applied to steel helmets and consisted of wide bands of contrasting colors separated by thin black lines. A second pattern was feathered daubs of paint applied with a wide brush, while a third resembled the hard-edged "lozenges" seen on aircraft, artillery pieces, and armor. Colors were mostly greens, ochres, and browns, but grays, blues, and purples were occasionally used as well. In addition, cloth camouflage covers were sometimes put on flamethrowers to prevent light from reflecting off the paint.

Hoses

The "jet-tube hose" (*Strahlrohrschlauch*) was made of rubber sheathed in linen and wrapped in steel wire to prevent it from being folded, kinked, or punctured. The wire was wrapped much more tightly at both ends, which were often covered with short linen sleeves.

Until 1917 both ends of the hose were fitted with threaded hex couplings. In the case of the *Wex*, however, a quick-release friction coupling connected the hose to the oil-tank outflow pipe so that operators could switch tanks in a matter of seconds. Previously, this action required a wrench and several minutes. There was also a brass-forked junction that allowed two *Kleif* to be hooked up to a single five-foot (1.5m) *Grof* lance to provide prolonged fire in areas where the large flamethrowers could not be transported.

The *Grof* hose was 16.4 feet long[24] and weighed forty pounds,[25] while the *Kleif* hose was five feet long[26] and weighed 6.8 pounds.[27] Since the hose used with the double *Kleif* was 9.8 feet long, it likely weighed about twice as much as the *Kleif* hose.

Igniters

The German flamethrower igniter (*Zünder*) was based on the percussion fuse used in projectiles.[28] It was essentially a double-walled tube filled with a combustible fusing compound and capped with a metal lid.

A.) First type of igniter - This model was made of brass, with a steel tube running through the center. At the base of the tube, a gelatin piston with a steel firing pin sat on a leather cushion. When the operator opened the stopcock of the lance, the pressurized oil drove the cushion, piston, and firing pin into an aluminum stopper that contained a capsule of fulminate of mercury. The entire unit was projected the length of the cartridge and struck the iron lid fixed to the end, causing the firing pin to detonate the fulminate of mercury. Cotton wicks in the iron lid transmitted the ignition through four vents bored in the walls of the aluminum stopper, lighting paraffined fuses that in turn ignited the combustible compound in the walls of the cartridge. The piston, firing pin, aluminum stopper, fulminate capsule, and iron lid were ejected by the initial gout of flame. Since the compound burned for approximately ninety seconds, the flamethrower operator could fire multiple bursts.

This igniter was 8.7 inches in length by 1.8 inches in diameter. The wooden base had a deep groove into which fit the two prongs of the retaining fork.

B.) Second type of igniter - This igniter was similar to the first type, with the following differences:

The double-walled shell was made of sheet tin instead of brass; the fulminate of mercury capsule was now fixed in place, protruding from the top of the cartridge; and the firing pin was attached to a metal spring on top of the gelatin piston instead of being attached directly to the piston itself.

The initial rush of pressurized oil drove the piston and firing pin down the interior channel and into the fulminate of mercury capsule. Four coal-dust wicks transmitted the ignition to the fusing compound within the walls of the sheet-tin shell, causing the metal envelope to become red hot and forming siliceous slag inside interior channel. The heat, the slag, and the flames from the fusing compound all helped ignite the oil as it passed. The initial burst of flame ejected the piston, firing pin, and spent fulminate of mercury capsule, leaving a clear passageway for the liquid. When the igniter burned out, the operator removed the two-pronged retaining key, and the spent shell was ejected by the igniter-holder spring.

The second type of igniter was 8.5 inches in length by 1.8 inches in diameter. The fusing compound was made up of 7.86 percent sulfur, 24.8 percent pitch, 60.01 percent potash nitrate, and eight percent coal.

C.) Third type of igniter - Produced in 1917 to coincide with the introduction of the *Wex* and the light *Grof*, it was said to be safer than earlier models of igniter.[29] It followed the same general layout as the first two types, with the following differences:

The primer was fixed inside the body of the igniter and was composed of black powder and magnesium instead of fulminate of mercury; the gelatin piston was replaced with one made from adhesive and glycerin; the double-walled shell of the igniter was changed from sheet metal to thin steel; and the wooden base was eliminated.

A protective steel lid covered the top half of the igniter, held in place by adhesive tape. Before firing, the operator removed the lid; as in the case of earlier igniters, the initial rush of pressurized oil pushed the firing pin through the interior channel into the primer, and cotton wicks were again used to transmit ignition to the fusing compound. However, the piston and firing pin were ejected from the nozzle only after the zinc blades holding them place had been melted by the heat.

The third type of igniter was 9.1 inches in length by 1.8 inches in diameter. The fusing compound consisted of nitrate of barium, potassium nitrate, magnesium, charcoal, and a "resinous substance."

Flame Oil

Charles Theune wrote that flame oil was composed of a mixture of coal-tar residue with other chemical additions, light and heavy hydrocarbons, coal-tar oil, and carbon disulphide.[30] It had a specific gravity of 1. The light materials heightened combustibility, and the heavy materials increased the range of the flame jet.

According to the French, the three different samples of German flame oil they tested had three different compositions. The first sample consisted mainly of wood distillate with acetone, methyl alcohol, ethylene hydrocarbons, carbolic acids, and pyridine bases. The second sample was composed of forty-two to forty-five percent oil of acetone (the residue of the manufacture of ordinary acetone) and fifty-five to fifty-eight percent wood tar free of pyroligneus acid (wood vinegar) and creosote. The third sample comprised thirty percent carbon disulfide, forty-five percent oil of acetone, and twenty-five percent pitch.[31]

There were four grades of flame oil, color coded by their thickness:

A.) Blue oil - The oil most employed in the field. Relatively thick flowing, it produced a heavy flame that heightened the adverse psychological impact on the enemy. Blue oil was susceptible to thickening further in severe cold, which could clog the flamethrower. Under such conditions, Yellow oil was substituted.

B.) Yellow oil - A thin, quick-burning oil that produced little smoke and a very hot flame. When Yellow oil was used, it was imperative that the valves and couplings of the flamethrower be tightened to prevent leakage, the major cause of accidental burns or explosions. Yellow oil was also dangerous to use in enclosed spaces such as dugouts and tunnels because of its strong fumes.

C.) Green oil - A mixture of one part Blue and three parts Yellow oil. It produced a heavy smoke but retained some of the heat of Yellow oil.

D.) Red oil - The cheapest, thickest grade of oil, used for training purposes only and never in the field. It produced more smoke than heat. When Red oil was used, the flamethrower had to be carefully cleaned afterward.

All four grades of flame oil decomposed over time, thickening into clumps and clogging the valves, nozzles, and hoses of flamethrowers. Regular cleaning and inspection of the equipment was paramount.

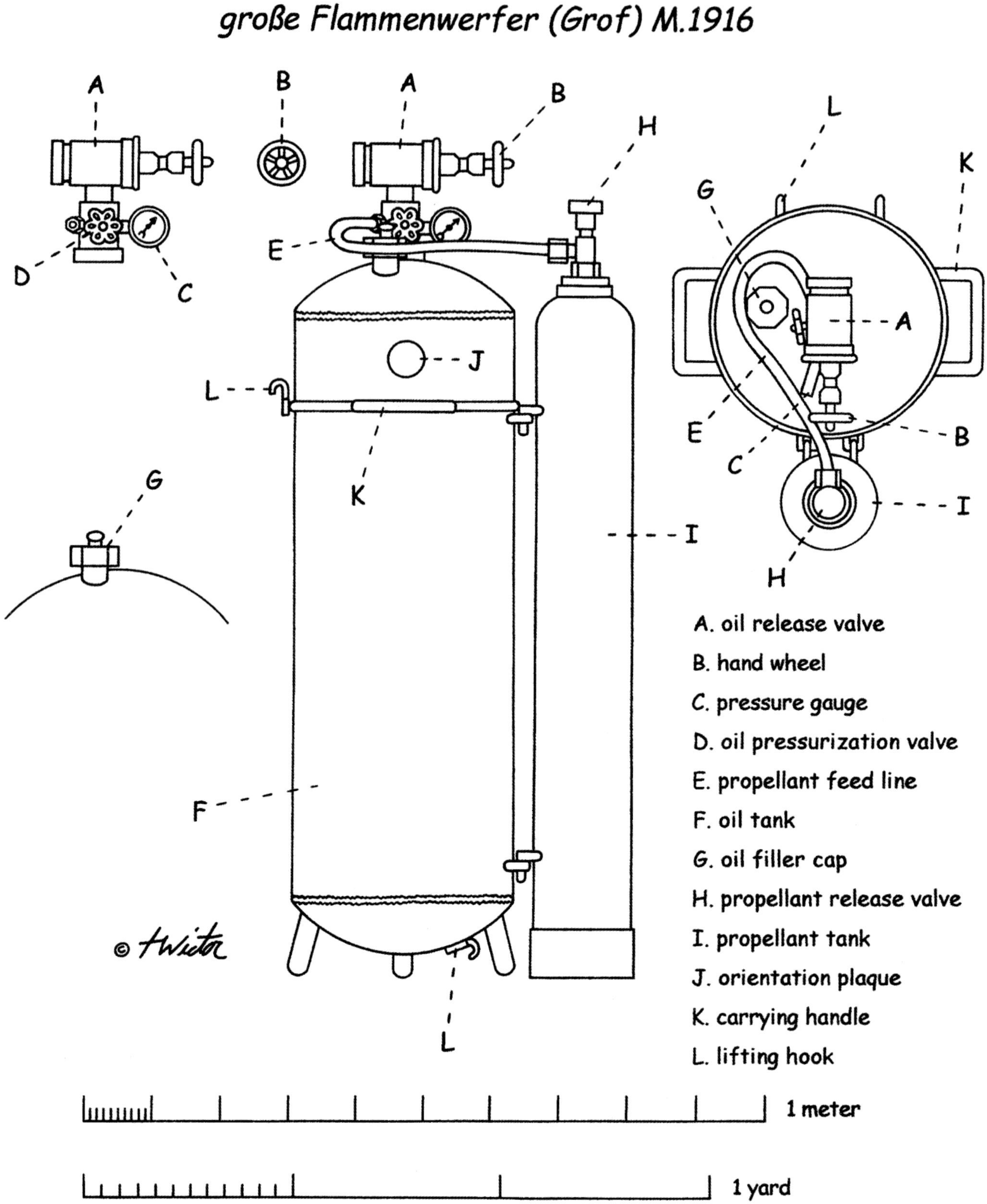
große Flammenwerfer (Grof) M.1916
A
B
A
B
H
L
K
G
E
D
C
J
L
A
E
B
C
K
I
I
G
H
F
© Twictor
L
A. oil release valve
B. hand wheel
C. pressure gauge
D. oil pressurization valve
E. propellant feed line
F. oil tank
G. oil filler cap
H. propellant release valve
I. propellant tank
J. orientation plaque
K. carrying handle
L. lifting hook
1 meter
1 yard

kleine Flammenwerfer (Kleif) M.1912

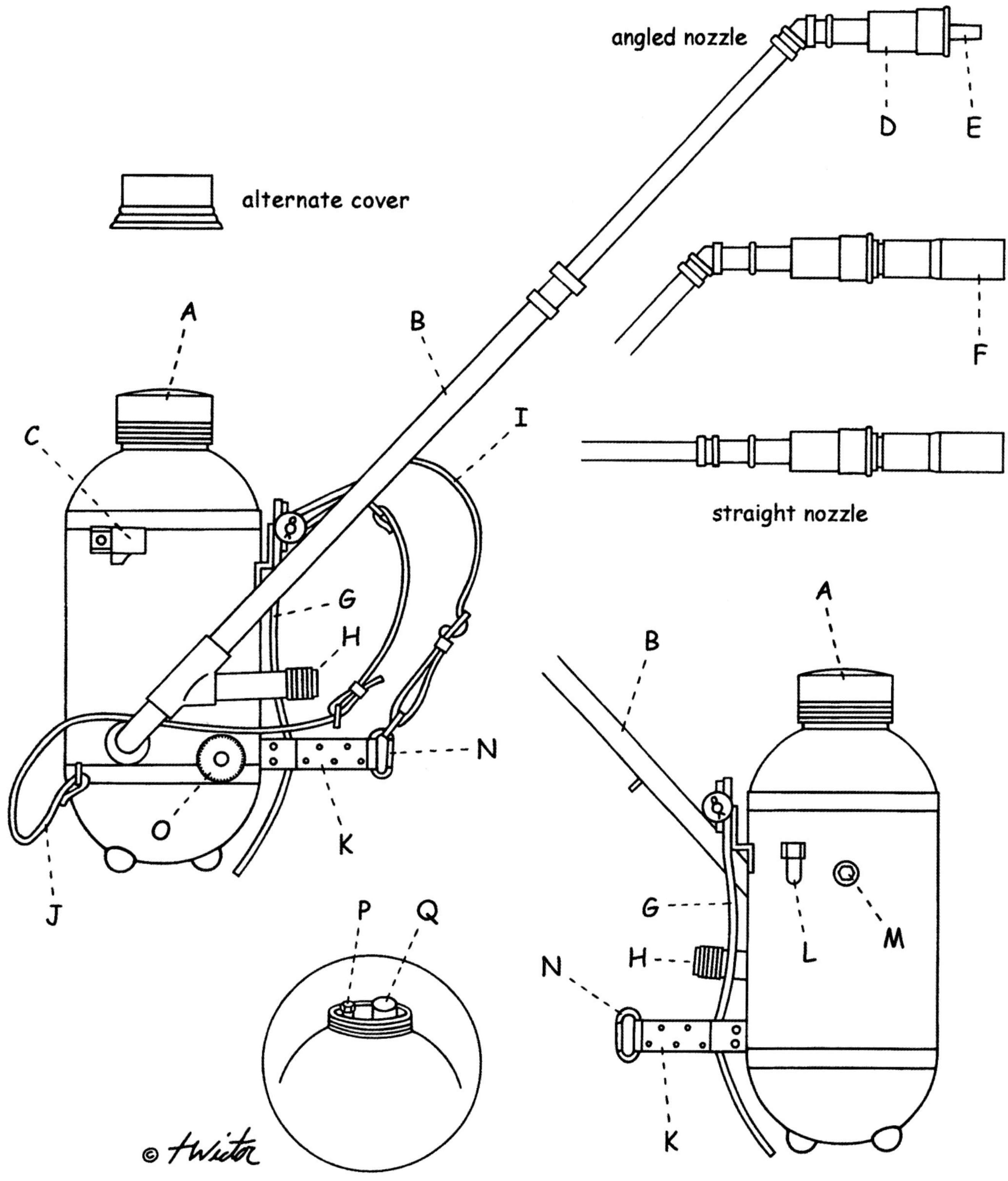

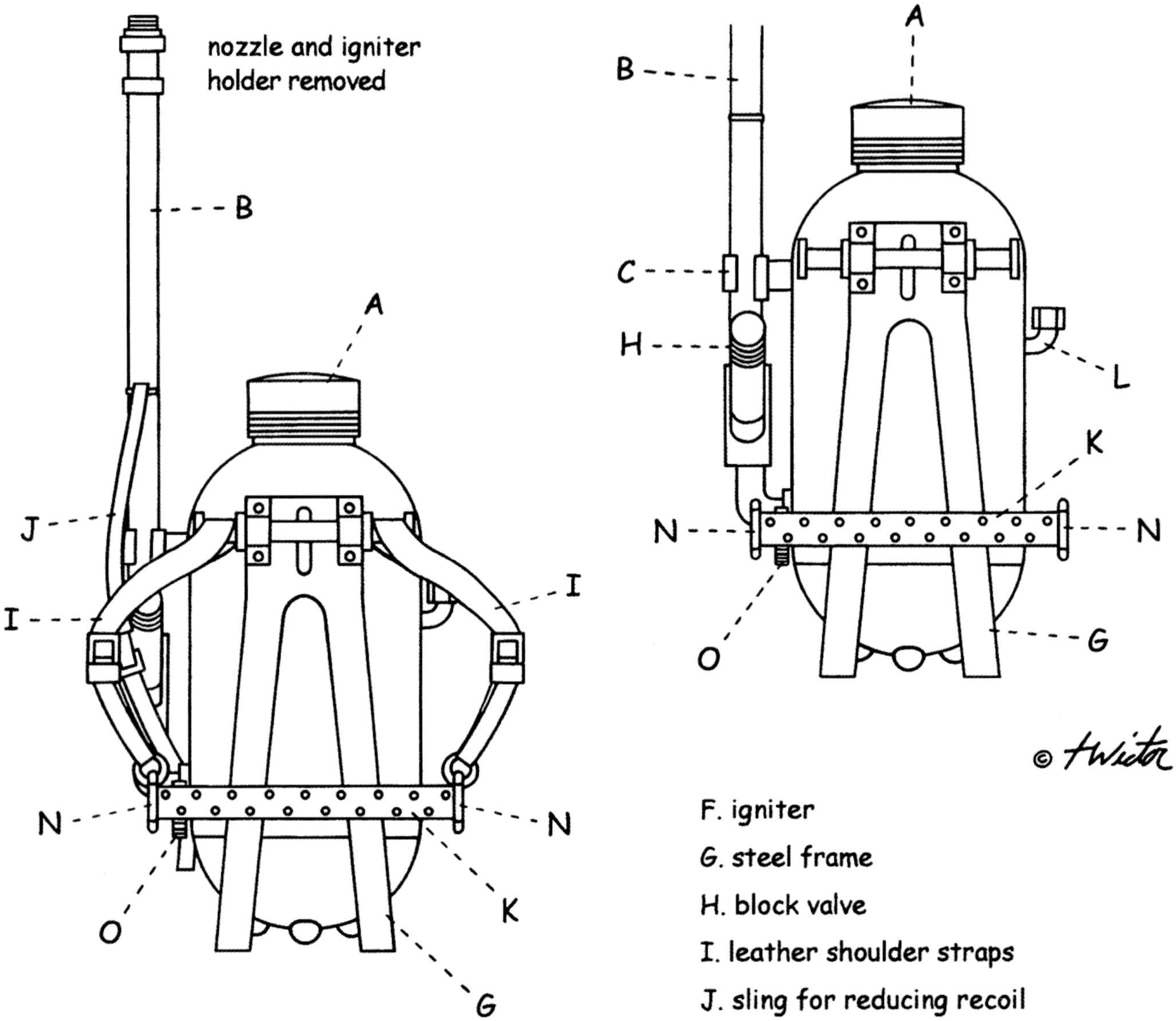

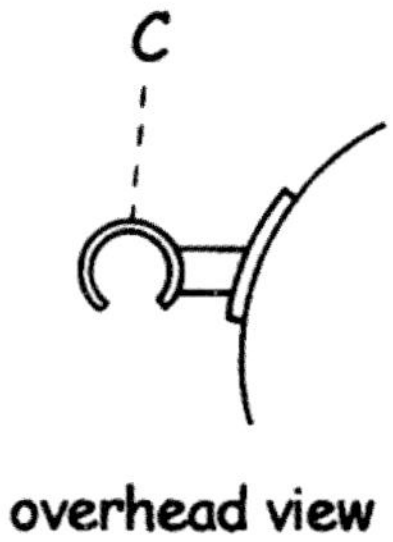

A. threaded cover
B. telescoping lance
C. retaining clamp for lance
D. igniter holder
E. nozzle
F. igniter
G. steel frame
H. block valve
I. leather shoulder straps
J. sling for reducing recoil
K. leather-padded steel waist support
L. oil filler tube
M. threaded relief plug
N. carabiner clip
O. propellant/oil release valve
P. pressure gauge
Q. propellant filler cap

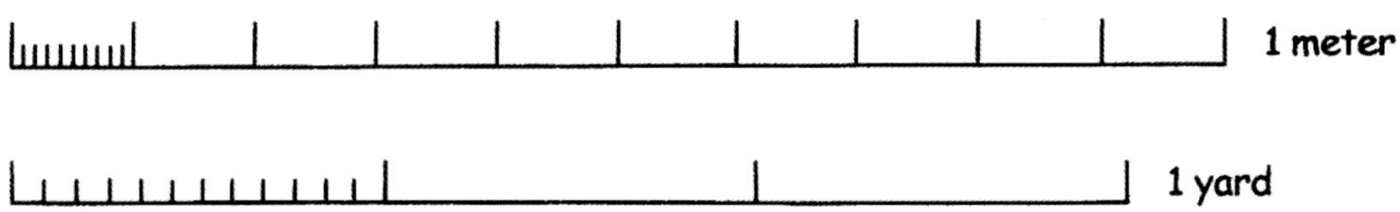

kleine Flammenwerfer (Kleif) M.1914

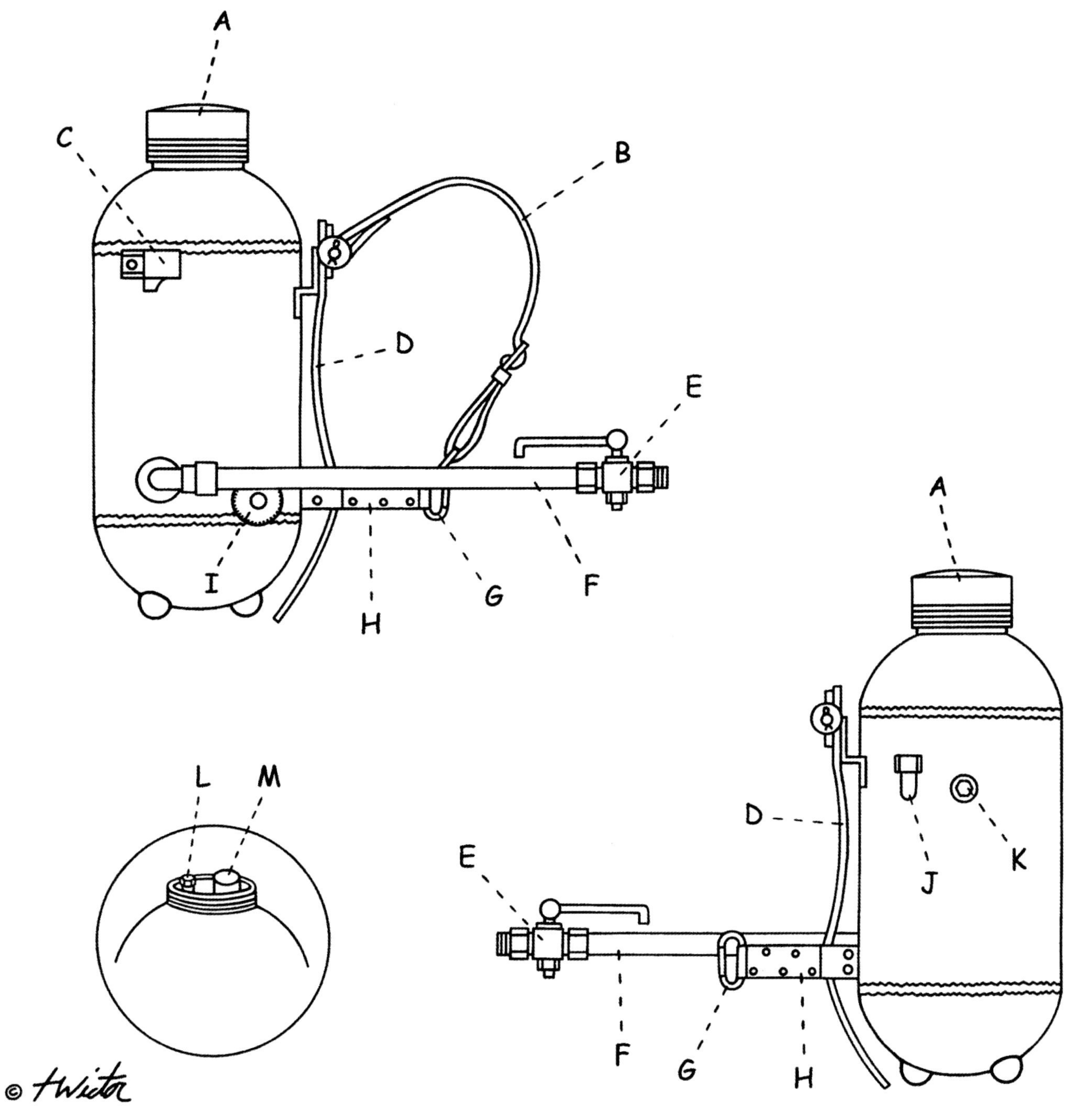

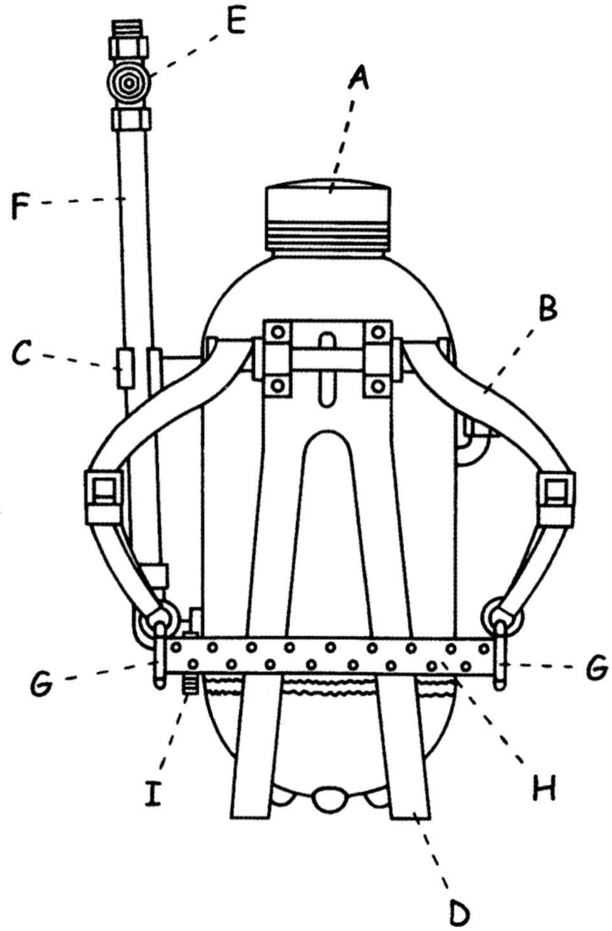

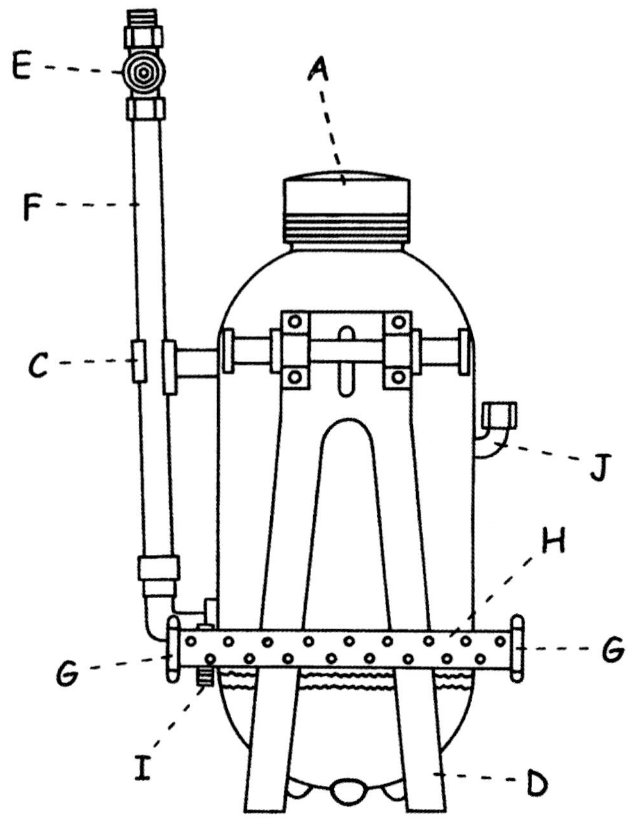

C. retaining clamp for oil outflow pipe

D. steel frame

E. oil release stopcock

F. swiveling oil outflow pipe

G. carabiner clip

H. leather-padded steel waist support

I. propellant release valve

J. oil filler tube

K. threaded relief plug

L. propellant filler cap

M. pressure gauge

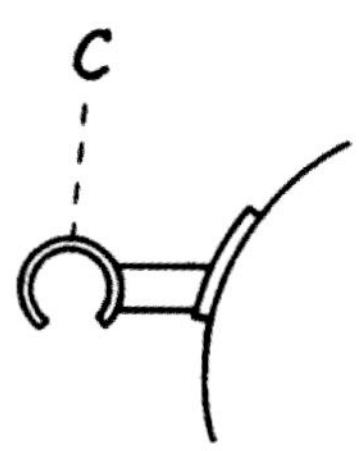

overhead view

© twitor

A. threaded cover

B. leather shoulder straps

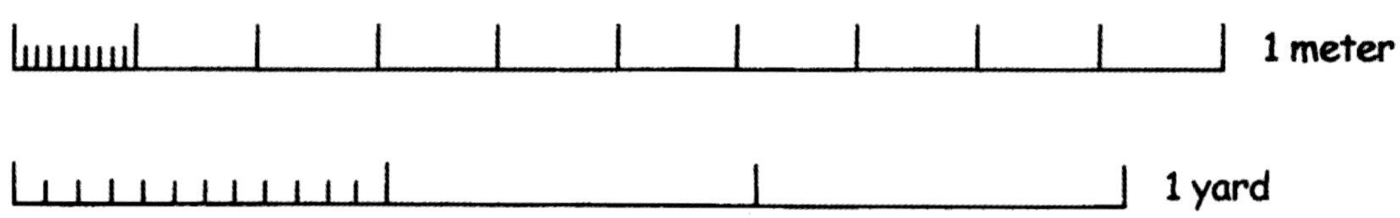

kleine Flammenwerfer (Kleif) M.1915

Early Model

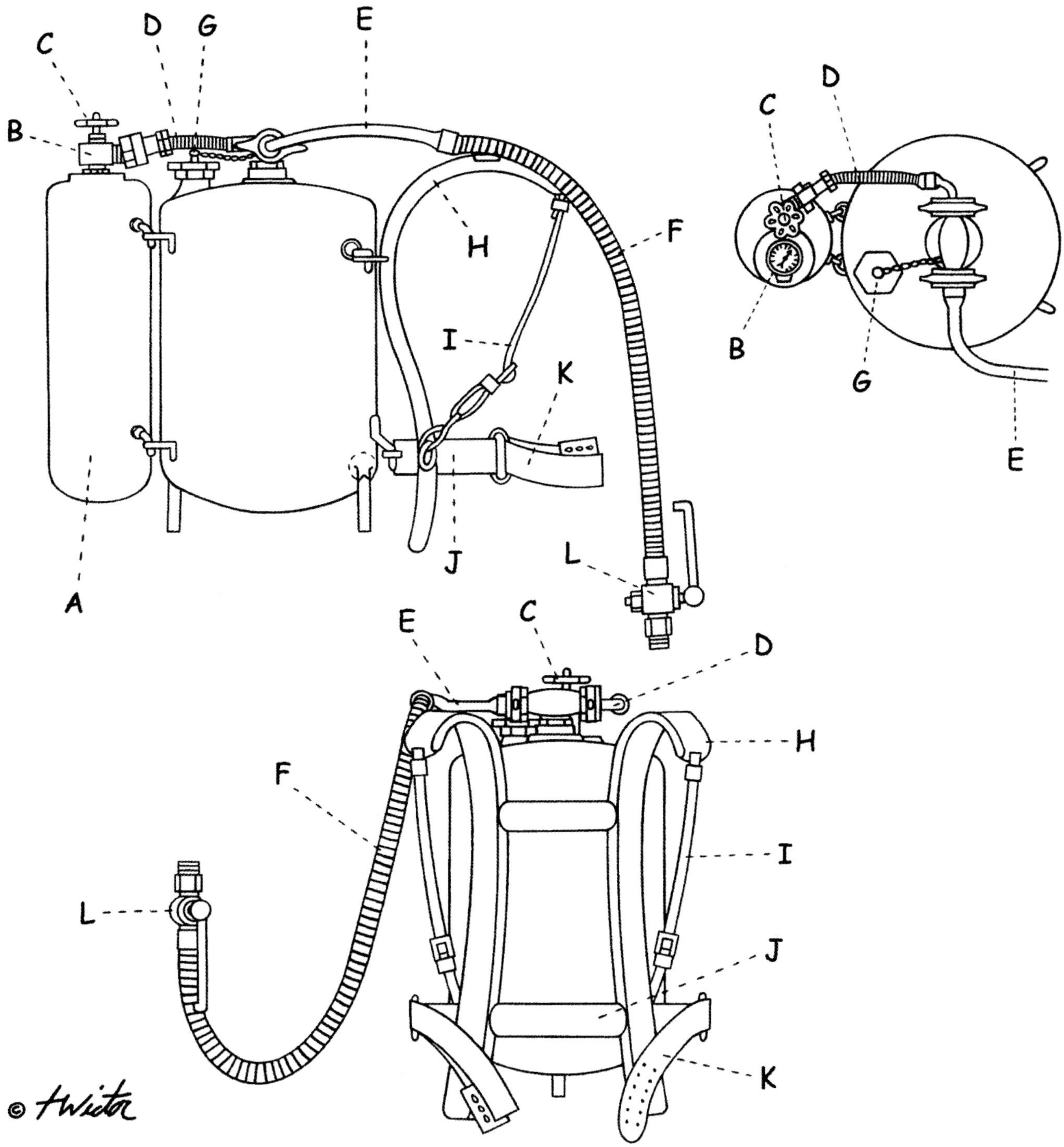

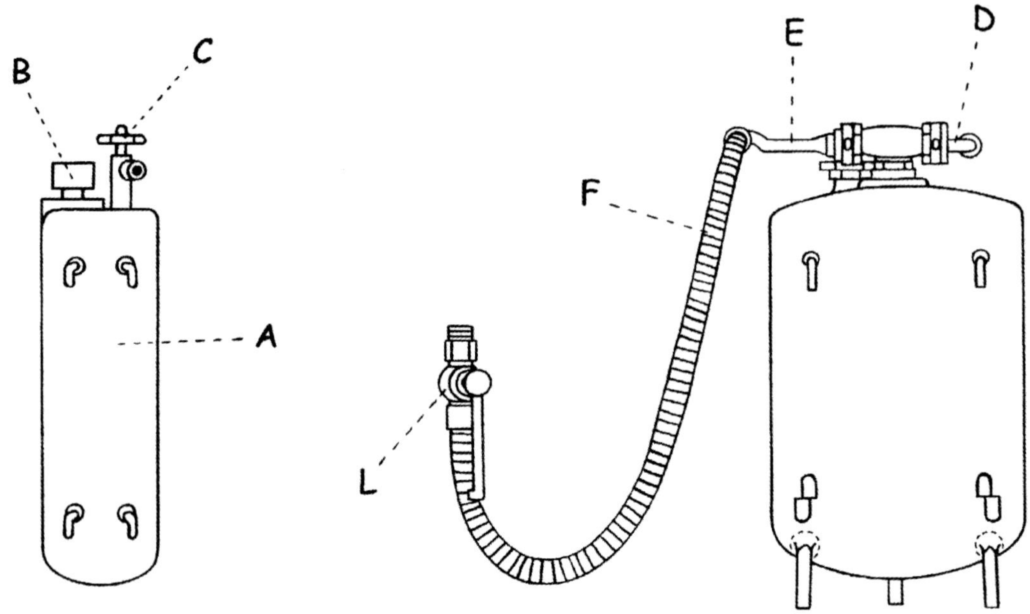

Most dimensions estimated from photographs.

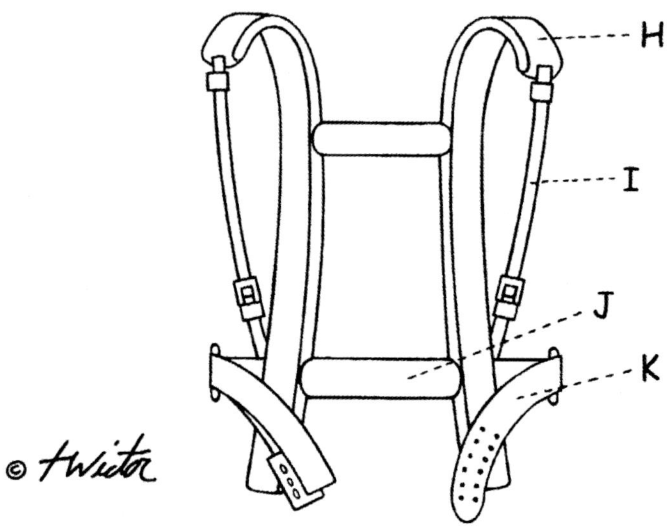

A. propellant tank
B. pressure gauge
C. propellant release valve
D. propellant feed line
E. oil outflow pipe
F. rubber outflow hose
G. oil filler cap
H. leather-padded steel frame
I. leather shoulder straps
J. leather-padded steel waist support
K. leather waist belt
L. oil release stopcock

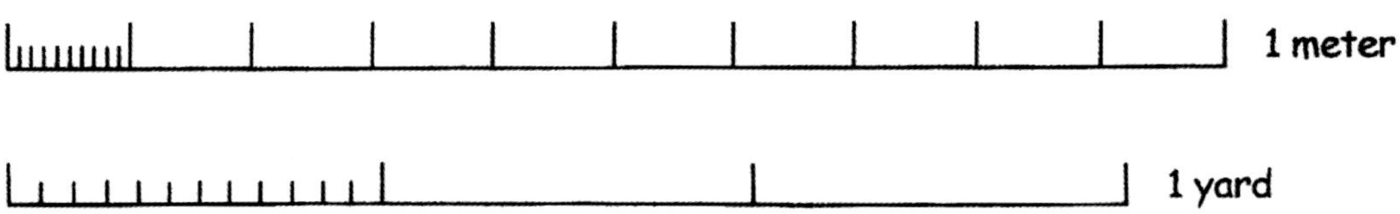

kleine Flammenwerfer (Kleif) M.1915

Late Model

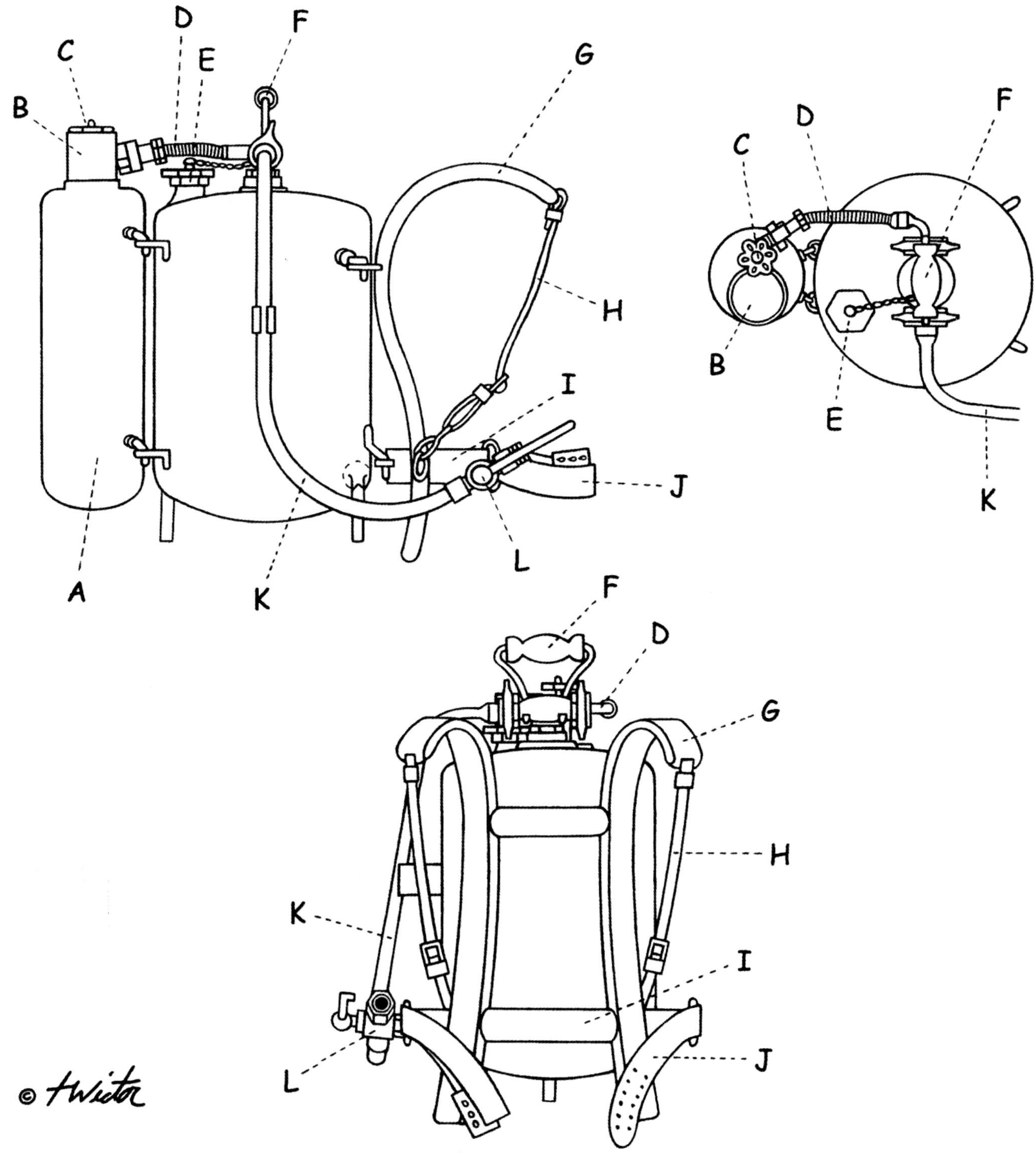

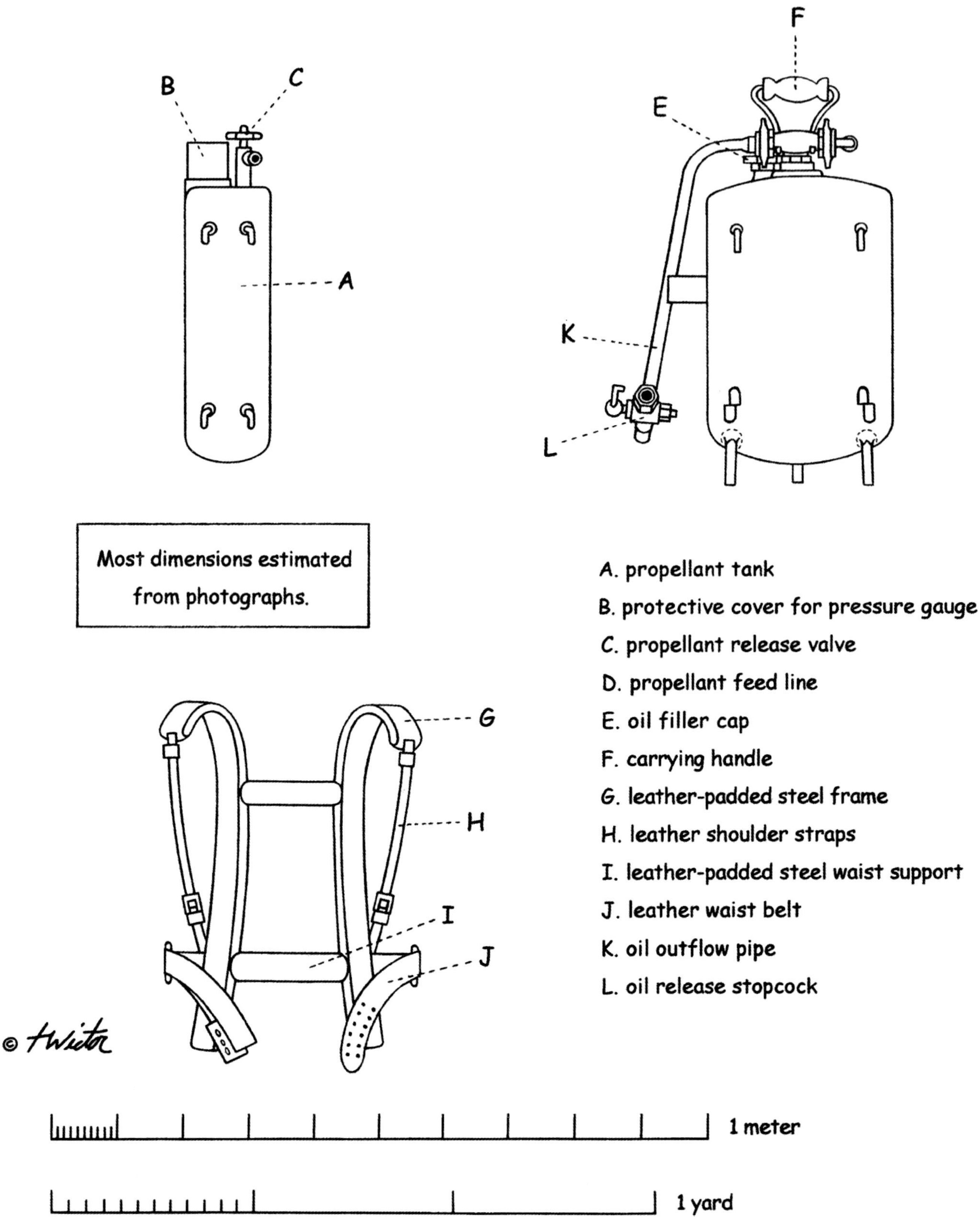
B
C
A
F
E
K
L
Most dimensions estimated from photographs.
A. propellant tank
B. protective cover for pressure gauge
C. propellant release valve
D. propellant feed line
E. oil filler cap
F. carrying handle
G. leather-padded steel frame
H. leather shoulder straps
I. leather-padded steel waist support
J. leather waist belt
K. oil outflow pipe
L. oil release stopcock
G
H
I
J
© twictor
1 meter
1 yard

kleine Flammenwerfer (Kleif) M.1916

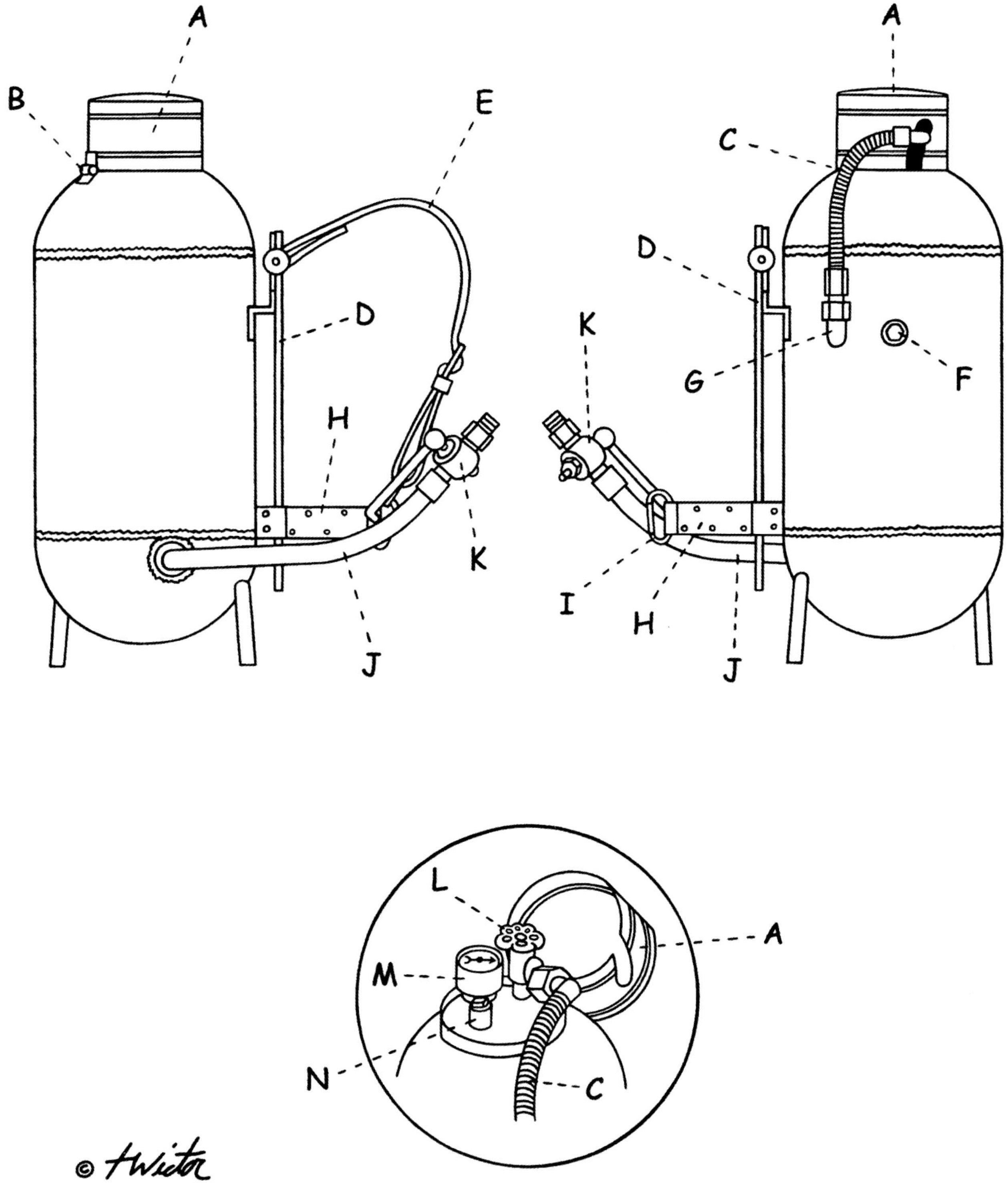

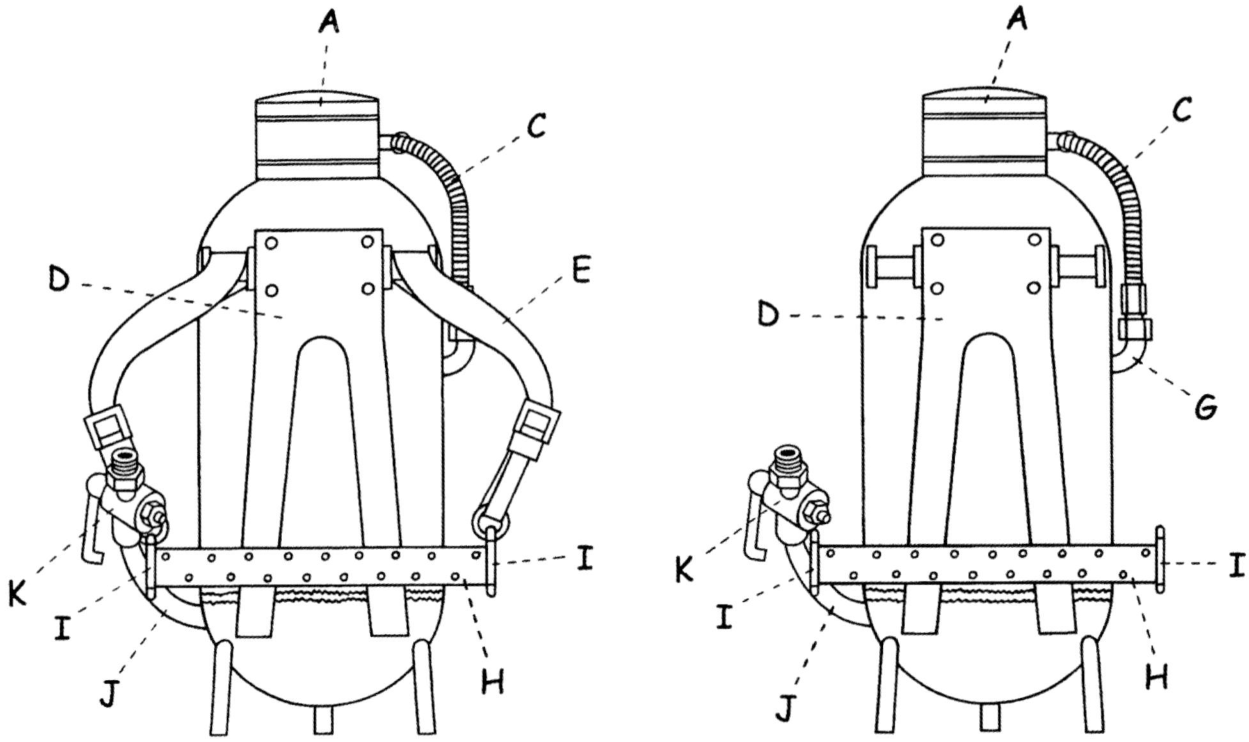

A. hinged cover
B. hinge
C. propellant feed line
D. steel frame
E. leather shoulder straps
F. threaded relief plug
G. oil filler tube
H. leather-padded steel waist support
I. carabiner clip
J. oil outflow pipe
K. oil release stopcock
L. propellant release valve
M. pressure gauge
N. propellant filler cap

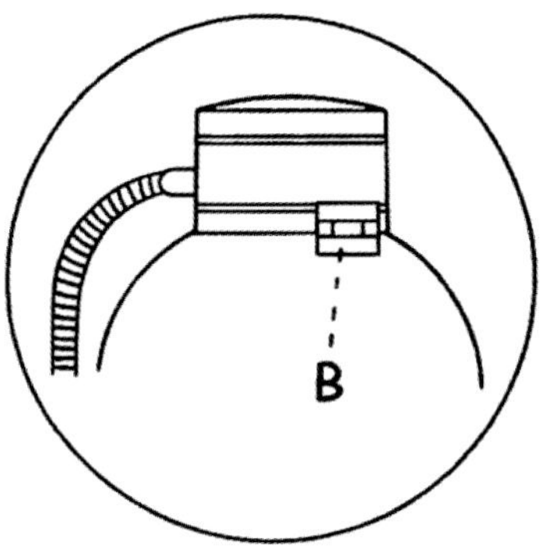

Rear view

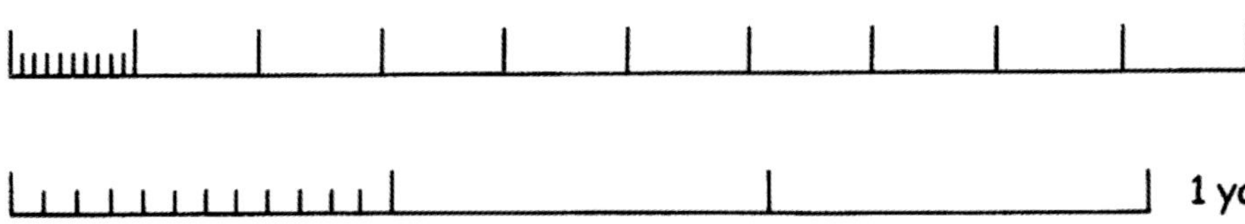

mittlere Flammenwerfer (Kleif) M.1917

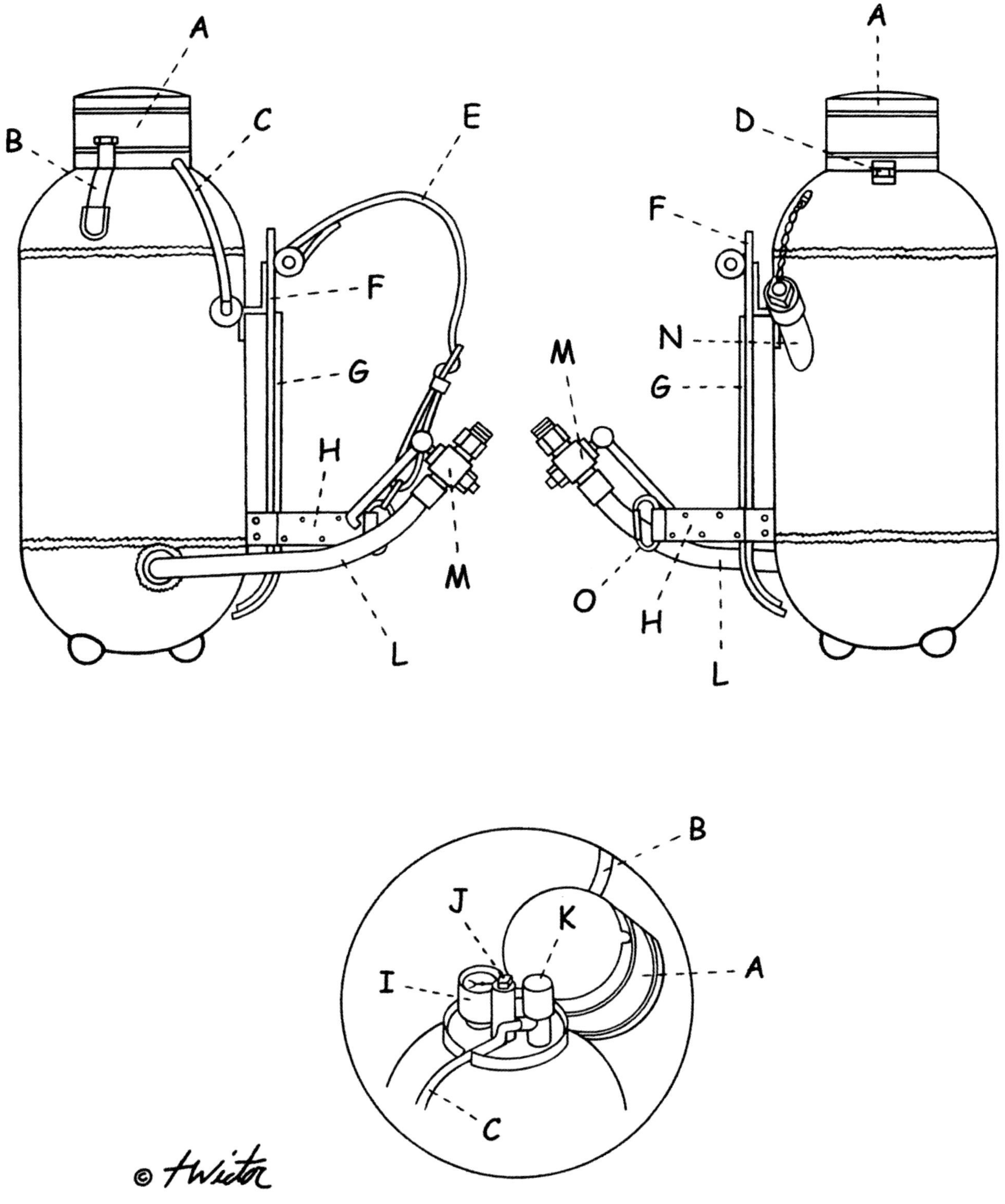

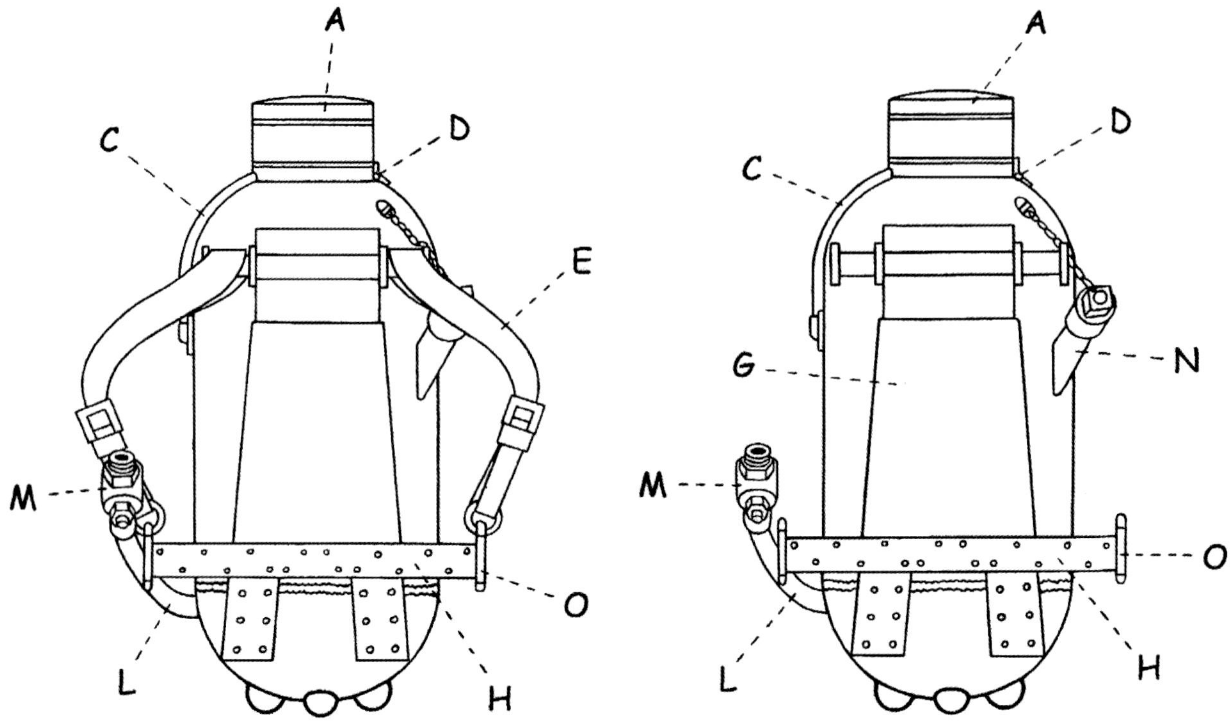

A. hinged cover
B. securing strap
C. propellant feed line
D. hinge
E. leather shoulder straps
F. steel frame
G. leather padding
H. leather-padded steel waist support
I. pressure gauge
J. propellant filler cap
K. propellant release valve
L. oil outflow pipe
M. oil release stopcock
N. oil filler tube
O. carabiner clip
P. orientation plaque

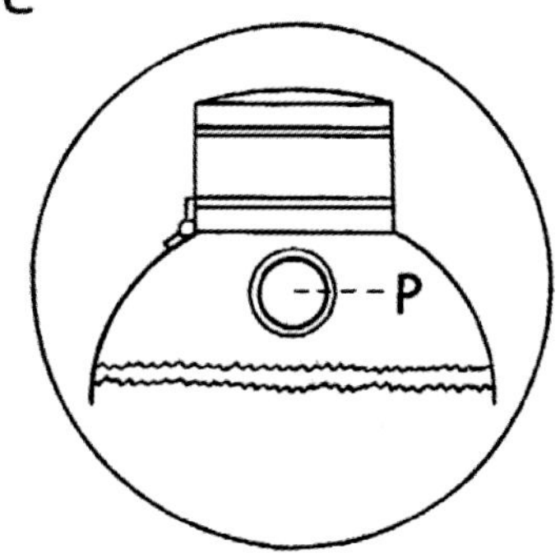

Rear view

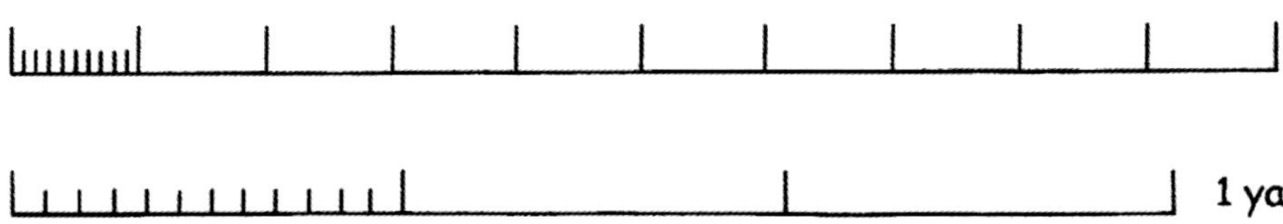

Wechselapparat (Wex) M.1917

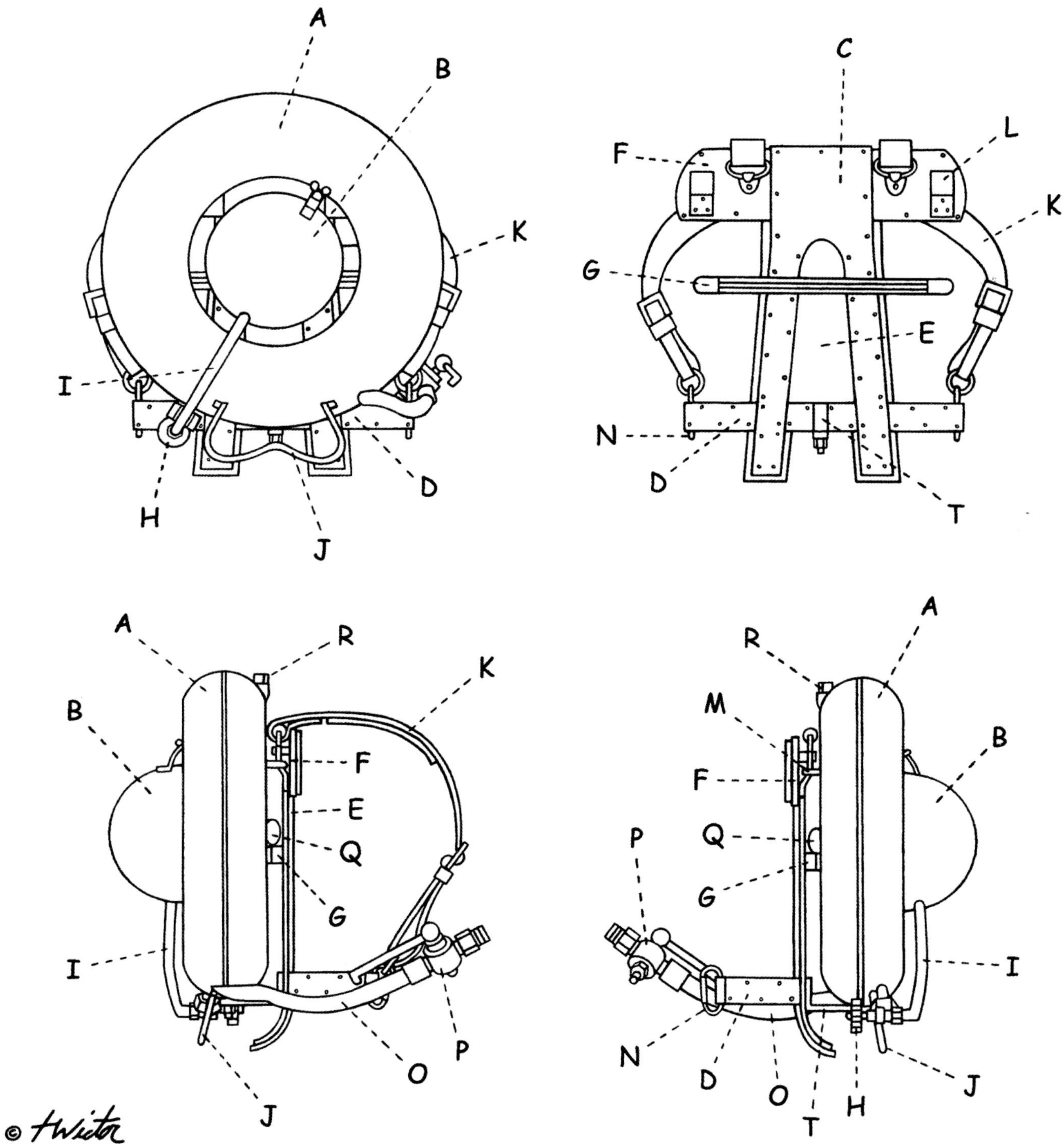

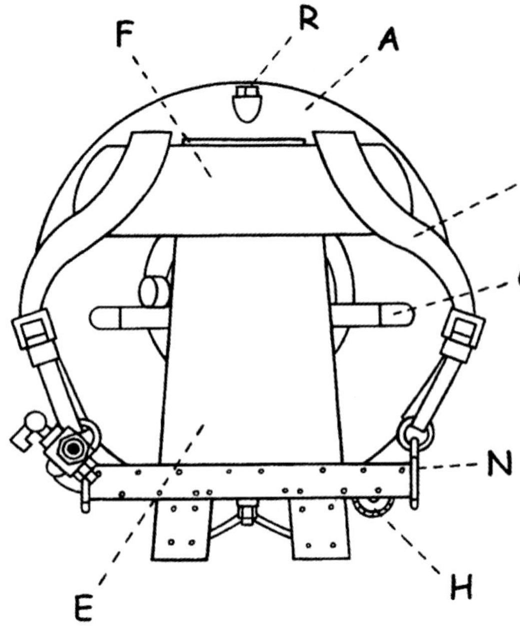

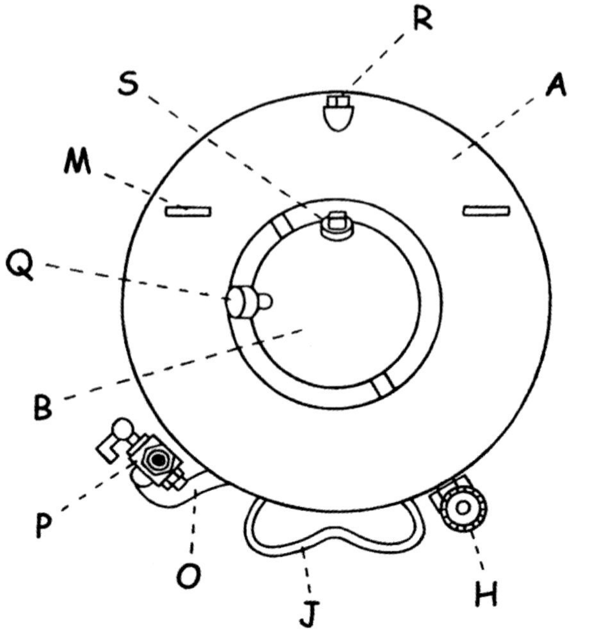

A. oil tank
B. propellant tank
C. steel frame
D. leather-padded steel waist support
E. leather padding
F. leather-padded steel back support
G. oil tank support brace
H. propellant release valve
I. propellant feed line
J. wire stand
K. leather or webbing shoulder straps
L. steel tongue
M. U-shaped support bracket
N. carabiner clip
O. oil outflow pipe
P. oil release stopcock
Q. pressure gauge
R. oil filler cap
S. propellant filler cap
T. L-shaped support bracket

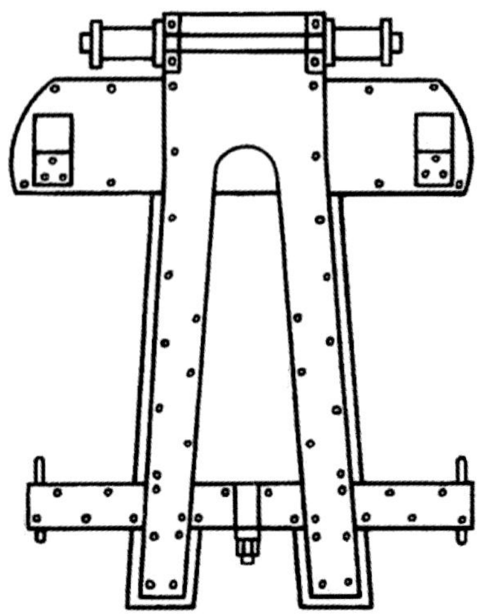
Early knapsack frame

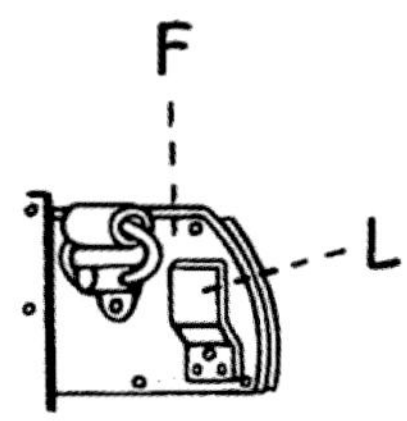

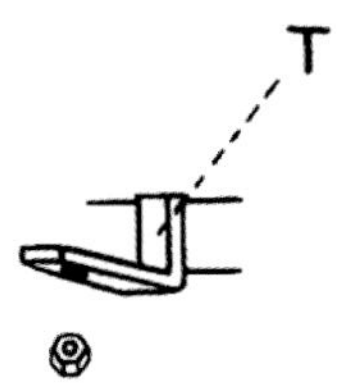

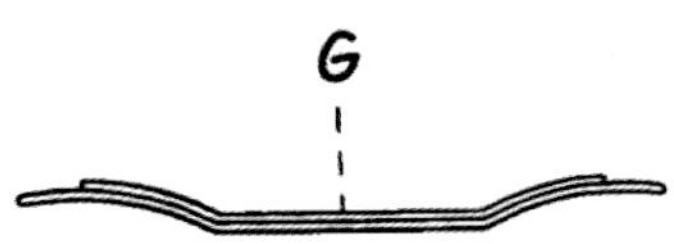

Overhead view

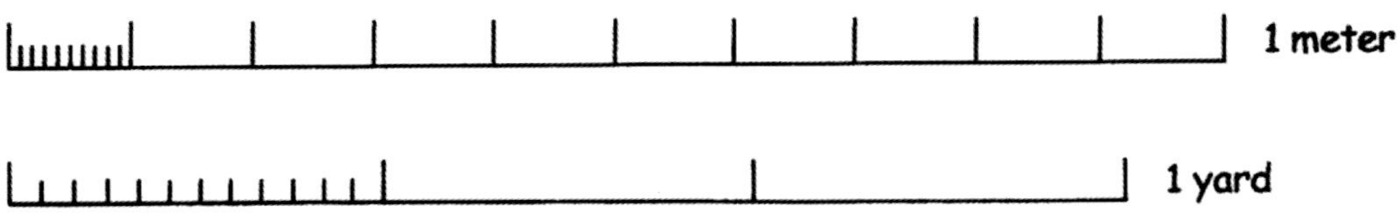

große Strahlrohr

Left:

M.1914 lance

5 ft (1.5 m) long

Right:

M.1917 lance

5 ft (1.5 m) long

große Strahlrohr

(Telescoping)

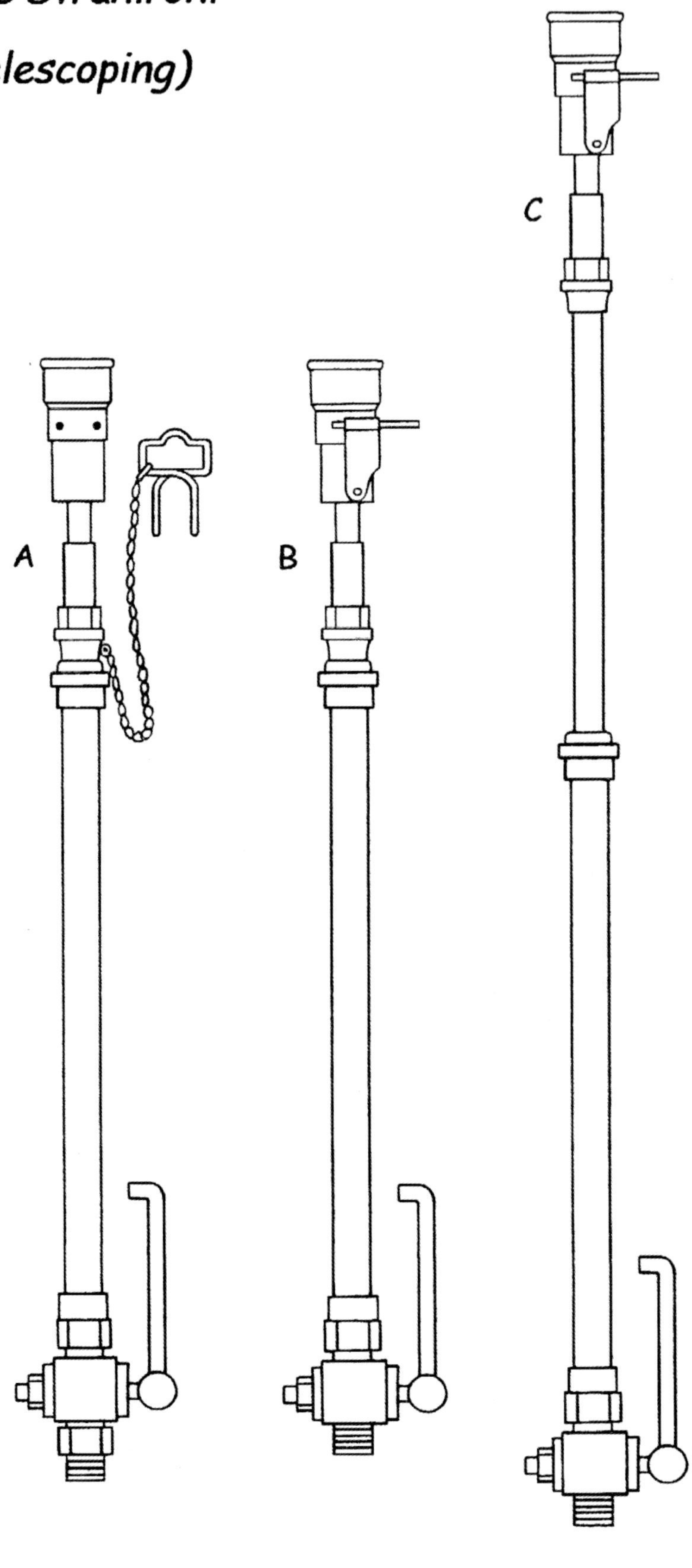

A. M.1914 lance retracted
4.5 ft (1.35 m) long

B. M.1917 lance retracted
4.5 ft (1.35 m) long

C. M.1917 lance extended
5.7 ft (1.75 m) long

kleine Strahlrohr M.1914

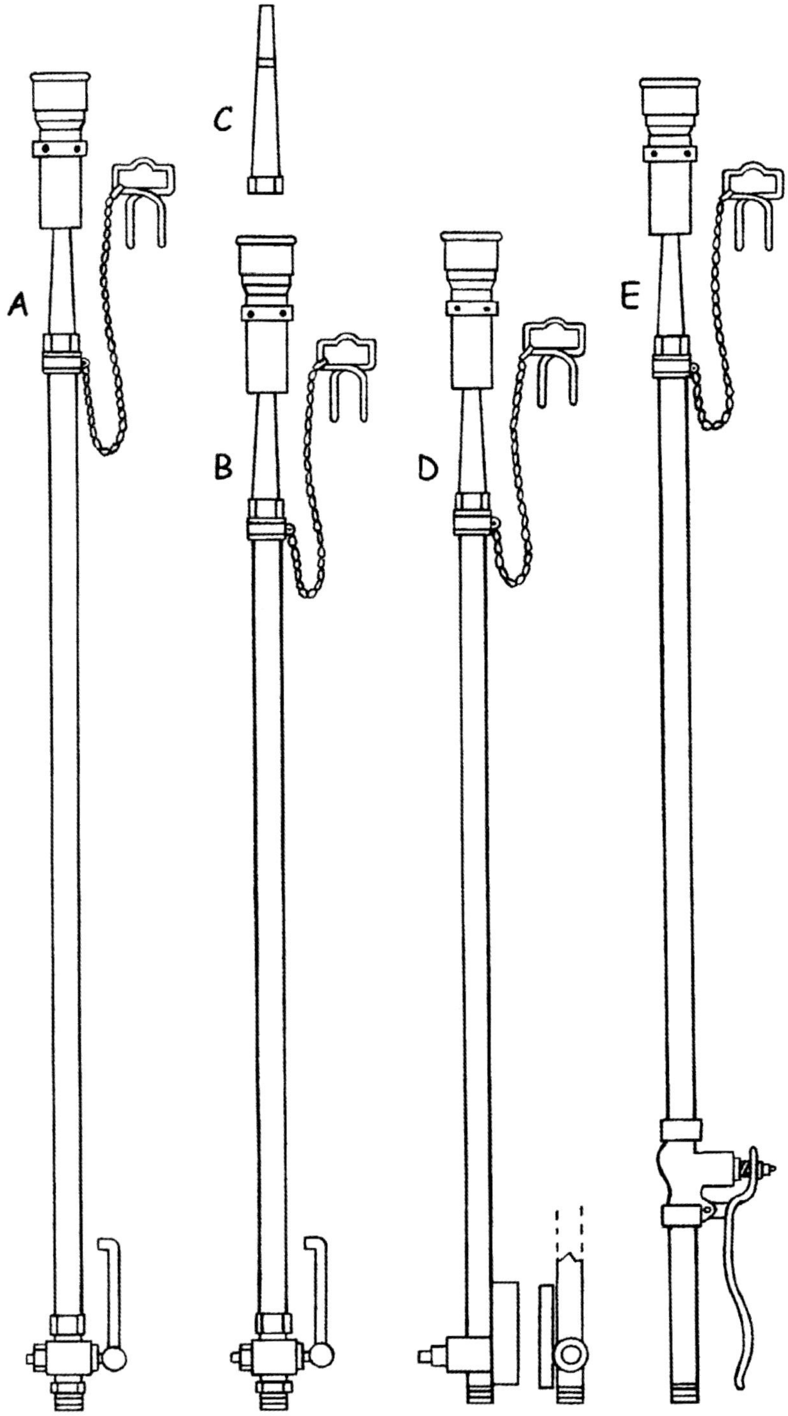

A. 4.6 ft (1.4 m) lance

B. 4 ft (1.2 m) lance

C. 0.3 in (8 mm) nozzle with painted red stripe

D. 4 ft (1.2 m) lance with early-model self-closing valve (side view provisional)

E. 4.6 ft (1.4 m) lance with late-model self-closing valve

kleine Strahlrohr

M.1916, M.1917, and M.1918

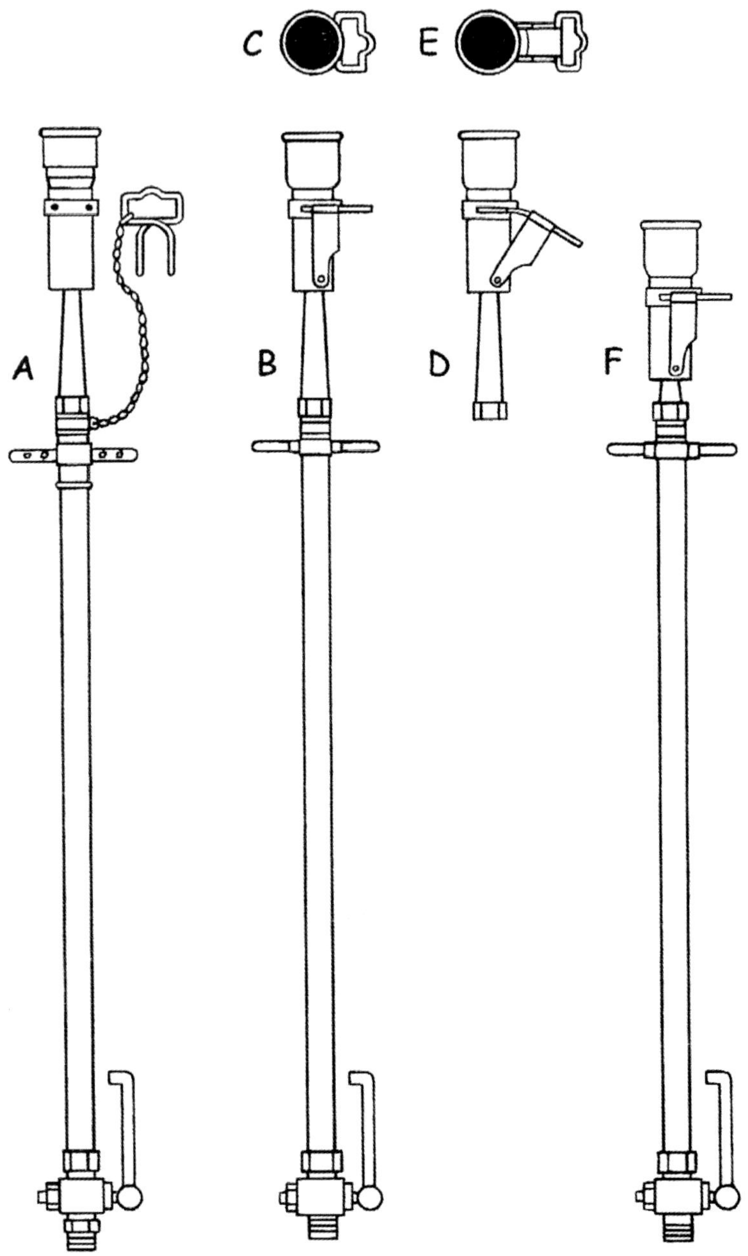

A. 3.6 ft (1.1 m) M.1916 lance

B. 3.6 ft (1.1 m) M.1917 lance; igniter fork in closed position

C. front view of igniter holder with igniter fork in closed position

D. M.1917 nozzle with igniter fork in open position

E. front view of igniter holder with igniter fork in open position

F. 3.3 ft (1 m) M.1918 lance

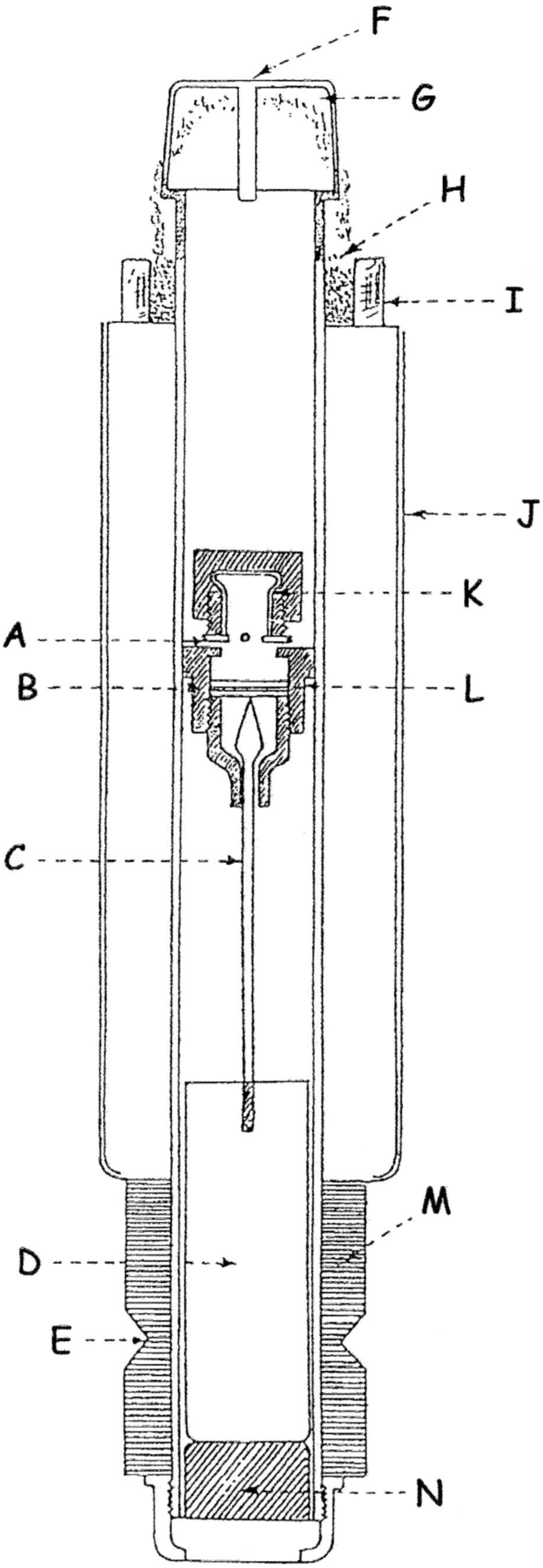

Small Igniter, First Type

length: 8.7 in

diameter: 1.8 in

A. ignition vent
B. aluminum stopper
C. firing pin
D. gelatine piston
E. groove for igniter fork
F. iron cap
G. cotton filaments
H. powdered charcoal
I. paraffined fuse
J. brass shell
K. fulminate capsule
L. two cardboard discs
M. wooden base
N. leather pad

Igniter, based on a drawing in Conférences de l'Ecole des gaz de combat: Les Lance-flammes. 3ème Conférence. Lance-flammes portatifs étrangers.

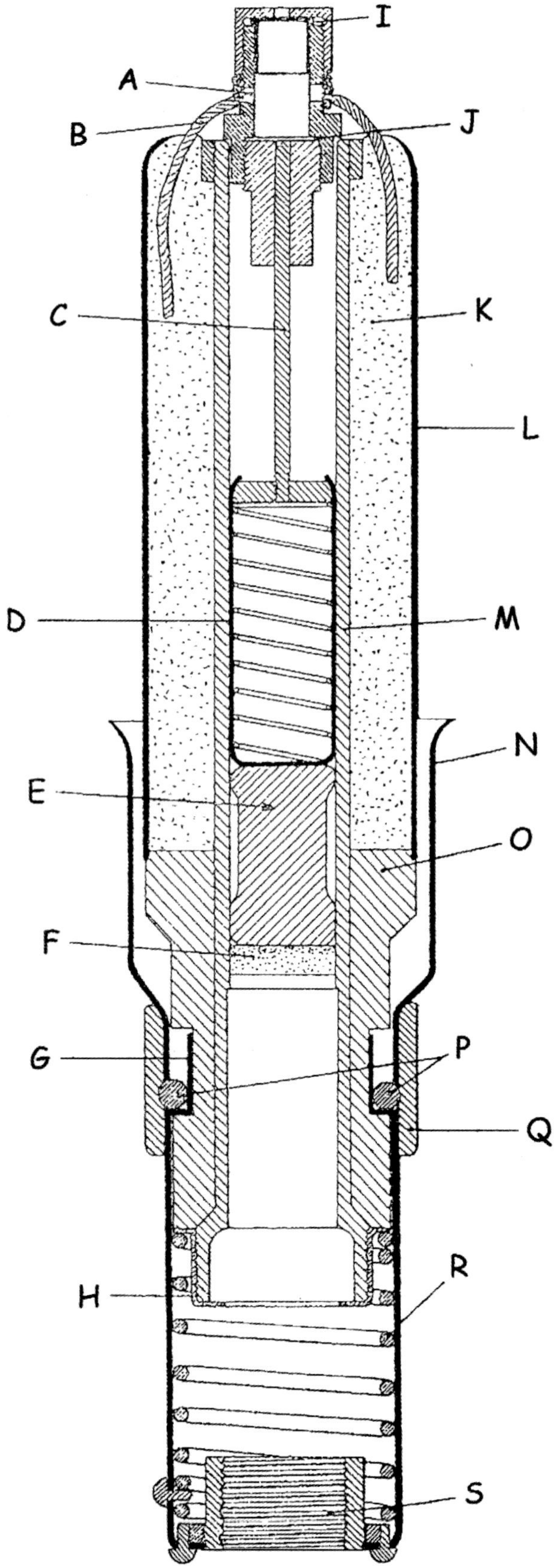

Small Igniter, Second Type

length: 8.5 in

diameter: 1.8 in

A. ignition vent

B. wick

C. firing pin

D. spring inside brass cylinder

E. gelatine piston

F. felt disc

G. protective sheet-metal sheath

H. protective sheet-metal cap

I. fulminate capsule

J. leather disc

K. fusing compound

L. sheet-metal shell

M. steel tube

N. igniter holder

O. wooden base

P. igniter fork tines

Q. igniter-fork retainer

R. spring for ejecting igniter

S. threaded socket for nozzle

Igniter, based on a drawing in Conférences de l'Ecole des gaz de combat: Les Lance flammes. 3ème Conférence. Lance-flammes portatifs étrangers.

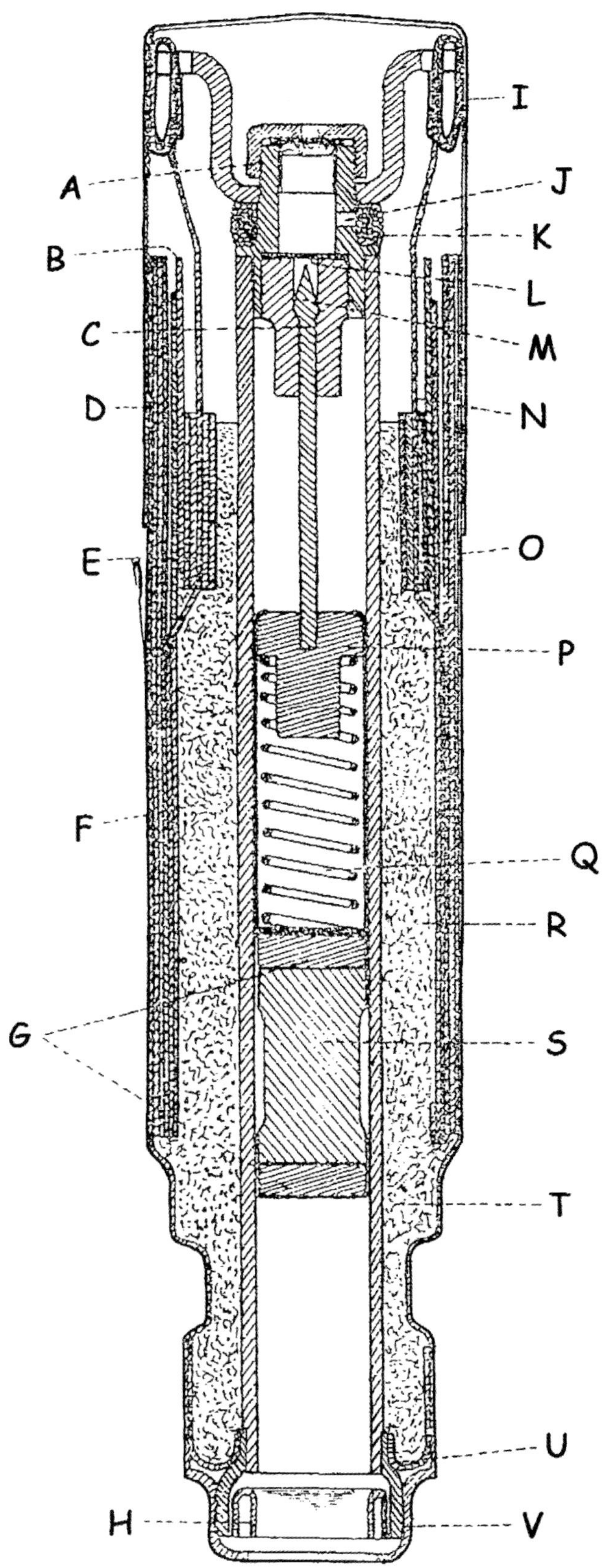

Small Igniter, Third Type

length: 9.1 in

diameter: 1.8 in

A. fulminate capsule
B. cloth
C. firing pin
D. sheet steel shell
E. adhesive cloth tape
F. fusing compound
G. felt pads
H. leather ring
I. protective steel lid
J. ignition vent
K. gun cotton
L. cardboard disc
M. tip of firing pin
N. zinc blades
O. sheet steel shell
P. piston
Q. spring
R. sand and fusing compound
S. cylinder of paste and glycerine
T. sand
U. soldered seam
V. threaded cap

Igniter, based on a drawing in Conférences de l'Ecole des gaz de combat: Les Lance-flammes. 3ème Conférence. Lance-flammes portatifs étrangers.

APPENDICES

Appendix 1
Uniforms of the Flamethrower Pioneers

Before the establishment of a separate flamethrower arm in late 1914, pioneer formations known to have used the weapon wore their own uniforms with no distinguishing badges or insignia. From March of 1915, all officially designated flamethrower troops wore the uniform of the Guard Pioneer Battalion (*Garde-Pionier-Bataillon*), with a few small distinctions. In September of 1918, pioneer companies on the western front were issued three small flamethrowers each, to be deployed by special units under the command of an officer.[1] These men retained their own field uniforms with no special insignia.

It appears that flamethrower operators of all assault battalions wore the uniform of the Guard Pioneers. The officers and men of the flamethrower detachment of *Sturmbataillon Nr. 5* (*Rohr*) were also awarded a special spiked helmet (*Pickelhaube*) as specified below.

The following are descriptions of the uniforms worn by all flamethrower formations.

Pionier-Versuchs-Kompagnie

Researched and developed flamethrowers from 1908 to 1912.

Prior to 1912, the Pioneer Experimental Company wore the M.1895 dark blue service jacket (*Dunkelblau* or *Waffenrock*) with black standing collar and black Swedish cuffs piped in red; black trousers and marching boots completed the uniform. The collar and cuffs displayed white Guard lace (*Garde-Litzen*) with black center lines (*Litzenspiegel*), and the shoulder straps were scarlet with a yellow chain-stitched Gothic V.

For barracks duty, the undress M.1903 smock (*Litewka*) in light gray was worn. It had a row of buttons concealed by a fly front, two breast pockets, and black patches with short white Guard lace affixed to the stand-and-fall collar. Officers wore a light-gray double-breasted smock piped in red, with black tabs on the collar and two rows of silver-plated buttons.

The M.1895 black-leather spiked helmet had trimmings in a white-metal alloy called "pioneer silver" and a helmet plate (*Wappen*) in the shape of a Prussian eagle with a Guard star superimposed. On formal occasions, the helmet spike was replaced by a silver cone (*Trichter*) surmounted by a black horsehair plume (*Paradebusch* or *Haarbusch*); to complete the elegant picture, the pioneer could don a light-gray greatcoat (Mantel) with scarlet shoulder straps and black panels (Mantelpatten) on either side of the collar, which displayed white Guard lace. Two styles of cap were issued: the peaked service cap (Dienstmütze or Schirmmütze); and the round, peakless field cap (Feldmütze or Kratschen). Both were in dark blue with black bands, red piping, and imperial and Prussian cockades.

On February 28, 1910, Kaiser Wilhelm II issued an All Highest Cabinet Order (*Allerhöchste Kabinetts-Ordre* or AKO) mandating the change of the uniform color from dark blue to field gray (*feldgrau*) for all land and air forces. It apparently did not affect the Pioneer Experimental Company because a later AKO dated May 28, 1912, stated that from November 1, 1912, the unit would wear a field-gray service jacket or field jacket (*Feldrock*) identical to that of Guard Pioneer Battalion.[2] The stand-and-fall collar and Swedish cuffs had white Guard lace with black center lines; piping was red on the front fly and rear skirts, black on the collar and cuffs. Shoulder straps were field gray, with red piping and a red chain-stitched V.

The spiked helmet remained as above, while the service and field caps were changed to field gray with black bands piped in red. In the field, a grayish-brown or light-green cloth helmet cover with no number on the front was worn as camouflage. Following mobilization, the scarlet shoulder straps of the greatcoat were changed to light gray piped in red.

Flammenwerfer-Abteilung Reddemann
Established at the end of 1914.

Most of the 48-70 men, one Offizier-Stellvertreter, and one Leutnant of Flamethrower Detachment Reddemann were reservists from the Posener Municipal Fire Brigade; the remaining positions were filled by young wartime volunteers. Although they arrived in Berlin in a variety of military and fire-brigade uniforms and civilian clothing, it is not known how they were outfitted in the field. One account of the first flamethrower attack refers to men of the detachment as the "black collars,"[3] which could mean that they wore firefighters' tunics.

The unit may also have been issued the Guard Pioneer's M.1910 service jacket in field gray, which was piped in red on the front fly and rear skirts, black on the collar and Swedish cuffs, and had plain field-gray shoulder straps piped in red, although on straps made after January of 1915 the piping was omitted as an economy measure. An AKO of March 3, 1915, authorized the simplified field jacket (*vereinfachte Feldrock*) with deep, unadorned turn-back cuffs and plain rear skirts. White Guard lace with black center lines decorated the collars and cuffs of the M.1910 service jacket but only the collar of the simplified field jacket. The March 3 AKO also ordered collar lace shortened in length by half.

Headgear and greatcoat were the same as the wartime Pioneer Experimental Company, except that the greatcoat shoulder straps were devoid of number or regimental cypher. The colors of the bayonet knot (Troddel) worn by Flamethrower Detachment Reddemann is not known.

III. Garde-Pionier-Bataillon
Established March 15, 1915.

The 3rd Guard Pioneer Battalion was raised in the Guard Pioneer Replacement Battalion (*Garde-Pionier-Ersatz-Bataillon*) and thus wore the field-gray uniform of its parent unit. As members of the third battalion, the men were issued bayonet knots with a yellow stem (*Stengel* or *Eichel*); the slider (*Schieber* or *Knopf*) and crown (*Kranz*) were white for the 9th Company, red for the 10th Company, yellow for the 11th Company, and blue for the 12th Company. The 13th and 14th Companies, added in October, and the 15th and 16th Companies, added in December, wore bayonet knots with blue stems. Sliders and crowns were white (13th Company), red (14th Company), yellow (15th Company), and blue (16th Company). The colors of the bayonet knots identifying the Replacement Company, Reserve Company (created in January of 1916), and workshop detachment are not known, but the stems may have been yellow.

The M.1910 service jacket and the simplified field jacket were joined by the blouse (*Bluse*) after the Kaiser signed AKO Nr. 735, dated September 21, 1915, which called for sweeping changes in the uniform of the German military. The loose-fitting M.1915 blouse featured the deep, unadorned cuffs and plain rear skirts of the simplified field jacket, with a collar faced in green badge cloth (*Abzeichen Tuch*), no piping, and buttons concealed by a fly front. For pioneers, Guard lace on the blouse collar was light gray with white center lines and black middle stripes (*Mittelstreifen*) or filling (*Füllung*) between the two bars. Standardization was never achieved, resulting in anomalies such as M.1915 blouses with long or short white Guard lace and M.1910 service jackets with light-gray Guard lace.

Another provision of AKO Nr. 735 changed the pioneer shoulder-strap color from field gray piped in red to black piped in red. Although this order was issued in September of 1915, photographic evidence shows that flamethrower pioneers continued to wear field-gray shoulder straps throughout the war. In addition, Guard lace was often eliminated from the cuffs of the M.1910 service jacket as an austerity measure.

AKO Nr. 735 also mandated the adoption of a field-gray peacetime jacket (*Friedensrock*) to replace the dark-blue tunic worn by Prussian units for generations. The M.1915 peacetime jacket was very similar in cut to the M.1895 service jacket, with a black standing collar, black Swedish cuffs, and eight rounded, silver-plated buttons. Piping was in red, while shoulder straps were black with no piping. Guard lace on the collar and cuffs was white with black center lines, as found on the M.1910 service jacket.

Officers wore two styles of double-breasted undress jacket: the light-gray peacetime M.1903 smock and the M.1915 small jacket (*kleiner Rock*), a tunic with a similar cut but in field-gray cloth. The M.1903 smock had "collar panels" (*Kragenpatten*) in black velvet with red piping and a silver button on the outer edge, shoulder straps in silver wire cord with black darts (*Faden*) on a red base, red uniform piping, horizontally cut pockets, and silver-plated buttons. On the M.1915 small jacket, the pockets were slanted upward from back to front, while the shoulder straps were of silver wire cord with black darts on a black velvet base with red piping.

The leather spiked helmet was worn formally until the end of the war, but Ersatz examples made of tin, cardboard, steel, fiber, and pressed felt began to appear in 1915. The German-silver fittings on enlisted men's helmets were changed to steel as an economy measure; these were usually painted field gray. The 3rd Guard Pioneer Battalion was also one of the first formations to receive the M.1916 steel helmet (*Stahlhelm*), which was painted field gray.

In late 1915, laced ankle boots, puttees, and trousers with leather knee patches were adopted by flamethrower pioneers and other newly formed assault units, and the stone-gray prewar greatcoat was replaced by the M.1915 model that featured turn-back cuffs, six buttons painted field gray, and a collar faced in green badge cloth.

Some reports state that flamethrower carriers retained their marching boots because they offered more protection in the event of an accidental fuel spill.[4]

IV. Garde-Pionier-Bataillon
Established in February of 1916.

This short-lived unit consisted of a battalion staff, a workshop detachment, and the 1st and 2nd Companies. Although uniforms were identical to those of the 3rd Guard Pioneer Battalion, the color of the bayonet-knot stem is not clear.

In the infantry, blue stems were used to denote the fourth battalion, but this color had already been assigned to the 13th through 16th Companies of the 3rd Guard Pioneer Battalion. It is possible that bayonet knots with blue stems were issued to the 4th Guard Pioneer Battalion regardless, which would certainly have created confusion.

II. Garde-Pionier-Ersatz-Bataillon
Established March 1, 1916.

Replacement battalion for all flamethrower troops, including those in Guard pioneer formations and infantry assault battalions. As members of the second battalion, the men wore bayonet knots with a red stem, while slides and crowns were in white, red, yellow, or blue, identifying the 1st through 4th Replacement Companies respectively. A Garrison Company (*Garnison Kompagnie*) also existed, but the colors of its bayonet knot are not known.

All other uniform and headgear details are the same as those of the 3rd and 4th Guard Pioneer Battalions.

Garde-Reserve-Pionier-Regiment
Established April 20, 1916.

Uniforms of the Guard Reserve Pioneer Regiment were identical to those of the 3rd and 4th Guard Pioneer Battalions. Ideally, members of the regiment should have worn only the M.1915 blouse with black shoulder straps, but photographs show that this goal was never achieved. Bayonet knots were issued with white, red, and yellow stems to identify the 1st, 2nd, and 3rd Battalions respectively; the four companies within each battalion were designated by sliders and crowns in white, red, yellow, or blue. The experimental company (*Versuchs Kompagnie*) wore a bayonet knot of as-yet unidentified colors: It appears that the slider and stem were white, while the crown was red and the fringe (Quast) was another color, possibly blue.

On July 28, 1916, the Kaiser signed an AKO awarding the regiment a death's head (Totenkopf) sleeve badge as an official commemoration of the 150th flame attack. Crown Prince Wilhelm recommended the badge and announced it in a letter to the regiment that praised the men's "death-defying joy of combat."[5] The Guard Reserve Pioneer Regiment and the flamethrower platoon of Assault Battalion No. 5 (Rohr) thus became the only units honored with this prestigious symbol during the war (see below).

The sleeve badge was a skull-and-crossbones done in the "Prussian" style, resembling the busby plate worn by Leib Hussar Regiment No. 1 (*Leib-Husaren-Regiment Nr. 1*). Cut from light-gray cloth for enlisted men or embroidered in silver thread for officers, both versions had ten white teeth and black velvet eye sockets and nasal openings.[6] They were mounted on field-gray ovals of no fixed size and sewn to the lower left sleeve. For officers and *Offizier-Stellvertretern*, the badge was always worn above the cuff, regardless of the jacket model. For enlisted men, the placement of the badge varied, although it is not known if this had significance. The death's head was always worn above the cuff of the M.1910 service jacket; in the case of the simplified field jacket and M.1915 blouse, the badge was worn either on the cuff itself or above it. It is possible that the higher position was used to identify men of the flamethrower platoon of Assault Battalion No. 5 (*Rohr*), which was separate from the Death's Head Pioneers.

The Crown Prince's letter authorized the flamethrower pioneers to wear the death's head only "for the duration of the war," which explains why the badge appears in so few photos of flamethrower pioneers taken after the Armistice.

Battle dress included marching boots or ankle boots and puttees, trousers with cloth or leather knee patches, steel helmets often camouflaged in disruptive patterns of three or more colors, and the M.1915 greatcoat. The staining caused by flame oil was enough of a problem that many flamethrower operators preserved their prestigious Death's Head Pioneer uniforms by wearing older and/or nonstandard items in the field.

As would be expected, members of the Guard Reserve Pioneer Regiment attached to assault battalions retained their own uniforms.

Sturmbataillon Nr. 5 (Rohr)

Developed from *Sturmabteilung Calsow*, established on March 2, 1915.

Flamethrower Platoon created on October 17, 1915.

The flamethrower platoon of Assault Battalion No. 5 (*Rohr*) had one officer and twenty-three men armed with six *Kleif*, as prescribed by War Ministry Order No. 355. 10. 15 A6.[7] Flamethrower operators of Assault Battalion No. 5 (*Rohr*) wore the uniform of the 3rd Guard Pioneer Battalion and later Guard Reserve Pioneer Regiment complete with death's head sleeve badge,[8] even though they were considered separate from the Death's Head Pioneers. Photos suggest that the members of Rohr's flamethrower platoon may have worn their death's head badges above the sleeve cuffs of their simplified field jackets and M.1915 blouses, possibly to differentiate themselves from Reddemann's men.

Prior to the awarding of the death's head sleeve badge to the Guard Reserve Pioneer Regiment, the Crown Prince requested that the Kaiser order a special helmet for the Rohr flamethrower detachment in recognition of its achievements. The AKO of June 6, 1916, defined the new helmet as a Guard Pioneer M.1897 *Pickelhaube* with a small silver-plated death's head affixed beneath the Guard star. The death's head was in the "Brunswick" style instead of the "Prussian" and as such was identical to the cap badge worn by Brunswicker Hussar Regiment No. 17 (*Braunschweigisches Husaren-Regiment Nr. 17*).[9] It is not certain if the helmet was delivered in significant numbers.

Jäger- (Sturm-) Bataillon Nr. 3

Established on July 8, 1916.

Formerly *Brandenburgerisches Jäger-Bataillon Nr. 3*.

Jäger (Assault) Battalion No. 3 was formed with an integral flamethrower platoon drawn from the 2nd Guard Pioneer Replacement Battalion. Although the platoon was a permanent component of the assault battalion, its individual members were rotated in from the Guard Reserve Pioneer Regiment. They therefore wore Guard Pioneer uniforms that after July 28, 1916, included the death's head sleeve badge.

Notes

1 Cron, *Imperial German Army 1914-18*, p. 158.
2 Kraus, *Die feldgraue Uniformierung des deutschen Heeres*, p. 653.
3 Von Schaewen, "Der erste Flammenwerferangriff," in *Das Ehrenbuch*, p. 525.
4 Larcade, p. 55.
5 Reddemann to Fries, p. 21.
6 Kraus, *Die feldgraue Uniformierung*, p. 656.
7 *Generallandesarchiv Karlsruhe*, 456 F3/966.
8 Kraus, *Die feldgraue Uniformierung*, p. 499.
9 Ibid.

Appendix 2
Evolution of Flamethrower Combat Formations 1914-1918

Field Pioneer Companies, Battalions, and Regiments
August-December 1914

One two-man flamethrower squad per platoon, for a total of three per company.

Each squad armed with one *Kleif*.

Flammenwerwer-Abteilung Reddemann
January-March 1915

Forty-eight (then 70) men, one *Offizier-Stellvertreter*, one *Leutnant*.

Armed with ten hand-pumped flamethrowers, two *Grof*.

III. Garde-Pionier-Bataillon
March 1915-January 1916

Four (then six, then eight) field companies of 139 men each.

Three combat platoons per company.

Each combat platoon armed with four to six *Grof*, six *Kleif*.

January-April 1916

Eight field companies of 200 men each.

Three combat platoons per company.

Combat platoon composed of five flamethrower detachments, one machine-gun detachment, one replacement detachment; two *Kleif* squads in each flamethrower detachment.

Each combat platoon armed with six to eight *Grof*, 18 *Kleif*.

IV. Garde-Pionier-Bataillon
January-April 1916

Two field companies of 200 men each.

Three combat platoons per company.

Combat platoon composed of five flamethrower detachments, one machine-gun detachment, one replacement detachment; two *Kleif* squads in each flamethrower detachment.

Each combat platoon armed with six to eight *Grof*, 18 *Kleif*.

Garde-Reserve-Pionier-Regiment
April-December 1916

Ten (then twelve) field companies of 200 men each.

Three combat platoons per company.

Combat platoon composed of five flamethrower detachments, one machine-gun detachment, one replacement detachment; two *Kleif* squads in each flamethrower detachment.

Each combat platoon armed with six to eight *Grof*, 18 *Kleif*.

December 1916-March 1918

Twelve field companies of 181-182 men each.

Five combat platoons per company.

Four combat platoons composed of four *Kleif* (then *Wex*) squads and one grenade-launcher or machine-gun squad each.

Two combat platoons included one squad of hand-grenade throwers each.

Fifth combat platoon detached for assault battalions; comprised of six *Kleif* (then *Wex*) squads.

Each combat platoon armed with four *Grof*, 10 or 11 *Kleif*; from May 1917 four *Grof*, four *Kleif*, six *Wex*.

March 1918-November 1918

Twelve March Companies of 200 men each.

Three combat platoons per company.

Combat platoon composed of four *Wex* squads, one machine-gun squad, one grenade-launcher squad; each *Wex* squad armed with two flamethrowers and reinforced with extra men. Grenade-launcher squad could be equipped as fifth *Wex* squad armed with two reserve devices.

Each combat platoon armed with six or seven *Grof*, six or seven *Kleif*, 10 *Wex*.

Pioneer Companies on the Western Front
September-November 1918

One flamethrower platoon per company.
Each platoon armed with six *Wex*.

Notes

The information in Appendix 2 is drawn from:
Cron, *Imperial Germany Army 1914-18*, p. 169.
Cron, *Geschichte des Deutschen Heeres im Weltkrige 1914-1918*, p. 174.
"Instructions for the Employment of Flame Projectors," p. 692.
Records of *Württembergisches Pionier-Bataillon Nr. 13*, M 200 Bü. 80.
Reddemann, *Geschichte*, pp. 11-13, 15-16, 38-39.
Theune, *Flammenwerfer und Sturmtruppen*, pp. 229-233.

Appendix 3
Organization and Equipment of Flamethrower Companies

A. Organization of a flamethrower company in the field, for position warfare (1914-18).

1 company commander
4 *Leutnants*
1 *Feldwebel*
1 *Vizefeldwebel*
20 *Unteroffiziere*
22 *Gefreite*
120-121 *Pioniere*
1 medical *Unteroffizier*
1 train *Unteroffizier*
8 grooms
2 motor-transport drivers
Total combat strength = 181-182 men

1st Combat Platoon (*Kampfzug*)
1 platoon leader (*Leutnant*, *Feldwebel*, or *Vizefeldwebel*)
4 flamethrower squads (2 *Unteroffiziere*, 2 *Gefreite*, 12 *Pioniere*)
7 hand-grenade throwers (1 *Gefreiter*, 6 *Pioniere*)
1 machine-gun squad or grenade-lancher squad (1 *Unteroffizier*, 5 *Pioniere*)
Total = 30 men

2nd Combat Platoon
1 platoon leader (*Leutnant*, *Feldwebel*, or *Vizefeldwebel*)
4 flamethrower squads (2 *Unteroffiziere*, 2 *Gefreite*, 12 *Pioniere*)
7 hand-grenade throwers (1 *Gefreiter*, 6 *Pioniere*)
1 machine-gun squad or grenade-lancher squad (1 *Unteroffizier*, 5 *Pioniere*)
Total = 30 men

3rd Combat Platoon
1 platoon leader (*Leutnant*, *Feldwebel*, or *Vizefeldwebel*)
4 flamethrower squads (2 *Unteroffiziere*, 2 *Gefreite*, 12 *Pioniere*)
1 machine-gun squad or grenade-lancher squad (1 *Unteroffizier*, 6 *Pioniere*)
Total = 24 men

4th Combat Platoon
1 platoon leader (*Leutnant*, *Feldwebel*, or *Vizefeldwebel*)
4 flamethrower squads (2 *Unteroffiziere*, 2 *Gefreite*, 12 *Pioniere*)
1 machine-gun squad or grenade-lancher squad (1 *Unteroffizier*, 6 *Pioniere*)
Total = 24 men

5th Combat Platoon (for an assault battalion)
1 platoon leader (*Leutnant*, *Feldwebel*, or *Vizefeldwebel*)
6 flamethrower squads (3 *Unteroffiziere*, 3 *Gefreite*, 18 *Pioniere*)
1 orderly (1 *Pionier*)
Total = 26 men

Replacement Platoon (***Ergänzungszug***)
1 platoon leader (*Leutnant*, *Feldwebel*, or *Vizefeldwebel*)
8 subordinates (*Kommandierte*) (2 *Unteroffiziere*, 6 *Pioniere*)†
4 orderlies (4 *Pioniere*)
21-22 reserve (3 *Unteroffiziere*, 9 *Gefreite*, 9-10 *Pioniere*)
Total = 34-35 men

†Subordinate section
1 clerk (*Pionier*)
3 cooks (1 *Unteroffiziere*, 2 *Pioniere*)
2 equipment managers (1 *Unteroffizier*, 1 *Pionier*)
1 shoemaker (*Pionier*)
1 tailor (*Pionier*)
Total = 8 men

The strength of individual platoons changed according to orders for engagements and the number of men available. In the case of high casualties among the men, several platoons were merged; preparing for a large-scale attack required another strengthening and concentration of the platoon to undertake shock-troop missions with small-flamethrower squads.

Platoon leaders and enlisted men were changed as seldom as possible, so that they got to know each other and their fighting abilities. Each trained flamethrower pioneer was required to be familiar with the operation of all flamethrower apparatuses and all auxiliary weapons.

B. Equipment of a flamethrower company in the field (1914-18) and the number of vehicles, horses, and auxiliary weapons (position warfare)

Small flamethrower (***Wex***)
30 *Wex* with pressure gauges
30 *Wex* carrying frames
30 *Wex* box wrenches
30 small adjustable wrenches for *Wex* and *Kleif*
60 6mm nozzles for *Wex* and *Kleif*
10 8mm nozzles for *Wex* and *Kleif* (red striped)
60 igniter holders for *Wex* and *Kleif* flamethrowers
20 *Wex* elbow joints
15 comparison pressure gauges with safety valves for *Wex*, *Kleif*, and *Grof*
20 *Wex* funnels
60 small lances for *Wex* and *Kleif* (without nozzles and igniter holders)
60 small lance hoses for *Wex* and *Kleif*
20 small hose couplers for *Wex* and *Kleif*
50 boxes of washers for *Wex*, *Kleif*, and *Grof*
20 hammers for all devices
20 cutting pliers for all devices
20 pipe pliers for all devices
20 screwdrivers for all devices
50 tool pouches for *Wex*, *Kleif*, and *Grof*
30 small igniter pouches for *Wex* and *Kleif*
10 spare pressure gauges for *Wex* and *Kleif*
10 spare *Dräger* valves for *Wex* and *Kleif*

Medium Flamethrower (***Kleif***)
20 *Kleif* with carrying frames and pressure gauges
10 forked couplers for Doppelkleif
20 *Kleif* adjusters
30 gas-filling hoses for *Kleif* and *Grof*
10 spare arming valves for *Kleif* and *Grof*

Large Flamethrower (***Grof***)
20 *Grof* with pressure gauges
15 *Grof* connecting hoses
40 *Grof* hoses
20 large lances (without nozzles and igniter holders)
25 *Grof* couplers
20 *Grof* carrying frames
20 *Grof* carrying harnesses
25 11mm nozzles
25 igniter holders
15 *Grof* adjusters
15 crescent wrenches (72mm)
15 large adjustable box wrenches
30 *Grof* carts
30 large-igniter pouches
10 spare *Grof* pressure meters

Oil Equipment
15 barrel wrenches
20 barrel spigots
3 oil pumps with oil hoses
40 large oil cans
20 small oil cans
6 cleaning pails
40 barrels of Blue oil, "iron" supply [meaning emergency or basic reserve supply]
10 barrels of Yellow oil, "iron" supply

Nitrogen Tanks
8 contents pressure meters, "iron" supply
50 large nitrogen tanks, "iron" supply
10 small nitrogen tanks, "iron" supply

Igniters
160 large igniters (4 cases), "iron" supply
240 small igniters (8 cases), "iron" supply

Accessories
10 tool cases
10 trench periscopes
20 20 m tape measures
10 flare pistols with ammunition
2 range finders Model 15
2 stopwatches

Means of Transportation and Horses
1 4.5-tonne cargo truck
5 2.5-tonne trailers; cargo trucks for the trailers are requisitioned for the individual situation
2 bicycles
5 field wagons (Field Wagon Model 95)
1 large field cooker
12 draft horses
5 riding horses

Auxiliary Arms
5 light machine guns
2 heavy machine guns
10 grenade launchers

For the advance during mobile warfare, the flamethrower company established a rear equipment depot, possibly in affiliation with a pioneer park, in which the spare equipment could remain behind under watch. The equipment that the flamethrower company used for mobile warfare was principally the small flamethrowers and a few medium and large flamethrowers. For mobile warfare, the flamethrower company was equipped with field wagons, horses, and grooms, in the manner of a pioneer field company.

Notes
The information in Appendix 3 is drawn from Theune, *Flammenwerfer und Sturmtruppen*, pp. 229-233.

Appendix 4

A. Arms and Ammunition of the Flamethrower Pioneers

Flame Jet

The flame jet is the most effective weapon of the flamethrower in close combat. Full technical control is only achieved after a thorough individual training process. With appropriate training and careful guidance, the flamethrower pioneer gains unconditional confidence in his flamethrower weapon every time he uses the jet of fire, overcoming circumstances in which he has only one chance of physical or moral success. Anyone who uses the flame jet against the enemy knows the effectiveness of this close-combat technique and understands the fear it instills in the enemy facing it.

Rifles and Carbines

The flame jet is often superior to the rifle and carbine in man-to-man combat. Rifles and carbines can support the efficacy of the flame jet through targeted fire.

The shooting skill of the flamethrower pioneers should not be neglected in favor of other duties. Flamethrower pioneers themselves must use their shooting skill if for some reason they cannot depend on the overall effect of the flame jet.

Careful individual training in shooting educates the flamethrower pioneers in the determined and deliberate action required during close combat.

Shooting at close and the closest ranges. Battlefield-condition shooting with live ammunition in groups. Folding targets set up, shot at quickly, and quickly dropped. Particular emphasis put on training in battlefield-condition quick firing. Flamethrower pioneers must make skillful, swiftly completed single shots with machine guns, grenade launchers, rifles, and pistols.

Pistols, Bayonets, Spades

Equipped with pistols, bayonets and sharpened spades for self-defense, the squad leader and flamethrower pioneers successfully launch into close combat when the flamethrowers are empty or disabled.

Machine Guns and Grenade Launchers

To provide worthwhile support and protection for the flame jet in battle, machine guns engage opponents outside of the trenches, and grenade launchers engage opponents in the trenches. Besides being used for the actual effect of their fire, both weapons are frequently employed for diverting the attention of the enemy and affecting his morale. In specific instances, the weapons are used to allow the flamethrower shock troops to advance within firing range. The cooperation between machine guns, grenade launchers, and the flame jet necessitates careful training. It is not enough that machine-gun and grenade-launcher personnel from the infantry join the flamethrower shock sections; a combined training exercise must frequently follow.

In specific instances when grenade launchers fire ahead along the route of the advancing flamethrower squads, or when our own machine guns shoot over the heads of the flamethrower squads, it is recommended that the machine guns and grenade launchers be served by officers or older noncommissioned officers of the flamethrower squads.

Hand Grenades

Hand grenades reinforce the effect of the flame jets. After a flame shock that either reaches the enemy trench or is delivered in it, the enemy retreats and groups together. Throw hand grenades into such accumulations of men!

The skillful throwing of hand grenades singly at fixed targets, then simultaneously in groups; throwing in parallel and hitting the target! The flamethrower pioneers must be able to throw hand grenades from every position: standing, kneeling, and prone, also with full apparatuses on the back and while wearing gas masks. Throwing over distant obstacles, over sandbag barricades, traverses, and during assault rushes!

It is important to be able to throw the hand grenade out of a trench, sap head, and shell hole when prone. Also sideways out of a trench onto a target or in the direction of the trenches. Also hitting specific parts of trenches, sap heads, and shell holes. Through competitive throwing and the giving of prizes, one can increase the pleasure that the men take from this duty!

B. Accouterments

In addition to the field-marching pioneer outfit or the assault uniform of the Infantry A.V.F. 160, each man will also receive a flamethrower-pioneer outfit suitable for his particular assault exercise and conforming to the task, the circumstances of the opponent, and the effects of other enemy weapons.

1. Equipment for operations on a larger scale

Squad leader for small, medium, and large flamethrowers
Steel helmet; slung rifle; no back pack; belt with bayonet; no cartridge pouches; 30 cartridges in jacket pockets and bread bag; pickax or pioneer spade with shortened handle hung perpendicularly on belt; adhesive tape; mess kit rolled in overcoat and ten empty sand bags (construction material) carried on back; bread bag; two water bottles; gas mask; rations. Screwdriver and small adjustable wrench in bread bag.

Individual squad leaders: wire cutters; flare guns; white cloth panels for signaling to aircraft.

Small and medium flamethrower carriers
Steel helmet; small or medium flamethrower; gas mask; pistol; bayonet; and no cartridge pouches.

Lance operator for small, medium, and large flamethrowers
Steel helmet; pistol; bayonet; mess kit; overcoat; bread bag; two water bottles; gas mask; flamethrower lance and hose; three igniters in an igniter case on belt; spare igniter fork.

Assistants and large-flamethrower assistants
Steel helmet; pistol; bayonet; mess kit; overcoat; bread bag; two water bottles; gas mask; two igniters; tool bag worn around the neck or on the belt, containing: 1 set of washers; 1 pair of pipe pliers; 1 spare igniter holder.

Provisions are as those of the hand-grenade throwers.

Hand-grenade throwers
Steel helmet; slung rifle or carbine; bayonet; no cartridge pouches; 30 cartridges in jacket pockets and bread bag; hand-grenade sacks with hand grenades (about 6 stick grenades or ten egg grenades in each).

One section of the grenade throwers issued pioneer shovels with shortened handles to be hung from the belt, the other section equipped with middle-sized wire cutters. Mess kit rolled in overcoat and ten empty sand bags carried on back. Rolled sand bags tied with cord and attached to the back; two water bottles; gas mask.

Provisions in bread bag and mess kit:

> 1 loaf of bread; 2 portions of meat; and two portions of dried fruit (each in a tin).

2. Equipment for Forcible Operations and Reconnaissance
In the case of small combat missions, patrols, and reconnaissance in force, in which surprise and mobility are necessary for success, the equipment is limited to the bare minimum of what is required. The amount of patrol accouterment carried is determined by the personal preferences of the flamethrower pioneers.

A flamethrower patrol without back packs, belts, bayonets, and ammunition pouches, with only:

field caps,
gas masks (without metal containers) tucked into field jackets,
pistols (without holsters) attached to bread-bag straps and carried in jacket pockets,
daggers carried in jacket pockets,
and laced shoes and puttees

Is more mobile and therefore more successful in surprising the enemy than a patrol in steel helmets and with full assault equipment.

Notes
The information in Appendix 4 is drawn from Theune, *Flammenwerfer und Sturmtruppen*, pp. 219-225.

Appendix 5

Not to be brought into the front lines!

Order T.17: Instructions on the Cooperation Between the Infantry and Flamethrowers.

I. Function of the flamethrower: close-combat technique which facilitates the advance of the infantry for:

- rolling up trenches,
- frontal attacks against blockhouses, machine-gun nests, etc.,
- fighting in woods and villages.

II. Flamethrower officers must always carry out preliminary reconnaissance!

III. Flamethrowers:

- do not explode when hit by projectiles;
- their stream of flame stops when the carrier or lance operator is wounded;
- one can calmly walk through flame oil burning on the ground without being burned.

IV. Organization of the infantry and flamethrowers:

a) Shock troop (however many flamethrowers in addition to 4-6 infantrymen trained as hand-grenade throwers): goes in front.

The leader is the flamethrower officer or noncommissioned officer.

b) Assault troops: follow behind.

V. Rolling up Trenches

a) Shock troop.

Only upon the order of the shock-troop leader, the assigned infantrymen throw hand grenades forward and sideways (egg hand grenades are best).

b) Assault troops

1. Not too many!

2. There must be two competent leaders assigned (one in front, one in the center).

3. The assault troops must always keep a few meters' distance from the shock troop. No man must run in front of the flamethrowers! The assault troops must absolutely remain on their feet and follow the flamethrowers! They will cause no harm to our side!

4. The assault troops must remain grouped together but not clumped up! There must be 1.5 to 2 meters between each man.

5. Men of the assault troops must never throw hand grenades forward into the trench. They must only throw sideways if necessary, to deal with enemies still present in the secondary positions, shell holes, etc.

VI. Frontal Attacks Against Blockhouses, Strengthened Machine-gun Positions, etc.

Do not use flamethrowers if it is not possible to creep up unnoticed to within 30 meters, and then only if there is cover (shrubs, small rises, shell holes, etc.).

a) Shock troop

1. The 4-6 infantrymen assigned to the troop carry wire cutters forward. After the flame attack, they must suppress any remaining resistance and disarm prisoners.

2. The advance of the shock troop: Short jumps from cover to cover. Also by crawling. Do not proceed in a straight line toward blockhouses etc., but describe a half circle depending upon the available cover. Never two or more men in a crowd! Do not offer easy targets! The shock troop is spread out, but it remains cohesive.

b) Assault troops

1. Success of the flame attack depends on the cover.

2. Draw the attention of the enemy away from the shock troop. (Heavy shooting with pauses, simulations of jumps ahead, etc.).

3. Advance immediately, as soon as the flamethrowers go to work and the enemy fire decreases in intensity.

VII. Fighting in Woods and Villages

As above (Paragraph VI).

Notes
The information in Appendix 5 is found in Hauptstaatsarchiv Stuttgart, *Generalkommando XIII*. AK M 33/2 Bü 236. Order of General Fritz von Below, German 1st Army, autumn of 1916.

Appendix 6
Flamethrower Shock Troop

The number of men in a flamethrower shock troop (*Flammenwerferstosstrupp*) seems to have varied. Charles Theune wrote that a *Kleif* shock troop (*Kleifstosstrupp*) or *Wex* shock troop (*Wexstosstrupp*) was composed of two small flamethrower squads, four infantry or pioneer hand-grenade throwers, and at least one shock-troop leader (*Stosstruppführer*). Each flamethrower squad included three or four men, which meant that a shock troop contained a total of eleven to thirteen members.

For rolling up a trench, the flamethrower shock troop formed a single-file column, attacking in the following order:

first lance operator
first flamethrower carrier
first assistant
first hand-grenade thrower
second hand-grenade thrower
first shock-troop leader
third hand-grenade thrower
fourth hand-grenade thrower
second lance operator
second flamethrower carrier
second assistant
second shock-troop leader (if present)
third shock-troop leader (if present)

The men advanced at intervals of about seven feet, followed by infantry assault troops (*Sturmtruppen*).

From his position in the middle of the column, the first shock-troop leader was in overall command. He led the fight, ordered the throwing of hand grenades, detailed the flanking troops, and was responsible for both the prompt employment of the flamethrowers and the efficient performance of his men.

If present, the second and third shock-troop leaders were in charge of maintaining communication among the men, the correct distances between them, and the security of the flanks. In addition, the rearmost shock-troop leader made certain that the infantry assault troops kept up.

A strengthened flamethrower shock troop (*verstärkte Flammenwerferstosstrupp*) included three *Wex* or *Kleif* squads, six hand-grenade throwers, and at least two shock-troop leaders.

Notes

The information in Appendix 6 is drawn from Theune, *Sturmtruppen und Flammenwerfer*, pp. 119, 122, 124-125, as well as photos.

Appendix 7
Wex March Platoon

Strength:
1 officer (platoon leader)
9 NCOs (squad leaders)
33 men, 1 runner.

Composition:
5 *Wex* squads, each comprised of: 1 NCO, 1 lance operator, 2 *Wex* carriers, 1 assistant
1 machine-gun squad: 1 NCO, 4 machine gunners
1 replacement troop: 3 NCOs, 9 men.

Each *Wex* squad armed with 2 apparatuses.

Side arms:
Enlisted men armed with pistols; NCOs leading the *Wex* squads armed with carbines.

The tools equipping a *Wex* squad are:
3 spades, 2 wire cutters, 1 wrench, 1 toolkit.

March formation - In 4 columns:
platoon leader
4 NCOs, squad leaders
4 lance operators
4 *Wex* carriers
4 *Wex* carriers
4 assistants
1 runner, 3 NCOs
2 replacements, 1 machine gunner, 1 lance operator
2 replacements, 1 machine gunner, 1 *Wex* carrier
2 replacements, 1 machine gunner, 1 *Wex* carrier
2 replacements, 1 machine gunner, 1 assistant
1 NCO, 1 replacement, 1 NCO

Notes
The information in Appendix 6 is drawn from Ministère de la Guerre, *Lance-flammes portatifs étrangers*, p. 18.

ENDNOTES

Introduction Notes

[1] Francis A. March, *History of the World War: An Authentic Narrative of the World's Greatest War* (Philadelphia/Chicago/Toronto: United Publishers of the United States and Canada, 1919), p.88.

Chapter One Notes

[1] Adrienne Mayor, *Greek Fire, Poison Arrows, and Scorpion Bombs: Biological and Chemical Warfare in the Ancient World* (Woodstock, New York; New York; London: Overlook Duckworth, 2003), pp.241-242.

[2] Harold Lamb, "Flame Weapons," *Chemical Warfare* Volume 13, Number 1 (January 15, 1927): 237, 245.

[3] Ibid.

[4] John W. Mountcastle, *Flame On! U.S. Incendiary Weapons, 1918-1945* (Shippensburg, Pennsylvania: White Mane Publishing, 1999), p.3.

[5] "Greenough's Liquid Fire," *Richland County Observer* (March 21, 1862), p.2, col.4. Additional details were found in an unidentified, undated newspaper article – possibly from the St. Peter Tribune of July 18, 1862 – pasted into a scrapbook.

[6] Mountcastle, pp.7-8.

[7] Most of the information on the development of Fiedler's flamethrower from 1905-1909 is taken from Charles Theune, *Sturmtruppen und Flammenwerfer* (Berlin: Landes-Verlag, 1921), pp.245-247.

[8] "German Patents of 1908 Reveal France's Blindness," *The Galveston Daily News* (June 26, 1921), p.29, col.8.

[9] Swiss Patent. No. 42243, filed January 3, 1908, p.1; and British Patent No. 216, filed January 3, 1908, and accepted August 20, 1908, p.2. Fiedler's German patent for this device cannot be found.

[10] See Chapter Three.

[11] See Chapter Eight.

[12] The information on fire tubes is taken from *Pionierdienst im Kampf um Festungen, Entwurf 1914* (Berlin: Reichsdruckerei, 1915), pp.135-137.

[13] "M. Erzberger is Murdered: Assassinated Near Offenberg, Baden; Notable Character," *Sheboygan Press and Sheboygan Telegram* (August 26, 1921), p.1, col.1.

[14] Herbert Corey, "Germans Squirt Flame into British Trenches to Burn Out Soldiers," *The Syracuse Herald* (September 7, 1915), p.5, col.2.

[15] Robert Lembke, telephone conversation with author, February 24, 2004. Robert Lembke is the son of Georg Lembke, a German flamethrower pioneer during the First World War. For more information on Wilhelm's apparently changed attitude toward flamethrowers, see Chapter Seven.

[16] Corey.

[17] *Rangliste der Königlich Preussischen Ingenieur- und Pionierkorps zum 1 Mai 1914*. (Berlin, 1914), p.88.

[18] Rangliste der Königlich Preussischen Armee und des XIII. (Königlich Württembergischen) Armeekorps für 1914 (Berlin: Ernst Siegfried Mittler und Sohn, 1914), p.423.

[19] Ibid., p.751.

[20] "Personalnachrichten," *Feuer und Wasser* No.30 (29 July, 1911), p.250.

[21] The *Rangliste der Königlich Preussischen Armee* gives 1911 as the date of Reddemann's promotion to Hauptmann, but the *Rangliste der Königlich Preussischen Ingenieur- und Pionierkorps* gives it as 1910.

[22] *Rangliste der Königlich Preussischen Armee*, p.995.

[23] Berliner Addressbuch 1929 (Berlin: Verlag August Scherl Deutsche Adressbuch-Gesellschaft, 1929), p.2832. In this telephone book, he is listed as "Dr. jur. Bernhard Reddemann."

[24] Hermann Cron, *Imperial Germany Army 1914-18: Organisation, Structure, Orders-of-Battle* (Solihull, West Midlands, England: Helion and Company, 2002), p.168.

[25] "Personalnachrichten," p.250.

[26] Bruce I. Gudmundsson, "These Hideous Weapons," in *The Great War: Perspectives on the First World War*, edited by Robert Cowley (New York: Random House, 2003). p.311.

[27] Bernhard Reddemann, *Geschichte der deutschen Flammenwerfer-Truppe* (Berlin: Verein ehem. Angehöriger der Garde-Reserve-Pionier-Regiments, 1933), pp.9-10.

[28] Ibid., p.10.

[29] *Dem Andenken unserer gefallenen Kameraden: Garde-Reserve-Pionier-Regiment (Flammenwerfer)* (Berlin: Kameradschaft der Flammenwerfer im NS.-Reichskriegerbund, 1931), p.18.

[30] Theune, *Sturmtruppen und Flammenwerfer*, p.247.

[31] Reddemann, *Geschichte*, p.8.

[32] Theune, *Sturmtruppen und Flammenwerfer*, pp.247-248.

[33] Reddemann, *Geschichte*, p.11.

[34] Bundesarchiv-Militärarchiv PH 5-II/496 contains a photo and text, while a handwritten report titled "Short Description of Our Close-combat Weapons" (*Kurze Beschreibung unserer Nahkampfmittel*) in PH 14/324, dated February 2, 1915, describes a "heavy flamethrower of cylindrical boilers, 180 liters [forty-five gallons] capacity, portable by two men when empty."

[35] "Liquid Fire as a Weapon," *The Literary Digest* Volume 53, Number 5 (July 29, 1916): 246-247.

[36] Mountcastle, p.11.

Chapter Two Notes

[1] Reddemann, *Geschichte*, p.8.

[2] Bernhard Reddemann, "Die Flammenwerfer," in *Unsere Pioniere im Weltkriege*, edited by Otto Riebicke (Berlin: Kyffhäuser Verlag, 1925), p.195.

[3] Philip Gibbs, *The Soul of the War* (New York: Robert M. McBride and Company, 1916), p.143.

[4] March, *History of the World War*, p.92. See also Edward Wright, "The Victories of Vimy and Arras, and the Rupture of the Hindenburg Line," in *The Great War*, Volume 9, edited by H.W. Wilson and J.A. Hammerton (London: The Amalgamated Press, 1917), p.318.

[5] Reddemann's service with Pioneer Battalion No. 29 is documented in Hans Tröbst and Artur Leipold, *Das posensche Pionier-Bataillon Nr. 29 und seine Kriegsforationen* (Berlin: Kolk, 1932), pp.33, 279.

[6] John Mosier, *The Myth of the Great War* (New York: Perennial/HarperCollins, 2001), p.157.

[7] Adolf Deutelmoser, *Die 27. Infanterie-Division im Weltkrieg 1914-18* (Stuttgart: Bergers Literarisches Büro, 1925), pp.24-25.

[8] Tröbst and Leipold, p.56.

[9] Jean-Joseph Rouquerol, *La Guerre en Argonne* (Paris: Payot, 1937), p.53.

[10] Ibid.

[11] Tröbst and Leipold, p.33.

[12] Reddemann, "Die Flammenwerfer," pp.195-196.

[13] *Ministère des Affaires Étrangères, Les Violations des Lois de la Guerre par l'Allemagne* (Paris/Nancy: Librairie Berger-Levrault, 1915), pp.171-172.

[14] Although this document, Order No. 365/11. 14. A6, is found in the German Bundesarchiv-Militärarchiv, the file number is not known. It cannot be easily traced because there are no precise lists for the contents of each file in the archive.

[15] Charles. H. Foulkes, *"Gas!" The Story of the Special Brigade* (London: William Blackwood and Sons, 1934), p.25.

[16] Ignatius Phraye, "Liquid Fire as a German Arm. Terrors of the 'Flame Projector,'" *The War Budget*, Volume VI, No. 11 (January 27, 1916): 329.

[17] Records of Württembergisches Pionier-Bataillon Nr. 13, Hauptstaatsarchiv Stuttgart M 200 Bü. 80.

[18] Ibid., M 209 Bü. 17.

[19] Reddemann, *Geschichte*, p.10.

[20] Theune, *Sturmtruppen und Flammenwerfer*, p.248.

[21] Reddemann, *Geschichte*, p.16.

[22] Records of *Württembergisches Pionier-Bataillon Nr. 13*, M 200 Bü. 80.

[23] Reddemann, "Die Flammenwerfer," pp.195-196.

[24] Reddemann never specified the exact date that his Detachment was founded, but modern writers provide conflicting information. On page 27 of Jim Hall and Chip Minx, "Die Totenkopf Pioniere," *Kaiserzeit* Volume VIII, Number 4 (Winter 1979), the date is given as January 15, 1915. On page 44 of Bruce I. Gudmundsson, *Stormtroop Tactics: Innovation in the German Army, 1914-1918* (Westport, Connecticut: Praeger Publishers, 1989), the date is January 18, 1915.

[25] Reddemann, *Geschichte*, p.11.

[26] Ibid., p.10.

[27] *Dem Andenken unserer gefallenen Kameraden*, p.16.

[28] Cron, *Imperial Germany Army*, p.168.

[29] Reddemann, *Geschichte*, p.12.

[30] Although this document, Order No. 4051/15. IV, is found in the German Bundesarchiv Militärarchiv, the file number is not known. It cannot be easily traced because there are no precise lists for the contents of each file in the archive.

[31] Hauptmann von Schaewen, "Der erste Flammenwerferangriff," in *Das Ehrenbuch Der deutschen Pioniere*, edited by Paul Heinrici (Berlin: Verlag Tradition Wilhelm Rolf, 1931), p.524-525.

[32] Ibid., p.525.

[33] Ibid.

[34] All technical details of the Detachment's first operation are taken from Reddemann, *Geschichte*, pp.11-13.

[35] Von Schaewen, p.525.

[36] Ibid.

[37] Reddemann, *Geschichte*, pp.12-13.

[38] Gibbs, *The Soul of the War*, pp.303-304.

[39] *Dem Andenken unserer gefallenen Kameraden*, p.21.

[40] Reddemann, *Geschichte*, pp.12-13.

[41] Von Schaewen, p.525.

[42] "Germans' Fluid Fire Caused Terrible Burns," *New York Times* (March 5, 1915), p.1, col.7.

[43] "Smoke Screened Assailants," *New York Times* (March 7, 1915), Section II, p.3, col.2, 3, 4.

[44] "Liquid Fire Attack Failed," *New York Times* (March 6, 1915), p.3, col.2, 4, 6.

[45] "Smoke Screened Assailants," p.3, col.2, 3, 4.

[46] Reddemann, *Geschichte*, p.13.

[47] Ibid., pp.13-14.

[48] Ibid., p.14.

Chapter Three Notes

[1] Cron, *Imperial Germany Army*, p.168.

[2] *Dem Andenken unserer gefallenen Kameraden*, p.32.

[3] Bernhard Reddemann to Brigadier General Amos A. Fries, Chief, Chemical Warfare Service, Thru: Major Herman H. Zornig, U.S. Army, Military Attache, U.S. Embassy, Berlin, February 29, 1928, Record Group 175, File #470.71/32, U.S. National Archives, p.5.

[4] Reddemann, *Geschichte*, p.14.

[5] Cron, *Imperial Germany Army*, p.168.

[6] Reddemann to Fries, p.10.

[7] Victor Lefebure, *The Riddle of the Rhine: Chemical Strategy in Peace and War* (New York: E. P.Dutton and Company, 1923), p.73.

[8] Reddemann, *Geschichte*, pp.14-15.

[9] Lembke, telephone conversation with the author. According to Georg Lembke, the Crown Prince personally bankrolled the development of the flamethrower battalion, as the high command was initially not enthusiastic about the idea.

[10] Bernhard Reddemann, "Die Totenkopf Pioniere," in *Das Ehrenbuch Der deutschen Pioniere*, p.516.

[11] Most of the information on combat equipment is found in Reddemann, *Geschichte*, pp.15-16.

[12] Reddemann, "Die Flammenwerfer," p.197.

[13] Bruce I. Gudmundsson, *Stormtroop Tactics*, p.53; and "These Hideous Weapons," in *The Great War: Perspectives on the First World War*, edited by Robert Cowley (New York: Random House, 2003), pp.312-313.

[14] Most of the information on flame tactics is found in Reddemann, "Die Totenkopf Pioniere," pp.516-524.

[15] Reddemann, *Geschichte*, pp.16-17.

[16] Wilhelm Balck, *Entwickelung der Taktik im Weltkriege* (Berlin: R. Eisenschmidt, 1920), p.73.

[17] Ibid.

[18] Reddemann, *Geschichte*, p.17.

[19] Reddemann, "Die Totenkopf Pioniere," p.520.

[20] Ibid.

[21] Ibid.

[22] Reddemann, *Geschichte*, p.18.

[23] Ibid., p.19.

[24] Although this document, No. 24309/2252, is found in the German Bundesarchiv Militärarchiv, the file number is not known. It cannot be easily traced because there are no precise lists for the contents of each file in the archive.

[25] "British Troops Capture German Liquid Fire Gun," *The Lima Daily News* (July 3, 1915), p.12, col.5.

[26] Reddemann, *Geschichte*, p.19.

[27] Ibid.

[28] Colin Mitchell, "Hooge (July 31st 1915)", in *A Deep Cry: First World War Soldier-Poets Killed in France and Flanders*, edited by Anne Powell (Phoenix Mill, Britain: Sutton, 1998), p.332. Rifleman Colin Mitchell served in the 8th and later the 3rd Battalions of the Rifle Brigade.

[29] Mountcastle, p.9.
[30] Philip Gibbs, *Now It Can Be Told* (New York and London: Harper and Brothers, 1920), p.103.
[31] Mountcastle, p.9.
[32] Private A. P.Hatton, "First Use of Liquid fire," *The Great War: I Was There!* Part 11 (December 13, 1938): 439-441.
[33] Gibbs, *Now It Can Be Told*, pp.103-104.
[34] "The Battle of Rue d'Ouvert and Stony Mountain and the Struggle Round Hooge," *The Great War*, Volume 4, pp.339-340.
[35] Gibbs, *Now It Can Be Told*, p.104.
[36] Stephen Bull, *World War I Trench Warfare* (1). Osprey Elite Series No.78 (Oxford: Osprey Publishing, 2002), p.50.
[37] Hatton, p.440.
[38] Gibbs, *Now It Can Be Told*, p.104.
[39] Mountcastle, p.11.
[40] Maj.-Gen. Leonard Wood et al. (eds.), *The History of the First World War*, Commemorative Edition, Volume 1 (New York: Grolier, 1965), p.290.
[41] Phraye, "Liquid Fire as a German Arm": 329.
[42] Most of the information on Sturmabteilung Calsow is found in Cron, *Imperial Germany Army*, p.119.
[43] The adjective *Kurhessisches* is derived from *Kurhessen*, or "Electoral Principality of Hessia."
[44] Information on this part of the attack is found in *Oberstleutnant* Clausius, *Erinnerungsblätter Deutscher Regimenter, Band 176*: *Infanterie-Regiment von Wittich (3.Kurhessiches) Nr. 83* (Oldenburg iO/Berlin: Verlag Georg Stalling, 1926), pp.50-52.
[45] Information on this part of the attack is found in Prof. Dr. Hartenstein, *Das Kurhessische Pionier-Bataillon Nr. 11 im Weltkriege 1914-1918* (Zeulenroda in Thüringen, Germany: Verlag Bernhard Sporn, 1936), p.26.
[46] "Germans Use Liquid Fire in Attack on Russians," *The Syracuse Herald* (March 10, 1915), p.2, col.6.
[47] Hartenstein, p.33.
[48] Ibid., pp.34-36.
[49] Theune, *Sturmtruppen und Flammenwerfer*, pp.97-98.
[50] "Germans Using Gas," *Fairbanks Daily Times* (June 8, 1915), p.1, col.2.

Chapter Four Notes

[1] Reddemann, *Geschichte*, p.19.
[2] War Diary of the General of Pioneers of *Armee-Abteilung Gaede*, Genrerallandesarchiv Karlsruhe 456 EV 105/57.
[3] Most of the information on the Schlayer gasoline sprayer is found in the War Diary of 1. *Landwehr-Pionier-Kompagnie XIV. Armee Korps*, Generallandesarchiv Karlsruhe 456 EV 105/98.
[4] War Diary of the Commander of Pioneers of *Landwehr Division Nr. 12*, Genrerallandesarchiv Karlsruhe 456 EV 105/69.
[5] War Diary of the General of Pioneers of *Armee-Abteilung Gaede*.
[6] War Diary of *Landwehr Division Nr. 12*, Genrerallandesarchiv Karlsruhe 456 EV 142/1.
[7] Gustav Goes, *Hartmannsweiler Kopf: das Schicksal eines Berges im Weltkriege* (Berlin: Traditionsverlag Kolk, 1930), p.101.
[8] War Diary of *Landwehr Division Nr. 12*.
[9] Reddemann, *Geschichte*, p.15.
[10] Ibid., pp.19, 50-51.
[11] "Liquid Fire Guns Russia's Terror, *Oakland Tribune* (March 28, 1915), p.2, col.2.
[12] Laura De Gozdawa Turezynowicz, *When the Prussians Came to Poland: The Experiences of an American Woman During the Invasion* (New York: G.P. Putnam's Sons, 1916), pp.153-154.
[13] "Austro-German Plans in East," *The Daily Gleaner* (June 21, 1915), p.1, col.3.
[14] "Checking of the Advance," *The Mansfield News* (September 25, 1915), p.2, col.1.
[15] Phraye, "Liquid Fire as a German Arm," 329.
[16] Ibid.
[17] Ibid.
[18] Cron, *Imperial Germany Army*, p.119.
[19] Generallandesarchiv Karlsruhe 456 F3/966.
[20] Graf Eberhard von Schwerin, *Königliches preussisches Sturm-Bataillon Nr. 5 (Rohr)* (Zeulenroda in Thüringen, Germany: Drud und Verlag von Bernhard Sporn, 1939), p.18.
[21] Ibid.
[22] Jürgen Kraus, *Die feldgraue Uniformierung des deutschen Heeres 1907-1918*, Vol. II (Osnabrück: Verlag Biblio, 1999), p.499.
[23] Von Schwerin, p.7.
[24] Ibid., p.18.
[25] Ibid., p.165.
[26] Theune, *Sturmtruppen und Flammenwerfer*, p.250.
[27] Cron, *Imperial Germany Army*, p.166.
[28] Gudmundsson, *Stormtroop Tactics*, pp.49-50.
[29] Goes, pp.104-114.
[30] Cron, *Imperial Germany Army*, p.119.
[31] "Instructions for the Employment of Flame Projectors," *The Infantry Journal* Volume 14, Number 9 (March 1918): pp.692-698. This translation of a German document dated December 12, 1915, describes the textbook combined stationary and pouncing attack.

Chapter Five Notes

[1] Most of the information on the preparations for the Verdun offensive is found in Reddemann, *Geschichte*, pp.20-21.
[2] *Oberleutnant* Dürning, "Die Kriegsformationen der Pionierwaffen," in *Das Ehrenbuch Der deutschen Pioniere*, p.63.
[3] Cron, *Imperial Germany Army*, p.169.
[4] Reddemann consistently calls them *Flammenstosstrupps*, but Charles Theune and other sources use the term *Flammenwerferstosstrupps*.
[5] Bundesarchiv-Militärarchiv W10/51589.
[6] Records of *Pioneer Regiment 23*, Bundesarchiv-Militärarchiv PH 14/218.
[7] Reddemann, *Geschichte*, pp.17, 20.
[8] Ibid, pp.21-24.
[9] *Dem Andenken unserer gefallenen Kameraden*, pp.21-25.
[10] Reddemann, *Geschichte*, p.22.
[11] A somewhat rough English translation of "Extract from a Report of the Commander of the 3rd and 4th Battalions of Guard Pioneers on the Subject of Recent Flame Fighting," dated April 20, 1916, is found in "Gases and Flame," Memorandum No.15, Headquarters Fort Niagra Training Camp (Fort Niagra, New York: Office of Senior Instructor, 1917), pp.60-62.
[12] Alistair Horne, *The Price of Glory: Verdun 1916* (London: Penguin Books, 1993), p.81.
[13] *Dem Andenken unserer gefallenen Kameraden*, pp.22, 25.
[14] This and the following two attacks are described in Reddemann, *Geschichte*, p.23.
[15] "Gases and Flame," p.62.
[16] "French Minister of War Pleased," *The Lincoln Daily Star* (March 4, 1916), p.4, col.3.
[17] Henry Sheahan, *A Volunteer Poilu* (Boston and New York: Houghton Mifflin Company/The Riverside Press Cambridge, 1916), pp.200-201.
[18] Hermann Cron, "Übersicht der Behörden und Truppen in der Kriegsformation, Band 8," 1918, Bundesarchiv-Militärarchiv PHD 6/181.
[19] Horne, p.162.
[20] Alexander Schwencke and Martin Reymann, *Die Tragödie von Verdun 1916. II. Teil: Das Ringen um Fort Vaux* Reichsarchiv Band 14 (Oldenburg, Germany: Drud und Verlag von Gerhard Stalling, 1928), p.15.
[21] Markus Klauer, *Die Höhe Toter Mann während der Kämpfe um Verdun in den Jahren 1916/1917* (Remscheid, Germany: Eigenverlag, 2001), p.81.
[22] Jean-Louis Larcade, *Deutsche Sturmtruppen: Troupes d'assaut allemandes (1914-1918)* (Les Jonquerets de Livet, France: Editions des Argonautes, 2002), p.130.
[23] Theune, *Sturmtruppen und Flammenwerfer*, pp.22, 155.
[24] Ibid., pp.136-137.
[25] Reddemann, *Geschichte*, p.23.
[26] Cron, *Imperial Germany Army*, p.168.

[27] Ibid.
[28] Much of the information on the formation of the *Garde-Reserve-Pionier-Regiment* is found in Reddemann, "Die Totenkopf Pioniere," in *Das Ehrenbuch der deutschen Pioniere*, p.524.
[29] Theune, *Sturmtruppen und Flammenwerfer*, pp.229-233.
[30] Reddemann, *Geschichte*, p.25.
[31] Lembke, telephone conversation with author.
[32] "Gases and Flame," p.60.
[33] Reddemann, *Geschichte*, pp.25-26.
[34] Lembke, telephone conversation with author.
[35] Reddemann, *Geschichte*, p.24-25.
[36] Ibid., p.25.
[37] Charles Theune, "The Flame Thrower," *Artilleristische Monatschafte* (January-February, 1921). Translated by the Military Intelligence Division of the U.S. War Department. Records of the Chief, Chemical Warfare Service, Record Group 175, File #470.71/1164, U.S. National Archives, pp.4-5.
[38] Reddemann, *Geschichte*, p.25.
[39] Christina Holstein, *Battleground Europe Series: Verdun-Fort Douaumont* (Barnsley, South Yorkshire, United Kingdom: Pen and Sword Books, 2002), p.67.
[40] P.C. Ettighofer, *Verdun: Das grosse Gericht* (Gütersloh, Germany: C. Bertelsmann, 1936), pp.157-160.
[41] Holstein, p.69.
[42] Ettighofer, p.163.
[43] Ibid., p.72.
[44] *Dem Andenken unserer gefallenen Kameraden*, pp.22-24.
[45] Reddemann, *Geschichte*, p.30.

Chapter Six Notes

[1] Charles Theune, "Der Flammenangriff im Caillettewald vor Verdun am 1. Juni 1916," in *Das Ehrenbuch Der deutschen Pioniere*, pp.525-527.
[2] Reddemann, Geschichte, p.30.
[3] Theune, "Der Flammenangriff im Cailettewald," p.527.
[4] Ibid.
[5] Ibid.
[6] Theune, *Sturmtruppen und Flammenwerfer*, p.165.
[7] Reddemann, *Geschichte*, p.30.
[8] *Dem Andenken unserer gefallenen Kameraden*, pp.21, 23-24.
[9] Schwencke and Reymann, p.39.
[10] *Dem Andenken unserer gefallenen Kameraden*, pp.22, 25.
[11] *Descriptive Account of the Fort of Vaux and its Role During the Battle of Verdun. The Battle of Verdun in History Series* (Frémont, Verdun: Les Éditions Lorraines), p.12.
[12] Horne, p.254.
[13] Account by German war correspondent Kurt von Reden, in the June 16, 1916, edition of the *Breisgauer Zeitung*, quoted in Henry Bordeaux, *The Last Days of Fort Vaux* (Paris: Thomas Nelson and Sons, 1919), p.231.
[14] Schwencke and Reymann, p.97.
[15] Bordeaux, pp.155-156.
[16] Schwencke and Reymann, p.108.
[17] Ibid.
[18] Ibid., pp.108-109.
[19] Bordeaux, pp.203-204.
[20] Colonel Sylvain-Eugène Raynal, *Le Drame du Fort de Vaux* (Frémont, Verdun: Éditions Lorraines, 1949), pp.121-124.
[21] Schwencke and Reymann, p.109.
[22] Bordeaux, p.204.
[23] Raynal, p.123.
[24] Bordeaux, pp.202-203.
[25] Schwencke and Reymann, p.110.
[26] Horne, p.258.
[27] Raynal, p.126.
[28] Ibid., p.145.
[29] Horne, p.260.
[30] Schwencke and Reymann, p.111.
[31] Ibid., pp.111-112.
[32] Raynal, p.164.
[33] Schwencke and Reymann, p.112.
[34] *Hauptmann* Lindow, "Das II/Pi. 20 (bestehend aus 3 Pionierkompagnien: I.K./Pi. 20, 2./Pi. 20 und 3./Pi. 20) bei Vaux," in *Das Ehrenbuch Der deutschen Pioniere*, p.239.
[35] Reddemann, *Geschichte*, p.24.
[36] *Dem Andenken unserer gefallenen Kameraden*, pp.32-33.
[37] Larcade, p.123.
[38] Reddemann, *Geschichte*, p.24.
[39] Ibid., pp.29-30.
[40] "Pressing the Foe," *The Daily Gleaner* (July 8, 1916), p.1, col.1.
[41] *Dem Andenken unserer gefallenen Kameraden*, p.22.
[42] Henry D. Sleeper (ed.), *Diary of Section VIII: American Ambulance Field Service* (Boston: Thomas Todd Co., 1917), pp.25-26.
[43] This information is found in Theune, *Sturmtruppen und Flammenwerfer*, pp.156-157.

Chapter Seven Notes

[1] Edward Wright, "The Victories of Vimy and Arras, and the Rupture of the Hindenburg Line," in *The Great War*, Volume 9, p.318.
[2] The information on the flamethrower regiment's experiences at the Somme, including individual flame attacks, is found in Reddemann, *Geschichte*, pp.31-32.
[3] Edmund Blunden, *Undertones of War*, (New York: Harcourt, Brace, and World, Inc., 1965), p.80.
[4] The Papers of Colonel Sir Eric Gore-Browne, Reference Number 88/52/1, Imperial War Museum.
[5] Rudyard Kipling, *The Irish Guards in the Great War: The First Battalion* (Staplehurst, Kent, United Kingdom: Spellmount, 1997), p.133.
[6] "Experience of the German 1st Army in the Somme Battle, by General von Bülow," Occasional Papers Number 56, Engineer School, United States Army (Washington Barracks, D.C.: Press of the Engineer School, 1917), p.27.
[7] Theune, "The Flame Thrower," p.184.
[8] Peter T. Scott, "An Awful Job," *Military Illustrated* Number 98 (July 1996): 36-40.
[9] Wright.
[10] Foulkes, p.165.
[11] Theune, "The Flame Thrower," p.6.
[12] Chris McCarthy, *The Somme: The Day-by-day Account* (London: Arms and Armour Press, 1993), pp.45, 51, 67.
[13] *Dem Andenken unserer gefallenen Kameraden*, pp.24-25.
[14] John Buchan, *The Battle of the Somme* (New York: Grosset and Dunlap, 1917), p.226.
[15] Ibid., p.242.
[16] "Experience of the German 1st Army," p.32.
[17] Gudmundsson, *Stormtroop Tactics*, p.79.
[18] Friedrich Müller, *Brandenburgerisches Jäger-Bataillon Nr. 3* (Oldenburg, Germany: Verlag Gerhard Stalling, 1922), p.51.
[19] H. Colin, *Le Fort de Souville: L'Heure Suprême à Verdun* (Paris: Payot, 1938), pp.118-122.
[20] Ibid., p.121.
[21] *Dem Andenken unserer gefallenen Kameraden*, pp.21-25.
[22] Reddemann to Fries, p.21.
[23] Reddemann, *Geschichte*, pp.48-49.
[24] Ibid., p.49.
[25] Ibid.
[26] Lembke, telephone conversation with author.
[27] In *Geschichte*, p.27, Reddemann wrote that the 4th, 5th, and 7th Companies were used, but in "Die Totenkopf Pioniere," in *Das Ehrenbuch der Deutschen Pioniere*, p.522, he wrote that an entire unidentified battalion of the regiment was deployed.
[28] Reddemann, *Geschichte*, p.26.

[29] Reddemann, "Die Totenkopf Pioniere," p.523.
[30] On page 523 of "Die Totenkopf Pioniere," Reddemann wrote that 130 *Kleif* were used, yet there were sixteen flame shock troops and twenty-four *Kleif* squads positioned behind them, for a total of 216 *Kleif*, the number of devices arming a battalion.
[31] Reddemann, *Geschichte*, p.27.
[32] Reddemann, "Die Totenkopf Pioniere," p.524.
[33] Reddemann, *Geschichte*, p.28.

Chapter Eight Notes

[1] The information on individual flamethrower attacks in 1917 is found in Reddemann, *Geschichte*, pp.32-36.
[2] *Unteroffizier* Officer Rudolf Falk, Reserve Pioneer Company 80, "O Deutschland, hoch in Ehren!", in *Das Ehrenbuch Der deutschen Pioniere*, pp.315-317.
[3] Gudmundsson, *Stormtroop Tactics*, p.114.
[4] *Dem Andenken unserer gefallenen Kameraden*, p.27.
[5] Theune, *Sturmtruppen und Flammenwerfer*, p.149.
[6] Reddemann to Fries, p.16.
[7] M.C. Ortner, *Österreichische Militärgeschichte 1998 - Folge 6. Die k.u.k. Sturmtruppen 1916-1918: Elitesoldaten Der Monarchie* (Vienna: Verlagsbuchhandlung Stöhr, 1998), p.47.
[8] The information on Austro-Hungarian flamethrower platoons and their weapons is found in *Anleitung für Flammenwerfer* (Vienna: Druckerei des k.u.k. Kriegsministeriums, 1916), pp.5-10.
[9] Ibid., p.2.
[10] Ortner, p.24
[11] Peter Jung, *The Austro-Hungarian Forces in World War I (2), 1916-18*, Osprey Men-at-Arms Series No. 397 (Oxford: Osprey Publishing, 2003), p.11.
[12] Ortner, p.24.
[13] Ibid., pp.32-34.
[14] M. Christian Ortner, *Storm Troops: Austro-Hungarian Assault Units, Commandos in the First World War: Tactics, Organisation, Uniforms and Equipment* (Vienna: Verlag Militaria, 2005), p.268.
[15] Ortner, *Die k.u.k. Sturmtruppen 1916-1918*, p.51.
[16] Ortner, *Storm Troops*, p.268.
[17] Ortner, *Die k.u.k. Sturmtruppen 1916-1918*, p.51.
[18] Ortner, *Storm Troops*, p.269.
[19] Keith A. Murdoch, "The Anzacs' Great Record During 1917," *The Great War*, Volume 11, p.320.
[20] B.V. Stacy, F.J. Kindon, and H.V. Chedgey, *The History of the First Battalion A.I.F., 1914-1919* (Sydney: First Battalion A.I.F. Association, 1931.), pp.73-74.
[21] *Dem Andenken unserer gefallenen Kameraden*, pp.26, 27.
[22] Murdoch.
[23] C.E.W. Bean, *The Official History of Australia in the War of 1914-1918, Volume IV: The A.I.F. in France 1917* (Sydney: Angus and Robertson, 1929), p.514.
[24] Ibid., pp.514-515.
[25] Ibid., pp.515-516.
[26] *Dem Andenken unserer gefallenen Kameraden*, pp.26, 27.
[27] Bean, p.515.
[28] Theune, *Sturmtruppen und Flammenwerfer*, pp.124-125.
[29] Von Schwerin, p.48.
[30] "'Stosstruppen' Battalion is Repulsed by Forty Frenchmen," *Warren Evening Times* (September 5, 1917), p.1, col.1.
[31] "German Shock Troops Meet 40 French Oui! Oui!," *The Lima Daily News* (August 17, 1917), p.11, col.1.
[32] "'Stosstruppen' Battalion is Repulsed by Forty Frenchmen," p.1, col.2.
[33] "German Shock Troops Meet 40 French Oui! Oui!"
[34] "How 'Stosstruppen' Fighting Lost Out," *The Clearfield Progress* (September 5, 1917), p.2, col.6.
[35] Von Schwerin, pp.150, 154, 165.
[36] *Dem Andenken unserer gefallenen Kameraden*, p.27.
[37] Edward Wright, "The Victory of Craonne and the Battle Along the Ladies' Walk," in *The Great War*, Volume 10, p.242.
[38] *Dem Andenken unserer gefallenen Kameraden*, p.25.
[39] Reddemann, *Geschichte*, p.28.
[40] Lembke, telephone conversation with author.
[41] Theune, *Sturmtruppen und Flammenwerfer*, pp.237-243.

Chapter Nine Notes

[1] Edward J. Erickson, *Ordered to Die: A History of the Ottoman Army in the First World War* (Westport, Connecticut: Greenwood Press, 2001), pp.139-141.
[2] Turkish General Staff, *Birinci Dünya Harbinde Türk Harbi-Avrupa Cepheleri (Ozet)* (Ankara: Genelkurmay Askeri Tarih ve Stratejik Etud Baskangligi, 1996) p.61.
[3] Erickson, p.233.
[4] S.S. McClure, *Obstacles to Peace* (Boston: Houghton Mifflin Company, 1917), p.340.
[5] Peter Downham (ed.), *Diary of an Old Contemptible* (Barnsley, South Yorkshire: Pen and Sword, 2004), p.136.
[6] W. Grant Grieve and Bernhard Newman, *Tunnelers* (London, 1936), p.200.
[7] Much of the information on Operation Beach Party is found in the War Diary of *Sturmabteilung Marinekorps*, Bundesarchiv-Militärarchiv RM 120/324.
[8] Reddemann, *Geschichte*, pp.34-35.
[9] Ibid.
[10] Edward Wright, "The British Offensive at Ypres and the Battle of Lens," in *The Great War*, Volume 10, p.436.
[11] Grieve and Newman, p.200.
[12] War Diary of *Sturmabteilung Marinekorps*.
[13] Australian War Memorial, Unit War Diaries 1914-18 War, *2nd Australian Tunneling Company*, Item No. 16/3/8.
[14] Theune, *Sturmtruppen und Flammenwerfer*, p.118.
[15] Ibid., p.121.
[16] Grieve and Newman, pp.200-201.
[17] Wright, "The British Offensive at Ypres," p.436.
[18] *Dem Andenken unserer gefallenen Kameraden*, pp.26-28.
[19] Reddemann, *Geschichte*, p.35.
[20] "For Valour: Heroes of the Victoria Cross in the Fourth Year of the War," in *The Great War*, Volume 12, p.377.
[21] *Dem Andenken unserer gefallenen Kameraden*, pp.26-27.
[22] Reddemann, *Geschichte*, pp.35-36.
[23] Edward Wright, "The Langemark Victory and the Menin Road Check," in *The Great War*, Volume 10, p.480.
[24] Ibid., pp.481-482.
[25] Reddemann to Fries, pp.9-10.
[26] Colonel W.W. Murray, *The History of the 2nd Canadian Battalion (East. Ontario Regiment) Canadian Expeditionary Force in the Great War 1914-1919* (Ottawa: The Historical Committee, 2nd Battalion, C.E.F., 1947), pp.199-200.
[27] Ibid., p.200.
[28] Ibid., p.201.
[29] Wright, "The Langemark Victory," p.482.
[30] Guy Chapman, *A Passionate Prodigality* (New York, Chicago, San Francisco: Holt, Rineheart, Winston, 1966), p.190.
[31] Ibid., p.193.
[32] *Dem Andenken unserer gefallenen Kameraden*, pp.26-27.
[33] Reddemann, *Geschichte*, pp.36-37.
[34] Lembke, telephone conversation with author.
[35] "German Morale is Rapidly Weakening Says British Officer," *The Olean Evening Herald* (November 19, 1917) p.2, col.3-4.
[36] Müller, pp.85-88.
[37] Edward Wright, "The Cambrai of Surprises: II. – From the Capture of Bourlon Ridge to the Retirement of Flesquières," in *The Great War*, Volume 11, p.254.
[38] *Dem Andenken unserer gefallenen Kameraden*, p.27.

[39] Ibid., pp.26-27.
[40] Anthony Livesey, *The Historical Atlas of World War I* (New York: Henry Holt and Company, 1994), p.139.

Chapter Ten Notes

[1] The information on flame battles and individual flamethrower attacks in this period is found in Reddemann, *Geschichte*, pp.37-38.
[2] Library and Archives Canada, *War Diaries of the First World War*, RG9, Militia and Defense, Series III-D-3, Vol. 4931, Appendix B, 21st Canadian Battalion Narrative of Enemy Raid Lens Section [online], 4 March 1918.
[3] *Den Andenken unserer gefallen Kameraden*, p.31.
[4] Theune, *Sturmtruppen und Flammenwerfer*, p.187.
[5] War Diary of *Sturmpanzerkraftwagen-Abteilung 1*, Bundesarchiv-Militärarchiv N 89/5, entry for February 12.
[6] Theune, p.187.
[7] The information on March Companies is found in Reddemann, *Geschichte*, pp.38-39.
[8] Reddemann, *Geschichte*, p.39.
[9] Ibid., p.39-40.
[10] Gudmundsson, *Stormtroop Tactics*, p.159; and Müller, p.94.
[11] Reddemann, *Geschichte*, p.40.
[12] Ibid., p.42.
[13] Ibid.
[14] Reddemann, *Geschichte*, pp.44-45.
[15] Ibid., p.45.
[16] "Huns' Torture of Prisoners," *The Fort Wayne Journal-Gazette* (August 19, 1919), p.5, col.5-6.
[17] Ibid.
[18] Ibid.
[19] Maxwell Hundleby and Rainer Strasheim, *The German A7V Tank and the Captured British Mark IV Tanks of World War I* (Sparkford, Nr Yeovil, Somerset: Hayes Publishing Group, 1990), p.34.
[20] Rainer Strasheim, e-mail to the author, April 10, 2005.
[21] Strasheim, e-mail to the author, April 16, 2005, quoting Erich Petter, *Kampfwagenabwehr im Weltkriege 1914-1918* (unpublished typewritten study, Berlin: 1932. Bundesarchiv-Militärarchiv Freiburg W10/50769), p.107.
[22] Hundleby and Strasheim, pp.98-100.
[23] Ibid., pp.107-108.
[24] Walter Greiff, "Durchbruchschlacht," in *Kreuz-Zeitung* No. 71 (March 24, 1935): 18.
[25] *Dem Andenken unserer gefallenen Kameraden*, p.31.
[26] "U.S. Sentry Traps Foe in Trench," *The Syracuse Herald* (March 9, 1918), p.1, col.8.
[27] "Yankees Fail to Show Fear at Flame Attack," *The Syracuse Herald* (March 9, 1918), p.2, col.4-5.
[28] "U.S. Sentry Traps Foe in Trench."
[29] "Yankees Fail to Show Fear at Flame Attack."
[30] Laurence Stallings, *The Doughboys: The Story of the AEF, 1917-1918* (New York: Harper and Row, 1963), p.60.
[31] Jean GrosJean, "The History of Company 'F.'" Diary of a sergeant in Company "F," 307th Infantry Regiment, 77th Division (Longwood, Long Island, New York, 1918).
[32] "Tales of the Thirty-second," *The Sheboygan Press* (September 10, 1926), p.15, col.3-4.
[33] War Diary of *Sturmbataillon Nr. 16*. Generallandesarchiv Karlsruhe 456 F 65/5.
[34] "Tales of the Thirty-second," p.15, col.4.
[35] War Diary of *Sturmbataillon Nr. 16*.
[36] *Dem Andenken unserer gefallenen Kameraden*, p.31.
[37] Historical Section, General Staff, *A Survey of German Tactics 1918: Tactical Studies* No.1 (The Base Printing Plant, 29th Engineers, U.S. Army, 1918), p.19.
[38] Reddemann to Fries, p.10.

Chapter Eleven Notes

[1] Reddemann, *Geschichte*, p.46.
[2] H.G. Proctor, *The Iron Division: National Guard of Pennsylvania in the World War* (Philadelphia: The John C. Winston Company, Publishers, 1919), pp.193-194.
[3] Hervey Allen, *Toward the Flame* (Lincoln: University of Nebraska Press, 2003), p.277.
[4] *Dem Andenken unserer gefallenen Kameraden*, pp.28-29, 31.
[5] L. Wardlaw Miles, *History of the 308th Infantry 1917-1919* (New York: G. P.Putnam's Sons, 1927), p.82.
[6] War Diary of *Infanterie-Division Nr. 29*, Bundesarchiv-Militärarchiv PH 8-I/205, 206, and 374.
[7] Ibid.
[8] Miles, pp.85-86.
[9] Ibid., pp.87-88.
[10] Ibid., p.88.
[11] Ibid., p.299.
[12] *Dem Andenken unserer gefallenen Kameraden*, pp.28-29.
[13] War Diary of *Infanterie-Division Nr. 29*.
[14] *Dem Andenken unserer gefallenen Kameraden*, pp.28-29, 31.
[15] Scott, Emmett J. Scott, *Scott's Official History of the American Negro in the World War* (Chicago: Homewood Press, 1919), pp.175-176.
[16] Ibid.
[17] *North Carolina Day. Friday, November 11th, 1921. Armistice Day. North Carolina in the World War*. Educational Publication No. 28, Division of Publication No. 3 (Raleigh, North Carolina: State Superintendent of Public Instruction, 1921), p.37.
[18] Scott, p.234.
[19] War Diary of *Sturmbataillon Nr. 16*, Generallandesarchiv Karlsruhe 456 F 65/5.
[20] Ministère de la Guerre, *Section technique des Etudes et Expériences chimiques, Conférences de l'Ecole des gaz de combat: Les Lance-flammes. 2ème Conférence. Lance-flammes légers portatifs* (Paris, 1920), p.59.
[21] Hermann Cron, *Geschichte des deutschen Heeres im Weltkriege 1914-1918* (Berlin: K. Siegismund, 1937), p.174.
[22] Thomas M. Johnson and Fletcher Pratt, *The Lost Battalion* (Lincoln, Nebraska: The University of Nebraska Press, 2000), p.206.
[23] Ibid., p.208.
[24] Ibid., pp.245-246.
[25] Laurence Stallings, *The Doughboys: The Story of the AEF, 1917-1918* (New York: Harper and Row, 1963), p.275.
[26] Johnson and Pratt, pp.58-59.
[27] War Diary of *Reserve-Division Nr. 76*, Bundesarchiv-Militärarchiv PH 8-II/86 and PH 8-II/87.
[28] Hall and Minx, "Die Totenkopf Pioniere,": 28.
[29] Reddemann, *Geschichte*, p.46.
[30] *Dem Andenken unserer gefallenen Kameraden*, p.32.
[31] Reddemann, *Geschichte*, pp.50-51.
[32] Ibid., pp.51-52.
[33] *Dem Andenken unserer gefallenen Kameraden*, pp.32-33.

Chapter Twelve Notes

[1] Richard M. Watt, *The Kings Depart: The Tragedy of Germany: Versailles and the German Revolution* (New York: Barnes and Noble Books, 2000), p.190.
[2] Theune, *Sturmtruppen und Flammenwerfer*, p.188.
[3] Reddemann's discussion of the postwar period is found in Reddemann, *Geschichte*, p.46.
[4] Theune, *Sturmtruppen und Flammenwerfer*, p.15.
[5] *Darstellungen der Nachkriegskämpfe Deutscher Truppen und Freikorps*, Volume 9 (Berlin, Mittler & Sohn, 1943), p.262; and Sean Dobson, *Authority and Upheaval in Leipzig, 1910-1920: The Story of a Relationship* (New York: Columbia University Press, 2001), p.287.
[6] Reddemann to Fries, p.21.
[7] Reddemann, *Geschichte*, p.5.

[8] Robert G.L. Waite, *Vanguard of Nazism: The Free Corps Movement in Postwar Germany 1918-1923* (New York: W.W. Norton and Company, 1969), pp.14-15.
[9] Ibid., p.38.
[10] Ibid, p.36.
[11] Ibid., p.38.
[12] The bulk of this information appears in *Darstellungen der Nachkriegskämpfe Deutscher Truppen und Freikorps*, Volumes 1-9 (Berlin, Mittler & Sohn, 1936-1943). Other sources cited as needed.

Berliner Freischützenkorps: photographic evidence.
Freikorps von Brandis: photographic evidence.
Detachment Gerstenberg: *Darstellungen*, Volume 6, p.208.
Deutsche Schutzdivision: Ibid., p.202.
Eiserne Division: Major Josef Bischoff, *Die letzte Front: Geschichte der Eisernen Division im Baltikum, 1919* (Berlin: 1935), p.77.
Freikorps Hülsen: *Darstellungen*, Volume 6, p.188.
Freikorps von Lützow: Ibid., Volume 4, p.198.
Freikorps Potsdam: Hans von Kessel, *Handgranaten und rote Fahnen* (Berlin: Verlag für Kulturpolitik, 1933), handwritten excerpt; no page number.
Freikorps Rossbach: Edgar von Schmidt-Pauli, *Geschichte der Freikorps 1918-24* (Stuttgart: Verlag Lutz, 1936), p.362, and Charles Woolley, *German Uniforms, Insignia, and Equipment 1918-1923* (Atglen, Pennsylvania: Schiffer Publishing, 2002), p.76.
Freiwilligen Landesjägerkorps: *Darstellungen*, Volume 6, pp.185-186.
Freiwilligen Landeschützenkorps: Ibid., p.220.
Freiwilligen Regiment Reinhard: Ibid., p.200.
Garde-Kavallerie Schützen-Division: Ibid., p.185.
Gruppe Division Münster: *Darstellungen*, Volume 9, p.262.
Kavallerie-Schützen-Kommando 14: *Darstellungen*, Volume 4, p.198.
II Marine Brigade Erhardt: Ibid., p.199.
III Marine Brigade Löwenfeld: Ibid., Volume 9, p.259.
Minenwerfer Detachment Heuschkel: Ibid., p.200.
45. Reserve-Division: Ibid., Volume 3, p.208.

[13] "Bolsheviks Mass for Big Assault," *Manitoba Free Press* (January 9, 1919), p.1, col.7.
[14] "Inner City of Berlin is Quiet," *Reno Evening Gazette* (January 10, 1919), p.8, col.3.
[15] Major von Stephani, "Der Sturm auf das Vorwärtsgebäde am 10. Januar 1919," in *Das Buch vom deutschen Freikorpskämpfer*, edited by Ernst von Salomon (Berlin: Verlag für ganzheitliche Forschung und Kultur, 1988), p.42.
[16] Lembke, telephone conversation with author.
[17] "Government Now in Control of Situation; Isolate Certain Areas," *Iowa City Daily Citizen*, (March 6, 1919), p.1, col.1.
[18] Ibid., (May 8, 1919), p.1, col.4.
[19] Dobson, p.247.
[20] "Government Appears to be Quelling New Revolt of Gerans," *Sandusky Star-Journal*, (March 6, 1919), p.1, col.2.
[21] *The Fort Wayne News and Sentinel* (April 16, 1919), p.6.
[22] *Fort Wayne Journal-Gazette* (April 11, 1919), p.1.
[23] "Death is Penalty for Spartacans Captured in Berlin," *Reno Evening Gazette* (March 8, 1919), p.1, col.7.
[24] Richard Grunberger, *Red Rising in Bavaria* (New York: St. Martin's Press, 1973.), pp.140-141.
[25] Jacques Benoist-Méchin, *Geschichte des deutschen Heeres seit dem Waffenstillstand 1918-1938*, Band 1 (Berlin: Verlag Dietrich Reimer, 1943), p.226.
[26] "Noske Breaks Up a Red Demonstration," *Evening State Journal* (July 23, 1919), p.2, col.3.
[27] Lefebure, pp.244-245.
[28] "Germany Slow to Reduce Army," *The Gettysburg Times* (May 11, 1920), p.2, col.3.
[29] "Germany Under Martial Law," *Syracuse Herald* (January 14, 1920), p.21, col.7.
[30] "Ebert Again in Control," *The Kansas City Times* (March 19, 1920), p.1, col.5.
[31] Dobson, p.287.
[32] Gerd Lüdersdorf, "Der Köpenicker Blutsonntag vom 21. März 1920," *Berlinische Monatschrift Heft 3* (Marz 2001): 37-45.
[33] "Begin War to Control City," *The Evening State Journal* (March 22, 1920), p.1, col.8.
[34] "Violent Disorders Reported from Every Section of German Empire," *The Clearfield Progress* (March 20, 1920), p.1, col.2.
[35] "Flame Throwers Used," *The Olean Evening Times* (April 8, 1920), p.7, col.3.
[36] William MacDonald, "What French Militarism Means," *The Nation* Volume 110, Number 2863 (May 15, 1920): 651.
[37] Norbert Fischer and Hanna Vollmer-Heitmann, *Chronik 1920: Tag für Tag in wort und Bild* (Dortmund: Chronik Verlag, 1990). p.138.
[38] *Reichsgesetzblatt* No. 28 (March 16, 1935): 369.
[39] E.J. Gumbel, "Disarmament and Clandestine Rearmament Under the Weimar Republic," in *Inspection For Disarmament*, edited by Seymour Melman (New York: Columbia University Press, 1958), pp.203-219.
[40] Philipp Scheidemann, *Die rechtsradikalen Verschwörer: Reichstags-Rede gehalten am 12 Mai 1923* (Berlin: Verlag für Sozialwissenschaft, 1923), p.20.

Chapter Thirteen Notes

[1] S.A. Dion, *Tanks, Gas, Bombing, Liquid Fire* (New York: George U. Harvey Publishing, 1917), p.154.
[2] Wright, "The Great British Battles of the Somme: IV. – Struggle on the Wings and the Thrust towards Bapaume," in *The Great War*, Volume 8, p.119.
[3] Foulkes, p.165.
[4] Amos A. Fries and Clarence J. West, *Chemical Warfare* (New York: McGraw-Hill, 1921), p.352.
[5] "The Battles of Hooge, Rouges Bancs, and Festubert," in *The Great War*, Volume 4, p.68.
[6] William T. Hornaday, *A Searchlight on Germany: Germany's Blunders, Crimes, and Punishment*. Preparation Pamphlet Series (New York: American Defense Society, 1917), p.24.
[7] Reddemann, *Geschichte*, pp.47-48.
[8] "3,000 Germans Perish in a Sea of Fire," *New York Times* (April 16, 1916), p.4, col.1, 2.
[9] *Dem Andenken unserer gefallenen Kameraden*, pp.22-26.
[10] "Caught in a Sea of Fire," *The War Illustrated* Volume 5 (September 16, 1916), p.114.
[11] Ibid.
[12] "The Nemesis of Flame," *Deeds of Heroism and Daring*, edited by Elwyn Barron (London/New York: Harper and Brothers, 1920), pp.18-20.
[13] Reddemann, *Geschichte*, pp.47-48.
[14] Ibid., p.47.
[15] Theune, "The Flame Thrower," pp.3-4.
[16] Ibid., p.9
[17] Military Attaché, the Hague, to Director of Military Intelligence Division, General Staff, War Department, April 18, 1921, Records of the Chief, Chemical Warfare Service, Record Group 175, File #470.71/1164, U.S. National Archives.
[18] Chief, Chemical Warfare Service, to Military Intelligence Department, General Staff, War Department, July 30, 1921, Records of the Chief, Chemical Warfare Service, Record Group 175, File #470.71/1164, U.S. National Archives.
[19] Bernhard Reddemann to Brigadier General Amos A. Fries, Chief, Chemical Warfare Service, Thru: Major Herman H. Zornig, U.S. Army, Military Attache, U.S. Embassy, Berlin, February 29, 1928, Record Group 175, File #470.71/32, U.S. National Archives
[20] Fries and West, p.401.
[21] Ibid., p.351.
[22] Ibid., p.401.

[23] Brigadier-General Amos A. Fries to Military Attache, U.S. Embassy, Berlin, Subject: Flame Throwers, 1 June, 1928, File #461/4788, Record Group 175, U.S. National Archives.

[24] "Gases and Flame," Memorandum No. 15, Headquarters Fort Niagra Training Camp (Fort Niagra, New York: Office of Senior Instructor, 1917), p.61.

[25] Reddemann, *Geschichte*, pp.49-50.

[26] Reddemann to Fries, p.16.

[27] Ibid., p.18.

[28] Ibid., p.13.

[29] Lefebure, p.44.

[30] Lectures of the French Army Chemical Warfare School, second lecture, File #MID 2314-C-90, Record Group 165, U.S. National Archives, p.79. Translation of French documents originally published in 1920.

[31] Georges Bertrand and Oscar N. Solbert, *Tactics and Duties for Trench Fighting* (New York: G. P.Putnam's Sons, 1918), pp.226-228.

[32] *Dem Andenken unserer gefallenen Kameraden*, p.18.

[33] Ibid., p.15.

[34] Ibid.

[35] Reddemann, *Geschichte*, p.52.

[36] *Dem Andenken unserer gefallenen Kameraden*, p.17.

[37] *Deutscher Feuerschutz*, No. 21 (1939): 635.

[38] Bernhard Reddemann, "Flammenwerfer vor die Front," *Der S.A.-Mann*, Folge 21 (26 Mai 1934): 15.

Chapter Fourteen Notes

[1] Reddemann, *Geschichte*, p.12.

[2] Bundesarchiv-Militärarchiv PH 5-II/496.

[3] Reddemann, *Geschichte*, p.11.

[4] Ibid., p.15.

[5] Ibid, p.24.

[6] The majority of the data presented in this section is found in Theune, *Sturmtruppen und Flammenwerfer*, p.99.

[7] Larcade, p.125.

[8] Records of *Württembergisches Pionier-Bataillon Nr. 13*, M 200 Bü. 80.

[9] Ministère de la Guerre, *Section technique des Etudes et Expériences chimiques, Conférences de l'Ecole des gaz de combat: Les Lance-flammes. 3ème Conférence. Lance-flammes portatifs étrangers* (Paris, 1920), p.8. Although a useful reference, this report also contains many inaccuracies and should be read with caution.

[10] Ibid., pp.9-11.

[11] Ministère de la Guerre, *Lance-flammes portatifs étrangers*, p.8.

[12] Theune, *Sturmtruppen und Flammenwerfer*, p.99.

[13] Ibid.

[14] Reddemann, "Die Flammenwerfer," in *Unsere Pioniere im Weltkriege*, p.199.

[15] Theune, *Sturmtruppen und Flammenwerfer*, p.60.

[16] "New Terror of War Invented by German," *The Syracuse Herald* (May 6, 1917), p.4, col.1. This article stated that the Germans have invented an improved apparatus for spraying liquid fire, which has a much greater range than that of earlier weapons. It was already in use by May 5, inflicting extremely heavy casualties on the French.

[17] Theune, *Sturmtruppen und Flammenwerfer*, p.99.

[18] Ibid., p.38.

[19] Ibid., pp.34-37.

[20] Ministère de la Guerre, *Lance-flammes portatifs étrangers*, p.10.

[21] Theune, *Sturmtruppen und Flammenwerfer*, p.86.

[22] Ministère de la Guerre, *Lance-flammes portatifs étrangers*, p.7.

[23] Theune, *Sturmtruppen und Flammenwerfer*, p.112.

[24] Ibid., p.32.

[25] Ibid., p.112.

[26] Ibid, p.32.

[27] Ministère de la Guerre, *Lance-flammes portatifs étrangers*, p.7.

[28] Ibid., pp.4, 14.

[29] Theune, *Sturmtruppen und Flammenwerfer*, p.250.

[30] Ibid., pp.19-21.

[31] Ministère de la Guerre, *Lance-flammes portatifs étrangers*, p.17.

BIBLIOGRAPHY

Primary sources

Government Documents and Public Records

Anleitung für Flammenwerfer. Vienna: Druckerei des k.u.k. Kriegsministeriums, 1916.

Annuaire Officiel de l'Armée Française pour 1913. Paris: Berger-Levrault, 1912.

Australian War Memorial, Unit War Diaries 1914-18 War, *2nd Australian Tunnelling Company*, Item No. 16/3/8.

Berliner Addressbuch 1929. Berlin: Verlag August Scherl Deutsche Adressbuch-Gesellschaft, 1929.

Cron, Hermann. "Overview of the Authorities and Units in the Wartime Formations, Volume 8" (*Übersicht der Behörden und Truppen in der Kriegsformation*, Band 8). Bundesarchiv-Militärarchiv PHD 6/181. The establishing of various Guard Pioneer Formations.

Experience of the German 1st Army in the Somme Battle, by General von Bülow. Occasional Papers Number 56, Engineer School, United States Army. Washington Barracks, D.C.: Press of the Engineer School, 1917.

"Gases and Flame." Memorandum No. 15, Headquarters Fort Niagra Training Camp.Fort Niagra, New York: Office of Senior Instructor, 1917.

Grand Quartier Général des Armées de l'Est, État Major. *Instruction Relative À L'Utilisation Des Compagnies Schilt: Projection Des Liquides Inflammables*. Paris: Imprimerie Nationale, 1916.

Grand Quartier Général des Armées du Nord et du Nord-est. *Instruction Relative À L'Utilisation Des Compagnies de Lance-flammes*. Paris: Imprimerie Nationale, 1918.

Historical Section, General Staff. *A Survey of German Tactics 1918: Tactical Studies No. 1*. The Base Printing Plant, 29th Engineers, U.S. Army, 1918.

History of Trench Warfare Material 1917-1919. Washington, D.C.: Army Ordnance, Government Printing Office, 1920.

"Instructions on the Cooperation Between the Infantry and Flamethrowers" (*Merkblatt für das Zusammenarbeiten der Infanterie mit Flammenwerfer*). Hauptstaatsarchiv Stuttgart, Generalkommando XIII. AK M 33/2 Bü 236.

Library and Archives Canada, War Diaries of the First World War, RG9, Militia and Defense, Series III-D-3, Vol. 4931, Appendix B, *21st Canadian Battalion Narrative of Enemy Raid Lens Section* [online], 4 March 1918.

Ministère de la Guerre, Section technique des Etudes et Expériences chimiques. Conférences de l'Ecole des gaz de combat: *Les Lance-flammes*. 2ème Conférence. Lance-flammes légers portatifs. Paris, 1920.

—. *Conférences de l'Ecole des gaz de combat: Les Lance-flammes. 3ème Conférence. Lance-flammes portatifs étrangers*. Paris, 1920.

Ministère de la Guerre, Direction de l'Infanterie. *Instruction Provisoire sur l'Utilisation des Appareils Lance-flammes et des Engins Incendiaires du 1er Février 1921*. Paris: Imprimerie Nationale, 1921.

Ministère des Affaires Étrangères. *Les Violations des Lois de la Guerre par l'Allemagne*. Paris/Nancy: Librairie Berger-Levrault, 1915.

Ministero Della Guerra, Sottosegretariato per le Armi e Munizoni. *Cenni Descrittivi Degli Apparati Schilt: N. 1 del 1° Luglio 1915*; N. 2 del 6 Luglio 1915; N. 3 del 6 Luglio 1915. Rome: Laboratorio Foto-Litografico del Ministerio Della Guerra, 1916.

Pionierdienst im Kampf um Festungen, Entwurf 1914. Berlin: Reichsdruckerei, 1915.

R. Esercito Italiano, Comando Supremo, Ufficio Tecnico. *Cenni Descrittivi Degli Apparecchi Lanciafiamme portatili*. 1918.

Rangliste des Königlich Preussischen Ingenieur- und Pionierkorps zum 1 Mai 1914. Berlin, 1914.

Rangliste der Königlich Preussischen Armee und des XIII. (Königlich Württembergischen) Armeekorps für 1914. Berlin: Ernst Siegfried Mittler und Sohn, 1914.

Records of *Armee-Oberkommando 9*. Bundesarchiv-Militärarchiv PH 5-II/496. Photos and descriptions of the grosse Flammenwerfer M.1912.

Records of the Chief, Chemical Warfare Service. Record Group 175, U.S. National Archives.

Records of *Pionier-Regiment No. 23*. "Enclosure 2 to Divisional Orders" (*Anlage 2 zu Division-Befehl*). Bundesarchiv-Militärarchiv PH 14/218. Instructions for the use of flamethrowers by 5th Infantry Division.

Records of *Württembergisches Pionier-Bataillon Nr. 13*. Hauptstaatsarchiv Stuttgart M 200 Bü. 80; M 209 Bü. 17.

"Short Description of Our Close-in Combat Means" (*Kurze Beschreibung unserer Nahkampfmittel*). Bundesarchiv-Militärarchiv PH 14/324. Contains a hand-written report, dated February 2, 1915, which describes the grosse *Flammenwerfer* M.1912.

Turkish General Staff. *Birinci Dünya Harbinde Türk Harbi-Avrupa Cepheleri (Ozet)*. Ankara: Genelkurmay Askeri Tarih ve Stratejik Etud Baskanligi, 1996.

"Use of the Flamethrowers" (*Verwendung die Flammenwerfer*). Pamphlet Ia No. 491 distributed by the Fifth Army High Command. Bundesarchiv-Militärarchiv W10/51589.

War Diary of *1. Landwehr-Pionier-Kompagnie XIV. Armee Korps*. Generallandesarchiv Karlsruhe 456 EV 105/98.

War Diary of the Commander of Pioneers of *Landwehr Division Nr. 12*. Generallandesarchiv Karlsruhe 456 EV 105/69.

War Diary of the General of Pioneers of *Armee-Abteilung Gaede*. Generallandesarchiv Karlsruhe 456 EV 105/57.

War Diary of *Infanterie-Division Nr. 29*. Bundesarchiv-Militärarchiv PH 8-I/205, 206, and 374. Composition of German shock troops attacking American positions on the Vesle, August of 1918.

War Diary of *Landwehr Division Nr. 12*. Generallandesarchiv Karlsruhe 456 EV 142/1.

War Diary of *Reserve-Division Nr. 76*. Bundesarchiv-Militärarchiv PH 8-II/86 and PH 8-II/87. Composition of assault unit sent against the "Lost Battalion."

War Diary of *Sturmabteilung Marinekorps*. Bundesarchiv-Militärarchiv RM 120/324.

War Diary of *Sturmbataillon Nr. 16*. Generallandesarchiv Karlsruhe 456 F 65/5.

War Diary of *Sturmpanzerkraftwagen-Abteilung 1*. Bundesarchiv-Militärarchiv N 89/5.

Books

Allen, Hervey. *Toward the Flame*. Lincoln: University of Nebraska Press, 2003.

Balck, Wilhelm. *Entwickelung der Taktik im Weltkriege*. Berlin: R. Eisenschmidt, 1920.

Bekleidung und Ausrüstung der Preussischen Feuerwehren. Leipzig: Verlag von Moritz Ruhl, 1901.

Bertrand, Georges, and Oscar N. Solbert. *Tactics and Duties for Trench Fighting*. New York: G.P. Putnam's Sons, 1918.

Bischoff, Major Josef. *Die letzte Front: Geschichte der Eisernen Division im Baltikum, 1919*. Berlin: 1935.

Bordeaux, Henry. *The Last Days of Fort Vaux*. Paris: Thomas Nelson and Sons, 1919.

Blunden, Edmund. *Undertones of War*. New York: Harcourt, Brace, and World, Inc., 1965.

Colin, H. *Le Fort de Souville: L'Heure Suprême à Verdun*. Paris: Payot, 1938.

Dem Andenken unserer gefallenen Kameraden: Garde-Reserve-Pionier-Regiment (Flammenwerfer). Berlin: Kameradschaft der Flammenwerfer im NS.-Reichskriegerbund, 1931.

Deutelmoser, Adolf. *Die 27. Infanterie-Division im Weltkrieg 1914-18*. Stuttgart: Bergers Literarisches Büro, 1925.

Dion, S.A. *Tanks, Gas, Bombing, Liquid Fire*. New York: George U. Harvey Publishing Company, 1917.

Downham, Peter (ed.). *Diary of an Old Contemptible*. Barnsley, South Yorkshire: Pen and Sword, 2004.

Ettighofer, P.C. *Verdun: Das grosse Gericht*. Gütersloh, Germany: C. Bertelsmann, 1936.

Foulkes, Charles. H. *"Gas!" The Story of the Special Brigade*. London: William Blackwood and Sons, 1934.

Fries, Amos A., and Clarence J. West. *Chemical Warfare*. New York: McGraw-Hill, 1921.

Goes, Gustav. *Hartmannsweiler Kopf: Das Schicksal eines Berges im Weltkriege*. Berlin: W. Kolk, 1930.

Heinrici, Paul (ed.). *Das Ehrenbuch Der deutschen Pioniere*. Berlin: Verlag Tradition Wilhelm Rolf, 1931.

Miles, L. Wardlaw. *History of the 308th Infantry 1917-1919*. New York: G. P.Putnam's Sons, 1927.

Moss, Jasper A. *Trench Warfare*. Menasha, Wisconsin: George Banta Publishing Company, 1917.

Müller, Friedrich. *Brandenburgerisches Jäger-Bataillon Nr. 3*. Oldenburg, Germany: Verlag Gerhard Stalling, 1922.

Raynal, Colonel Sylvain-Eugène. *Le Drame du Fort de Vaux. Frémont, Verdun*. Éditions Lorraines, 1949.

Reddemann, Bernhard. *Geschichte der deutschen Flammenwerfer-Truppe*. Berlin: Verein ehem. Angehöriger der Garde-Reserve-Pionier-Regiments, 1933.

Riebicke, Otto (ed.). *Unsere Pioniere im Weltkriege*. Berlin: Kyffhauser Verlag, 1925.

Rouquerol, Jean-Joseph. *La Guerre en Argonne*. Paris: Payot, 1937.

Salomon, Ernst von (ed.). *Das Buch vom deutschen Freikorpskämpfer*. Berlin: Verlag für ganzheitliche Forschung und Kultur, 1988.

Schwencke, Alexander, and Martin Reymann. *Die Tragödie von Verdun 1916*. II. Teil: *Das Ringen um Fort Vaux*, Reichsarchiv Band 14. Oldenburg, Germany: Druck und Verlag von Gerhard Stalling, 1928.

Schwerin, Graf Eberhard von. *Königliches preussisches Sturm-Bataillon Nr. 5 (Rohr)*. Zeulenroda in Thüringen, Germany: Drud und Verlag von Bernhard Sporn, 1939.

Scott, Emmett J. *Scott's Official History of the American Negro in the World War*. Chicago: Homewood Press, 1919.

Sheahan, Henry. *A Volunteer Poilu*. Boston and New York: Houghton Mifflin Company/The Riverside Press Cambridge, 1916.

Sleeper, Henry D. (ed.). *Diary of Section VIII: American Ambulance Field Service*. Boston: Thomas Todd Co., 1917.

Theune, Charles. *Sturmtruppen und Flammenwerfer*. Berlin: Landes-Verlag, 1921.

Tröbst, Hans, and Artur Leipold. *Das posensche Pionier-Bataillon Nr. 29 und seine Kriegsforationen*. Berlin: Kolk, 1932.

Turezynowicz, Laura De Gozdawa. *When the Prussians Came to Poland: The Experiences of an American Woman During the Invasion*. New York: G.P.Putnam's Sons, 1916.

Wilson, H.W., and J.A. Hammerton (eds.). *The Great War*. London: The Amalgamated Press, 1915-1918.

Articles

"Caught in a Sea of Fire," *The War Illustrated* Volume 5 (September 16, 1916): 114.

Deutscher Feuerschutz, No. 21 (1939): 635.

Greiff, Walter. "Durchbruchschlacht," *Kreuz-Zeitung* No. 71 (March 24, 1935): 18.

Hatton, Private A.P."First Use of Liquid Fire," *The Great War: I Was There!* Part 11 (December 13, 1938): 439-441.

"Instructions for the Employment of Flame Projectors," *The Infantry Journal* Volume 14, Number 9 (March 1918): pp.692-698.

"Les Nouveaux Lance-flammes des Allemands," *Le Miroir* Number 208 (November 18, 1917): 2.

"Liquid Fire as a Weapon," *The Literary Digest* Volume 53, Number 5 (July 29, 1916): 246-247.

MacDonald, William. "What French Militarism Means," *The Nation* Volume 110, Number 2863 (May 15, 1920): 651.

"Personalnachrichten," *Feuer und Wasser* Number 30 (July 29, 1911): 250.

Phayre, Ignatius. "Liquid Fire as a German Arm. Terrors of the 'Flame Projector'," *The War Budget* Volume VI, Number 11 (January 27, 1916): 329.

Reichsgesetzblatt No. 28 (March 16, 1935): 369.

Newspapers

"Austro-German Plans in East," *The Daily Gleaner* (June 21, 1915), p.1, col. 3.

"Begin War to Control City," *The Evening State Journal* (March 22, 1920), p.1, col. 8.

"Bolsheviks Mass for Big Assault," *Manitoba Free Press* (January 9, 1919), p.1, col. 7.

"British Troops Capture German Liquid Fire Gun," *The Lima Daily News* (July 3, 1915), p.12, col. 5.

"Checking of the Advance," *The Mansfield News* (September 25, 1915), p.2, col. 1.

Corey, Herbert. "Germans Squirt Flame into British Trenches to Burn Out Soldiers," *The Syracuse Herald* (September 7, 1915), p.5, col. 1-5.

"Death is Penalty for Spartacans Captured in Berlin," *Reno Evening Gazette* (March 8, 1919), p.1, col. 7.

"Ebert Again in Control," *The Kansas City Times* (March 19, 1920), p.1, col. 5.

"Flame Throwers Used," *The Olean Evening Times* (April 8, 1920), p.7, col. 3.

"French Minister of War Pleased," *The Lincoln Daily Star* (March 4, 1916), p.4, col. 3.

Fort Wayne Journal-Gazette (April 11, 1919), p.1.
The Fort Wayne News and Sentinel (April 16, 1919), p.6.
"German Morale is Rapidly Weakening Says British Officer," *The Olean Evening Herald* (November 19, 1917), p.2, col. 3-4.
"German Patents of 1908 Reveal France's Blindness," *The Galveston Daily News* (June 26, 1921), p.29, col. 8.
"German Shock Troops Meet 40 French Oui! Oui!," *The Lima Daily News* (August 17, 1917), p.11, col. 1.
"Germans' Fluid Fire Caused Terrible Burns," *New York Times* (March 5, 1915), p.1, col. 7.
"Germans Use Liquid Fire in Attack on Russians," *The Syracuse Herald* (March 10, 1915), p.2, col. 6.
"Germans Using Gas," *Fairbanks Daily Times* (June 8, 1915), p.1, col. 2.
"Germany Slow to Reduce Army," *The Gettysburg Times* (May 11, 1920), p.2, col. 3.
"Germany Under Martial Law," *Syracuse Herald* (January 14, 1920), p.21, col. 7.
"Government Appears to be Quelling New Revolt of Germans," *Sandusky Star-Journal*, (March 6, 1919), p.1, col. 2.
"Government Now in Control of Situation; Isolate Certain Areas," *Iowa City Daily Citizen*, (March 6, 1919), p.1, col. 1-4.
"Greenough's Liquid Fire," *Richland County Observer* (March 21, 1862), p.2, col. 4.
"How 'Stosstruppen' Fighting Lost Out," *The Clearfield Progress* (September 5, 1917), p.2, col. 6.
"Huns' Torture of Prisoners," *The Fort Wayne Journal-Gazette* (August 19, 1919), p.5, col. 5-6.
"Inner City of Berlin is Quiet," *Reno Evening Gazette* (January 10, 1919), p.8, col. 3.
"Liquid Fire Attack Failed," *New York Times* (March 6, 1915), p.3, col. 2, 4, 6.
"Liquid Fire Guns Russia's Terror, *Oakland Tribune* (March 28, 1915), p.2, col. 2.
"M. Erzberger is Murdered: Assassinated Near Offenberg, Baden; Notable Character," *Sheboygan Press and Sheboygan Telegram* (August 26, 1921), p.1, col. 1.
"New Terror of War Invented by German," *The Syracuse Herald* (May 6, 1917), p.4, col. 1.
"New Verdun Line Holds as German Renew Attacks," *New York Times* (April 12, 1916), p.1, col. 3.
"Noske Breaks Up a Red Demonstration," *Evening State Journal* (July 23, 1919), p.2, col. 3.
"Pressing the Foe," *The Daily Gleaner* (July 8, 1916), p.1, col. 1.
"Smoke Screened Assailants," *New York Times* (March 7, 1915), Section II, p.3, col. 2, 3, 4.
"'Stosstruppen' Battalion is Repulsed by Forty Frenchmen," *Warren Evening Times* (September 5, 1917), p.1, col. 1.
"3,000 Germans Perish in a Sea of Fire," *New York Times* (April 16, 1916), p.4, col. 1, 2.
"Violent Disorders Reported from Every Section of German Empire," *The Clearfield Progress* (March 20, 1920), p.1, col. 2.

Pamphlets and Special Publications

The Crimes of Germany. Special supplement by The Field. London: The Field and Queen (Horace Cox), Ltd., 1916.
Descriptive Account of the Fort of Vaux and its Role During the Battle of Verdun. The Battle of Verdun in History Series. Frémont, Verdun: Les Éditions Lorraines.
Hornaday, William T. *A Searchlight on Germany: Germany's Blunders, Crimes, and Punishment*. Preparation Pamphlet Series. New York: American Defense Society, 1917.
North Carolina Day. Friday, November 11th, 1921. Armistice Day. North Carolina in the World War. Educational Publication No. 28, Division of Publication No. 3. Raleigh, North Carolina: State Superintendent of Public *Instruction, 1921*.
Scheidemann, Philipp. Die rechtsradikalen Verschwörer: Reichstags-Rede gehalten am 12 Mai 1923. Berlin: Verlag für Sozialwissenschaft, 1923.
Sleeper, Henry D. (ed.) *Diary of Section VIII: American Ambulance Field Service*. Boston: Thomas Todd Co., 1917.

Other Contemporary Documents

The Papers of Colonel Sir Eric Gore-Browne, Reference Number 88/52/1, Imperial War Museum. Description of British training in how to survive flamethrower attacks.
GrosJean, Jean. "The History of Company 'F'." Diary of a sergeant in Company F, 307th Infantry Regiment, 77th Division. Longwood, Long Island, New York, 1918. Description of German flamethrower attack.

Communications with the Author

Lembke, Robert. Telephone conversation with author, February 24, 2004. Information about Georg Lembke, former member of the 2nd Company of the Guard Reserve Pioneer Regiment.
Schleichert, Sabine. Letter to author, November 26, 2003. Information about the postwar career of Bernhard Reddemann.
Strasheim, Rainer. E-mails to author, April 10 to April 16, 2005. Updated information about the role of flamethrowers in the development of the German A7V tank.

Secondary Souces

Books

Barron, Elwyn (ed.) *Deeds of Herosim and Daring*. London/New York: Harper and Brothers, 1920.
Bean, C.E.W. *The Official History of Australia in the War of 1914-1918*, Volume IV: *The A.I.F. in France 1917*. Sydney: Angus and Robertson, 1929.
Benoist-Méchin, Jacques. *Geschichte des deutschen Heeres seit dem Waffenstillstand 1918-1938*, Band 1. Berlin: Verlag Dietrich Reimer, 1943.
Bruce, Robert. *Live Firing Classic Military Weapons in Colour Photographs: Machine Guns of World War I*. London: Windrow and Greene, 1997.
Buchan, John. *The Battle of the Somme*. New York: Grosset and Dunlap, 1917.
Bull, Stephen. *Brassey's History of Uniforms: World War One: German Army*. London: Brassey's, 2000.
—. *Stormtrooper: Elite German Assault Soldiers*. London: Publishing News, Ltd., 1999.
—. *World War I Trench Warfare* (1). Osprey Elite Series No. 78. Oxford: Osprey Publishing, 2002.
Chapman, Guy. *A Passionate Prodigality*. New York, Chicago, San Francisco: Holt, Rineheart, Winston, 1966.
Clausius, *Oberstleutnant. Erinnerungsblätter Deutscher Regimenter*, Band 176: *Infanterie-Regiment von Wittich (3. Kurhessiches) Nr. 83*. Oldenburg iO/Berlin: Verlag Georg Stalling, 1926.
Cowley, Robert (ed.). *The Great War: Perspectives on the First World War*. New York: Random House, 2003.
Cron, Hermann. *Imperial Germany Army 1914-18: Organisation, Structure, Orders-of-Battle*. Solihull, West Midlands, England: Helion and Company, 2002.
—. *Geschichte des deutschen Heeres im Weltkrige 1914-1918*. Berlin: K. Siegismund, 1937.
Darstellungen der Nachkriegskämpfe Deutscher Truppen und Freikorps, Volumes 1-9. Berlin: Mittler & Sohn, 1936-1943.
Dobson, Sean. *Authority and Upheaval in Leipzig, 1910-1920: The Story of a Relationship*. New York: Columbia University Press, 2001.
Erickson, Edward J. *Ordered to Die: A History of the Ottoman Army in the First World War*. Westport, Connecticut: Greenwood Press, 2001.
Fischer, Norbert, and Hanna Vollmer-Heitmann. *Chronik 1920: Tag für Tag in Wort und Bild*. Dortmund: Chronik Verlag, 1990.

Fitzsimons, Bernard (ed.). *Tanks and Weapons of World War I*. London: Beekman House, 1973.

Gibbs, Philip. *Now It Can Be Told*. New York and London: Harper and Brothers, 1920.

—. *The Soul of the War*. New York: Robert M. McBride and Company, 1916.

Gray, Randal. *Kaiserschlacht 1918: The Final German Offensive*. Osprey Campaign Series No. 11. London: Osprey Publishing, 1991.

Grieve, W. Grant, and Bernhard Newman. *Tunnelers*. London: 1936.

Grunberger, Richard. *Red Rising in Bavaria*. New York: St. Martin's Press, 1973.

Gudmundsson, Bruce I. *Stormtroop Tactics: Innovation in the German Army, 1914-1918*. Westport, Connecticut: Praeger Publishers, 1989.

Hartenstein, Prof. Dr. *Das Kurhessische Pionier-Bataillon Nr. 11 im Weltkriege 1914-1918*. Zeulenroda in Thüringen, Germany: Verlag Bernhard Sporn, 1936.

Haselgrove, Michael J., and Branislav Radovic. *Helmets of the First World War: Germany, Britain, and Their Allies*. Atglen, Pennsylvania: Schiffer Publishing, 2000.

Hicks, James E. *German Weapons - Uniforms - Insignia 1841-1918*. La Cañada, California: James E. Hicks and Son, 1958.

Hoffschmidt, E.J., and W.H. Tantum IV. *German Army and Navy Uniforms and Insignia 1871-1918*. Greenwich, Connecticut: WE Inc., 1968.

Holstein, Christina. *Battleground Europe Series: Verdun-Fort Douaumont*. Barnsley, South Yorkshire, United Kingdom: Pen and Sword Books, 2002.

Horne, Alistair. *The Price of Glory: Verdun 1916*. London: Penguin Books, 1993.

Hundleby, Maxwell, and Rainer Strasheim. *The German A7V Tank and the Captured British Mark IV Tanks of World War I*. Sparkford, Nr Yeovil, Somerset: Hayes Publishing Group, 1990.

Johnson, Thomas M.; and Fletcher Pratt. *The Lost Battalion*. Lincoln: The University of Nebraska Press, 2000.

Jones, Nigel H. *Hitler's Heralds: The Story of the Freikorps 1918-1923*. New York: Dorset Press, 1992.

Jung, Peter. *The Austro-Hungarian Forces in World War I (2), 1916-18*. Osprey Men-at-Arms Series no. 397. Oxford: Osprey Publishing, 2003.

Jurado, Carlos Caballero. *The German Freikorps 1918-23*. Osprey Elite Series No. 76. Oxford: Osprey Publishing, 2001.

Kessel, Hans von. *Handgranaten und rote Fahnen*. Berlin: Verlag für Kulturpolitik, 1933.

Kipling, Rudyard. *The Irish Guards in the Great War: The First Battalion*. Staplehurst, Kent, United Kingdom: Spellmount, 1997.

Klauer, Markus. *Die Höhe Toter Mann während der Kämpfe um Verdun in den Jahren 1916/1917*. Remscheid, Germany: Eigenverlag, 2001.

Koch, Fred. *Flamethrowers of the German Army 1914-1945*. Atglen, Pennsylvania: Schiffer Publishing, 1997.

Kraus, Jürgen. *Die feldgraue Uniformierung des deutschen Heeres 1907-1918*, Vol. I and II. Osnabrück: Verlag Biblio, 1999.

—. *The German Army in the First World War: Uniforms and Equipment - 1914 to 1918*. Vienna: Verlag Militaria, 2004.

Kreutz, Heinrich; Rolf Hofmann; Thomas M. Johnson; and J. Rex Reddick. *Edged Weapon Accouterments of Germany 1800-1945*. Pottsboro, Texas: Reddick Enterprises, 2002.

Larcade, Jean-Louis. *Deutsche Sturmtruppen: Troupes d'assaut allemandes (1914-1918)*. Les Jonquerets de Livet, France: Editions des Argonautes, 2002.

Lefebure, Victor. *The Riddle of the Rhine: Chemical Strategy in Peace and War*. New York: E. P.Dutton and Company, 1923.

Livesey, Anthony. *The Historical Atlas of World War I*. New York: Henry Holt and Company, 1994.

Lübbe, Klaus. *German Uniforms and Bayonets 1841-1945*. Hamburg: Niemann Verlag Hamburg, 1999.

March, Francis A. *History of the World War: An Authentic Narrative of the World's Greatest War*. Philadelphia/Chicago/Toronto: United Publishers of the United States and Canada, 1919.

Mayor, Adrienne. *Greek Fire, Poison Arrows, and Scorpion Bombs: Biological and Chemical Warfare in the Ancient World*. Woodstock, New York; New York; London: Overlook Duckworth, 2003.

McCarthy, Chris. *The Somme: The Day-by-day Account*. London: Arms and Armour Press, 1993.

McClure, S.S. *Obstacles to Peace*. Boston: Houghton Mifflin Company, 1917.

Melman, Seymour (ed.). *Inspection For Disarmament*. New York: Columbia University Press, 1958.

Mosier, John. *The Myth of the Great War*. New York: Perennial/HarperCollins, 2001.

Mountcastle, John W. *Flame On! U.S. Incendiary Weapons, 1918-1945*. Shippensburg, Pennsylvania: White Mane Publishing, 1999.

Murray, Colonel W.W. *The History of the 2nd Canadian Battalion (East. Ontario Regiment) Canadian Expeditionary Force in the Great War 1914-1919*. Ottawa: The Historical Committee, 2nd Battalion, C.E.F., 1947.

Ortner, M.C. *Österreichische Militärgeschichte 1998 - Folge 6. Die k. u. k. Sturmtruppen 1916-1918: Elitesoldaten Der Monarchie*. Vienna: Verlagsbuchhandlung Stöhr, 1998.

—, M. Christian. *Storm Troops: Austro-Hungarian Assault Units, Commandos in the First World War: Tactics, Organisation, Uniforms and Equipment*. Vienna: Verlag Militaria, 2005.

Powell, Anne (ed.). *A Deep Cry: First World War Soldier-Poets Killed in France and Flanders*. Phoenix Mill, Britain: Sutton, 1998.

Proctor, H.G. *The Iron Division: National Guard of Pennsylvania in the World War*. Philadelphia: The John C. Winston Company, 1919.

Saunders, Anthony. *Weapons of the Trench War 1914-1918*. Phoenix Mill, Stroud, Gloustershire: Sutton Publishing, 1999.

Schmidt-Pauli, Edgar von. *Geschichte der Freikorps 1918-24*. Stuttgart: Verlag Lutz, 1936.

Stacy, B.V., F.J. Kindon, and H.V. Chedgey. *The History of the First Battalion A.I.F., 1914-1919*. Sydney: First Battalion A.I.F. Association, 1931.

Stallings, Laurence. *The Doughboys: The Story of the AEF, 1917-1918*. New York: Harper and Row, 1963.

Waite, Robert G.L. *Vanguard of Nazism: The Free Corps Movement in Postwar Germany 1918-1923*. New York: W. W. Norton and Company, 1969.

Watt, Richard M. *The Kings Depart: The Tragedy of Germany: Versailles and the German Revolution*. New York: Barnes and Noble Books, 2000.

Wood, Maj.-Gen. Leonard et al. (eds.). *The History of the First World War*, Commemorative Edition, Volume 1. New York: Grolier, 1965.

Woolley, Charles. *German Uniforms, Insignia, and Equipment 1918-1923*. Atglen, Pennsylvania: Schiffer Publishing, 2002.

Articles

Hall, Jim, and Chip Minx. "Die Totenkopf Pioniere," *Kaiserzeit* Volume VIII, Number 4 (Winter 1979): 26-30.

Klietmann, Dr. Kurt-Gerhard. "Der Offizierhelm des Flammenwerfertrupps des Sturm-Bataillons Nr. 5 (Rohr) vom Jahre 1916," *Orden- und Militaria-Journal* No. 21 (April 1977): 473-476.

Lamb, Harold. "Flame Weapons," *Chemical Warfare* Volume 13, Number 1 (January 15, 1927): 237, 245.

Lüdersdorf, Gerd. "Der Köpenicker Blutsonntag vom 21. März 1920," *Berlinische Monatschrift* Heft 3 (Marz 2001): 37-45.

Reddemann, Bernhard. "Flammenwerfer vor die Front," *Der S.A.-Mann*, Folge 21 (26 Mai 1934): 14-15.

Scott, Peter T. "An Awful Job," *Military Illustrated* Number 98 (July 1996): 36-40.

GLOSSARY

Aufrollen - rolling up a trench with grenades and often flamethrowers. Conceived by *Leutnant* Beumelberg of *Pionier-Bataillon Nr. 30.*

behelfsmässigen Stockzünder - makeshift stick fuse. A stick or board with a bundle of kerosene-soaked rags on the end, used when the flamethrower igniter had burned out.

Brandgranate (also *Brand-Handgranade*) - incendiary hand grenade. Used to ignite oil stream of early flamethrowers. *See Flammenkugel.*

Brandröhre - fire tube. Incendiary device consisting of sheet-metal tube filled with fusing compound. Used by pioneers and assault troops.

Brandröhrentrupp - fire tube squad. Consisted of one NCO (as needed) and five pioneers. Two carried a guide pole and three carried armed fire tubes.

Deckungsstrahl - covering jet. A burst of smoke and flame that provided cover for advancing troops.

Doppelgrof - double large flamethrower. Two large flamethrowers attached to one lance. *See Grof.*

Doppelgroftrupp - double large-flamethrower squad. Consisted of:
squad leader (*Führer*: *Gefreiter* or *Unteroffizier*),
lance operator (*Strahlrohrführer*),
assistant directly behind lance operator (*Hilfsmann*),
three oil-tank operators (*Grofleute*),
See Doppelgrof, Grof.

Doppelkleif - double small/medium flamethrower. Two *Kleif* attached to a single large lance. *See Kleif.*

Doppelkleiftrupp - double small/medium-flamethrower squad. Consisted of:
squad leader (*Führer*: *Gefreiter* or *Unteroffizier*),
lance operator (*Strahlrohrführer*),
assistant directly behind lance operator (*Hilfsmann*),
two *Kleif* carriers (*Kleifträgern*),
assistant to carry hose (*Hilfsmann*),
See Doppelkleif, Kleif.

Fang - (abbr.) flame attack. *See Flammenangriff.*

Fert - (abbr.) flame defense. *See Flammenverteidigung.*

Fl.W. - (abbr.) flamethrower. *See Flammenwerfer.*

Flammenangriff - flame attack. *See Fang.*

Flammenbegleittrupp - flame accompanying squad. Flamethrower squad attached to an infantry assault unit.

Flammenkugel - flame ball. Incendiary hand grenade used to ignite flame oil. *See also Brandgranate.*

Flammenschütze - flame shooter. Term used by Austro-Hungarian army to describe the lance operator of a flamethrower squad.

Flammenstoss - flame shock or flame attack; also flame burst.

Flammenstosstrupp - flame shock troop. Assault unit consisting of small-flamethrower squads and infantrymen armed with grenades, rifles, and light machine guns.

Flammenverteidigung - flame defense. *See Fert.*

Flammenwerfer - flamethrower.

Flammenwerferkompagnie - flamethrower company.

Flammenwerferstosstrupp - flamethrower shock troop. Consisted of:
One or more shock-troop leaders (*Stosstruppführern*),
Two, three or four-man flamethrower squads (*Flammenwerfertrupps*),
four grenade throwers (*Handgranatenwerfern*).
See Flammenstosstrupp, Flammenwerfertrupp, Stosstrupp.

Flammenwerfertrupp - flamethrower squad of four men.

Grof - (abbr.) large flamethrower. *See grosse Flammenwerfer.*

Grofleute - large-flamethrower staff. Oil-tank operators for large flamethrower. *See Grof, grosse Flammenwerfer.*

Groftrupp - large-flamethrower squad. Consisted of:
squad leader (*Führer*: *Gefreiter* or *Unteroffizier*),
lance operator (*Strahlrohrführer*),

assistant directly behind lance operator (*Hilfsmann*),
two oil-tank operators (*Grofleute*).
See Grof, grosse Flammenwerfer.

grosse Flammenwerfer - large flamethrower. *See Grof.*

Halbkleiftrupp - half *Kleif* squad. A flamethrower squad armed with a *Kleif* filled only halfway with oil, in order to improve speed and mobility. *See Kleif.*

Halbzug - half platoon. Thirteen men armed with three portable flamethrowers, often attached to assault units for the short term.

Handgranatenwerfer - hand-grenade thrower.

Heeresflammenwerfer - army flamethrower. Weapon of the officially designated flamethrower sections, as opposed to a device built by another unit.

Hilfsmann - assistant. Also served as replacement and grenade thrower in small/medium-flamethrower squads.

indianermässigen Vorpirschen - Indian-style Forward Stalking. A method of moving forward indirectly, in small leaps and bounds, while taking advantage of the natural cover provided by the terrain.

Kleif - (abbr.) small flamethrower. After 1917, called "medium flamethrower." *See kleine Flammenwerfer, mittlere Flammenwerfer.*

Kleifbegleittrupp - small/medium-flamethrower accompanying squad. *Kleif* squad attached to an infantry unit. *See Kleif, kleine Flammenwerfer, mittlere Flammenwerfer.*

Kleifstosstrupp - small/medium-flamethrower shock troop. Consisted of:
One or more shock-troop leaders (*Stosstruppführern*),
Two, three or four-man Kleif squads (*Kleiftrupps*),
four hand-grenade throwers (*Handgranatenwerfern*).
See Kleif, Kleiftrupp.

Kleifträger - small/medium-flamethrower carrier. *See Kleif, kleine Flammenwerfer, mittlere Flammenwerfer.*

Kleiftrupp - small/medium-flamethrower squad. Consisted of:
squad leader (*Führer*: *Gefreiter* or *Unteroffizier*),
lance operator (*Strahlrohrführer*),
Kleif carrier (*Kleifträger*),
assistant (*Hilfsmann*).
See Kleif, kleine Flammenwerfer, mittlere Flammenwerfer.

kleine Flammenwerfer - small flamethrower. Before 1917, this term used to describe *Kleif*; after 1917, this term used to describe *Wex*. *See Kleif, mittlere Flammenwerfer, verbesserte kleine Flammenwerfer, Weschelapparat, Wex.*

Leichtgrof - light *Grof*. The *Grof M.1916*, a lightened version of the *Grof M.1912*.

Messertaktik - Knife Tactic. A tactic in which long, narrow formations of flamethrower shock troops attacked the enemy line perpendicularly.

mittlere Flammenwerfer - medium flamethrower. Before 1917, this flamethrower was called the *kleine Flammenwerfer*. *See Kleif, kleine Flammenwerfer, verbesserte kleine Flammenwerfer.*

springenden Angriff - pouncing attack. An assault using only small portable flamethrowers. *See vereinten stehenden und springenden Angriff.*

stehenden Angriff - stationary attack. An assault using only large emplaced flamethrowers. *See vereinten stehenden und springenden Angriff.*

Stosseinheit - shock unit. Consisted of flamethrower shock troops and infantrymen or pioneers armed with machine guns, grenade launchers, trench mortars, and explosives. *See Flammenwerferstosstrupp.*

Stosseinheit in Rudelform oder in Form eines Angriffskeils - shock unit in the form of a flock or an attacking wedge. Consisted of:
three *Wex* or *Kleif* shock troops,
four light machine-gun squads,
four grenade-launcher squads,
two infantry groups,
one group of pioneers with explosives,
one infantry half group as machine-gun ammunition carriers,
one infantry group as grenade-launcher ammunition carriers,
one infantry half group as hand-grenade throwers.
See Kleifstosstrupp, Wexstosstrupp.

Stosseinheit in Schlangen-, Säulen-, oder Reihenform zum Aufrollen eines Schutzengrabens - shock unit in snakelike, column, or single-file form for rolling up a trench. Consisted of:
two *Wex* or *Kleif* shock troops,
two light machine-gun squads,
two grenade-launcher squads,
one infantry group.
See Kleifstosstrupp, Wexstosstrupp.

Stosstrupp (pl. Stosstrupps) - shock troop. Small unit such as a squad, section, or platoon of assault infantry or pioneers.

Stosstruppen - shock troopers. Assault infantrymen or pioneers, members of a *Stosstrupp*.

Strahlrohr - jet tube or lance.

Strahlrohrführer - jet-tube director or lance operator.

Strahlrohrschlauch - jet-tube hose or lance hose.

Sturmtrupp - (pl. *Sturmtrupps*) - assault squad or troop.

Sturmtruppe - (pl. *Sturmtruppen*) - assault unit.

Sturmtruppen - assault troops. Assault infantrymen or pioneers, members of a *Sturmtruppe*.

Trupp - (pl. *Trupps*) - squad or troop.

Truppe - (pl. *Truppen*) troops, corps.

verbesserte kleine Flammenwerfer - improved small flamethrower. Another name for *Kleif M.1917*. *See Kleif, kleine Flammenwerfer, mittlere Flammenwerfer.*

vereinten stehenden und springenden Angriff - combined stationary and pouncing attack. An assault using large emplaced flamethrowers and small mobile flamethrowers. *See springenden Angriff; stehenden Angriff.*

verstärkter Kleifstosstrupp - reinforced small/medium-flamethrower shock troop. Consisted of:
two or more shock-troop leaders (*Stosstruppführern*),
three- or four-man *Kleif* squads (*Kleiftrupps*),
six hand-grenade throwers (*Handgranatenwerfern*).
See Kleiftrupp, Kleifstosstrupp.

verstärkter Wexstosstrupp - reinforced *Wex* shock troop. Consisted of:
two or more shock-troop leaders (*Stosstruppführern*),
three- or four-man *Wex* squads (*Wextrupps*),
six hand-grenade throwers (*Handgranatenwerfern*).
See Wextrupp, Wexstosstrupp.

Wechselapparat - Interchangeable flamethrower. Small, ring-shaped flamethrower introduced in 1917. *See kleine Flammenwerfer, Wex.*

Wex - (abbr.) Small, ring-shaped flamethrower. *See kleine Flammenwerfer, Wechselapparat.*

Wexbegleittrupp - *Wex* accompanying squad, attached to an infantry unit. *See Wechselapparat, Wex, Wexstosstrupp.*

Wexstosstrupp - *Wex* shock troop. Consisted of:
one or more shock-troop leader (*Stosstruppführer*),
two, three or four-man *Wex* squads (*Wextrupps*),
four hand-grenade throwers (*Handgranatenwerfern*).
See Wextrupp.

Wexträger - *Wex* carrier. *See Wechselapparat, Wex.*

Wextrupp - *Wex* squad. Consisted of:
squad leader (*Führer*: *Gefreiter* or *Unteroffizier*),
lance operator (*Strahlrohrführer*),
Wex carrier (*Wexträger*),
assistant (*Hilfsmann*).
See Wechselapparat, Wex.

Zangen-taktik - Pincers Tactic. Squeezing the target between machine-gun and grenade-launcher fire and a flamethrower assault.

Zünder - igniter.

Zünderhalter - igniter holder.

INDEX